When Sun Meets Moon

Islamic Civilization and Muslim Networks
Carl W. Ernst and Bruce B. Lawrence, editors

Highlighting themes with historical as well as contemporary significance, Islamic Civilization and Muslim Networks features works that explore Islamic societies and Muslim peoples from a fresh perspective, drawing on new interpretive frameworks or theoretical strategies in a variety of disciplines. Special emphasis is given to systems of exchange that have promoted the creation and development of Islamic identities—cultural, religious, or geopolitical. The series spans all periods and regions of Islamic civilization.

A complete list of titles published in this series appears at the end of the book.

SCOTT KUGLE

When Sun Meets Moon

Gender, Eros, and Ecstasy in Urdu Poetry

The University of North Carolina Press *Chapel Hill*

Publication of this book was supported in part by a subvention from Emory University.

© 2016 Scott Kugle
All rights reserved
Designed and set in Merope Text by Rebecca Evans. Manufactured in the United States of America. The University of North Carolina Press has been a member of the Green Press Initiative since 2003.

Cover illustration: "The Sun and the Moon" by Rudra Kishore Mandal (double portrait of Mah Laqa Bai and Siraj Awrangabadi, courtesy of the artist)

Library of Congress Cataloging-in-Publication Data
Names: Kugle, Scott Alan, 1969– author.
Title: When sun meets moon : gender, eros, and ecstasy in Urdu poetry / Scott Kugle.
Description: Chapel Hill : The University of North Carolina Press, [2016] | Series: Islamic civilization and Muslim networks | Includes bibliographical references and index.
Identifiers: LCCN 2015042774| ISBN 9781469628912 (cloth : alk. paper) | ISBN 9781469626772 (pbk : alk. paper) | ISBN 9781469626789 (ebook)
Subjects: LCSH: 880-01 Siraj Awrangabadi, 1712–1763—Criticism and interpretation. | 880-02 Mah Laqa Bai, 1768—Criticism and interpretation. | Urdu poetry—18th century—History and criticism. | Urdu poetry—19th century—History and criticism. | Love in literature. | Ecstasy in literature.
Classification: LCC PK2168 .K84 2016 | DDC 891.4/391009—dc23 LC record available at http://lccn.loc.gov/2015042774

TO B. PRABHUWARA KUMAR —

a true friend,

a defender of the vulnerable,

a teller of Deccan tales

CONTENTS

Acknowledgments xi

Translation and Transliteration from Urdu and Persian xiii

Introduction 1

1 Celestial Bodies Seen from Deccan Soil 8

FIRST ORBIT *Siraj the Sun* 25

2 Siraj's Bewilderment 29

3 Siraj's Silence 47

4 Eros and Spirit 71

5 Poetry as Music 100

6 Transit—When Sufis Meet Shi'is 120

SECOND ORBIT *Mah Laqa the Moon* 141

7 Mah Laqa Bai's Radiance 147

8 Mah Laqa Bai's Men 166

9 Mah Laqa Bai's Shame 185

10 The Performance of Gender 210

11 Mah Laqa Bai's True Love 235

Conjunction—When Sun Meets Moon 254

Notes 267

Bibliography 295

Index 305

FIGURES, MAPS, AND PHOTOGRAPHS

Figures

Initiatic lineage of Siraj Awrangabadi 54

Family lineage of Mah Laqa Bai 192

Maps

South and West Asia with Deccan region detail 14

Awrangabad City in the late eighteenth century 49

Hyderabad City in the early nineteenth century 134

Photographs

The dargah (tomb-shrine) of Shah Siraj, located in Awrangabad 28

The dargah of Nizam al-Din Awrangabadi, located in Awrangabad 51

Mah Laqa Bai portrait, oil painting from mid-nineteenth century, housed at the Archaeology Museum in Public Gardens, Hyderabad 144

Pavilion housing the tomb of Mah Laqa Bai and her mother, Raj Kanvar Bai, located at the foot of Mawla ʿAli Hill, outside Hyderabad 156

Prime Minister Aristu Jah and the second nizam, miniature painting housed at the Archaeology Museum in Public Gardens, Hyderabad 168

Tombs of Mah Laqa Bai and her mother, Raj Kanvar Bai 191

ACKNOWLEDGMENTS

Researching and writing this book has been a labor of love and an excellent adventure. It kept me flitting from America to India for many years, with crucial stops in London and Pakistan. I am grateful to many people and institutions that supported me along the way.

While completing this book, I was generously funded by the Mellon Foundation New Directions Grant. The Fulbright Foundation financed initial research on Sufi and Shiʻi pilgrimage sites in Hyderabad. Specialized research on Mah Laqa Bai was funded by the American Institute of Indian Studies. The U.S. Ambassadors Fund for Cultural Preservation funded a project to restore Mah Laqa Bai's built heritage; I was privileged to serve as director and am grateful to Juliet Wurr (public diplomacy officer at the U.S. Consulate in Hyderabad) and her assistant, Salil Kader, who supported the project despite all obstacles. My associates on the project, including Oudesh Rani Bawa (my Urdu teacher), Vasant Kumar Bawa (founder of the Center for Deccan Studies), Sajjad Shahid (heritage activist), and G. Shashidhar Reddy (architectural and graphic designer), were wonderful partners.

Colleagues at Emory University invited me to give talks on Shah Siraj and Mah Laqa Bai, and supporters from my Department of Middle Eastern and South Asian Studies include Roxani Margariti, Vincent Cornell, Rkia Elaroui Cornell, Elliot McCarter, Ruby Lal, and Velcheru Narayana Rao, while Juana Clem McGhee diligently looked after the details. In the field of performance studies, Pallabi Chakravorty and Joyce Flueckiger helped with delightful discussion and probing questions. I am also thankful for the keen eye of Stephanie Yep, an intrepid doctoral student, who helped edit the manuscript.

Oudesh Rani Bawa deserves special thanks for reading Mah Laqa Bai's poems with me; she tirelessly helped explain their linguistic and cultural nuances as the power went out and the monsoon rains darkened the skies. The people of Hyderabad—scholars, poetry lovers, musicians, and journalists—encouraged me, argued with me, and delighted me in discussions; they all deserve my heartfelt thanks, especially Siraj Kamal Sohrab Alam (heritage collector), Jayanthi Rajagopalan (cultural tourism entrepreneur), Mohammed Suleman Siddiqi (professor of Islamic studies), and Mohammad Aslam Khan and his late father, Saeed ur-Rahman Khan (both musicians of Sarangi).

Research for this book was conducted in archives whose caretakers deserve praise for helping me access rare manuscripts. At the National Museum in Delhi, my research was facilitated by Dr. Tripati and the staff in charge of Islamic manuscripts. At the Andhra Pradesh State Oriental Manuscript Library, I was aided by the director and two archivists, Drs. Rafath Rizwana and Fathima Tanweer. At the Salar Jung Museum's library, I was helped by the director, Dr. A. N. Reddy, and his assistant, Veerender Mallam, along with the library staff. (But those in charge of the Idara-e Adabiyat-e Urdu should be spanked for having lost an irreplaceable handwritten *divan* of Mah Laqa Bai!)

Many institutions have invited me to speak about the topics in this book, and those were critical moments to share and receive feedback. In addition to Emory University, I thank Western Michigan University, Cornell University, the Nehru Center in London, and the Dance Matters Conference at Jadhavpur University in Kolkata.

Sufi communities in the Deccan supported me in countless ways. In Hyderabad, I am deeply grateful to members of the Khanqah-e Kaleemi and to its late leader Syed Mohammed Rasheed-ul-Hasan Jeeli-ul-Kaleemi (may God grant him compassion), his family, and his followers. I thank Syed Moinuddin Mohammad Mian, the kind custodian at the dargah of Nizam al-Din Awrangabadi, along with his family and his supporters.

This book is the fruit of residing in Hyderabad. There I found a second home because of the welcoming embrace of Rudra Kishore Mandal, Syed Ali Arif, Aditya Kini, and Sonam Gyamsto. The love of such friends illumines the city more than Divali lamps or Muharram torches. I would have never arrived in Hyderabad if not for Seemi Bushra Ghazi, Zia Inayat Khan, and Omid Safi, with whom I first explored ghazals—may the light in your hearts never fade!

TRANSLATION AND TRANSLITERATION FROM URDU AND PERSIAN

All texts and poems in the book are original translations by the author unless otherwise noted. This book refers to terms in Urdu and Persian, which are defined in context the first time they are used. The transliteration system is adapted from the *Annual of Urdu Studies* journal. Letters of Urdu are given below with representation in roman script with diacritical marks; Persian and Arabic terms are transliterated according to the Urdu system. The transliteration system below follows the consonant alphabetic pattern for Urdu dictionaries.

Consonants

ب	b	bē	ذ	ż	żāl	ع	ʿ	ʿain
پ	p	pē	ر	r	rē	غ	gh	ghain
ت	t	tē	ڑ	ṛ	ṛā	ف	f	fē
ٹ	ṭ	ṭā	ز	z	zē	ق	q	qāf
ث	s̱	s̱ē	ژ	ž	žē	ک	k	kāf
ج	j	jīm	س	s	sīn	گ	g	gāf
چ	ch	chē	ش	sh	shīn	ل	l	lām
ح	ḥ	ḥē	ص	ṣ	ṣuād	م	m	mīm
خ	kh	khē	ض	ẓ	ẓuād	ن	n	nūn
د	d	dāl	ط	ṯ	ṯoē			
ڈ	ḍ	ḍā	ظ	ẓ	ẓoē			

ہ	h	*hē*, when voiced at a word's end, is written, as in *nigāh* (sight); as a silent consonant that is not vocalized, it is not written, as in *irāda* (will)
ھ	ḣ	*dō-chashmī hē* is not a separate letter but is appended to consonants when they are aspirated, as in *k̇hēl* (game) or *hāṫh* (hand) or *ṗhūl* (flower)
و	v	*vōv* a consonant as in *valī* (saint) or *sakhāvat* (generosity)
ی	y	*yē* a consonant as in *yasmīn* (jasmine) or *ayāt* (signs)
ں	ñ	*nūn ghuna* represents the nasalized *n* in Urdu, as in *maiñ hūñ* (I am) or *nahīñ* (no)

Vowels

ا	ā	
ی		ī or ē, depending on pronunciation, as in *shēr* (lion) or *shīr* (milk)
ای		ai or ei, a semi-vowel (diphthong), as in *shaikh* (elder) or *meiñ* (in)
اے		ay, a semi-vowel (diphthong), as in *ay ṣabā* (oh breeze)
و		ū or ō, depending on pronunciation, as in *sujūd* (prostration) or *khusrō* (prince)
او		aw, a semi-vowel (diphthong), as in *awliya* (saints) or *awrang* (throne)
وا		wa, a semi-vowel commonly pronounced as *ā*, as in *khwāja* (master) or *khwāb* (sleep)
◌َ		a *zabar*, a short vowel, as in *khabar* (news) or *jamāl* (beauty)
◌ِ		i or e *zer*, a short vowel depending on pronunciation, as in *vilāyat* (sanctity) or *sheʿr* (couplet)
◌ُ		u or o *pesh*, a short vowel depending on pronunciation, as in *upar* (above) or *tohmat* (suspicion)
ء		*hamza* (connection between two vowels) as in *sāʾil* (petitioner) or *kōʾī* (anyone)
◌ِ		–e or-ye *izafa* ("of" relation between two nouns) as in *vaḥdat-e vujūd* (oneness of being) or *shāh-e mardān* (king of men) or *khwāja-ye khwājagān* (master of masters)
و		o *wāw* ("and" conjunction between two nouns) as in *āb o havā* (water and air)

Diacritics are not used in names and terms appearing in the main text. The endnotes and bibliography provide diacritics for book titles and authors, technical terms, and poetic citations to aid readers who know Urdu and Persian or require details. Exceptions are made for terms that are already commonly adopted into English, such as Qawwali (not Qavvali) and Deccani (not Dakkani). Terms that are frequently used after being defined in the text are not italicized, such as ghazal, shaikh, and imam.

When Sun Meets Moon

Introduction

Don't you see how God created seven heavens in ascending stages
And in them made the moon a light and made the sun a lamp?
God made you sprout from the earth as a plant grows
Then returns you to the earth and will bring you forth anew.

—Qur'an, 71:15–17

The Qur'an portrays the sun and moon as signs of God's majesty. In their motion, moods, and illuminating power, they seem to soar above humankind. We live by the soil and inevitably return to dust, while above us the sun and moon witness our plight. The Qur'an hints that the sun and moon have character, as if they are personalities who serve a transcendent will: *Glory be to the One who created the pairs of every type. . . . The sun moves along a course set for her—that is a decision of the mighty One, the One who knows all things. And the moon, for him we decreed progressive stages until returning to his former slender curve* (Q 36:37–39).[1] Sun and moon display the power of the unseen creator in their harmonious movements and altering light.

We often project gender upon the sun and moon, as if they are man and woman. They appear as competitors chasing each other, or as lovers longing for the other's distant embrace. The Qur'an flirts with our all-too-weak human understanding, and in its Arabic the sun and moon do have genders, the sun being feminine and the moon masculine.[2] But the Qur'an flirts with us in order to warn us. Observing their personalities should lead us not to worship the sun and moon as gods but rather to acknowledge the greatness of God, who created them: *Blessed is the One who set constellations in the heavens, and made within them the sun as a lamp and set the moon shining, the One who made day and night follow in succession, desiring us to stay mindful and to give thanks* (Q 25:61–63). To live humbly and stay conscious of God requires constant reminders. For Muslims, the Qur'an is the prime reminder as its words resound through prayer, recitation, calligraphy, and sometimes even poetry and song.

In addition to the Qur'an and the Prophet who delivered it, poets also remind us effectively of our true nature. The metaphors of poets bridge these two realms—our bewildering life on earth mired in trials and the fascinating hints of a life beyond our routine limitations. Poetic words offer hints of transcendence even as they are rooted in everyday language. In Islamic culture, poets are admired for their power to propel listeners through their art from the earthly to the celestial and inspire in them to ascend through the dimensions of sound, meaning, and spirit. Muslim poets with a mystical orientation cultivate love poetry that is purposefully ambiguous, fusing erotic love (for an embodied beloved) with spiritual love (for a transcendent divinity). This book will explore the verse of two Urdu poets whose earthly lives, though very different in circumstance, meet in the ethereal realms of imagination. One is a man named Siraj, the sun, while the other is a woman named Mah, the moon. They both lived in the Deccan region of South-Central India, but they never met. Their lives interacted and corresponded without ever meeting, just like the Qur'an tells about the moon and the sun: *It is not to be that sun meets moon, and it is not to be that night overtakes day—each glides on a sphere of its own* (Q 36:40).

Shah Siraj Awrangabadi (1716–63) was an ascetic who, after a youthful homosexual love affair, gave up sexual relationships to follow a higher calling of personal holiness. Mah Laqa Bai Chanda (1768–1824) was a courtesan dancer who transposed her seduction of men into pursuit of mystical love. Both elevated earthly love to a spiritual quest, yet neither married or produced children. Both were devoted Muslims, yet neither fulfilled the legalistic prescriptions of the *shariʿa*. The man was Sunni while the woman was Shiʿi, yet both shared a mystical orientation and skill in the art of love poetry in Urdu. The basic goal of this book is to retrieve marginalized gendered subjectivities, such as Shah Siraj's and Mah Laqa Bai's, from oblivion in order to challenge heterosexist and androcentric interpretations of the Islamic tradition. Other voices and experiences did exist but are too often ignored. They spoke out through an abundant conception of human spirituality in an Islamic idiom, spirituality that incorporates the messy and mundane worldly dimensions of life, together with the most sublime experiences and transcendent yearnings.

Mah, the moon, and Siraj, the sun: neither could meet, yet each moved in a sphere that rhymed. In the Qur'an God swears a moral oath on their constant difference: *I swear by the sun and her brightening and by the moon as he follows her, by the day when it displays her and by the night when it veils* her. I swear . . . by the soul and what formed her and what revealed her debased or faithful revealed her. Whoever honors the soul flourishes but those fail who defile her (Q 91:1–10). Through archetypes of the sun and moon, the Qur'an evokes moral principles that govern human destiny—that those who honor and care for their souls during the trials of this world flourish in the next world, but those who defile and corrupt their souls fail. Both personalities compared in this book, Mah and Siraj, strove to live up to this principle amid the bewildering circumstances of their earthy lives. Both left eloquent words as testimony to their struggles.

It is the responsibility of intellectuals today to contemplate the yearnings and experiences of individual subjects (from the past or the present) to create meaning in their lives amid the often restrictive and conflict-ridden but altogether dynamic structures and processes of daily living. This book takes up this responsibility, with two subjects who are more eloquent than most and who left a lasting legacy of their joys, trials, aspirations, and pains. I investigate the varying ways in which each of these two poets, by virtue of their gendered subjectivity and erotic feelings, lived in the face of seemingly overwhelming social structures; they navigated these structures, or resisted or reinforced them, all the while crafting exquisite mystical love poetry and interacting with society in rich, multidimensional ways. I hope that their comparative examples will help us rethink our normative understandings of the relationships between gender, sexuality, and spirituality, both in their context of South Asia and in the reader's own context.

Shah Siraj and Mah Laqa Bai lived just after the Mughal conquest of the Deccan. This period witnessed the rapid growth of the Urdu *ghazal*, a genre of lyrical poetry (explained in detail in chapter 1). As poets, the two have much in common, reflecting the cultural unity and uniqueness of the Deccan region where they lived. Yet they contrast in many ways, revealing the diversity inherent in Islamic culture there. This study compares these two poets at three levels: literary, personal, and historical. The literary level can be conceived as subjective (as life experienced by the one living it), as both poets gave voice to their own experiences through musical words. The personal level can be conceived as biographical (as life perceived by contemporary observers), as both poets inhabited a distinct social network that shaped and was shaped by their personalities. Finally, the historical level can be conceived as structural (as life constrained by forces in time, space, and culture), as each poet lived in a society that was evolving beyond his or her awareness or control. All three levels involve the symbolic realm, through the spheres of poetic imagination, personal spirituality, and organized religion. In all three levels, gender is an important constraint to behavior and an essential element in identity. In all three spheres, sexuality is a dynamic force that always energizes and often threatens the social order. Gender and sexuality are important components of the lives of these two poets, as they are in the lives of everyone. Yet because Siraj and Mah Laqa were poets, gender and sexuality emerge through their words in expressive ways that are particularly illuminating and invite deeper analysis.

This book has a wide, multidisciplinary scope, encompassing mysticism, world literature, gender studies, and queer studies, all framed by the Islamic cultural history of the Deccan region. I am emboldened in this audacious approach by the magisterial work of Walter Andrews and Mehmet Kalpaklı titled *The Age of Beloveds*. They address the Ottoman-era ghazal written in Turkish, through which they pose questions about the relationship between gender and sexuality to social order and political power. They indicate a new approach to literary study of the ghazal, one that does not separate the poems from the intimate lives of those who wrote them or from the grand structures of power and status, claiming that a careful rereading of "what we think of as literary sources" can provide vivid

> evidence for societal practices, behaviors, attitudes, and patterns of thought that, we believe, inform, structure, and help us interpret literary products. The circularity of this depiction, however, stems from the equally circular notion that societal behavior is scripted behavior. This is simply to say that such things as love and sex are not biological realities (the way that reproductive sexual intercourse is). They are social constructs given form and shape by the way they are put into language, the ways they are talked about and understood at particular times in particular cultures.[3]

Seeing poetry as a social construct, Andrews and Kalpaklı unpack the product and lives of poets to address issues of sex, sexuality, and the pursuit of pleasure; yet they also translate the Ottoman ghazals in a captivating and evocative way, giving the poetry its rights as world literature. They chart a boldly "circular" argument that literature constructs society, which constructs literature. Cutting this circle in order to straighten it into a line, to assert that society is primary and literature is its reflection (or conversely, that litterateurs are visionary geniuses who inspire society), does damage to the subtle and constant interaction between social norms and the imaginative use of words. Andrews and Kalpaklı "take the position that cultural products, symbols such as words and pictures, are not merely reflective of social behavior and emotional states but actually constitutive of behavior and emotion in a complex set of interactions marked by mutuality of origination."[4] I also take this position and apply it to Urdu poetry in the Deccan during the late Mughal era, just as Andrews and Kalpaklı do for poetry in Anatolia and Europe during the high Ottoman era.

The canvas of Andrews and Kalpaklı is bewilderingly vast, centered in Istanbul yet extending through Venice, Paris, and London in comparing Ottoman society with early-modern Europe. My book lovingly uses their methodology but takes up a much more intimate comparison. Rather than compare poetry from two disparate but connected regions, I compare two poets from the same region. In this way, I hope to address gender and sexuality as it plays out in the nuanced lives of two individuals instead of in normative social scripts. But of course, individual lives and social norms are deeply connected—one reveals the other. Making a comparison of a male poet with a female poet will draw out larger social structures and patterns of normative behavior in ways that focusing on just one poet could not.

This comparison proceeds in eleven chapters organized through images of heavenly bodies. The first chapter, "Celestial Bodies Seen from Deccan Soil," describes the growth of a distinctive culture of Islam in South Asia and especially in the Deccan; this will provide readers with essential background information to appreciate the two poets and their literary works. Chapters 2–5 make up the "First Orbit," focusing on Siraj Awrangabadi, whose name invokes the sun; his life, longing, and literary activities as a Sufi within the Sunni community form the content of these four chapters. Chapter 6, "Transit—When Sufis Meet Shiʿis," takes its name from the astronomical term for the occasion when one celestial body appears to cross another's path; this middle chapter describes the creative ways that Sufis and Shiʿis met and forged commonalities in the Deccan and built a devotional topography of land that brought these two poets together despite their sectarian differences. After this, chapters 7–11 make up the "Second Orbit," focusing on Mah Laqa Bai, whose name evokes the moon; her life, love, and literary ambitions as a courtesan within the Shiʿi community form the content of these five chapters, which mirror the section on Siraj.

Finally, after Shah Siraj has met Mah Laqa Bai through this extended comparison, the final chapter draws conclusions. "Conjunction—When Sun Meets Moon" refers to the astronomical term for an apparent meeting of two celestial bodies that in reality are far separated. The two poets never met in real life, but their poetry and personas have: they wrote in a single literary tradition and pursued spiritual goals that intersected. Both poets lived in an Islamic culture in the Deccan in which Shi'i and Sufi coexisted, overlapped, and often reinforced each other. These three terms—coexist, overlap, and reinforce—are different, and their difference is important. Coexist means that Sufism and Shi'ism both exist in the same social space. Overlap means that they share some common characteristics despite their difference. Reinforce means that the characteristics they share are essential to both, such that the existence of one mutually supports the existence of the other and that both thrive together rather than merely coexist. Coming to a nuanced understanding of the confluence and divergence of Sufism and Shi'ism is the most ambitious goal of this book, and it is the ultimate reason for engaging in such an unusual comparison: to see what happens when the sun meets the moon.

The multidisciplinary approach used here will engage a broad audience. For readers of world literature, this book offers translations of Urdu poets who have rarely been found in English volumes before. Those interested in gender studies can follow the biographies of courtesans, concubines, eunuchs, transvestites, and celibate men as models that challenged—but only obliquely—the normative structures of femininity and masculinity in a particular patriarchal society. For those pursuing sexuality studies, this book meditates on sexual orientation in a society before that term was invented and offers nuanced life histories of religious-minded artists who did not separate eros from devotion. Those involved in Islamic studies will find many angles of interest; this book addresses how the arts (poetry, song, and dance) expressed Islamic ideals, explores mysticism not only in Sufism but also in Shi'i communities, and illuminates the complexity of Shi'i and Sunni sectarian interactions as they overlap with common mystical orientations and devotional practices.

Those fascinated by South Asian history can explore the little-known cultural history of the southernmost fringe of the Mughal Empire—the Deccan province—which was its prize and also its peril. Those interested in Urdu literature can better understand the role of the Deccan in giving birth to the ghazal as an Urdu poetic genre. The eighteenth-century

Deccan is often overlooked in South Asian history because in many ways it is betwixt and between. In terms of space, it is between North India and South India, affected by both but belonging to neither. In terms of time, it is betwixt the medieval era of Mughal glory and the modern era of European domination, never fully pulled into the decline of the former or totally absorbed into the ascendance of the latter.

Being neither here nor there, however, the Deccan was never a void. It was full of creative possibilities in politics, religion, and literature, and it gave rise to a strong cultural florescence in the eighteenth century. The evidence of that florescence lingers in poems and pavilions, songs and dances. This legacy was shaped by a man named after the sun and a woman named after the moon. Come, let us leave this introduction and explore their lives and writings.

CHAPTER ONE

Celestial Bodies Seen from Deccan Soil

When Abraham observed the moon ascend, he said, "This is my Lord!" But when it set he said, "If my Lord had not given me guidance, I would surely be among those who are astray." When he observed the sun rise, he said, "This is my Lord—this is greater than all others!" But when it set he said, "O my people, I do not equate God with anything as you do."

—Qur'an 6:76-79

Shah Siraj and Mah Laqa Bai were poets in the eighteenth-century Deccan, but they were Muslims first. This initial chapter will explain how Islam developed in the Deccan, because religion and region shaped these poets' experiences of gender, sexuality, and poetry. It will illustrate the development of Islam in various contexts, including religious, social, and literary contexts.

Celestial and Terrestrial Contexts

The Qur'an declares that the sun, moon, and stars are not divine, challenging the old gods of earth, water, wind, and fire. It tells the story of Abraham—the archetypal monotheist—rebelling against his father and tribe. Ostracized for rejecting their idols, he wandered in search of a true deity. He observed the stars, moon, and sun yet rejected each in favor of a singular immaterial God. The Qur'an uses both narrative and poetry to convey its message through the story of Abraham and many subsequent prophets, including Moses, Jesus, and Muhammad. Poetically it argues that all things, including the sun and moon, worship God, who creates and sustains them. In worshipping the one God, each being acknowledges its ephemeral nature while reaching in humility toward the one who is eternal.

As the people of ancient cultures, like the Arabs, Persians, Africans,

Berbers, and Turks, increasingly converted to Islam, ancient deities of the moon and sun were displaced. To reinforce the idea that the sun and moon submit to the monotheistic faith, Muslims told of miracles by Muhammad and his closest follower, ʿAli ibn Abi Talib (died 661). The Prophet pointed to the full moon and it split, demonstrating his mission to the pagan Arabs; the Qurʾan refers to this event when it recites, *The time drew nigh and the moon split in two, but when they see a miracle they turn aside muttering, "Clearly it's sorcery"* (Q 51:1–2). ʿAli caused the sun to reverse its course after he missed the time for afternoon prayer because the Prophet had fallen asleep with his head cradled in ʿAli's lap; the sun moved back across the sky and gave ʿAli a second chance to fulfill his obligatory prayer.[1] Rather than propitiate the sun and moon, Muslim worshippers were to imitate their qualities: their submission to God's will, moving invariably along a determined path, serving with inerrant timing and exhibiting patient endurance in constant motion. Bowing in submission, people on earth could find the balance, dynamism, and harmony displayed by the heavens and its illuminated celestial bodies.

Muslims brought a religious message and also engineered a political revolution. Uniting various nations and tribes under one religion created a force that was political and civilizational. It elevated one book—the Qurʾan—as sacred above all others but also encouraged literacy and scholarship, creating a veritable explosion of the written word. Over time, military conquest matured into stable administration and urban prosperity, which promoted courtly love and the literary pursuit of beauty. Whether strolling in a garden, engaging in repartee at a tavern, or reciting at nighttime gatherings, poets kept their *divans* handy. The divan was a collection of poetry, especially the short lyrical love poems called ghazals, the symbol of cultivating a refined romantic and spiritual personality.

Mah Laqa Bai and Shah Siraj both compiled poetic divans. Yet before examining the poems and personas of Shah Siraj and Mah Laqa Bai, we have to understand how their Islamic society in the Deccan was formed. The terrestrial context will extend into three long-duration views: first, a view of Islamic civilization in South Asia from the perspective of religious history; second, a view of gender and sexuality in Islamic cultures from the perspective of sociology; and third, a view of love poetry from the perspective of comparative literature with a focus on Persian and Urdu. We could call these three different views "rites for sects," then "rhythm of sex," and finally "rhymes in sets."

Religious Context: Sectarian Competition and Coexistence

Muslims forged their new religion into a city-state, then a commonwealth, and then an empire. The Prophet Muhammad first ruled as mediator, religious guide, and lawgiver at Medina. He and his companions then formed a commonwealth that united Arab tribes along with former slaves and clients, including as allies some Jews and Christians, some of whom later converted to Islam. Within three decades, a faction led by the Umayyad Arab clan claimed the right to rule Islamic domains as an imperial dynasty, expanding its boundaries of control, fostering interregional trade, and generating enormous wealth for an aristocracy that accepted their terms.

However, this faction's success in empire building engendered conflict in theology as well as in politics. In the beginning, the Prophet, who spoke for God, brought the divine presence directly into the community and inspired unity among fractious tribes. But Muhammad's death created a deep crisis. Senior male followers selected a caliph (*khalifa* or "authoritative follower") who would rule, perpetuating an Arab tribal custom of electing an elder male leader. Four consecutive caliphs guided the nascent Islamic community through rapid expansion while factions formed through tribal chauvinism, regional power, and personal enmity. After a complex struggle, a governor of Syria took power as a king, setting up his family as the Umayyad dynasty. This usurpation led to sectarian formations that persist today. Many Muslims accepted the king as providing stable continuity, while others rejected his unjust usurpation of power that betrayed the Prophet's teachings. Some abhorred kings but feared politics and so turned toward morality. Each reaction gave rise to a different kind of Islamic practice.

Those who accepted kings who took power by fiat evolved into a sectarian allegiance called Sunni (which is short for Ahl al-Sunna wa'l-Jamaʿa). They asserted that an elected caliph was legitimate and that kings were acceptable if they enabled Muslims to live securely and fulfill their religious duties. Sunnis accepted kings as a necessary evil and focused on building a system of Islamic moral order called *shariʿa*. Those who rejected the dynastic usurpation developed into a sectarian allegiance called Shiʿi (which is short for Shiʿat ʿAli). Shiʿi loyalists asserted that only members of the Prophet Muhammad's immediate family should lead. They held that the Prophet designated his cousin and son-in-law, ʿAli, to be leader in both spiritual and political affairs. Members of the Shiʿi community developed a devotional ethos and theological outlook linked to their political dissent, asserting that the light of guidance that provided Muhammad with charismatic authority and intuitive knowledge was passed on genealogically. From the descendants of Muhammad's daughter Fatima (died 632) and her husband, ʿAli, one male in each generation was to be designated as the imam who perpetuated the Prophet's charisma. Some Shiʿi groups rebelled against rulers they saw as illegitimate and many of the imams were martyred, and so the Shiʿi community formed a vibrant minority with many varieties in devotional life and theological discourse.

In the face of opposition and rebellion, Muslim kings claimed to rule on behalf of the caliph, whom they upheld as a political pawn.[2] This concession created a stable pattern of governance for many centuries, producing an affluent urban society under an expansive empire, but it did not live up to Qurʾanic ideals. Shiʿi rejection and calls for justice highlighted the system's inequities but did not resolve them. Suppressed rebellions caused schismatic differences within the Shiʿi community, which fractured into competing factions. The largest Shiʿi community is called the "Twelver" group or "Imami" Shiʿis, who believe in a lineage of imams descended from ʿAli through twelve generations.[3] Twelver Shiʿis believe that the imams were created from one preexisting light and through them the universe came into being and is sustained.[4] They are the most excellent of all beings after the Prophet Muhammad and are superior to angels and previous prophets; they are immaculate and protected from sin.[5]

Some Muslims tired of political wrangling. They preached detachment from worldly ambition in order to draw closer to God through personal piety, mystical contemplation, and communitarian living. This movement was advocated by ascetics, philosophers, and mystics who were eventually called Sufis. The term Sufi has various etymologies: it could mean an ascetic who wears rough wool, or a sage who loves wisdom, or a contemplative who seeks ecstatic experience. Sufis created a subculture based upon a charismatic teacher (spiritual master or *shaikh*) who imparts the inner meaning of Islam. Sufi practice of Islam was not defined by political domination or messianic justice but rather by a constant struggle to stay conscious of the presence of God in all situations—in work as well as in prayer, in enjoyment as well as in suffering. Eventually, Sufis organized themselves into discrete communities with different methods of practicing Islam with a mystical orientation. Once so organized, Sufis could occasionally influence politics and social norms and thus were not individual quietists, such as the label "mystic" might imply.

Both Sunni and Shi'i Muslims were drawn to Sufi practices. Sufi lineages included as spiritual masters several of the Prophet Muhammad's family members who were considered by Shi'is to be imams. Sufis shared with Shi'is the concept that the Prophet was more than a mortal human. Both groups believed that he was also a spiritual principle: he was imbued with divine light through which God created the world. After the death of the Prophet's material body, his presence lives on through the divine light that shines through his closest followers, the imams for Shi'is and the saints (*awliya*) for Sufis. In the medieval period, political events led Sufis to identify mainly with the Sunni sect, while Shi'is began to distinguish themselves from Sufis.[6]

The esoteric teaching of Sufi masters filled a gap in Sunni communities, as the caliph system lost ideological force and political persuasiveness and actual power devolved onto regional sultans (meaning "authority" or ruler by might rather than by any divine right). Many Sunnis were attracted to Sufi leaders as "spiritual kings" whose prayers and devotions helped to prop up the "worldly kings" who ruled by violence and coercion. Sufis built a powerful institution called a *tariqa* (sometimes translated as "Sufi order" or "brotherhood"). Multiple orders proliferated, spreading variations of basic Sufi practices of prayer, meditation, music, and ecstatic devotion. After Mongol invasions of the thirteenth century, many Sunnis looked to Sufi leaders as anchors of the Islamic social order because strongmen, chiefs, and kings came and went in quick succession. In response, many Shi'is of the Twelver community disparaged the term "Sufi" as a marker of a mere subculture aligned to Sunni interests. Yet mystical concepts and practices advocated by Sufis were cultivated by many Shi'is under a different name—not Sufism but *'irfan*, or "mystical knowledge."

In short, there were different orientations within Islam broadly categorized as Sunni, Shi'i, and Sufi. Sunni and Shi'i were sectarian groups, whose split was over political issues, social allegiances, and theological assumptions. The third group, Sufi, was not a sect but rather a mystical movement. This movement was found mainly among Sunnis but shared many concepts with mystical currents among Shi'is. This background is important for the history of Islam in the Deccan, where all three groups were found, and each has played important roles, interacting with the others in complex ways.

Sufism in South Asia was largely shaped by the Chishti Sufi community. Khwaja Muʿin al-Din Chishti (died 1236) brought Sufi practices from Afghanistan and settled in Rajasthan. He taught that a Muslim should cultivate magnanimity like the sun, generosity like a river, and humility like the earth. Three generations later, Nizam al-Din Awliya (died 1325) systematized the core practices of the Chishti community, centered on ascetic renunciation, focused meditation, popular poetry, and devotional music. He sent his delegates to all corners of the Islamic empire ruled by the Delhi sultans, who controlled large tracts of South Asia. His disciples included courtiers who were the best poets of their age, like Amir Hasan Sijzi (died 1336) and Amir Khusro (died 1325), who left a literary and musical legacy that continues today.[7]

In the fourteenth century, many poets, administrators, and scholars moved south to Dawlatabad (a fortress town close to Awrangabad), sparking a florescence of Islamic devotional and artistic activity. Nizam al-Din sent disciples to Dawlatabad in the Deccan region, most notably Burhan al-Din Gharib (died 1337). The poet Amir Hasan shifted south and became a devoted follower of Burhan al-Din.[8] Chishti Sufis set the tone for popular religious piety among Sunni communities in the Deccan due to their admirable ethics and their lyrical activity.[9]

By the sixteenth century, the Deccan region split into five states ruled by Muslim kings (Bijapur, Golkonda, Khandesh, Ahmadnagar, and Berar) and one state ruled by a Hindu king (Vijayanagar). The king of Golkonda, Sultan Quli Qutb-Shah (ruled 1518–43), declared Shiʿism to be the official faith, buttressing his independence from the Sunni dynasty in Delhi. He fostered cultural and commercial relationships with the Shiʿi Safavid dynasty that ruled Iran. The Qutb-Shahi dynasty of Golkonda imported prime ministers from Iran, such as Mir Muhammad Muʾmin (died 1625), an impressive scholar-administrator who helped to design the new city of Hyderabad in 1592. The Qutb-Shahi rulers expressed Shiʿi piety in building shrines dedicated to Hazrat ʿAli, Imam Husain (died 680 at Karbala), and other Shiʿi heroes and heroines. Sufi masters' tombs and Shiʿi relic shrines were important sites of religious devotion and had intense syncretic potential. Hindus engaged in worship there in an Islamic environment, transferring Hindu practices onto Islamic foci of devotion.

As Islamic communities expanded in the Deccan, they witnessed a

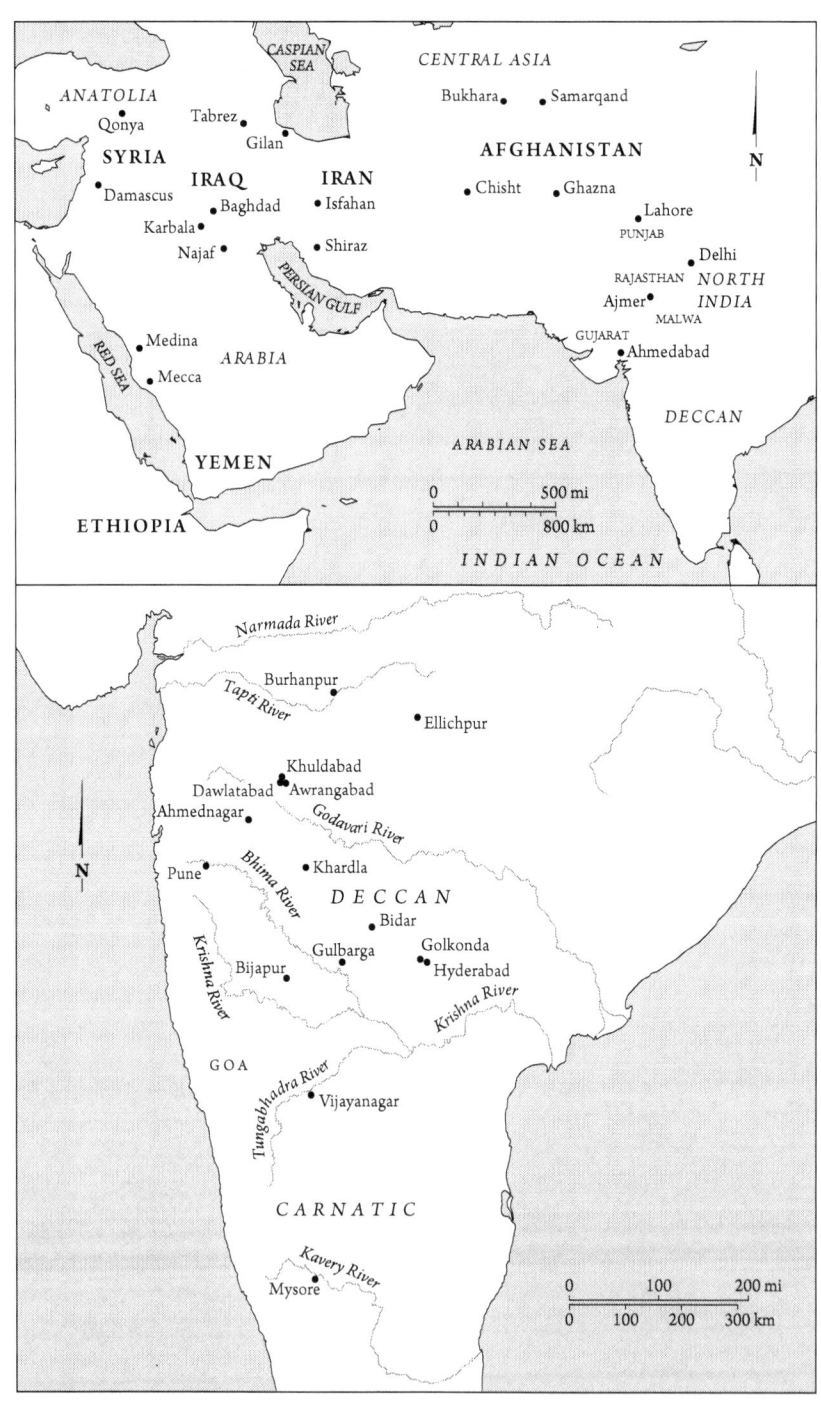

South and West Asia with Deccan region detail

variety of sectarian, theological, and political movements. Initial conquest was by the sultans of Delhi, Sunni warlords who saw Islam as submission to God and obedience to rulers. Sufis promoted community involvement, presenting Islam as inner transformation, ethical refinement, and mystical insight. Political and ritual innovation by Shi'i groups presented Islam as protest against injustice and revival of rightful claims. Historically these forces acted in waves, one supplanting the next, but socially and devotionally each wave left a deep imprint on the cultural life of Deccan Muslims. By the end of the seventeenth century, all three of these religious orientations — Sunni, Sufi, and Shi'i — coexisted in the Deccan in a complex interplay and delicate balance.

In the late seventeenth century, Mughal conquest of the Deccan shook this balance and brought this southern region under the centralized rule of Delhi once again. Shah Siraj and Mah Laqa Bai lived after the Mughal conquest, yet it is important to understand the three religious orientations that predate the Mughal era because they so deeply affected these two poets' personalities. Shah Siraj was a Sunni and a Sufi, while Mah Laqa Bai was a Shi'i with a mystical orientation. Before we can embark on a study of these two poets' spirituality and literature, we must take another long-duration view of their environment from the viewpoint of gender, for this study compares these two poets — one male and the other female — neither of whom lived a conventional sexual life.

Social Context: Gender and Sexuality in Islamic South Asia

The Qur'an disparages the idea that the sun and moon are gods: *Among God's signs are the night and day, the sun and moon. So never prostrate in worship to the sun or the moon — rather prostrate to God who created them both* (Q 41:37). But the allure of nature deities was hard to displace. Many in ancient societies found compelling how nature deities interacted through sex and war, such that sexual activity between people was often seen as ritual. Sexual activity echoed the drama of the gods' creative acts, and often a king's sexual potency mirrored the political vitality of his kingdom. The king's ritual intercourse with a priestess, often on a new year's holiday, recreated the mythic coupling that engendered the cosmos, commemorating the potency of the sky god and the fertility of the earth goddess.

Islam displaced such elaborate rituals and sexualized myths, but it did not suppress sexual pleasures. Islamic culture fostered a sense of sexual pleasure as being good, willed by God, and facilitated by Islamic legal norms. Some Muslim ascetics decried sex, but most Muslim theologians saw sexual pleasure as a blessing from God. Muslim jurists tried to "domesticate" sexual practices with rules about marriage, privacy, and propriety; such rules were a mixture of penalty and permissiveness. Islamic law formalized marriage as a contract, not a sacrament, allowing divorce, encouraging remarriage, permitting polygyny, and legalizing concubines.[10] The pursuit of sexual pleasure was refined into romance in prosperous urban centers, royal courts, and Sufi hospices. Romance blossomed outside the boundaries of married partnership as wives were increasingly sequestered behind patriarchal privacy. The heroes of romantic culture were male poets (often courtiers, scholars, or travelers) and female singers (often slave-artists or concubines). Outsiders from other civilizations or religious allegiances often looked aghast at Islamic culture's permissiveness.

Persianate Islamic culture fostered romantic literature and mystical pursuit of illumination, in which sexual pleasure and aesthetic refinement were seen as mutually reinforcing. With conquest, trade, and migration, this Persianate Islamic culture spread throughout South Asia, where Muslim views of sex and gender were further complicated. An indigenous Hindu culture that saw women as impure during menstruation strengthened patriarchal Islamic notions about female seclusion and prevented them from entering places of worship. The Brahmanical tradition of holy ascetic life (*brahmachariya*) reinforced some strands of Sufi thought that perceived married life as worldly entanglement. Chishti Sufis harbored an ideal of celibacy for their spiritual masters; not all of them refused marriage and those who did never imposed celibacy upon their followers, but it remained a potent ideal for many Chishtis. They stood on the crossroads between Hindu custom that equated holiness with sexual renunciation and Islamic culture that pictured sex with women as entanglement in worldly affairs.

Yet Islamic culture in South Asia also nurtured the opposite extreme of luxurious indulgence. Muslim aristocrats amassed wealth and power, acquiring multiple wives and retinues of concubines, female slaves, eunuchs, musicians, and dancers (eunuchs will be met in chapter 6 and concubines in chapters 8 and 9). In South Asia, both Shi'i and Sunni jurists allowed sexual relations of a male slave owner with his female slaves.[11] In addition, the Twelver Shi'i community allowed *mut'a* or "temporary marriage" (in Persian, *izdivaj-e muvaqqat*), through which a man took wives for a limited period of time in a legal union for the purpose of sexual pleasure or social companionship rather than for procreation. Debate over this practice sparked sectarian rivalry between Sunni and Shi'is, but it was practiced in premodern South Asia.[12] From the viewpoint of gender and sexuality, South Asia was largely patriarchal. Hindu and Muslim views stressed women's inferiority and restricted their mobility and opportunity. Within Muslim communities, both Sunnis and Shi'is, despite their other differences, stressed fidelity to legal norms that kept daughters and wives under the authority of men. Yet there were always important exceptions to general rules.

In all communities, aristocratic women had power to act independently as older matrons, even if they had endured stifling restrictions in younger years before strategic marriage into other aristocratic families. In Sufi communities, there was comparatively more flexibility about sexuality, even if gender norms were rigid. Through celibacy and poverty, both female and male Sufis escaped some of the burdens of being a householder as imposed by patriarchy. In Shi'i communities, the institution of "temporary marriage" could potentially give women a social and sexual life that was not defined by childbearing and marital restrictions, though in practice it may not have allowed women to transcend patriarchal limitations. Courtesans who were mainly Shi'i provide the most dramatic example of women who lived beyond the boundaries imposed by marriage and child-rearing. Yet courtesans also negotiated patriarchal forces and were often victims if they remained financially dependent on rich men for support.

Islamic society in premodern South Asia accepted courtesans and concubines as part and parcel of the aristocratic class. The distinction between courtesan and concubine was a subtle but important one. Concubines were female slaves owned by men primarily for sexual satisfaction. Courtesans were women raised by other women in order to be artists, performers, and seductresses of wealthy male patrons; they were not owned by men, though they did elicit support from men or, in lower-class circles, rented themselves to men for entertainment of an artistic, conversational, or possibly sexual nature. Courtesans thrived by appearing independent of male control, yet this autonomy was an illusion since they were most often financially supported by courts or estates run by men. Still, the illusion of independence was powerful and alluring, symbolized most strongly by the courtesan's status of not being married and being able to compete with men in the arts of music, dance, and conversation.

Through the early-modern period, concubines and courtesans were distinct from mere prostitutes. With prostitutes, sexual gratification was directly related to monetary payment, unmediated by other structures. For concubines, sexual relations with men were mediated by ownership, which made intercourse with them legal under Islamic law. A courtesan's sexual relations with men were mediated by art and aesthetics, as her role was seen primarily as entertaining performance, erudite company, and artistic refinement, which may or may not have included intimacy. Since it was ambiguous whether courtesans were involved in sexual relations with their patrons, it is no surprise that in Islamic society in South Asia, many courtesans were avowedly Shiʿi. The Shiʿi legal allowance for temporary marriage regulated this tension and provided legal and moral mechanisms to justify sexual relations if and when they might arise, without compromising the allure of the courtesan as a woman beyond the bounds of married householder, the status upon which her charm and social power depended.

In modern times, the distinction between courtesan and concubine collapsed. With colonial intrusions, the wealth and prestige of royalty and lower aristocrats faded, and courtesans lost their patronage. Victorian values were imposed on society, which denigrated sensual art forms as merely licentious. Concubines and courtesans became lumped into the category of "prostitutes" under the forces of colonial domination, decay of royal patronage, and impact of Islamic reform movements.[13] Mah Laqa Bai was fortunate to live in the early-modern period, before these social changes set in that erased the very possibility of her existence as a courtesan of high standing, artistic excellence, and acknowledged spirituality.

Few courtesans reached the position of independent noblewomen, as did Mah Laqa Bai. Few Sufis were completely celibate as adults outside the burdens of a household, as was Shah Siraj. Shah Siraj and Mah Laqa Bai were exceptions to the rules, but their cases illustrate the power of rules that held under their sway the great majority of their coreligionists. These two figures were also exceptions in another way: they broke through the silence of routine life with eloquence. Most people live, love, and die without leaving a record of their feelings, but Shah Siraj and Mah Laqa Bai belonged to the strange class of people—poets—who defy the rule of silence. Despite their difference in sectarian allegiance and beyond their binary opposition in gender, Shah Siraj and Mah Laqa Bai belong together as poets. But before we can compare them, we need to take a third long-distance view of Islamic society in South Asia, this time from the vantage point of literature.

Literary Context: Love Poetry in Islamic Culture

The Prophet Muhammad delivered a universal message adapted to Arab culture. Bedouin Arabs did not invest in arts like sculpture, architecture, or written literature that required settled life. Instead, they devoted their artistic skill to language. Their highly refined oral poetry told narratives of their tribal heroes, lovers, and rogues. Beauty of expression became a cipher for truth, both in terms of tribal identity and supernatural power.[14] In this environment, the Prophet Muhammad presented the Qur'an in Arabic, which was uniquely powerful and beautiful, but his people mistook him for a poet-soothsayer. Such poets were *manic* as understood by the Greeks like Socrates: they were inspired by a muse who dictated rhythmic words from beyond their rational faculties in fits of inspiration like madness.[15] Arab soothsayers incanted rhymes about future calamities inspired by their deities, while Arab vagrant poets spoke in epics inspired by jinn, disembodied beings of a fiery nature that roamed the desert. Calling Muhammad a poet-soothsayer, his society rejected his claim to transmit messages from God. Muhammad's revelations, however, asserted that he was not a possessed poet but rather a messenger sent by God—just as were Abraham, Moses, David, and Jesus before him.

In response, the early Muslim community rejected poets, who were seen as the spokespersons for the pagan gods and ancient rites of nature deities.[16] Yet Islamic denunciation of poetry relaxed once the religion was firmly established. Arab Muslims took great pride in their literary heritage consisting of both the Qur'an and pre-Islamic odes in Bedouin Arabic. Some Muslim poets turned to themes of erotic love amid wine parties in an ecstatic mode. Others cultivated themes of passionate love amid courtly etiquette in a chaste romantic mode. Still others explored themes of spiritual love amid ascetic rigor in a mystical mode.

This love poetry had a great impact on Persian and later Urdu literature in South Asia. Persian language changed with the new Islamic environment.[17] Sultan Mahmud of Ghazna, the first Muslim ruler to conquer large areas of South Asia (ruled 998–1030), patronized medieval Persian poets who adopted themes of love developed in Arab poetic circles. The introductory elegy for a lost love (*nasib*) detached from the Arab ode to become a Persian love lyric known as the ghazal. It evolved from the thirteenth century into a refined form that invented ways of speaking to an absent beloved in romantic and mystical registers. The ghazal was the favorite genre for love poetry in Persian and later in Urdu.

Saʿdi of Shiraz (died 1292) raised the romantic ghazal to heights of sweetness and grace. He reputedly visited South Asia, and Muʿin al-Din Chishti used to quote his verses fondly. One generation later in Delhi, Amir Khusro in Chishti Sufi circles—inspired by Saʿdi—composed courtly love poems that can be read as mystical allegory. His friend Amir Hasan cultivated the ghazal in the Deccan.[18] Hafiz (died 1389) intensified the genre's complexity and subtlety. He was invited to move to the Deccan, but the poet balked at the sea voyage and sent this ghazal to the Deccan ruler who had invited him:[19]

> Getting a world of joy is not worth even a moment of pain
>   Sell my Sufi cloak for a bottle of wine?—that's a net gain
> A sultan's crown is radiant but constant fear of death lurks in it
>   A much coveted headdress, for sure—but will the head remain?
> The wine-seller's door opens just enough to offer a mere cup
>   I got just a sip—and my pious prayer mat bears its stain
> At first, a breezy whiff of profit made anxiety at sea seem easy
>   I was wrong—a hundred pearls ain't worth the waves and rain

Hafiz illustrates the ghazal's rhyme structure and also reveals how it was the preeminent form of poetic expression in Persian in medieval Iran and South Asia. A fine ghazal was worth its weight in gold and pearls if it caught the ear of a royal patron. Yet a good poet would never allow his ghazal to be valued in mere gold.

The ghazal's rhyme and rhythm stands as a literary symbol for Indo-Persian culture.[20] Its structure and imagery are well illustrated by Amir Hasan in the following poem, which invokes the moon and sun:[21]

> Just tonight, you moon among beauties, be my guest for a while
>   Let the sun of your visage light me like dawn's bright smile
> My heart is a furnace holding you, my Abraham, my bosom friend
>   Favor me just once and make the flames into a garden domicile
> Your black ensnaring curls have thrown into disarray my piety
>   Now with the liquor of your gaze let my body roll and spirit rile

> This wretch Hasan informs you that your lovers all seem content
> I'm not qualified to join them, but won't you treat me as worthwhile?

The ghazal is written in couplets. The first couplet's lines end in a rhyming sound (*radif*), which may be embedded in a longer word or phrase (*qafiya*). The first line of each subsequent couplet is free within the rhythm of the poem, but the second line must echo the rhyme. The ghazal's beauty is in seeing how far the imagery can extend or how wide a thought can wander before it is pulled back to the rhyme that finishes the couplet, stringing it like pearls on a silken thread. Hasan's ghazal displays another characteristic of the form, the poet's citation in the final couplet of his or her own persona as if by a third-person observer. Hasan means "good" but is also his pen name (*takhallus*), and he plays on the imagery of a good thing—namely himself—being deemed worthless by an arrogant lover. Word play involving the poet's pen name is a feature of the ghazal giving it irony, sarcasm, and humor.

In the Persian ghazal there are gender ambiguities that English translation cannot express. Ghazals have been translated as the speech of a love-struck man entreating an aloof female beloved. Yet the Persian ghazal does not specify the genders of either lover or beloved, because Persian language does not express gender in grammar: there is no difference between "she," "he," or "it," either as the subject of an action or as the referent of a pronoun. In many Persian ghazals the gender ambiguity is inflected toward a male lover with a male beloved, as in this ghazal of Amir Hasan. The speaker's gender is only hinted at in the last couplet with the poet's pen name, Hasan, a male name. The gender of the object of desire is specified only once in comparing the beloved to Abraham, *Khalil* or "the bosom friend."[22] The poem hints that the love described could be between two males, but other couplets describe a love that is completely ambiguous in terms of gender pairing.

The poet, Amir Hasan, was an intimate friend of Amir Khusro; they were so close that some sources portray them as having been deeply in love.[23] Could the poem's imagery of the beloved residing in Hasan's heart, like Abraham in the burning furnace, allude to his real-life bosom friend, Amir Khusro? The poem's delicious ambiguity allows it to be sung in Qawwali performances where Sufi listeners can create their own associations to refine whatever love they feel. Whether love portrayed in ghazals reflects the biography and person of the poet will be addressed as this book examines gender and sexuality in Urdu poetry. This ghazal by Amir Hasan alerts us to the complexity of this terrain as it was handed down through Persian poetry to Urdu authors.

The ghazal was cultivated across South Asia in Persian and was adapted to Urdu in the Deccan. The Deccan's syncretic and multicultural forces allowed Urdu to grow not only as a spoken vernacular but also as literary expression. Though many poets later composed in Urdu across North India, the roots of Urdu literature are in Deccan soil. This book's focus on two poets in the Deccan will help shift attention of scholars to this much-neglected region, to balance previous studies that skew Urdu's literary history northward.

One of the pioneering Western scholars of Urdu and Persian literature, Annemarie Schimmel, has pointed out that Urdu developed in the Deccan.[24] Chishti Sufis in the Deccan were instrumental in forging Urdu into a literary language. Shi'i poets also wrote lamentations about love for and martyrdom of the imams (*marsiya*), adding to the growing literary status of the Deccani dialect of Urdu. Deccani Urdu was different in many ways from dialects of Urdu in Northern India, which developed as spoken vernaculars without being used as a poetic medium. In the north, the cultural weight of the Mughal Empire pushed poets to compose in Persian, and other poets adopted Hindi written in Devanagari script. In the Deccan, authors innovated by using Persian script to write the Deccani vernacular language, which mixed local Indian languages with Persian, Turkish, and Arabic expressions. This was the seed of Urdu as a literary language.

In the Deccan, different communities met and mingled without being dominated by one overarching imperial power. This led to a great flourishing of creativity, innovation, and syncretism until the Mughal Empire absorbed the Deccan into its polity based in Agra and Delhi. In the next section, we will consider the cultural potential of the Deccan region before and after the Mughal conquest.

Temporal Context: The Deccan after Mughal Conquest

In the sixteenth century, kingdoms in the Deccan (which could be labeled "South Indian Shi'i-Sufi hybrid states") cultivated creativity in architecture, painting, poetry, and devotional life. Deccan kingdoms like Golkonda turned with increasing intensity to their local soil—languages, landscapes, and devotional idioms—to articulate an independent Deccan culture that was Islamic but open to cooperation and co-adaptation with the wider South Asian environment that was largely Hindu. By the seventeenth century, the Deccan kingdoms came under increasing pressure from the Sunni Mughals. Starting with Akbar (ruled 1556–1605), Mughal emperors pushed south and reinforced explicitly Sunni allegiance to counter intensifying conflict with the Safavid Empire in Iran that espoused Shi'ism.[25] After a century of pressure, attrition, diplomacy, and occasional battles, the emperor Awrangzeb (ruled 1658–1707) championed a Sunni fideism to justify conquering the Deccan kingdoms. He built up Awrangabad as a military base to conquer the farthest southern kingdom, Golkonda, with its vibrant capital city of Hyderabad, "The Abode of 'Ali."

Awrangzeb conquered Golkonda in 1687 but snatched that gem at a high price. Three decades of campaigning dangerously overextended Awrangzeb's empire. His trusted military courtier Nizam al-Mulk (died 1748) became governor of the Deccan province. Taking the royal title Asaf-Jah, Nizam al-Mulk acted as independent ruler in the Deccan though he professed allegiance to the Mughal emperor, with whom he shared ties of Central Asian ancestry and Sunni allegiance. Nizam al-Mulk's descendants established the Asaf-Jahi dynasty; known more popularly as the nizams, they maintained an army and minted their own coins. Their Deccan territory was a successful state with territory as large as France holding ports on the Arabian Sea and the Bay of Bengal. The nizams ruled with stability as the rest of the Mughal realm broke up and regional strongmen—some Muslim, some Hindu, and some Sikh—jostled for power.

While the nizams remained Sunni and promoted Mughal political norms, the local population persisted in their distinctive Deccan mix of sectarian hybridity that allowed Hindu and Muslim to coexist and allowed Shi'i and Sunni to thrive side-by-side along with Sufi mystics. The nizams gained a loyal following by promoting the shrines and festivals of diverse religious groups, turning confessional holidays into civic spaces for public merriment. Music and poetry were central to such events. Artistic production, religious life, and scholarly activity were dominated by the two urban centers at opposite ends of the road that traversed the Deccan plateau: Hyderabad in its southeastern heartland and Awrangabad at its northwestern gateway.

These two urban centers flourished during the eighteenth century. The Sufi poet Shah Siraj lived in Awrangabad, whose environment promoted his blend of mystical devotion and erotic aesthetics. The courtesan poet Mah Laqa Bai lived in Hyderabad, whose court was the stage for her flashy dance and her fleshly skill of seduction. On the surface, the contrast between these two poetic voices could not be starker. One is a man, in his youth a homosexual bon vivant who was in love with a soldier and renounced sexual fulfillment to sublimate his erotic energy into mystical verse. The other is a woman who carefully cultivated the arts of poetry, song, and dance in her youth in order to seduce powerful men in her mature years.

Yet despite these apparent contrasts in gender and propriety, there are deep currents that bind them together: currents of eros, ecstasy, and aesthetics. Though Siraj renounced sexual activity in favor of devotional intensity, he remained an artist whose poetry was deeply shaped by eros—though it was oriented toward refinement into spirituality, Shah Siraj never denounced erotic energy in an ascetic gesture of defiance. He remained to the end of his life a lover whose sexuality (and sexual orientation) was an important aspect of his personality and his art, though he shied away from sexual acts. In the case of Mah Laqa Bai, her erotic energy was on public display, but she was never reduced by her culture to her sexuality. As a courtesan, she was an admired artist and a publicly respected personality in court as well as in religious arenas. Though she brazenly transgressed Muslim jurists' notions of Islamic propriety, she inhabited a space of tolerance in her Islamic society and was deeply involved in promoting religious devotion.

Religiosity and sexuality were not contradictory forces in the Islamic culture of the Deccan. This is evident in the life stories of these two poets and is an essential feature of their verse. The garden imagery of their Urdu poetry represents both the paradise of devotional bliss and the rose arbor of sensual dalliance. In this garden, the sun meets the moon. Here, contradictory opposites dance together, leaving a whirl of paradox in their wake, which bewilders the tyranny of reason and releases the songbird of desire from its cage. It is the garden of Urdu poetry that Siraj and Mah Laqa share, and they are brought together through its ideal of love, embracing both erotic and ecstatic experiences. This book explores these insights through their two life stories to discover their interconnections and express them through English translations of their verse.

FIRST ORBIT

Siraj the Sun

Were the crescent moon polite, on seeing your brow
 It would bow day or night when you meet with salams
What's this you do, Siraj, just like the sun?
 Each dawn that idol's house you greet with salams

—*verses from a ghazal by Siraj*

In four chapters, this section traces the personality, poetry, and music of Siraj Awrangabadi. His formal name was Sayyid Siraj al-Din Husaini, but he is best known by his pen name, Siraj, which means the sun.[1] In the verses quoted above, he plays with the homology between his pen name and his radiant namesake.[2] Siraj was born in Awrangabad around 1716 and died there in 1763. Histories of Urdu literature note his importance but usually mention only that he was a younger contemporary of the poet Vali Deccani (1667–1707), who brought the new style of writing the ghazal in Urdu to Delhi. After this, most histories are content to follow the development of romantic and mystical poetry in the north. Siraj remains in the shadows, and few of his poems have been translated into English or analyzed in detail.

As a Sufi poet who mastered the mystical tone of Urdu love poems, Siraj is important. His life and writing highlight how Urdu originated in the Deccan and how Sufis were instrumental in cultivating the language as a literary and theological medium; Siraj prods us gently to keep our focus on the Deccan region, despite how historians of Urdu have veered persistently to the north. More important, Siraj has an intriguing and rare personality as a man dedicated to love but who never married;

in terms of gender and eros in Islamic societies, Siraj offers a particularly rich example of the patriarchal demands of masculinity at odds with one man's artistic and spiritual goals. His spiritual aspiration diverted him from composing poetry just as he was reaching maturity. The complex relationship between his spirituality and his art is better documented in Siraj's case than in that of most Urdu poets because he was a Sufi master and his religious practices were at the center of both his literary life and social persona. For these interlinked reasons, he deserves a close look.

The aim of this First Orbit is to understand the richness of Siraj's spiritual life and the tensions in his artistic vocation as a poet, as both impacted his social life as a Muslim man. Fortunately, the means to realize this aim exist in profusion. There are numerous texts that are important resources on his life and poems, some published and some in archival manuscripts. There are also sound recordings of his poetry sung in the Qawwali tradition that he patronized so strongly.

Most important is his collection of poems, or *Kulliyat*. It includes 515 ghazals and 11 *masnavis* or epic odes, along with a few from more rare poetic forms. The ghazals contain glimpses of the author's spiritual insights and concept of love, while one masnavi has an autobiographical narrative that reveals much about his early life. Siraj gives a brief autobiographical account in the introduction to his selection of favorite Persian ghazals, *Intikhab-e Davavin-e Farsi* (also known as *Intikhab-e Divanha*). While no copy of this book appears to be extant, the text of Siraj's autobiography is preserved for us in "Shafiq" Awrangabadi's memorial of Persian poets in India, titled *Gul-e Raʿna* or "The rose of beauty."[3] This collection of biographies was completed in 1768, only several years after Siraj's death, by an author who knew him personally. The same author wrote another collection of biographies, *Chamanistan-e Shuʿara* or "The poets' garden," two years before Siraj's death. We also have a book by "Qaqshal" (whose given name was Afzal Beg Awrangabadi) titled *Tuhfat al-Shuʿara* or "Gift of the poets," composed in 1752 while Siraj was still alive.[4] An account of a tour of Awrangabad was written shortly after 1774 by Khaksar Sabzavari, titled *Savanih* or "Life and travels."[5] The author, a Sufi visitor to Awrangabad, recorded with admiration the city's sites and

Sufi tomb-shrines called *dargahs* (along with those in the outlying towns of Dawlatabad and Khuldabad). He mentions Siraj primarily as a saint who had died eleven years earlier and thus as one of the most recent of the great Sufi masters whose tombs were places of pilgrimage in the city. Siraj is mentioned last—being most recently deceased—in a list of famous Chishti, Qadiri, Naqshbandi, Shattari, and Qalandar saints.

Siraj's reputation as a saint and his tomb as a place of pilgrimage did not survive to the present. This section will illustrate the tension between Siraj's roles as poet, Sufi master, and man who lived outside the gender norms imposed by his society. Its chapters will explore many sources of information about him, from biographies to hagiographies to his poems as written or sung. These sources demand that we use the tools of several intellectual disciplines for a holistic analysis, and the following chapters therefore use approaches from religious studies, literary analysis, theology, and gender studies.

Besides his voluminous collection of Urdu poems and his letters to friends, little remains of Siraj's legacy. None of his Sufi disciples wrote a memorial of their teacher, and he penned no systematic theological treatises. His legacy is primarily oral, in his poems that were composed to be sung. Siraj himself did not collect them in written form; rather his friends compiled a book from them on his behalf. Without these loving friends, his literary legacy would be as bare as his tomb, which is lonely and rather dilapidated. Though it still stands in Awrangabad, in the center of a grassy park littered with stray plastic bags, nothing remains of the *takiya* or Sufi center where he thrived and taught.[6]

If Siraj could witness this sorry state of affairs, he would most likely laugh. What seems like a deplorable situation to a scholar would seem to a Sufi perfectly natural. Of course a lover's home is in ruins and the turning of this world effaces his every trace. For one dedicated to love, what use is there in buildings, followers, power, or fame? Life's success is measured only in the quality of moments with one's beloved. If that is the case for the lover of a person, what is the state of one who has given up loving a person for the love of God? The worse his or her worldly state gets, the better it is for one who strives to be God's lover, for Muʿin al-Din Chishti

The dargah (tomb-shrine) of Shah Siraj, located in Awrangabad
(photo by Scott Kugle)

taught that "He indeed is the true lover who welcomes with delight the sorrows and pain received from his Friend [*yar*, meaning God]."[7]

Siraj would laugh and maybe sing his own poem about "the world's abode as just a vast emptiness." As we begin to explore this eloquent, intriguing, and unconventional Islamic personality, let us listen to his whole ghazal:[8]

> Worshipping God is best achieved by self-worshipping
>   True being is in nothingness and nothingness in being
> My heartfelt wine companion, clear my head of pain
>   I'm drunk, so give me a goblet of eternal spirit's inebriating
> Whoever sees the world's abode as just a vast emptiness
>   Grasps that in the heart's realm alone a lover stays residing
> There's hope that my sweetheart will give me just a glimpse
>   After such tyrannous teasing and just before exile's agonizing
> One night, while burning slowly the candle told me, Siraj,
>   In the end, every lofty thing is heading for a humbling

CHAPTER TWO

Siraj's Bewilderment

Hear news of love's bewilderment
—*first phrase of the first verse of a ghazal by Siraj*

The best way to start this series of chapters about Siraj is to listen to his voice. This means we should listen to Qawwali, the Sufi devotional music in which his poetry is still sung. I heard Siraj's most famous ghazal in an all-night music session, sung during the ʿurs celebration—honoring the death anniversary of a saint—of Shaikh Nizam al-Din Awrangabadi (died 1729) to whose Sufi lineage Siraj belonged. This chapter offers an English translation of this poem so that we can understand the states of mystical love that it portrays and can reflect upon them in the light of the poet's own personality.

This popular poem has received wide acclaim, and Urdu audiences often know by heart its evocative opening line: *khabar-e tahayyur-e ʿishq sun*.[1] An English translation might read like this:

> Hear news of love's bewilderment:
>   no beauty remains, no feverish madness
> No you remains, no I remains—
>   all that remains is unself-consciousness
> A wind blew in from the unseen world,
>   scorching the garden of appearances
> On pain's bare branch, just one bud—
>   call it the heart—remains in greenness
> Just now, the king of oblivion has bestowed
>   upon me nakedness's royal robe
> No stitch of discernment's propriety remains,
>   no veil-rending insanity's lewdness
> With what tongue can I express complaint
>   against my beloved's negligent gaze?
> Take from my heart's wine-vat a hundred cups—
>   it remains brimming in fullness

> Your beauty's power stirs up bewildering
> tumult here to such extent that
> The mirror reflects no charred devotee,
> no idol—its face remains imageless
> An amazing moment it was, when I
> first learned from passion's pages
> Ever since, reason's tome stood on the shelf
> and remains right there, readerless
> Passion's flames reduced to ash
> Siraj's uncomplaining, speechless heart
> No caution remains, no second thought—
> all that remains is fearlessness

This English translation tries to capture the *radif*, the ghazal's original rhyme, with the use of the verb "remains" followed by a rhyming sound "-ess" at the end of the second line of each couplet.

The English translation offered above tries to convey this grammatical dynamism with rhyme words that not only end in a similar sound, "-ess," but are delivered by syllables of either "-less" or "-ness" or a combination of the two. The choice of these rhyming words in English suggests a tension between fullness and emptiness—their opposite nodes create a whirl of meaning that pulls and tugs the reader into an abstracted state that is both-empty-and-full (bewilderment) or neither-empty-nor-full (equanimity). Let us enter this perplexing struggle one couplet at a time.

News of Love's Bewilderment

Every ghazal begins with an opening couplet (*matlaʿ* or point of arising) that sets up the rhyme. Both lines of the first couplet end with the rhyme that sets up the sonic thread that will echo through the second line in each subsequent couplet.

> Hear news of love's bewilderment:
> no beauty remains, no feverish madness
> No you remains, no I remains—
> all that remains is unself-consciousness

Often in the ghazal, this sonic thread is all that binds the couplets together, since they do not require any narrative or continuous theme.

However, in Siraj's ghazals in general, and in this one in particular, the opening couplet does more than set up the rhyme: it introduces a theme that pervades all the couplets, giving the ghazal an unusual unity. That theme is bewilderment (*tahayyur*), which results from persisting with love beyond the stages of pleasure and pain.

For Siraj, this bewilderment is more than mere confusion (whether information gathered by the senses is true) or simple perplexity (if a deduction by reason is correct). The major spiritual teacher in Siraj's Sufi order, Shaikh Kalimullah Shahjahanabadi (died 1729), explains the importance of bewilderment:

> The first stage of the spiritual path is repentance and the final stage is bewilderment (*hairat*).... The beauty and perfection of the divine essence is such that it calls for bewilderment rather than mere doubt.... Bewildered wonder at some object comes from a person's knowing and perceiving the essence of that object, in contrast to doubt which comes from a person's ignorance and misunderstanding. So bewilderment comes from a person's presence with a thing while doubt comes from a person's absence from that thing. A bewildered person ascends, with each passing moment, upward toward the pinnacle of knowing something because of his passionate desire to know that thing. In contrast, the doubtful person descends, with each passing moment, down into ignorance about the reality of a thing because of his lack of attention to it.[2]

For Siraj, bewilderment is a spiritual state resulting from absolute resignation, which is the highest form of love.

The couplet's first line lures the listener with familiar tropes of love poetry: "Hear news of love ..." The first two words allude to the morning breeze that acts as a messenger, carrying news of the alienated lover's condition over the distance of separation to the beloved. The name of this poetic genre, ghazal, means "weaving words of love," and the breeze acts as a personified metaphor for the poet's own breath, whose art pronounces delicate tones that balance symbols conveying love's moods. In the ghazal, the distant beloved, whose hair is tousled by the breeze, may or may not care to hear the message it whispers, but even if the beloved openly disdains and belittles the message, the breeze's seductive play through his or her hair only rouses the lover to further unrealistic hope and savory pain.

The message in the first line is not an ordinary amatory overture that declares the yearning of desire and the burning of separation. Rather, the lover sends a strange message to the beloved—that love has burned him out: "Hear news of love's bewilderment..." The lover announces his state of bewilderment; he has persisted so long in love's throes that he no longer maintains a strong focus on the beloved person. The subject-object relationship of such personalized love, which requires a forceful ego to maintain, is no longer tenable. As the line flows along toward the first statement of the rhyme, it becomes about what the lover has lost in this state of bewilderment and not about what he hopes to gain: "Hear news of love's bewilderment: no beauty remains, no feverish madness." Beauty stands for the beloved, a beauty (*pari*) whose appearance and manner is captivating like a fairy or possessing spirit. Madness stands for the lover, who is captive to a feverish insanity (*junun*) like the famous lover of Arabian odes, Majnun, whose reason is unhinged by Laila's beauty as he wanders through the wastelands, seeing her image everywhere.

These two icons of lover and beloved are the two poles between which the fabric of love stretches, enabling words to be woven in the ghazal. Yet in this first line, the icons of lover and beloved are present only in their absence: they are mentioned only to report that they no longer remain! The fascinating power of the beloved's beauty has fired the lover's fever of passion to such a heat that is has melted down his subjectivity. He has pushed through the straits of love's torment only to find on the other side a desert expanse with no identifiable features, in which one can never establish one's orientation. It is the wilderness of bewilderment in which the self, once hitched to love's dynamism, has now become unhinged: "No you remains, no I remains..." Love's bewilderment allows the poem to speak more directly and to eschew the complexity of Persian formality and grammar, which had structured the first line. In very simple Urdu, shedding Persianate phrases and garden imagery, the line states the news succinctly: there is no I and there is no you.

The first line says "Hear news of love" and the second line clarifies the news: the game of passion has reached a new plateau in which passion has burned itself out. But to what effect? That is left open, creating a series of possibilities for the poem's later couplets to explore, yet the poem's tone is not melancholy spiced with sarcasm but is rather deep with despair. The second line flows toward its restatement of the rhyming phrase, "No you remains, no I remains—all that remains is unself-consciousness." Again, the speaker takes recourse to apophatic language, that which says by unsaying, to express the unique potency of bewilderment, which Michael Sells, meditating upon the Sufi thinker Ibn 'Arabi (died 1240), called "the station of no-station."[3] All that remains is what is not! No lover's passion, no beloved's beauty, no I and no you—all that remains is unself-consciousness. This is, of course, a paradox. It is not routine consciousness, yet it is not unconsciousness, for even in bewilderment there is a persistent awareness and the voice continues to speak. It is unself-consciousness (*be-khabari*) a state in which one has no news of oneself. The positive and assertive expression of this state is rapture (*vajd*), while its negating and dissolving expression is bewilderment (*tahayyur*), to which the first couplet inexorably leads us listeners.

An Unseen Wind

How did the poetic voice get to this vast void of bewilderment? What willful acts brought him here, and does being lost in its expanse represent a triumph for the lover or utter defeat? To answer these questions, the following couplet returns to classical images of desire's garden but turns them on their head:

> A wind blew in from the unseen world,
>   scorching the garden of appearances
> On pain's bare branch, just one bud—
>   call it the heart—remains in greenness

In the opening couplet, the morning breeze, which carries a message to the beloved, brings only the message that there no longer remains beloved or lover. Similarly, in this couplet, the spring wind is supposed to spread the fragrance of blooming roses and set the tree blossoms quivering in a captivating dance for the pleasure of the lovers in a garden who stroll along its lanes or secretly meet in its bowers. To understand more fully the power of this couplet, we must hear it against the backdrop of garden imagery in Urdu poetry, which forms one of its most alluring pool of resources to speak about love.

As a hybrid, Deccani Urdu adapted images and themes from Persian poetry to the local soil, giving them simplicity and directness often lacking in the complex and overtly crafted Persian poetry of Mughal times. Images of springtime verdure and pleasure gardens made up one language environment where Persian and Urdu overlapped (another being the court and a third being the tavern). Urdu poets not only preserved the nightingale and rose, the proud tulip and coy narcissus (which populate Persian poetry and represent the emotional dynamics of love), but also sang of Indian flora with particularly heart-ravishing effect, and their devotional landscape was inhabited by Brahmins, idol temples, and dance circles of Krishna devotees rather than by Magian taverns or Syriac monasteries.

Whether the flowers are Persian or Indian, they represent the sensual appearance of a life force that was hidden and in this sense stand both for romantic love that approaches intimate union and for divine solicitous care that calls to us through the world, not despite it. The beauty of flowers, like the beloved, fuses the pursuit of metaphorical love to ultimate love. The garden is a place to pursue love, whether this is love for aesthetic beauty (with the color and fragrance and kaleidoscopic patterns created by flowers) or longing for a beloved partner. In Islamic theology, the garden represents paradise. But Muslims went far beyond mere theology and constructed actual gardens, especially in the Persianate world that included South Asia. The garden is a place of leisure, where strolls and picnics provide the context for roving eyes and chance meetings, where lush verdure provides cover for secret meetings, where arbors harbor trysts that are impossible or dangerous in the routine spaces of social life.

In the garden, one's longing for an absent beloved can be transposed onto one's yearning for God, such that the two kinds of love do not compete but rather reinforce each other. In this way, Urdu poetry uses the imagery of gardens both as reflections of romantic love and as allegories for mystical experience that derives from loving God. Such mystical experience can involve visions or flashes of insight that convey a kind of knowledge (gnosis or *ma'rifa*) that cannot be transmitted through reasoned discourse. Mystical experience can also manifest in moments of ecstasy (*be-khudi*), or literally being-not-self—that is, standing outside the self. In these moments, free of egoistic limitations, the self can experience spaceless expansion, timeless eternity, or boundless union with the whole cosmos. These moments of unself-consciousness may come unbidden as one confronts an overwhelming beauty or may be sparked by spiritual exercises. But while intense moments of ecstasy are blissfully energizing, if they become durative and long-lasting, they lead to a more painful state of oblivion and bewilderment.

This is where Siraj's phrase "A wind blew in from the unseen world, scorching the garden of appearances" is leading us, however reluctant we are to leave the fragrance of flowers. For the wind in this couplet is not a mild spring breeze that caresses the garden into full bloom but rather a hot summer wind that tears through the garden, scorching its blooms and raking them off the branches. It is a wind that does not represent the joy of spring but rather comes from the unseen world (*ghaib*). This wind does not coax one gently through the world of sensual appearances but rather strips one bare of anything other than the world of spiritual realities.

The imagery of flowers and spring greenery represents a theology of *jamal* or divine beauty. Beauty is God's quality, one the ninety-nine names of God, evoking manifestation, bringing into the world of appearances the comforting and captivating presence of God, and calling those who witness it to an intimate play of love (*naz o niyaz*). But beauty is only part of the story, and a theology of *jamal* can become indulgent or shallow if not balanced by experience of *jalal* or divine might. God's qualities comprehend opposites in ways human beings find frustratingly contradictory. Flowers fade. Lovers depart. Spring dries up in summer's heat. As ecstatic states flee by, we either crash down into routine time or soar too high and are scorched by the sun's majesty. These are expressions of *jalal*, which can manifest as overwhelming power or wrath in Islamic theology. When *jalal* storms through our human world, the effect is extinction (*fana'*) that overwhelms any manifestation and overshadows any trace of intimacy. It "blows away" the existence of contingent beings in the face of absolute being (*vujud-e mutlaq*).

In this ghazal, Siraj bemoans just such an experience of extinction, of being blown away. It is painful, and the only end to the pain is bewilderment, a condition worse than pain. The wind's blowing conveys a fire — "scorching" in the poem — that strips away the inessential parts of life and cooks what was raw, transmuting it into something refined. Images of wine, fire, and music are central to the Chishti Sufi tradition. The living heat of the human soul was originally sparked by God's breath, as the Qur'an says: *I blew into the human being of my own spirit* (Q 38:71). Despite this original intimacy, which was a breath closer than a kiss, the human being has gotten lost in distraction and requires systematic *zikr* or meditation to recall God's presence. Zikr focuses on regulating and retaining the breath while reciting God's names (both beautiful and mighty) to rekindle mindfulness. In addition to the systematic breathing of zikr, we also need periodic doses of a stronger wind that can blow the embers of spiritual memory into flame and give rise to more radical burning and boiling that alone can transform our raw humanity into wise maturity. The Persian Sufi poet ʿAbd al-Rahman Jami (died 1492 near Herat) stated that the jurist who forbids music and musical instruments has not understood the secret of "I blew into the human being of my own spirit," for when God breathed the soul into Adam's body, the "sound" that was created by this action was the origin of music, which takes us back more powerfully than language to that moment of primal contact and essential intimacy with God.

Jami's Persian ghazals are often sung in Qawwali performances, and couplets of his are often "knotted" into Siraj's poem as it is sung. Jami's theology is hopeful, for despite human frailty and failings, there is in our hollow body and porous personality the lingering potential to resonate when brought in contact with the divine breath of God. Ascetic simplicity, self-abnegating humility, the painful search for wisdom, and intoxicating love can combine to give us that resonance. Likewise, there is a kernel of optimism hidden in Siraj's couplet, after the burning wind of the unseen world razes the garden of appearances. The second line of the couplet states that there is "on pain's bare branch, just one bud—call it the heart," hinting that when love burns away all that one has, one finds one's heart like a bud. In the tight constriction of a state of despair (*qabz*) lies latent the possibility of future expansion into a state of joy (*bast*): "just one bud—call it the heart—remains in greenness." However, before reaching the long-deferred word "greenness," one must survive the burning, for in Urdu poetry the bud of the heart grows only after being charred.

The paradox of a charred branch bringing forth a green bud captures in poetic imagery a deep philosophical concept central to Sufi thought. Hovering between being and nothing (*vujud o ʿadam*) is the state of "contingent being," of those who are created in this world, suffer love, and die. Ibn ʿArabi's philosophical Sufism, which is often termed *vahdat al-vujud* or "the unity of being," systematized this conceptual scheme. We are neither self-subsisting and autonomous nor totally void and nonexistent—our lives are best understood as reflections in the realm of imagination (*ʿalam-e khayal*) when the true force of absolute being confronts the blank void of nonbeing. We have some substance, like a mirror's metal and glass, but the vivid images that give it character as they play along its polished surface do not belong to the mirror itself and do not arise out of its substance. These terms are adopted from Ibn ʿArabi's mystical philosophy, which Sufi poets in South Asia expressed in the Persian ghazal long before. The first among them was Fakhr al-Din ʿIraqi (died

1289), while in Chishti circles the first was Mas'ud Bakk (died 1387). Poets after the fourteenth century took this philosophical idea of contingent being for granted, latent as it was in poetic images of a face reflected in a mirror, bubbles quivering in a wine glass, dew drops gathered on rose petals, or dust motes whirling through sunbeams. 'Abd al-Rahman Jami was an interpreter of Ibn 'Arabi, most beloved in South Asia, for he wrote in both philosophical prose and colorful poetry. Siraj certainly takes for granted this concept of contingent being that can be absorbed back into absolute being through a process of spiritual refinement. Siraj trusts that his listeners will understand this complex scheme of ideas if he simply says, "No you remains, no I remains . . ."

The Royal Robe of Nakedness

The erotic potential of the ghazal, which was central to its success among courtesans and still makes it popular among film fans, is a theme that emerges in the next couplet as we return to Siraj's poem. Here oblivion, the overriding theme of the ghazal, takes on the personality of a king. Through the king, Siraj explores the ideas of agency and respectability. If oblivion is a state of being in which the subject recognizes "neither me nor you," then to whose agency should that state be attributed? This is especially crucial if the state of being lasts long and has a creative role to play in the formation of a spiritually mature personality, as our discussion of the previous couplet suggests. To address this ethical question, Siraj clothes it in metaphor:

> Just now, the king of oblivion has bestowed
> upon me nakedness's royal robe
> No stitch of discernment's propriety remains,
> no veil-rending insanity's lewdness

The word translated as "royal robe," *libas*, literally means clothing. In this phrase it is rendered as "royal robe" because it is coupled with the verb "bestowed." The image is of a king giving a gift to honor a courtier, court poet, artisan, or visitor who has done a worthy deed. Such a gift was usually a robe that the king had worn, taken off his own shoulders or out of his own wardrobe, and bestowed upon the honored guest.

Sufis transformed this custom into an initiation ritual in which the shaikh, as a spiritual king, bestows upon a disciple a cloak as a sign of investing him with spiritual authority to represent him and the lineage of past masters. In contrast to the royal robes given by kings, Sufi cloaks were usually of wool or other rugged cloth, were dyed blue-black (*kabud*) to symbolize renunciation and to prevent them from looking dirty even when they were old, and were often patched as they wore out as a sign of embracing poverty, embodying the Prophet Muhammad's statement "My poverty is my pride."[4]

These two contexts, royal and spiritual, came together in Sufi communities. By the time of Siraj, Sufi masters were commonly addressed as shah, or "king," by devotees in the Deccan. In his divan, the poet himself is given the formal address Shah Sayyid Siraj al-Din Husaini, marking his spiritual nobility as a result of his Sufi initiation (and also his genealogical nobility as a descendent of the Prophet's family through Imam Husain). In gatherings for *sama'*, the Sufi ritual of listening to devotional music in which Qawwali is performed, this royal symbolism is embodied as the Sufi master sits at the head of a "court" and his subjects approach, when inspired by the song, with gestures of subservience to dedicate offerings (*nazr* or *nazrana*) as requests for intimacy or favor.

The Sufi master presiding may show acceptance of disciples or of the wider listening audience by accepting monetary offerings, allowing the hem of his robe or his feet to be felt or his hand to be kissed, touching a prostrating disciple's shoulder or head in blessing, or embracing a disciple (especially one who has just come out of a moment of ecstasy). Such gestures have increased emotional intensity when Qawwali is held during an 'urs; this is true especially when the spiritual master presiding is a direct descendant (spiritual or genealogical, often both) of the saint commemorated. The sensual and even erotic elements of the 'urs at Chishti shrines in Awrangabad, where Siraj must have attended Qawwali sessions, are well described by Nile Green.[5] Such occasional gestures of acceptance and favor are intensified in a disciple's once-in-a-lifetime experience of being bestowed a robe or cloak of initiation, signaling that he has become an authorized representative or khalifa.

However, when Siraj says, "The king of oblivion has bestowed upon me nakedness' royal robe," his robe subverts both aristocratic and Sufi norms. He is given neither a jeweled robe nor a woolen cloak but rather the robe of nakedness. It is bestowed upon him not by a sultan or a shaikh but by the king of selfless oblivion (*shah-e be-khudi*). In these processes of spiritual discipleship, the issue of agency is key and complex. The disciple advances through spiritual stations (*maqamat*) by abandoning self-will, which is clearly a paradox, since the whole process takes high aspiration and hard work. Disciples negotiate this dangerous territory by attributing all progress along the path to the agency of their spiritual master or shaikh. Whatever good they experience they attribute to him, and whatever bad they experience they attribute to themselves, to their own base qualities. This opens up in the disciple a vulnerability to the deep influence of another. In this way, disciples hope that their base qualities might be transmuted into reflections of the shaikh's good qualities, as if he were an alchemist in possession of wisdom's mythic red sulfur and the disciple were mere lead.

Siraj knew this dynamic well, since he lived for many years as the disciple of a Chishti spiritual master, as we will explore in detail. Siraj attributes to his shaikh whatever knowledge of love that he has, expressing it in poems to his shaikh. He describes his teacher, like the beloved of Persian and Urdu love poetry, as having a powerful beauty with an almost martial penetration that invites comparison to a soldier. Sufism has often been called "the science of hearts" (*'ilm al-qulub*) since at least the time of Junaid of Baghdad (died 910), which is supremely ironic since it rests upon intuition and not reason. Calling it a "science" is only a way to attract theologians and philosophers to its potential richness and to invite them to give up their obsession with reasoned knowledge, which can never lead them out of the snare of egoism. As the mature disciple of a Chishti spiritual master, Siraj was an adept in the science of love. He might be expected to boast a bit about his master, as a direct way of showing his love for him and as an indirect way of boosting his own authority. That would be a subtle (but certainly common and forgivable) form of human arrogance.

However, the voice in Siraj's poem denounces such subtle arrogance—claiming a place in Sufi hierarchy and institution—as manifest hypocrisy. He does this through *malamati* themes of courting the blame of others as a way of humbling the self. In his state of unself-consciousness, he sees the king not as a locus of agency who grants to others their own power. Rather, he is the king of oblivion, and it is ambiguous whether he is a king who gifts oblivion to others or a king who is himself oblivion, beyond either existence or nonexistence. In either case, the king of oblivion bestows upon his supplicant a rare gift, the robe of nakedness. It is a gift that does not robe him in power or cloak him with wisdom but rather leaves him staggering in naked vulnerability.

As the couplet flows into its second line, Siraj takes advantage of the erotic force of the word "nakedness" (*barahnagi*): "No stitch of discernment's propriety remains . . ." Having achieved intimacy with oblivion, he is completely stripped of reason and discernment—not a stitch of it remains to clothe him in propriety and modesty. Some Sufis took this ideal quite literally, translating nakedness as nudity. They shed all clothing as a *malamati* strategy to keep themselves from taking themselves too seriously, from being admired by the public or patronized by kings. In Siraj's own generation, the Sufi poet Sarmad Shahid (died 1662) wandered from Sindh to Delhi without clothes. He defended his controversial appearance with a couplet of poetry, saying, "Those with deformity, God has covered with clothes / To the immaculate, God gave the robe of nudity."[6] Despite the controversy he aroused, Sarmad impressed the Mughal prince and heir apparent Dara Shikoh (died 1659), who respected the Sufi's insights in the oneness of all existence. But Dara Shikoh lost the battle for succession and was executed by his younger and more militant brother, Awrangzeb; shortly thereafter, Sarmad too came under threat. Even facing death, Sarmad upheld his dress code and his Sufi worldview, through which he saw everything as an emanation from God; in another of his Persian quatrains, he said, "The sweetheart with naked sword in hand approached / In whatever garb you come—I recognize you!"[7] When his undressed vulnerability was confronted with a naked sword, he did not cower but lauded his approaching death as a blessed opportunity to meet his beloved, God. Awrangzeb had Sarmad executed in Delhi.

Closer to Awrangabad, the Deccan had its own nude saints. One of them, Shah Mangi or "The Borrower King" (died 1713), was instrumental in helping Awrangzeb conquer the Deccan kingdom of Bijapur. "He was completely drawn out of his wits by divine distraction (*majzub-e kamil*) and was so intoxicated by love he could not reason (*mast la ya'qilu*). He stayed day and night wandering the world of oblivion."[8] Before his descent into holy irrationality, he was an ordinary Sufi disciple of Shah Murtaza Qadiri (died 1613).[9] As he took to going about naked and speaking madness, he used to say, "I will call the Mughal and give him Bijapur as a gift (*nazr*)." To this, his companion Shah Umangi or "The Ecstasy King" used to say, "If you call the Mughal, he'll make you wear pants!" When Awrangzeb conquered Bijapur, he heard reports of this naked Sufi. He summoned the Sufi to ascertain whether he went around without covering his genitalia, but Shah Mangi refused to attend. In the end, Awrangzeb ordered the Sufi to be "forced into pants."

Awrangzeb pushed farther south into the Deccan to conquer Hyderabad. There lived a Sufi named Shah Barahna or "The Naked King," a disciple of Sarmad whose tomb is still a place of visitation (died 1653–54).[10] Despite the powerful poetic image of reason lost to nudity, most Sufis kept their clothes on and opted for more socially acceptable roles. However, in the gathering for samaʿ, there was license to express lament or rapture by tearing the collar of one's shirt, as depicted in many Mughal-era paintings of Sufi gatherings. This is a more modest mark of leaving reason behind without the radical stance of nudity.

Siraj refers in the next phrase to an opposing image: "no veil-rending insanity's lewdness." That is not stripping oneself in order to keep others away but rather invading someone's privacy by tearing through the veil that shields the other. This refers to a state of love-frenzy when desire boils over and courtly etiquette of restraint (*adab*) is lost. The impassioned lover then storms the gates, so to speak, tearing away the veil of decorum and, in the process, probably losing any chance of sustained intimacy with the beloved. It is pure passion. Like nudity, it is a sign that love is so intense that it breaks down the conventions of romantic love.

The nakedness of the poet's voice in Siraj's ghazal is a result of passion that has blown itself out. He is neither clothed in reason nor tearing madly at the veil that separates him from his beloved. Neither lover nor beloved exist for him, for his love has reached the critical point of transmuting into bewilderment where "neither I nor you" remain.

The Readerless Tome of Reason

The next two couplets extend Siraj's exploration of paradox from the clothing of nakedness to other metaphors like the mirror or the wine-vat. But let us skip ahead to the couplet about the book of love. It is ironic that Siraj takes us to school when bewilderment is a state that confounds reason. Bewilderment is the very negation of reason's discrimination that asserts a dualistic separation between this and that, between right and wrong, between you and me. To assess bewilderment as a positive spiritual state, as union, is a subsequent step reintroducing reason (though from a perspective modified by wisdom).

For those in the throes of bewilderment it is only loss, the loss of firm mooring in the routine rationale of calculation. This is why the images in this ghazal, whose basic theme is bewilderment, are colored by terror, weighted by loss, and steeped in melancholy. This sixth couplet, which is also the next-to-last couplet, tries to turn this mood around and give a more positive explanation of the explorations of the earlier couplets. To do so, it sets passionate love over and against discriminating reason:

> An amazing moment it was, when I
> first learned from passion's pages
> Ever since, reason's tome stood on the shelf
> and remains right there, readerless

The couplet clothes the spiritual debate in metaphors of school (*dars*). It returns us listeners to our childhood, when we were made to value reason and subdue our passions in order to study, thereby rendering ourselves up for judgment by the teacher. We certainly have a lot of forgetting to do if we are to really learn about love's passion and lay aside our reliance on reason. Very aptly, reason is compared to a book. But this couplet is set in the school of love, not that of reason: "An amazing moment it was, when I first learned from passion's pages . . ." It is passion's pages that are read and memorized. To delve into passion's epic, the tome of reason must be closed. To learn of love, the poem's speaker has left reason's tome sitting on the shelf, where it remains to this very hour with no one to read it.

On the one hand, this couplet makes a complex theological argument about the limits of reason in comprehending God. Sufis had long since leapt into the fray that began among Muslim theologians and philosophers over who best understood the nature of divinity. Sufis like Jami not only illustrated in poetry but also argued in prose, as in his "Precious Pearl Establishing the True Relationship between Sufis, Theologians and Philosophers," which maintained that Sufi wisdom encompassed rational theology and philosophy while transcending their limitations by sparking the heart to realize its own nonbeing in confrontation with God's pure being.[11]

The message is that one should set one's attention with a full heart and total sincerity in one direction alone—toward the beloved. If reason or learning interferes, then all that distracts, whether books or reason that hopes to gain authority by reading books, must be burned. The Qur'an declares that God has not made two hearts in one person (Q 33:4). Whatever attracts our attention becomes the beloved of the heart, and singleness of attention is the only path forward in spiritual refinement. Yet singleness of attention means forcefully rejecting all that distracts, and burning is the most apt metaphor for this rejection.

Reason's tome stands on the shelf because the lover's dedication to passion has burned up any distraction, and the lover has been propelled beyond the confines of reason's jurisdiction. Siraj's ghazal holds out a more haunting possibility. Perhaps reason's tome stands on the shelf "and remains right there, readerless," because there is no subject to read it. There is nothing left of the heroic lover who renounces reason for passion. It is not reason's books that are burned in the fires of passion but rather the lover's subjectivity, which has burned away to such an extent that the expanse of bewilderment has opened around it. In contrast, the tome of reason seems to have fared much better—it may be readerless on the shelf, but it is still standing!

What Remains after Passion's Flames

The image of burning books leads directly to the closing couplet (*maqta'* or place of leaving off). In it the poet addresses himself as another in a gesture of self-alienation that simultaneously inscribes the poem with his authorial signature.

> Passion's flames reduced to ash
> Siraj's uncomplaining, speechless heart
> No caution remains, no second thought—
> all that remains is fearlessness

The poet's voice asserts in elegiac tones that passion's flames have burned not books but rather the heart of Siraj. This final couplet is an apt conclusion, resonating as it does with images and questions from earlier couplets. His heart is speechless (*be-nava*) and unable to complain, reminding us listeners of the fourth couplet. It resounds with the opening couplet through its rhyme, as the word for caution (*khatar*) and fearlessness (*be-khatari*) differ in only one consonant from the opening couplet's word for news (*khabar*) and unself-consciousness (*be-khabari*). It states with simple clarity why the mirror's face reflects no image, why reason's tome remains unread, and why the garden's branch is bare: it is because the speaker's heart has been burned away to almost nothing.

Yet this burning has left some residue—his heart has been reduced to ash, yet ash is a very potent substance. The couplet actually signifies ash with the word for dust (*khak*), from which we English speakers get our color khaki. It is the color of the earth when so dry that it can actually take on a personality by swirling and flying. Even as the dust dances, we understand that its motion is delivered by the wind—a mote of dust would never claim agency for itself. The very beauty of its dance, as when it glows in a sunbeam, comes from the fact that its choreography is drawn by the invisible power of an absent presence. Dust is an apt symbol for oblivion that is the central theme of the ghazal, for it describes the state of one who still lives, moves, wonders, and sings but has no awareness of these actions and cannot ascribe them to his own agency. However, this closing couplet does not speak of dust in general but of ash.

Ash is the dust that remains when the living tissue of the body is burned away. In South Asia, where Hindu bodies are burned rather than buried, ashes take on a greater significance. Yogis devoted to Shiva, for instance, smear themselves with ash to symbolize death and rebirth, the mark of one who has renounced this world, thereby gaining power in it to act on behalf of the next world. While Islamic culture has nothing so visceral as this, it does use substances like ash-colored antimony (lead sulfur) as collyrium to beautify the eyes, its silvery gray dust turning to lustrous black when moistened by the tears of its wearer. In the ghazal, the lover often compares himself to dust lying on the doorstep of the beloved's home, or uses this dust mixed with tears as *kohl* (in Arabic; *surma* in Urdu) to beautify his eyes and clear his vision of anything except the image of the beloved. The eye, the very window into the soul, becomes erased and replaced with something of the beloved. As Siraj sings in one of his ghazals, "When I find dust from his foot, I smear it in my eyes as surma . . . I'm dying of thirst, pour for me just once / In my soul's last gasp, the liquor of seeing you."[12]

Ash is more than dust. It is the proof of death and evidence of the body's destruction. However, it is also the evidence of an alchemical transformation in which the self becomes something else, passing away from its former nature to something more sublime. The use of ash in this couplet captures the ambivalence of burning in passion's flames. These flames certainly destroy and cause intense pain. However, if seen from an idealistic and optimistic perspective, its flames can be understood to burn only what is impure. There is no need to mourn the ash that is left behind, as it is just the condensed form of all the impurities that held the person back from achieving spiritual purity. Only in a state of purity can the lover approach intimate union with the beloved.

The ash, then, is a reminder that the one who is burning has found in the fire of passion a hidden treasure—real existence (*baqi*) that is existence of remaining with God and through God. The subject of obliteration is oblivious to this potential "finding the real" or rapture (*vajd*), for he is aware only that the pain has become so intense that he strangely no longer feels any burning. The poet's voice in the ghazal is cognizant only of his silence, accustomed as he was to being a nightingale singing of separation from the rose. He does not yet understand that his nightingale nature has been transmuted into a phoenix.

Conclusion

This ghazal, translated and interpreted couplet by couplet, is surely Siraj's most famous poem. It is most famous for many reasons. It is a beautifully constructed poem with a complex rhyme and ingenious rhythm. It is a profound poem because it invokes many of the crucial symbols and paradoxes of Sufi thought. It is a haunting poem through its insights into the pain of love, which almost all share. It is also his most famous because it is the poem most often sung in Qawwali—or perhaps it is sung because it is most famous. Surely the causation is circular.

There is a persistent divergence between the poem as read on the page and the poem as sung in Qawwali performance. In setting the lyrics to music, the Qawwals interpret the poem. We could say they give it "a certain spin" when they place it in motion through melody. They do this by omission and commission. They abbreviate the ghazal and choose which couplets to omit. They mix into the ghazal improvised additions, commissioning other poets to lend their voice with similar images but perhaps a different tone or even a completely different message. In general, the Qawwals give an upbeat and optimistic interpretation to the verses, pushing the listening audience to enthusiastically embrace love and discard reason and to see the lover as heroic in courage, stamina, and ultimate triumph.

The ghazal's own voice is far more tentative, contemplative, and befuddled. The bewildered voice of the ghazal as a poem has lost sight of any goal; it is suspended in the experience of obliteration. The enthused melody of the ghazal as sung, in contrast, has a definite goal and a dynamic sense of progress. It aims to spark in listeners the fire of passion, to move them quickly through bewilderment as only a stage in the progress toward the goal of union expressed as the ultimate triumph. We might summarize that the music's motion provides a certain teleological thrust to the ghazal that its words actually resist or suspend. The singers push the lyrics toward the final phrase, "all that remains is fearlessness."

In singing the ghazal, the Qawwals offer listeners this "fearlessness" as the poem's gift. The Qawwals urge them to adopt boldness in the pursuit of love, disregarding the disorientation that most of the poem so effectively describes.

Analysis of this poem provides the reader with a grounding in the ghazal form, a background in Sufi thought, and a glimpse into the Deccan imagery that nourished Siraj. The coming chapters will present his personality and history in more detail, for he certainly exhibited the "fearlessness" evoked by those who sing his poem. He was not just a poet but was also learned in music, religion, and love. He was an avid listener to sung poetry. As a Sufi master, he was the institutional patron of assemblies for samaʿ. In fact, he may have composed this poem specifically for the purpose of being sung in Qawwali style in a gathering whose purpose was to move listeners into states of mystical insight. Chapter 3 will examine closely the poetic language and style of Siraj, and only then can we address the question of how and why he composed poems to be sung in Qawwali.

CHAPTER THREE

Siraj's Silence

How strangely does the path of love twist
    Each of its twists is twisting with a twist
What secret signs lovers find in its way
    They keep hidden—what more can one say
It's best to stop speaking, Siraj, for sure
    Now only in silence can one be secure

—*three couplets from a masnavi by Siraj*

Siraj's biography is full of riddles. He claims to have begun composing poetry without any conscious decision. In his youthful years, he received poems as inspiration; in a frenzy of love madness, he wandered the hills reciting them in the wastelands to nobody in particular. As he matured and mastered Urdu poetry, he still claimed not to compose for its own sake but only to express his own states of love in ways that might inspire others; he wrote his poems to be sung, and they were written down not at his own bidding but rather by friends who collected them into a book. Just as he reached his artistic maturity, he took a vow to stop composing poetry—"It's best to stop speaking, Siraj," as he says in the masnavi quoted above.[1] Yet he took this vow not by his own volition.

Siraj's Sufi master had commanded him to stop composing poetry, and he complied. Why the command and why the compliance? This chapter will explore Siraj's silence—how he began to compose ghazals in Urdu and how he was restrained from continuing to express his genius in that form. It suggests that his Sufi master perceived the erotic elements of his poems as threatening. They were especially threatening since his poems were not meant for private reading or isolated contemplation but rather for community listening with dynamic rhythm and melody. The Sufi master's command encourages us to look beyond Siraj's poems for the real reason behind the order to stop composing poetry.

Sufi Roots in Awrangabad

To comprehend Siraj's imposed silence, we first have to understand how in his youth he began to speak in Persian poetry and then shifted to compose Urdu ghazals. Siraj lived during the initial flowering of Urdu poetry, when it grew up from under the shade of Persian poetry in South Asia. He was born in Awrangabad in 1716. The Mughal emperor Awrangzeb founded the city in 1681, renamed it after himself, and declared it his new capital.[2] Enormous material and cultural resources were then invested in the city. One literary newcomer to the capital wrote this account in 1773: "In the region of Hindustan, the capital city of Shahjahanabad [Delhi] is like the beautiful mole on the cheek of the kingdom. And in this land of the Deccan, the rival to that city is Awrangabad which is like its reflection. May God preserve it from defect and calamity and let it ever enjoy peace and security."[3]

The new capital generated great excitement and cultural energy. Soldiers and courtiers, administrators and scribes, merchants and mendicants flocked to the city to take part in its flourishing, as Awrangabad eclipsed Delhi in the north and overshadowed the former capitals of independent Deccan kingdoms like Hyderabad and Bijapur.[4] These Deccan cities had been vital centers of early Urdu literature but were largely ruined by Mughal conquest. Eventually, after 1712, the Mughal capital shifted back to Delhi, but the investment of money, building, and cultural institutions lasted much longer and Awrangabad remained a vital city.

Siraj composed in the Deccani dialect of Urdu, along with his elder contemporary Vali Deccani. Before the Mughal conquest, the Deccan was fertile ground for Urdu poetry, whereas in the northern cultural capitals, where Mughal rule weighed heavily, Persian was promoted as an administrative, courtly, and literary language. The earlier local dialects of Gujari and Deccani developed from the fifteenth through the seventeenth centuries into early Urdu (which is recognizable to modern Urdu speakers, though in an idiom that might sound archaic). Chapter 1 discussed how Chishti Sufis contributed to the development of this language in both its spoken form and its written expression. Urdu poetry has two tones — romantic and mystical. The two are in constant interaction, like different octaves of a single instrument. Romantic Urdu poetry celebrates the garden — its roses that attract the nightingale, its cypress trees that strut proudly, and its narcissus that lower their eyes seductively; this garden is the enclosed secret world where the lover searches for, finds, and

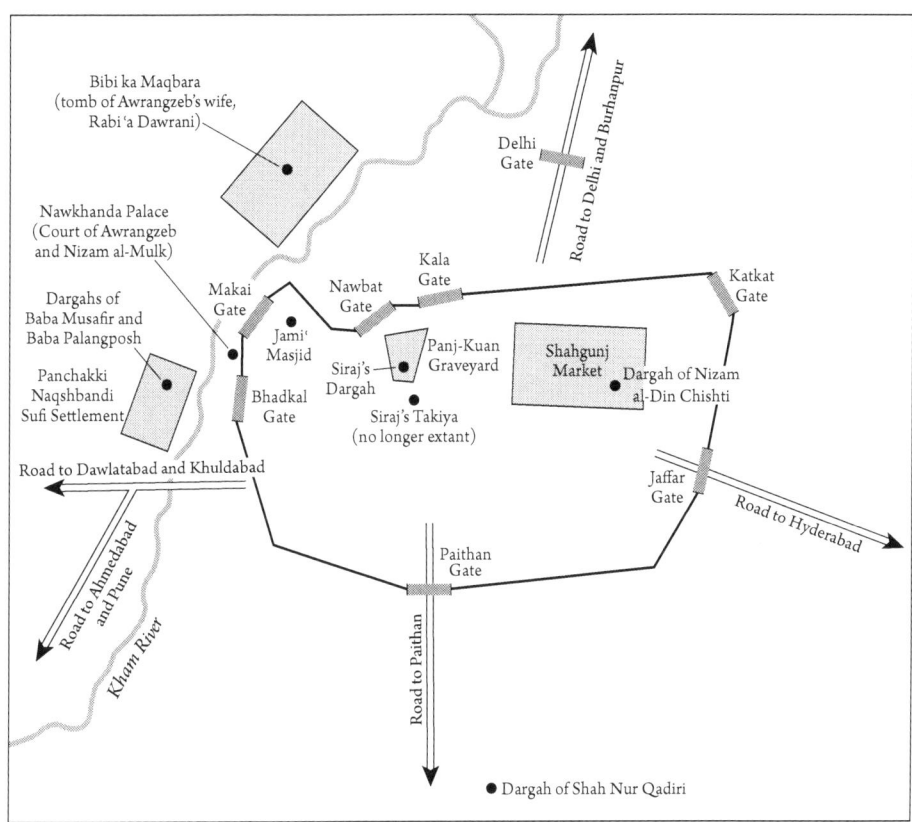

Awrangabad City in the late eighteenth century

loses the beloved. Romantic Urdu poetry has its origins in the Deccan's courtly capitals, where gardens were actively cultivated as pleasure parks, mortuary gardens, and refined retreats.[5] In early forms, romantic Urdu appeared in the court of Golkonda with Sultan Muhammad Quli Qutb-Shah (died 1611) and his court poets and in that of Bijapur with Ibrahim 'Adil Shah (died 1627) and his court poets. In modern form, it appeared in Awrangabad when it became the center of Mughal culture under the courtly patronage of Awrangzeb and Nizam al-Mulk, the first nizam of the Asaf-Jahi dynasty (ruled 1724–48).

By the eighteenth century, Awrangabad had inherited this linguistic and literary legacy, which was promoted by both Vali and Siraj. According to some Urdu scholars, Vali was the first romantic Urdu poet to mix mystical meanings into his verse on love and thereby assert that worldly love is metaphorical and can lead to deeper spiritual love that is absolute.

Earlier Urdu poets in the Deccan were reluctant to mix romantic love with mystical love for God and maintained a more solidly sensual focus on this-worldly beauties.[6] But Vali's new style in Deccani Urdu bursts with confidence and optimistic self-assertion; he transplanted it to Delhi where romantic poets like Mir Taqi Mir (1723–1810) cultivated it to bring out its different hues.[7]

Like Vali, Siraj mixed romantic and mystical registers in the Urdu ghazal. However, Siraj leaned more toward the mystical element in poetry. To understand how and why he did this, we need to go back to Siraj's youth. He grew up in Awrangabad when the city nourished a local flowering of the Chishti community, led by Shaikh Nizam al-Din Awrangabadi. Siraj's family kept him occupied in studies, religious and literary, until he was twelve. Early on he had a deep appreciation for classical Persian ghazals, which was only to be expected in a household descended from Sufi teachers, as the earliest full biography about him, found in *Tuhfat al-Shu'ara* (Gift of the poets), asserts.[8] But studying Persian ghazals at an early age may not have been good for his psychological stability. At the age of sixteen, Siraj experienced a kind of wildness (*vahshat*) that "found its way into his temperament," and spiritual urges (*jazbat*) drove him away from family and town into the wilderness.

He wandered outside of Awrangabad, weeping and singing Persian ghazals that his feverish imagination devised. His biographers say that he acted "as if insane, beyond personal will or choice, and wandered the mountains and deserted places." This may have been too much even for a Sufi family, and his father is reported to have chained him up. He fled his family and took refuge in the tomb of Burhan al-Din Gharib, that exemplar of the Chishti community in the Deccan. His dargah in Khuldabad, the mortuary center a short distance away from Awrangabad, was a safe haven for exiles of all kinds. Siraj stayed at the dargah for a period of seven years.

Then, in his early twenties and "having fallen into poverty," Siraj began to think about joining a Sufi community. The biography written about him by "Qaqshal" continues to state, "From the influence of a perfected spiritual guide (*sahib-e kamal*), Siraj took off his clothes and became acquainted with the delights of dervish life." These metaphors in his biography echo the third couplet of the ghazal that chapter 2 analyzed in which Siraj says, "The king of oblivion has bestowed upon me nakedness's royal robe." Taking off the clothes and wearing a cloak of initiation at the hand of a Sufi teacher is a metaphor for renouncing worldly life.

The dargah of Nizam al-Din Awrangabadi, located at Shahgunj in Awrangabad (photo by Scott Kugle)

His teacher was 'Abd al-Rahman Chishti (died 1747 in Ellichpur).[9] In a rare Persian ghazal of his that is preserved, Siraj refers obliquely to his new Sufi master:[10]

> Oh grace of Rahman, my guide and my leader you are
>   Chosen of the court of the singular creator you are
> Traveler on mystic paths, sage of gnostic wisdom
>   Intimate of reality's secret, a mighty ruler you are
> Master of pious knowledge, knower of secrets divine
>   Guide to the way of God, the king whose minister you are
> From your face shines the light of divine majesty
>   A ray of the beauty of the essence beyond compare you are
> No desire has Siraj except some hope of meeting you
>   Lord of nobles, refuge for souls, pointer for prayer you are

This may be the last Persian ghazal that he composed, for upon taking initiation with ʿAbd al-Rahman Chishti, the poet Siraj began to compose in Urdu. In one Urdu poem, he memorialized his Sufi master, whom he calls Shah Rahman:[11]

> I'm tongue-tied as a result of my love's curls' warp and weft
>   I'm deep in a well of sorrows as a result of his chin's lovely cleft
> This ghazal of Siraj is a brand igniting the gut, but like a candle
>   The heart glows because of blessings that in him Shah Rahman left

In other poems, Siraj simply calls him Rahman, leaving a delightful ambiguity between his spiritual guide and the all-merciful God. He does this, for example, in the closing line of this ghazal:[12]

> From chasing sudden beauties, distress eventually
>   Makes my heart spin in bewilderment eventually
> Torment's brand makes a lover's heart eventually
>   Into a garden glade with blazing roses eventually
> Leave your sorrows, Siraj, since now Rahman
>   Will make your every difficulty easy eventually

Thus Siraj embraced the innovation of writing ghazals in Urdu rather than in Persian. He wrote in a style that writers in Persian called Rekhta-ye Hindi. His intimate friend and fellow disciple ʿAbd al-Rasul Khan collected his Urdu poetry and organized it into the divan that survives for us today. Siraj composed Urdu poetry for about four or five years in his Sufi community.[13]

Siraj's Persian poetry, recited to the silent hills and baffled beasts, was never collected and is largely lost. However, contemporaries who wrote about him reported that "if his Persian ghazals had been committed to paper, they would constitute a thick divan and if people read them, they would consider them a miraculous act of God."[14] Strangely, though Siraj claims his Persian poems were lost in the wilderness and his contemporary admirers rued their loss, at least a few were preserved. "Qaqshal" collected the biographies and samples of poets of Awrangabad in his *Tuhfat al-Shuʿara*, written in 1752, and in it he preserves a few Persian ghazals of Siraj.[15] These reveal that even in his youth, Siraj was familiar with conventional Sufi imagery yet was also cultivating an experimental boldness in poetic innovation.

When he was composing these Persian poems, Siraj was not yet in the practice of Sufi discipline. He was rather caught in a loop of madness, revisiting his painful loss in love, which further fueled his flight from society. One of his Persian poems concludes, "This closing couplet will remain as Siraj's heart-felt constant refrain / Yet again, as at the start, the brand of madness falls on my heart." All of the few Persian poems we have of Siraj seem to capture the despair of this youthful tragedy. A couplet from another Persian ghazal complains, "I am stained with accusations and my secrets are unjustly known to all / How low have I fallen into ruin! Doesn't innocence matter at all?"[16] This study will explore Siraj's youthful love affair in detail to explain how it fueled his spiritual quest later in life.

Islamic Mysticism in the Urdu Ghazal

Siraj composed his entire divan of Urdu ghazals during a four- or five-year period while he was a Sufi disciple in the Kalīmi Chishti order. When Siraj reached his mid-twenties, his Sufi teacher, ʿAbd al-Rahman Chishti, commanded him to stop composing poems soon after 1739. Siraj's autobiographical statement tells us of his joy at finding a spiritual guide: "He [Siraj himself] set out in search of the rare pleasure of spiritual realization. This desire resounded in his very pulse until that need was fulfilled by a happiness-inspiring initiation with Khwaja ʿAbd al-Rahman Chishti (may God sanctify his holy secret) whose divine union occurred in AH 1160 [1747 CE]. He opened the door to divine direction and this poor wretch drank, as deeply as he was able, the wine of guidance from that *saqi* in the assembly of divine care."[17] Siraj implies that this spiritual initiation is what gave him the expansive joy, the incisive insight, and the peace of mind to begin composing his mature poems in Urdu. According to "Shafiq," a poet from Awrangabad who penned a biography of Siraj, "In those days, it occurred to a dear friend and brother in the Sufi path, ʿAbd al-Rasul Khan, to gather together in writing most of his free flowing verse in Urdu (*zaban-e rekhta*) and put it in good order. So he took those scattered gems that amount to almost five thousand couplets and strung them together in alphabetical order according to their rhyme and made of them a proper divan, and gave them to be shared with those special loved ones."[18]

Siraj's mysticism in the Chishti path was not just about listening to music or composing poems to be sung in a ritual setting where they might be put into musical motion that would inspire insight and ecstasy. His mysticism also involved more solitary pursuits, like meditation. He

Kalīmī Lineage	Other Chishti Sufis	Sufi Poets
Nizam al-Din Awliya (d. 1325 in Delhi)		Amir Khusro (d. 1325 in Delhi)
Nasir al-Din Chiragh (d. 1356 in Delhi)	Burhan al-Din Gharib (d. 1337 in Khuldabad)	Amir Hasan Sijzi (d. 1336 in Khuldabad)
Kamal al-Din 'Allama (d. Delhi in 1358)	Zayn al-Din Shirazi (d. 1369 in Khuldabad)	
Siraj al-Din (d. 1397 in Patan, Gujarat)	Mas'ud Bakk (d. 1387 in Delhi)	Hafiz Shirazi (d. 1389 in Shiraz, Iran)
'Ilm al-Din (d. 1480 in Patan)	Gesu Daraz (d. 1422 in Gulbarga)	
		'Abd al-Rahman Jami (d. 1492 in Jam, Afghanistan)
Mahmud Rajan (d. 1494 in Patan)	'Azizullah Mutawakkil (d. in Ahmedabad)	
Jamal al-Din Jaman (d. 1534 in Patan)	Rahmatullah Mutawakkil (d. in Ahmedabad) — Shah Bajan (d. 1507 in Burhanpur)	
Hasan Muhammad Chishti (d. 1583 in Ahmedabad, Gujarat)		
Shaikh Muhammad Chishti (d. 1630 in Ahmedabad)		
Yahya Madani (d. 1689 in Medina)	'Ali Riza Faruqi (d. 1730 in Ahmedabad)	Vali Deccani (d. 1707 in Ahmedabad)
Shaikh Kalimullah (d. 1729 in Delhi)	Yusuf and Sharif al-Din (d. 1710 in Hyderabad)	
Nizam al-Din Awrangabadi (d. 1729 in Awrangabad)	Sharif Chishti (d. 1750 in Awrangabad)	
Mawlana Fakhr al-Din (d. 1785 in Delhi)	Isma'il Bukhari Chishti (d. in Awrangabad)	
	'Abd al-Rahman Chishti (d. 1747 in Awrangabad)	Siraj Awrangabadi (d. 1763 in Awrangabad)

——— initiation and successorship in the Chisti lineage
- - - - initiation in the Chishti lineage

Initiatic lineage of Siraj Awrangabadi

mentions zikr, or recitation, as in this example from the very first poem of his divan:[19]

> With your name alone begins this, my poems' edition
> It's my tongue's recitation — my soul lives by its repetition
> With your whole heart, remember *the face of your Lord remains*
> While keeping thoughts away from *everything passes to extinction*
> I am ever expectant, O Muhammad, of your noble kindness
> Unveil in me faith and tell me secrets of the human condition
> You are the unique One, your name is Ahmad without the *mim*
> Every page of the Qur'an is beautified by your attribution
> Let me go unconscious, my beloved, with the wine of longing
> Give me a cup overflowing with your intoxicating intuition

Because this poem initiates his entire divan, it is more programmatic than an ordinary ghazal. The first couplet announces that his divan begins in the name of God, who is addressed in mystical tenderness with second-person familiarity. Without actually saying God's name — Allah — the couplet asserts that Siraj lives only by reciting this name, silently within every breath or aloud in every poem.

The second couplet invokes the *hamd* or praise of God, who is eternal and everlasting while all else ephemeral is passing away. His poem includes interlinear citations of the Qur'an in Arabic (*iqtibas*), specifically from Surat al-Rahman: *Everything passes to extinction in this world yet the face of your Lord remains* (Q 54:26-27). The mystic's consciousness is in tension between focusing awareness on perceiving God's face in all things while keeping attention away from clinging to anything that is ephemeral. The soul's eternal life consists in only this impossible quest, to see in greater clarity and deeper refinement the eternal face of God. The third couplet includes *naʿat* or praise for the Prophet Muhammad, who taught how to proceed on this quest, for the Prophet reveals the human condition and how to transcend it. The fourth couplet revels in the spiritual intimacy between Muhammad and God, for the Prophet transmitted to humanity the speech of God, which he could hear because he had refined his soul to a reflective transparency.

In this state of reflexivity, the Prophet was reported to have heard God say to his inner ear, "I am Ahmad without the *mim*," that is, without the letter *m*.[20] In this speech, God identifies as Ahad, the unique One — one of God's many names. Instead of saying this directly, God says it in a riddle that invokes one of the honorific names of Muhammad — Ahmad, the most praised one. Ahmad without the *m* is Ahad; that is, Muhammad was so intimate with God that only a single letter separated them. This image captures the idea, central to Islamic spirituality, that the Prophet Muhammad was the embodiment of an eternal light, which emanated with God before there was any otherness of the cosmos and its creation. This light was reflected in every human being and manifested more brightly in the chain of prophets, until in Muhammad it reached its clearest brilliance not obscured by any egoistic pretense. For this reason, Muhammad could perceive, receive, and preserve the speech of God, resulting in the Qur'an and founding Islam as a path of returning to God.

Like all Sufis, Siraj looked upon Muhammad as the wellspring of his mysticism and the focus of his love. He regarded Muhammad as a beautiful beloved, not just as a lawgiver, communal leader, or mouthpiece for revelation. This leads Siraj to his final couplet, where he invokes the beloved and longs to be ever intoxicated with his spiritual cup. Here, the notion that Muhammad is the beautiful exemplar flows seamlessly to yearning for one's beloved in whatever form she or he might appear. The beloved becomes the *saqi* or divine wine-pourer who leads the mystic beyond clinging to sensation and relying on reason into the walled garden of love. Without naming the beloved, Siraj raises the possibility that Hazrat 'Ali is the primordial saqi, since through Hazrat 'Ali the Prophet Muhammad's inner teachings were preserved and spread, making 'Ali the prototype for saints. In this world, the saqi appears in the guise of human teachers, sages, and spiritual teachers, from whom one can receive initiation and training as if sipping the wine of love. In the next world, the saqi will be Imam 'Ali, who pours out for the souls in paradise the potent drink of *kawsar*, the river of wine that runs through the garden of eternal intimacy.

The themes of Siraj's poetry are profound when viewed as Sufism. Each image has a resonance with the complex theology of Islamic mysticism. Interpreting the poem, it is easy to get caught up in theology. Yet Siraj is not offering theology as rational discourse about God. Rather, he is offering poetry whose essence is rhythmic meter and sonorous rhyme. With these musical elements, Siraj desires to sidestep reason. He does not want to convince readers but rather wants to move them. He does not desire to prove an argument but rather aims to ignite a yearning. Like his poetry, Siraj's spirituality was shaped by music more than by any other kind of ritual or devotional practice.

The Discipline of Silence

Siraj implies that these poems, which others found lovely, were the cause of trauma for him. After his friends began to write his poems down and circulate them, Siraj became famous. In an autobiographical statement, Siraj writes of himself, "Gradually, he began to receive fame far and wide, even with the common people. After a while, this poor wretch became outstanding in the rich clothing of 'my poverty is my pride' and at that time, in accord with the command of his spiritual guide, he restrained his hand and tongue from grasping the hem of metered speech, after having been composing for seventeen years."[21] These seventeen years of composing poetry include the four or five years that he wrote in Urdu plus his earlier period of writing in Persian, which must have begun when Siraj was about seven years old. It must have been a shock for one so accomplished in poetry to refrain from writing. Siraj presents his compliance with the command of his Sufi master but does not explain it. He claims that his Sufi practice led him to embody the famous saying of the Prophet Muhammad "My poverty is my pride."[22] Since his poetry was bringing him worldly renown, he implies, he abstained from it in order to deepen his spiritual poverty. So it was not mere poetic exaggeration when he described his renunciation of composing poetry by writing that he "restrained his hand and tongue from grasping the hem of metered speech."

Siraj's spiritual master, ʿAbd al-Rahman Chishti, appears to have told him that composing poetry was a form of acquisitiveness. Whether or not he intended it, Siraj's poetry garnered him fame in the eyes of others, and so he was grasping at the hem of poetry, meaning that he was begging for riches or renown from the world through his words. His Sufi master seems to have told Siraj that his poetry was not a pure expression of his spirituality but rather was an obstacle to refining his spiritual state. Presented in this way, Siraj had little choice but to acquiesce in hopes of progressing further by earning his master's approval.

For those who love Siraj's ghazals, it is hard to not to resent his spiritual teacher for forbidding the poet to compose. Nile Green, historian of Sufism in Awrangabad, notes caustically that "his command banning Siraj from composing any more poems is among the most notorious examples of the authority of the master in Sufi history."[23] Green means that it was an instance of the abuse of authority. How are we to understand this surprising command? It might have been because Siraj's poetry was too effective when he directed Qawwals to recite and sing. Perhaps he became too famous too quickly, as people memorized his poems and repeated them far and wide; by 1743, only four years after he stopped composing, his ghazals had reached Gujarat and North India.

It is difficult to attribute motives to ʿAbd al-Rahman Chishti's commands, because we know so little about him. We know only his name, the city in which he lived, date of death in a provincial town, and that he lived near the dargah of Nizam al-Din Awrangabadi and is reported to have written a book on Sufi discipleship, which is now untraceable. There were many poets active in the circle of Nizam al-Din Awrangabadi, yet we find no precedent in this Chishti tradition of a Sufi master silencing a poet-disciple.

We can indirectly infer something about Siraj's master from the few references that Siraj makes to their relationship. Siraj attributes whatever knowledge of love that he has and expresses in poems to his shaikh. He describes ʿAbd al-Rahman Chishti like the beloved of Persian and Urdu love poetry, as having a powerful beauty with an almost martial penetration that invites comparison to a soldier, as reflected in this ghazal:[24]

> The armies of anxiety have assaulted my heart
>   No wonder the forces of life are in utter disarray
> My beloved's beauty reached worldwide fame
>   No wonder the alleys and markets are in a riot
> Perhaps your mouth is the gem of Solomon's ring
>   No wonder nature's demons and fairies oblige you
> Your silvery cheek and ebony curls allow no escape
>   No wonder Ethiopian and Greek armies agree about this
> In growing intimate with your dagger of a glance
>   No wonder a prone lover suffers multiple lacerations
> My heart has not found one drop of life's liquor
>   No wonder, since I'm exiled from your company
> My kind teacher, Siraj, taught me well to have
>   No wonder that no science tops knowledge of love

As the mature disciple of a Chishti spiritual master, Siraj was an adept in the science of love. What he learned from his teacher is that nothing is as important or incisive in life as love and that eventually all others things — all other ways of knowing and apprehending reality — become obstacles to love. He might be expected to boast a bit about his master, as a direct way of showing his love for him and an indirect way of boosting his own authority. That would be a subtle (but certainly common and forgivable) form of human arrogance. But for Siraj, all human arrogance, even the most common and forgivable kind, should be obliterated. And the only force strong enough to do that is the fire of love.

Love alone can melt the human character like metal in a furnace and purify it of the dross of egoism. Of course, Siraj is speaking ultimately about love for God, which has this purifying effect. But in a more proximate way, it is one's love for a spiritual guide that leads one to love for God. The Chishti path always praised the disciple's self-consuming love for his spiritual master as the most basic enabling attitude on the spiritual path. Chishti teachings recommend that disciples should always keep the image of one's spiritual teacher in their minds (*tasavvur-e shaikh*). Especially when engaged in ritual activities like prayer, the disciple should concentrate so intently on his spiritual guide that it is as if the guide were present praying with him, or even praying in place of him. This concentration upon the image of the teacher should ultimately give rise to obliteration of the self within the personality of the teacher (*fana' fi'l-shaikh*).

While expressed directly in language, this process is said to result in the humbling or negating of the self. It leads a disciple to perceive himself as "a corpse in the hands of the one who washes him," malleable to his every command and never resisting his direction.[25] The shaikh is perceived to be like the prophet Solomon, a king whose seal ring commanded forces of nature and supernatural beings, as alluded to in Siraj's poem above (with the added simile of the beloved's red lips being more compelling than the carved ruby seal ring of the king): "Perhaps your mouth is the gem of Solomon's ring / No wonder nature's demons and fairies oblige you." But when expressed indirectly in poetic images, the process of a disciple submitting wholly to a master is said to be freeing and enabling, even enrapturing. The gaze of the beloved shaikh is as penetratingly sharp as a dagger: "In growing intimate with your dagger of a glance / No wonder a prone lover suffers multiple lacerations." But instead of killing the disciple, it cuts through his attachments to all other things that alienate him from God, freeing the disciple from the fetters of his own ego. The spiritual master's gaze is more potent than wine and should with a single glance give lifelong intoxication to the disciple, allowing him to leave self-concern and sparkle with the ferment of love.

Siraj lays out the basic metaphors of wine and love in comparatively simple terms in another of his ghazals:[26]

> Whoever once tastes your intoxicating glance
>> Spends day and night gazing in worship of wine
> If it knows of the moth's perilous burning
>> The candle looks on with just a smile
> So you're effaced, yet still want eternal life?
>> Just see nothingness as the pith of existence
> Stroll in gardens of "whoever knows the self"
>> If you aim for a taste of worshipping what's real
> What now, Siraj, there's no storm outside!
>> Your eyes rival the clouds in this downpour

The hopeful message of this poem is that, although love leads to suffering, through suffering comes wisdom. Serving a spiritual teacher might be painful, but this painful cutting through egoistic obsessions is the key to gaining wisdom.

This wisdom is encapsulated in the famous saying, to which the poem alludes, "Whoever knows the self knows the Lord." Sufis attribute it to either ʿAli or the Prophet Muhammad, and it was given a systematic interpretation by Ibn ʿArabi.[27] Like all mystical aphorisms, it urges the listener to seek direct knowledge of God, but to know God one needs to clearly analyze and understand the self. From this aphorism, Sufis glean the insight that one cannot analyze oneself directly but can do so only by looking at one's reflection in another. The shaikh acts as a mirror to reveal one's inner self—to test one's motives, clarify one's intentions, and restrain one's excesses.

Sufis who compose ghazals might add another phrase to this aphorism: "Whoever knows the self knows the Lord—and no one knows the self who does not love another." The ideals of burning with love and reflecting like a mirror are combined in the complex image of the saqi or wine-pourer. His beauty inspires passionate love, which burns one's heart, and he pours out wine that intoxicates one's reason. Yet the saqi offers a goblet of wine whose surface is like a mirror, and his offering can be accepted only while looking down, with such humility that the saqi's face is reflected in the wine. This seductive play of love offers a sensual complex of images that relate to an internal spiritual disposition. Loving another should transform the lover. Loving another is not about possessing him or her but about allowing oneself to be possessed by that love.

The person whose selfishness is burned away by love's fire becomes clear like a mirror and reflects the real One, true being, which is in a proximate way the reality of the cosmos and in an ultimate way is God. One gets everything by embracing nothing: "So you're effaced, yet still want eternal life? / Just see nothingness as the pith of existence." If nothingness is the pith of existence, then silence is the ultimate form of expression. Siraj accepted this message, as difficult as it was for a poet to accept silence. In a dramatic illustration of "obliteration in one's spiritual teacher," Siraj accepted his Sufi master's command to cease composing poetry.

Analyzing the relationship between master and disciple helps us to understand why Siraj complied willingly with the command to stop composing poetry. But it does not completely explain why 'Abd al-Rahman Chishti gave this command. This question is especially vexing because both master and disciple belonged to the Chishti path that had long cultivated poetry and music as the most effective way to communicate spiritual insights. The crucial issue that must have motivated this command could not have been the composition of poetry but rather the content of the poems or their social effect when sung.

Erotic Imagery and Mystical Insight

The content of poems and their effect upon the receiving audience are integrally linked. What affects both is the dangerous ambiguity of Siraj's love poetry, which was most likely what alarmed Siraj's Sufi teacher. This chapter has argued that Siraj's poetry is a masterful blend of the mystical and romantic dimensions of Urdu ghazal writing, but it has so far emphasized the mystical dimension. At this point in the analysis, the opposite must be emphasized. Though his poetry is leavened with mysticism, it is still robust love poetry, with erotic attraction, romantic longing, titillating flirtation, and sarcastic criticism, all woven deep into its fabric.

Siraj does not always push the ghazal's conventional images toward an interior intensity through Sufi devotions. He also plays the ironic game in which the ghazal taunts both the readers (who think they know the conventions) and the beloved (whose indifference tortures the poet). A fine example of this strategy is the following poem:[28]

> In the fire of exile don't give me punishment
> Like a puddle of quicksilver don't make me restless
> You deserve a golden beauty like sandalwood paste
> To ease your headache, don't apply my rosewater

> Enough pain from your ecstatic eyes, my saqi!
>   To bring me to my senses don't give me wine
> To the narrow-minded ascetic don't give any wine
>   Burn thorns and brambles, don't give them water
> Isn't it best not to disturb your den of snakes?
>   To your musky ringlets don't give a coiling shake
> "Do all lovers take pleasure courting a bad name?"
>   Your usual bastards don't get such a direct address
> O river of beauty, to my lips dying of thirst
>   Who told you, "Don't give a single drop"?
> Sugared words are a heedless, ignorant man's work
>   Siraj, hold your tongue—don't give them an answer

This ghazal is romantic and erotic rather than mystical. The sarcastic tone in which the lover addresses the beloved expresses love that is thwarted by continued rejection. Pursuing the beloved's beauty has already ruined the speaking lover's body, mind, and reputation, and he responds by telling the beloved not to do all the things he's been longing for. The beloved is told not to shake out the perfumed coils of hair that are more deadly than black snakes. The saqi is requested not to revive the speaker after his drunken collapse with another bout of wine but rather with a glimpse of his beautiful face. The desperate lover also turns all criticism into a compliment; when the beloved scoffs at him saying, "Do all lovers take pleasure courting a bad name?," he consoles himself by noting that the circle of rivals who receive the beloved's attention—"your usual bastards" (*kamine*)—never get a direct address like the scorn he just received. None of these romantic images is given a mystical orientation by raising the image into a religious or philosophical register.

Further, beneath the sarcastic tone of romantic poetry runs a current of erotic energy in this poem. Rosewater is a medical treatment for headache and fever (in *unani tibb*, the Islamic tradition of herbal medicine), but the lover suggests that it is not good enough for a beloved who is as beautiful as gold. Instead, sandalwood paste should be applied. On the surface there is a playful competition between two intense perfumes, rose and sandal, with sandal winning because it has a beautiful pale gold hue whereas rosewater has no color. Rosewater loses like the lover who speaks this ghazal, for it is "my rosewater" that is not worthy to anoint such a radiant forehead and ease its feverish ache. But all listeners would know that sandalwood paste and rosewater are applied together to prepare a young groom on his wedding day; the aromatic combination prepares him for the erotic encounter of union with his bride. So the lover's perception of a competition between these two ingredients that prepare the beloved for his sexual union only underlines his pain, for this beautiful groom is being prepared to meet someone else.

As if acknowledging the controversy of a Sufi poet writing romantic verse with erotic power, Siraj disparages his own poem in the last couplet. Even when he plays the more conventional ghazal game, Siraj ends up disapproving of poetry that seeks to win a prize—whether success in romance, fame in literature, or money in patronage—as simply language candy: "Sugared words are a heedless, ignorant man's work / Siraj, hold your tongue—don't give them an answer." His own spiritual nature, whether expressed in poetry or exercised through more devotional means, surpasses them. He does not deign to compete with other heedless, ignorant men in composing love poetry but urges himself to take refuge in silence.

Yet despite disparaging the game of poetry for the sake of fame, romance, or art itself, Siraj often took to playing that game. He was keen to push Urdu poetry to new heights of intricacy and to innovate with its images in a worldly game of artistic expertise. Take for example the ghazal below, which has an unusual structure called *baz-gasht* in which each couplet "returns back" to the phrase with which it began. This returning quality makes each couplet not just a line ending with the required rhyme but rather a line wrapped in a circle. Not only does the end of each couplet have to rhyme with the end of every other couplet, but also the end of each couplet has to repeat the phrase that began it (which is independent in an ordinary ghazal). The following English translation gives a sense of the "returning back" in the poem and its artistic innovation but cannot capture the rhyme that links each couplet in the Urdu poem:[29]

> Breathing my last I am, where is my sweet sorcerer?
>   My sweet sorcerer's absence has me breathing my last
> Impudence never deserves to be looked at face to face
>   Face to face that mirror looks at you full of impudence
> Without just cause, the innocent are free of punishment
>   Punishment of death why give me without just cause?
> The night is like your hair and your cheek rivals the sun
>   The sun is now your cheek and your hair is the night

> Anger unjustly you use to pierce my heart, my dear
>> My dear, your indifference in my view is unjust anger
> This chosen line of rhyme goes straight for my lover
>> My lover arched his brows to bend this chosen line
> Demands of love's religion are that you leave all else
>> Leave all else now, Siraj, if that is what love demands

In this "returning back" ghazal, Siraj speaks of love in a romantic way without giving the images a mystical twist. His energy goes instead into the formal complexity of the poem with its intricate interplay of repetition and rhyme. He even makes an ironic commentary on writing such a ghazal, in the couplet where he says, "This chosen line of rhyme goes straight for my lover / My lover arched his brows to bend this chosen line." The simple ghazal consists of couplets that head straight for the rhyming phrase that must close each couplet and link each with the one that came before. But in this ghazal, the couplets cannot run straight for that rhyming sound but rather have to be bent back to repeat the opening phrase of the couplet. Siraj attributes this formal complexity to the power of his beloved's beauty: the arched brows bend the straight line of the forehead into a captivating curve; the line that Siraj chooses to describe his beloved must also bend back upon itself to achieve the description.

The final couplet seems to disavow the whole poem that leads up to it. The poem is mainly romantic, but the final couplet speaks about religion, specifically the religion of love (*mazhab-e ʿishq*): "Demands of love's religion are that you leave all else / Leave all else now, Siraj, if that is what love demands." Siraj acknowledges that playing with poetry for its own sake is frowned upon by his commitment to mystical love; in fact, that love might demand that he renounce all else, including the composition of poetry. Despite composing poetry that could be largely if not totally romantic, Siraj seems to recoil from this practice.

This reveals a tension in his personality that is reflected in his poems. It is as if, after composing poetry that is romantic and even erotic, he asserts in compensation that his poetry should lead to silence, contemplation, and self-abandonment. In this sense, the erotic energies that arise in the poem's images are meant to be sublimated. In the following poem, Siraj speaks of union with the beloved, loss of ego, and melting into vulnerability. It has both a mystical thrust and an erotic force to its images, and thus it is no surprise that Qawwals often weave its opening couplet into their songs.[30]

> Dual-colored's no good, go become one single tone
> > Be head-to-foot soft wax or go become a stone
> You're tight as a bud yet with the aroma of a flower
> > Heart narrow and wine vast, how'll you go swallow
> O sorrow, what ill-tempered fate told you
> > To let my heart's mirror go become overcast?
> O path of sorrow, may you live long, I pray
> > With just one step it seems I go a hundred miles
> Go put on the ruinous Sufi cloak stitched with *alif*
> > Your reputation's lost before you go suffer the *a* of "ah"
> With steady feet walk through separation's fire
> > Take on the color of the candle—just go now, Siraj

These poems suggest that Siraj's poetry, despite its mystical tone, had an underlying erotic force. It bubbled up beneath the more placid surface of mystical imagery and expressions of tranquil contemplation.

This erotic force expressed in Siraj's ghazals contributed to his Sufi master's command that he stop composing. This order was given not only because of the love imagery in Siraj's poems but also because of their social reception. His poetry was not written as a private pursuit of symbolic meanings but was composed in a highly oral and musical context. Siraj's words had their force because of their performance in musical assemblies of Qawwali. In this setting, their mystical images reinforced Siraj's own authority as an ethical exemplar and Sufi master, whose spiritual presence called the Qawwali gathering into being. In this setting also, the romantic and erotic images could have a powerful impact on the audience, but they might also call into question the propriety of Siraj himself. This is because of Siraj's social persona: he was not just a poet but also a mystic, and more important for his social persona, he was an unmarried man.

The Dangers of Sexuality

Siraj's unmarried status was a point of controversy. On the one hand, it highlighted his spiritual aspiration of nonattachment to worldly concerns. Chishti Sufi masters had long emphasized voluntary poverty, and some took this to an ascetic extreme of not saving money or storing provisions. For Chishtis who took these teachings to heart, it was almost impossible to support a family (with wife or wives, children, and possibly wives' extended family). Those Chishtis who became popular leaders of communities were often under enormous pressure to care for the needs of a wide circle of disciples and daily visitors, which demanded the time and energy that most men invested in their immediate family. In such situations, marrying and having children would be unjust if they could not provide for a family's material and emotional needs. In addition, as Muslims adjusted to the South Asian environment, they adopted the preexisting culture of radical renunciation that asserted a dichotomy between the life of a householding male and a spiritually adept male. Restraining sexual activity and sublimating erotic energies were seen to be the very basis of refining one's spiritual power.

This preexisting cultural attitude toward spirituality had shaped Hindu, Buddhist, and Jain notions of sacred power, and it also deeply influenced Islamic society in South Asia. Nizam al-Din Awliya, for example, never married. He admitted that the Prophet Muhammad's public example (*sunna*) favored marriage in general; Nizam al-Din upheld this example for common people but claimed a personal exemption from this rule for himself in recognition of his own spiritual aspiration. His own aspiration was to live a life dedicated to loving God and serving the public, to which the consequences of marriage would be an impediment. But he never advocated that his disciples or successors follow his personal example, as if it overrode that of the Prophet Muhammad. Despite this nuanced stance, though, some of Nizam al-Din's followers did follow his lead. Burhan al-Din Gharib in the Deccan refused to marry. Siraj also followed their example.

It was not controversial in Chishti circles for a Sufi master to be unmarried, though it remained unusual. Most Sufi masters did in fact marry and raise children (in the Chishti and other Sufi communities). Despite this, Siraj in eighteenth-century Awrangabad would be an acceptable figure to his surrounding society, even if his chosen path of life was quite different from the average Muslim male's in Mughal culture. However, his status as an unmarried adult male does raise questions about his ascetic rigor and manly vigor. Where did his erotic energies go if they were not released through sexual relations with a wife and channeled into family bonds? Can a man's erotic energies be diverted, dissipated, or disintegrated? If so, how? And if a man is freed from erotic energies, in what way is he masculine? Such questions raise a host of issues about gender, sexuality, and religious devotion that this section will try to address.

Chishti Sufis had a very rigorous approach to ascetic morality. They demanded that a serious mystic control his sexual appetite just as he should minimize his appetite for food through fasting, limit his sleep by devotional vigils, and renounce wealth and power. Even if a Chishti were to marry, he was expected to restrain his appetite for sexual pleasures. A good example of this is Shaikh Nasir al-Din Chiragh-e Delhi (died 1356), the principal successor to Nizam al-Din Awliya in Delhi. By all accounts, Nasir al-Din was more rigid in following the example of the Prophet Muhammad through legal norms of the *shari'a* than was his teacher and guide. Therefore, he married despite the personal example of Nizam al-Din Awliya.[31] However, he married after a long period of celibacy during which he struggled to eliminate the power of sexual drives over his consciousness. As the Sufi historian Khaliq Ahmad Nizami reports, "Shaikh Nasir al-Din struggled hard in his early years to control the calls of flesh in him. He reduced his diet to almost the starvation point and whenever sex-desire troubled him he said to himself: 'Death is preferable to a life of sex-desire' and drank so much lemon juice that he brought himself to the verge of death."[32]

The problem with Shaikh Nasir al-Din's approach to erotic forces is in the way he saw them as "calls of the flesh." Erotic energies are as much inherent in the human mind as they are in the flesh of the body. Seeing the erotic drive as "urges of the flesh" was simply a strategy to try to overcome it by pitting mind against body. Some ascetic-minded devotees promoted this strategy, and it might have been effective in suppressing erotic energies, but it is not an accurate description of their origin or force within the human personality.[33] There is a different approach that takes the reality of eros into account, one upheld by other Chishti Sufis. It sees eros as a powerful force originating in the soul, not merely in the body. Eros permeates all dimensions of the human personality—body, mind, and heart. This approach does not reduce eros down to sexual urge (sensual response of the body) but sees eros also as attraction (aesthetic response of the mind) and passion (emotive response of the liver) and love (spiritual response of the heart). If a mystic took this more holistic approach to eros, then the question would be not how to suppress or eliminate erotic energies but rather how to channel them. What dimension of the personality would they energize, and how could this flow be directed? Do erotic energies fuel one's sexual urges, or do they spark one's aesthetic enjoyment, or do they ignite one's passion for love? Sublimation rather than suppression is the goal of this strategy, which was upheld by Nizam al-Din Awliya and Burhan al-Din Gharib among early Chishti exemplars.

If one adopts this approach toward the problem of erotic energy, as did Siraj, then mere brutal asceticism and self-denial are not sufficient strategies. One would need to take a more subtle approach that appreciates the force of eros while trying to direct its flow. Listening to love poetry set to music in a ritual gathering would become the major strategy to try to elicit erotic responses while redirecting them away from sexual lust. The following ghazal provides a lens through which we can analyze this approach, for its opening couplet sets us in the gathering of lovers, listening to devotional music:[34]

> This party's heating up, O God! If only he were here—
>   He, my beloved who lights the assembly—it would be rapt
> My heart's blood is showing up in my tears
>   Spilling, they tint everyone a sweet shade of red
> As a dowry, my heart walked off with sorrow's brand
>   But we had only asked for the sterling of a meeting
> The ascetic deserves just a tight and narrow cell
>   Lovers' garden is reserved for those devoted to openness
> In the face of your negligence, my heart has become
>   The nightingale for spring's scarlet rose of wrath
> The heart's estate is in the abode of beauty
>   Since it was promoted in the company of love
> As soon as I fail to achieve union with him
>   Then and only then will I let my desire die
> Don't be provocative like a rose's open petals
>   Keep your lips closed tight like the merest bud
> Tell us now, Siraj, how the moth assaults the candle
>   For a sincere heart, politeness is in transgressing

Siraj describes his approach to mysticism by contrasting a bare cell to an expansive garden: "The ascetic deserves just a tight and narrow cell / Lovers' garden is reserved for those devoted to openness." Siraj may have lived in voluntary poverty and freed himself from family burdens, but he was no ascetic. He caricatures the ascetic as hard-hearted and devoid of love, whereas for lovers, the world is a garden and everywhere one turns there are flowers, like manifestations of God's beauty. When one's attraction to beauty is raised from the level of craving possessiveness and lustful manipulation to the level of spiritual love—through sublimation of desire—then everything in the garden becomes sublime, a manifestation of God's own beauty.

In the sphere of ritual, the world is a garden for Chishti Sufis when they are gathered for sama'. In the sphere of theology, they assert that God's beauty appears most powerfully in the image of the human being.[35] When these two spheres overlap—held together through the poetry whose music fills the space and whose words invoke theology—the intensity and power of the experience can be overwhelming. They overlap when one sits in a gathering where devotional music is played and sung while one contemplates the beauty of a person whom one loves. This is the practice of *shahid-bazi* or "playing the witness," in which one perceives in the beauty of another person the beauty of God's creation.

Siraj alludes to this practice when he sings, "This party's heating up, O God! If only he were here— / He, my beloved who lights the assembly—it would be rapt." Just as every evening assembly of music and poetry has a candle that lights up the space, so also every assembly includes someone who strikes one as particularly beautiful and draws one's attention away from self-concern. Contemplating that person's face and form can lead one toward a deeper appreciation of God's own beautiful qualities reflected in divine creation. The emotional reaction to this experience is rapture or weeping, or perhaps both together. This experience Siraj describes by saying, "My heart's blood is showing up in my tears / Spilling, they tint everyone a sweet shade of red." His rapture is not just a personal and private experience. Rather, in sama' it becomes very public and social. One's tears can cause others to also weep, and one's rapture can spark joy in others—the spiritual state of one person can tint the hue of everyone who surrounds her or him.

The ghazal above reveals the erotic force that pushes up against the surface of Siraj's poetry. The beloved in this ghazal appears very clearly to be an actual person, an intimate friend or a young man whose presence lights up the assembly. Siraj lived a celibate life after joining his Sufi community, with no wife or children. Yet no matter how he may have sublimated his erotic drives in real life, eros gives his poetry force and would erupt rather dramatically in sama'. The voices of his friends interject in the closing couplet, "Tell us now, Siraj, how the moth assaults the candle," and we must remember that the candle is, from the first couplet, the beloved "witness" whose beauty lights the assembly. The poetic voice speaking for Siraj replies, "For a sincere heart, politeness is in transgressing." If one is a sincere lover, then transgressing decorum is the only way of being polite. Siraj's poems certainly did push the limits, even if in real life he was restrained.

Conclusion

For Siraj's Sufi teacher, these expressions may have transgressed the limit. Shah Rahman may not have doubted Siraj's sincerity, but he may have been alarmed at the heat and hubbub generated by Siraj's poems when they were sung in gatherings of Qawwali. He may have admired Siraj's inner state but moved to curtail its social manifestation in others through the medium of his poems. Why would these erotic images raise Shah Rahman's alarm, when they are quite common in the ghazal? To find an answer to this question, the next section will return to Siraj's early life, to examine the forces of gender and sexuality that shaped his personality. Though "playing the witness" and its homoerotic bonding may have been common practice among Chishti Sufis, the youthful history of Siraj reveals that he approached it from an unusual position. The command to cease composing ghazals encourages us to look beyond Siraj's poems for its real cause. It leads us to reexamine his youthful life and discover what experiences shaped his artistic use of erotic images, which was so adroit as to make his poems a threat to public morality.

CHAPTER FOUR

Eros and Spirit

Whoever looks upon your beauty it seems
    Walks a path paved with the sun's beams
In love's realm I've been appointed king
    God is bountiful beyond my wildest dreams

—*verses from a ghazal by Siraj*

Siraj might have been chaste but his lyrics were not, and that only heightened their effectiveness in the gatherings of samaʿ. This is perhaps because his lyrics resound too strongly with Siraj's earlier life, before he formally entered the Sufi community. To understand more fully why his Sufi master forbade Siraj from composing poems, this chapter will go back to his early life and examine erotic longing—that is, the gazing at beauty to which he refers in the ghazal quoted above, as in many others—as a force in his personal development and his spirituality.[1] This section will explore the forces of gender and sexuality that shaped his personality before he submitted to a Sufi master and embraced the Chishti Sufi community. It argues that Siraj's personality was of a type that is now—in modern psychological terminology—known as homosexual. This personality developed considerably before Siraj renounced sexual activity altogether in hopes of loving God alone. Renunciation of sexual activity changed his life path, but it did not change his personality in its deepest psychological structure. The erotic forces that he suppressed in practice resurfaced in his ghazal poetry with effective artistic force. Siraj hoped that rechanneling his erotic energy—what we call "sublimation of desire"—would fuel his spiritual life in his quest to love God alone.

Sexuality and Sanity in Siraj's Early Life

Before turning to the early life of Siraj and his first love affair, we must define some key terms that are crucial for discussing sexuality. These terms are often misunderstood, though they developed over the last century through clinical psychiatry. Sexuality refers to self-awareness that is not just an urge (like lust) but also a passion that moves us toward existential coming-to-completeness through encountering another person in a way that unites body, sensation, soul, and spirit. Sexual acts can be an expression of one's sexuality, or they can express other things such as social conformity or domination or even torture. Sexuality is an intimate part of each individual's personality and an integral component in each person's appreciation of beauty or apprehension of emotional intensity. Sexuality consists of many components, including strength of sex drive, frequency of sexual contact, a continuum of style (from aggressively passionate to delicately tender), and variation in intensity of response. A central component of sexuality is sexual orientation. This refers to whether one is attracted to a partner of the same gender or of the opposite gender (or perhaps to both and possibly to neither). Homosexuality refers to the sexual orientation through which one is attracted to a partner of the same gender for sexual fulfillment.

Modern psychiatry holds that sexual orientation is an inherent part of an individual's personality, elements of which may be genetic, influenced by hormonal balances in the womb, and shaped by early childhood experiences, the cumulative effects of which unfold during adolescence and early adulthood. Sexual orientation—both homosexuality and heterosexuality—belongs to the prerational level of a person's psyche; as such, sexual orientation cannot be consciously changed, though sexual behavior might be modified. Most psychiatrists assert that attitude toward one's sexual orientation is largely cultural and that behavior based upon one's sexual orientation is subject to rational control and clinical modification, but the underlying sexual orientation is not. Thus homosexuality as sexual orientation should not be confused with modern subcultures that uphold this term. In modern subcultures, men who experience homosexuality increasingly adopt the term "gay" to describe themselves and their community, while women who experience homosexuality increasingly adopt the term "lesbian." However, most all cultures have different names for homosexuality and those persons who experience it. The underlying phenomenon—which is arguably universal to all cultures—should not be confused with different cultural responses to it, responses that vary widely and alter over time and transform with social change.

In analytical terminology, one must carefully differentiate sexual orientation from gender identity. Gender refers to whether one identifies as a male, female, both, or neither—within any specific cultural definition of those roles. In patriarchal cultures, however, there is persistent social pressure to define homosexual orientation as a problem with one's gender identity. That is, a man who experiences sexual attraction to and fulfillment with another male is misunderstood to be acting like a woman and is censured for being effeminate or for betraying the norms of masculine behavior. Conversely, a woman who experiences sexual attraction to and fulfillment with another female is misunderstood to be acting like a man and is censured for betraying the norms of feminine behavior. In both cases, censure is often violent.

In patriarchal societies, the issue of sexual orientation is forcefully conflated with gender identity, to the point that the two elements of personality—sexual orientation and gender identity—become confused and juxtaposed. In every society there are people who have nonnormative gender identity; that is, a person may be perceived by others to be male (on the basis of anatomy, ascribed name, or outward appearance) but feels internally like a female, such that "he" may exhibit qualities associated with women in "his" society, unless such exhibition is censured. Conversely, a person may be perceived by others to be female yet feel internally like a male and may express qualities or behaviors associated with men. Such persons may feel "trapped" in a body of wrong anatomy. Such persons can be said to have "gender dysphoria" or disharmony between their assigned gender (as imposed by others) and their own gender identity (as perceived by the self). Some may feel this dysphoria only mildly and resolve it by wearing clothes or adopting behaviors typifying the gender with which they identify. Others may feel this dysphoria so strongly that they alter their body to conform more closely to the anatomical features of the gender with which they identify, in what can be called "transsexual" behavior. There are others whose sense of gender is ambiguous, who feel that they are neither "male" nor "female" but rather both—such persons used to be called hermaphrodites and are increasingly choosing the label "intersex." Others may feel ambiguous in the sense of being neither "male" nor "female" and assert that they belong to a "third gender," as is the case with hijras in South Asia, who are men who choose castration and dress and speak like women but live in separate communities of their own "third gender" family.

Finally, there are persons whose nonnormative gender identity arises not from their own choice but by its having been imposed by society, often through the institution of slavery. This is the situation for eunuchs, who are castrated in youth to serve in aristocratic households, especially those that practice gender segregation, as did many Islamic societies. Eunuchs grow up male and internally identify as men, but the anatomical features associated with masculine sexual activity are removed against their will. In Islamic cultures, eunuchs were considered to be "neither men nor women" and thus had to stand during prayer in a mosque behind the men but before the women. This genital removal does not affect a eunuch's sexual orientation, though it does affect his sexual behavior; if the testes are removed at an age before the onset of puberty, this will also affect a eunuch's sexuality in terms of diminished sex drive and hormonal imbalance. In chapter 6, we will discuss one eunuch who played a significant role in the spiritual heritage of the Deccan, who belonged to an influential class of persons.

The results of the above analysis demonstrate that homosexuality should be carefully differentiated from gender identity. Yet in contemporary South Asia, homosexual men are often thought to be eunuchs, and eunuchs are routinely identified as hijras. In reality, each of these categories is different, and the psychology of those who inhabit a category is distinct. When we apply modern clinical terms to the personality of Siraj, we find that he had a homosexual orientation but did not question his gender identity: he identified as male with no evidence of "effeminacy" but was sexually attracted to another male and not to females.

There is currently an intellectual debate over whether terms like "homosexual" can be properly applied to personalities and behaviors in premodern or non-Western societies. In the heyday of the gay liberation movement in the 1970s and 1980s, scholars found evidence of homosexuality in world history and literature in every era, and labeling it as such was used to fuel a movement for rights and pride in Western countries. In reaction to this, Michel Foucault noted that the category "homosexual" was invented in Europe in the 1880s and therefore should not be applied to sexual behaviors and gendered identities in previous eras or other lands; he contended that sexuality and sexual categories are part and parcel of European modernity's drive to power.[2] Foucault's ideas have been taken up as ideology by scholars like David Halperin, a scholar of ancient Greece, and Joseph Massad, a scholar of modern Arab politics.[3] Both deny that homosexuality has any meaning outside of modern Euro-America such that imposing it upon other cultures leads to distortion; they see sexuality in terms of dominance, status, and insertion roles rather than in terms of gendered subjectivities and object-choice.

Despite this growing chorus of "constructivist" discourse, some scholars have held that in fact object-choice is an important element of sexuality before and beyond European modernity, even if it was referred to by cultural terms more subtle or coded than "homosexuality." This position is maintained by Jonathan Boswell, a scholar of medieval Christendom, and Bernadette Brooten, a scholar of Hellenistic late antiquity; they see homosexual object-choice as a distinct feature of individuals and subgroups that get interpreted differently in different cultures, eras, and political dispensations.[4]

Lately, Halperin has modified his stand in response to the careful research of historians like Brooten. He now holds that homosexuality is not a modern "invention" but rather a modern "reconfiguration" of several elements of gender and sexual identity that were independent before European modernity.[5] This is a more subtle and useful approach that is similar to the approach of Khaled El-Rouayheb's survey of Arab-Islamic literature about same-sex relationships in the early-modern period.[6] Other scholars, when examining the literary output of Muslim societies from this era, sidestep this acrimonious debate by avoiding the term "homosexual" and adopting other terms. Walter Andrews and Mehmet Kalpaklı use "the beloved" to highlight the fluidity of sexual object-choice in Ottoman lands. Ruth Vanita and Saleem Kidwai use the term "same-sex love" in South Asia to focus on the importance of sexual object-choice while stressing the emotional quality of love as key.[7]

I find the approach of Andrews and Kalpaklı along with that of Vanita and Kidwai to be most promising. They are interested in investigating the subtleties of non-Western literature on its own terms while being attentive to issues of same-sex eroticism, repression or acceptance, and social flexibility despite legal norms. They do not intend to build academic careers by staking positions in an ideological debate. The position of this book is that same-sex attraction did and does occur in Islamic societies—in the Deccan as elsewhere—in both premodern and contemporary eras. It could be expressed in loving relationships between same-gendered partners; such relationships were accepted in certain conditions but repressed if they challenged patriarchal norms in the political or religious realms. For some individuals, same-sex attraction was such an integral part of their personality that their life choices were predicated upon it, even to the point of challenging family norms or daring social censure. I call such relationships "homosexual" not because they are exactly the same as modern Euro-American experiences; rather, the term homosexual is readily understood and has become a standard term for describing the psychological outlook shaped by same-gender sexual attractions, behaviors, and relationships. After all, scholars discuss "women" or "peasants" or "landlords" as universal phenomena that are nevertheless inflected by culture. Why not allow this careful extension of the expression "homosexual"? Why is it that terms regarding sexuality are somehow more incendiary than terms for describing gender or class?[8]

Returning to Siraj, we can note that homosexual orientation affected his social behavior in observable ways. He experienced profound trauma as a youth, fled his family obligations and expectations, and never married a woman or fathered children. Yet his sexual orientation did not overdetermine his behavior. He apparently chose to live a celibate life without sexual contact or romantic attachment once he entered adulthood. This does not mean that he was "asexual" and did not feel sexual attraction but rather that he restrained his sexual behavior to conform, as far as possible, to an Islamic moral code upheld by his community.

In many ways, Siraj was more stringent with himself in terms of sexual behavior than his Mughal society in general imposed. Mughal society was patriarchal but comparatively lenient in allowing that men could be sexually attracted to other men, as long as that did not entail taking a sexually "submissive" role associated with feminine behavior—in particular taking a receptive role in penetrative sexual acts.[9] This censure was based on Mughal understandings of gender identity rather than on homosexual orientation as such. The Mughal environment was "homosocial," meaning that men formed affectionate bonds and emotional attachment largely with other men, and women formed them largely with other women. Homosocial bonds could develop into homoerotic ones, when friendship and affection became charged with feelings of love, but this too did not imply any sexual activity. The prevalence of homosocial bonding was one consequence of a highly gender-segregated social order. The one great exception was the affection and companionship that men found in female courtesans, as this study will examine in greater detail in the case of Mah Laqa Bai. Men in this Mughal environment found it easy to express affection, love, and even passionate attraction to other men without that being assumed to be a sign of homosexual orientation.

This definition of terms has noted that each culture espouses different norms and reactions to these variations in sexual orientation and gender identity, which persistently occur in every culture. The Mughal culture in which Siraj thrived was both Islamic and patriarchal but showed remarkable toleration for homosocial bonding and even homosexual relationships, as long as they did not threaten the patriarchal social order based on property ownership, inheritance by legitimate children, and male control of female wives, sisters, and daughters.[10] Simon Digby has studied a chronicle of the Naqshbandi Sufi community in Awrangabad in the same era as the one in which Siraj lived and found that most discussions of erotic sentiments, attachments, and relationships of the Sufi lives documented there were homosexual in orientation; one was so open that it led to a youth stabbing to death the man who was in love with him.[11] The historian Gijs Kruijtzer also notes that Awrangabad under Mughal rule offers several examples of Sufis who were involved in homoerotic relationships, including Siraj.[12] The homosexual orientation of Siraj and the gender transgression of Mah Laqa Bai were largely accepted by their society without upsetting the general order of daily life, marriage and procreation, and Islamic norms.[13]

As this chapter examines Siraj's early life, it is best to start with his own autobiographical statement. He briefly describes himself before taking initiation with a Sufi master by saying, "This poor wretch (*faqir*) was overcome with passionate love at about the age of twelve. For approximately seven years, he donned the clothing of nakedness (*jama-ye 'ariyana*), and suffered the pains of intoxication (*nasha*) and oblivion (*be-khudi*). Most nights until daybreak he spent in the vicinity of the blessed tomb of Shah Burhan al-Din Gharib."[14] This description covers his puberty, adolescence, and early adulthood years—from age twelve to his early twenties—when one's sexual anatomy matures, one's erotic awareness dawns, and one discovers that social relationships can be sexually charged. It is a frightening and exhilarating time fraught with possibility and danger (though one's passage through it is deeply shaped by social expectations, cultural norms, and religious ideals that differ from era to era and place to place). Siraj's brief description uses poetic terms that are common in the ghazal to characterize these stages of his early life, but they are terms deeply resonant with erotic force. He wore the clothing of nakedness, suffered pains of intoxication, and enjoyed the rapture of oblivion.

While it hints at sexual awakening, Siraj's description conceals more than it reveals. This is not surprising, because Siraj fell in love with another male in his early years and suffered terribly as a result. Siraj speaks about this affair indirectly in an epic poem, as we will see below, but he avoids mentioning it directly in his autobiographical statement. The affair was disastrous for Siraj not because of its homosexual character but because his lover was not loyal and supportive. It was this affair spiraling into disaster that probably spurred Siraj's insane flight from the city of Awrangabad and his family.

During the seven years of his "insanity," he worked through this experience of wildness and exile. Taking refuge at the dargah of Burhan al-Din Gharib, he quieted his Persian poetic rage and quelled his erotic attractions until "cooled down" enough to join a Sufi community and take initiation with a teacher. Through this strategy, he sublimated his erotic drives without dissipating them altogether. In fact, joining a Sufi community was probably the only way he could reintegrate into his urban society, though we must acknowledge that he never really integrated fully with his family (by marrying and raising children to perpetuate his Sayyid clan). The Sufi community gave him a surrogate family, with a father-figure shaikh and fellow-disciple brothers, and this buffered him from his sexuality somewhat. Yet had he been buffered too much, his poetry would lack the force that it clearly had upon immediate audiences in samaʿ gatherings and still has.

It is generally not a safe practice to read ghazals for biographical information about the author. The ghazal is not a genre that lends itself to accurate representations of reality, let alone a chronological narrative. However, Siraj seems to have seeded his ghazals with oblique references to his actual experience and certainly turned to autobiography in his epic masnavi, titled "The Fragrant Garden of Imagination" (*Bustan-e Khayal*). This epic tells of the homosexual love affair that shaped his later life so deeply. It records real incidents—though exaggerated for poetic effect—without a sense of shame. The theme of homoerotic love in an epic romantic poem is not unusual in the later Mughal period, and other examples exist that can be compared with Siraj's poem.[15] Siraj wrote his story with the understanding that young lust led him through suffering to a spiritual sublimation of erotic urges that were refined into spiritually pure love directed toward God. That is the role of imagination, to lead the lover through infatuation with persons and images into a deeper longing for spiritual presence and insight.

Though Siraj's autobiography elides the details of his affair, his biographers hint at this erotic crisis in their accounts. These accounts differ widely, depending on how open the writer was to the erotic dimension of his personality. Some biographers preferred to cover over this dimension, to the extent that they altered the text of his biography while having it copied in order to erase the details of his erotic development. The able scholar 'Abd al-Qadir Sarvari has uncovered this discrepancy while editing Siraj's poems. Sarvari noted that there are two different manuscript copies of the text *Tuhfat al-Shu'ara* or "Gift of the Poets" by "Qaqshal," an author contemporary with Siraj. The two copies of the same text are held by two different libraries in Hyderabad. These two copies are almost identical up to the entry on Siraj, but their accounts of him differ widely. The version of the text held at the Andhra Pradesh State Oriental Manuscript and Research Library gives only the briefest outline of his early years: "Shah Siraj al-Din Awrangabadi, who wrote under the name Siraj, first found employment with military service. Presently, he left earning a livelihood through such employment and for some years donned darvesh dress. He put much thought into composing verse in Urdu (*rekhta-ye hindi*). He has arranged a divan [of ghazals] in Urdu. He also turns his attention to composing verse in Persian."[16]

The second version of the text exists in a copy of the book by "Qaqshal" held at the Salar Jung Museum Library. It was copied at an unknown date but was apparently an earlier version.[17] This version is much richer in information about Siraj's early life:

> Shah Siraj al-Din Awrangabadi came from a Sayyid family. His ancestors were Sufi masters. Until the age of twelve, his elders kept him engaged in studies. When he reached the age of fifteen, wildness (*vahshat*) found its way into his temperament. For a period of seven years, he remained like a madman in the dargah of Burhan al-Din Gharib—may God keep his heart holy. At nights, impelled by forces beyond his rational choice, he would wander the hills and wastelands. His father, named Sayyid Darvesh, placed chains around his ankles. After a time, he fell into poverty and the idea occurred to him to join the Sufi community (*fuqara'*). Under the influence of a spiritual guide, he shed his clothing and became intimate with the delights of being a Sufi. He has poetry. In Urdu, he is a powerful writer. Because of passion for poetry in Urdu, his house is thronged with handsome young men. One of those in his circle, 'Abd al-Rasul Khan, has collected and organized his divan [of ghazals]. He also turns his attention to composing verse in Persian.[18]

These two accounts, supposedly belonging to the same text, differ so radically that the discrepancy begs for an explanation.

Sarvari discovered this incongruity and timidly ventures the opinion that the copyist of the shorter entry made a simple mistake. He suggests that the copyist might have inadvertently incorporated information from the biography of Mir Fakhr al-Din Awrangabadi (1717–85) into the biography of Siraj, for Fakhr al-Din in his youth joined the military and then renounced worldly pursuits to become a Sufi.[19] Though Sarvari finds several other examples of such biographical conflation in this text, this explanation is unsatisfactory in the case of Siraj. Fakhr al-Din Awrangabadi was no obscure poet whose details would get mistaken for Siraj's life story; rather, he was the son of Nizam al-Din Awrangabadi, the leading Chishti figure of his generation. Fakhr al-Din was a famous personality in Awrangabad and Delhi and became the spiritual adviser to high Mughal officials, including, by some accounts, the Mughal emperor Shah ʿAlam (ruled 1759–1806). He authored several texts and many texts were written about him, some by highly placed political figures in the Deccan such as the first nizam's grandson, who was his admirer.[20] Yet Sarvari contends that their biographies got conflated to explain why one version says that Siraj joined the military in his youth while the other version does not mention this. He finds it implausible that Siraj would have joined the military as a young man; in Sarvari's view that would be a deviation in his life trajectory of spirituality and poetry. In fact, many Sufis in Awrangabad and the wider Deccan worked as soldiers, courtiers, or administrators while developing into Sufi masters and poets.[21] So Sarvari's theory of a biographical conflation due to a copyist's error is weak. It does not account at all for the most glaring difference: the elimination of information about his youthful wildness, exile, being chained by his family, and taking refuge at the dargah of Burhan al-Din.

This study respectfully differs from the timid theory of Sarvari. The textual alterations are not a conflation of two different people, which would have added extraneous information, but rather a drastic abridgment that deleted selective information. This alternative explanation accounts for why the abridged version has the same beginning and ending. An identical beginning and ending would not be likely if parts of a different person's biography were mistakenly conflated with Siraj's biographical entry. Asserting that the shorter version is an abridgment also makes sense when one considers what information went missing: all mention of erotic awakening, insanity, and social conflict. The shorter version has been cleaned of controversial episodes in order to make Siraj's personality more acceptable to patriarchal norms. It is therefore not surprising that the shorter version — missing all details of Siraj's youthful controversies—is the text that has been published (on the margins of the main publication, *Chamanistan-e Shuʻara*).²² This is because it is more acceptable to modern Muslim sensibilities that have been deeply impacted by Victorian British morality and reformist currents of Islamic piety. What gets erased is Siraj's only real love affair with another male and his spending time with throngs of "handsome young men" (*amrad-e khub-surat*) later in life, with whom he shared his passion for Urdu poetry.

Making Love in the Garden of Imagination

Fortunately, we do not have to rely on biographers of Siraj, some of whom seem more intent on silencing their subject than on letting him speak. To make sense of Siraj's formative years, we can turn to his own writings. His autobiographical prose might be humbly meager, but his poetic recreation of his youthful adventures, in the epic *Bustan-e Khayal* or "The Fragrant Garden of Imagination," abounds in details that take 1,162 couplets to recount. This poem is based upon his own experience, though clothed in florid metaphor, and through it we learn that in his early adolescence Siraj fell in love with another young man, who was apparently a Hindu soldier.²³ They were happily in love despite vicious gossipers and jealous rivals who tried to target them, until the soldier shifted to Hyderabad, then a provincial city ruled from Awrangabad. Siraj left his family to run after him but found that, upon moving, his lover had grown cold. Siraj was abandoned and went mad. This episode was indicated in coded hints in the longer version of his biography but was erased in the shorter biography and replaced by the statement that Siraj had joined the military. That is a clever way of implying that Siraj left his family and home while not saying that he ran away to join a lover in the military.

Before we turn to Siraj's compelling narrative, we must warn against imposing on eighteenth-century Awrangabad the standards and assumptions of twenty-first-century modernity, whether Muslim or secular, Western or South Asian. For the purpose of analysis, we will call the love between Siraj and his soldier a homosexual affair. This is because it was a romantic and emotional bond between two males that was expressed in physical intimacy. But we must refrain from imposing contemporary understandings of homosexuality upon Siraj, especially understandings that position homosexuality as a political identity in oppositional contradiction to Islam as a religious identity. For a man to fall in love with a man (particularly if one, or both, were not socially "mature") was not deemed unusual in the Mughal context; aside from a small class of jurists, Mughal-era aristocrats and educated gentry did not perceive a man loving another man as anything sinful against Islam. What was deemed shameful and dangerous was to allow lust or infatuation to overwhelm one's sense of decorum and status. This was especially the case if a mature man let a younger person (of lower rank or social status), whether male or female, exercise influence or mastery over him. In other words, a "noble" man could romantically love or even sexually interact with another man but must refrain from falling into the classic poses of the lover in the ghazal. The decorum of male lovers was especially precarious in musical performances, as demonstrated ably by the recent research of Katherine Butler Schofield.[24] For Mughal men, love affairs were probably easier with another man or boy than with a woman or girl. The gender of one's beloved did not seem to matter much, as long as one's attitude toward him or her was oriented toward mastery and status maintenance. It was life orientation that mattered far more than sexual orientation.

Siraj found it hard to abide by this attitude. He was too passionate a lover and too affected by beauty to maintain Mughal standards of decorum and patriarchal mastery. Siraj seems to have taken ghazal imagery very literally as a code to live by, if his account in "The Fragrant Garden of Imagination" is to be believed. The literary critic Sarvari admits that this masnavi is autobiographical, calling it "outwardly a love story which in reality interweaves events in the author's life."[25] In a prose summary by the able hand of Saleem Kidwai, the basic features of Siraj's autobiographical poem emerge:

> There was a time when I was with my flower-faced beloved and life felt divine. Always together, hand in hand, we would talk and drink wine. The nights were moonlit, every gesture an embrace, and together we would recite ghazals. We did what we wanted, the drums of pleasure beating in our ears. Even silence was a treasure for life was brimming with pleasure. With my beloved beside me, I had no fear of the future. This sounds like a fairy tale from the past—that happiness unfortunately did not last.

Before he tells the story of his affair, he describes the seductive beauties of Awrangabad—and they are all men—"like a thousand Josephs," the prophet whom the Qur'an upholds as the paragon of male beauty. While some of the descriptions are ambiguous in terms of gender, like "putting a mirror to shame," most of them are clearly masculine, as the beauties have facial hair and wear turbans, strings of flowers around their wrists, and swords strapped about their loins.[26]

Then Siraj turns to the crux of his story, for he fell in love with a Hindu youth:

> I have been the victim of another faithless one who did not know what promises meant, yet for the dust of whose feet I still crave. I was seven, had just discovered poetry, when I first saw him. Seven years passed, and I learned the ways of life. I became renowned for my knowledge and he for his beauty.... We were one, by passion engulfed. People talked and the envious were incensed. His people were outraged. It's inappropriate, this friendship with a Muslim, they said. We will cast you out of the community, they threatened. I don't care, he said, as long as I have my Siraj.... People saw the truth, this welding of hearts. The gossip died and so did the strife. I was lucky and felt like a king. I had found a beloved with the heart of a lover. We were going to be together forever. I had no idea what fate held for me. I did not know that this friend would become my enemy.[27]

Others' envy, families' cunning, and friends' deceit all teach Siraj hard lessons, as he recounts in this masnavi, and his beloved betrays him. After mourning for years and spurning the advances of all others, a handsome son of a military commander courts Siraj and pledges his love. Siraj repudiates this generous gesture, but it moves him to tell his story to the soldier's son. In telling it, Siraj relives the love affair, and his heart is sparked to give up life in Awrangabad and flee to Hyderabad, where the faithless beloved is now living. In Hyderabad, he meets his past love, only to be tricked yet again. In the end, he concludes,

> The ways of the beautiful are fake and their words untrustworthy.... I lost my mind, banged my head on stones and wandered off again into the wilderness. Death seemed the only solution and much as I tried, it wouldn't come. Then it struck me that the only solution was to turn my heart to God.... Save me from the chains of their beauty, let me not taste the honey from their lips. Save me from the beautiful ones so that I may see your beauty.[28]

There, in these few lines, he sums up the stages of his adolescence and coming-of-age: first his childhood pursuit of religious knowledge and study of poetry and then his teenage love affair with a Hindu youth. Some lines suggest that he even faced danger; speaking to God he implores, "Give me means to escape the snare of these beauties' curls, save me from the sorcery of their bewitching eyes. Don't let me be tangled in the clothes of their allure, don't let the hem of their tunics pull me along! Don't allow me to be locked up in chains of their intimacy, don't let me be thrown into the dungeons of punishment! Don't let my heart incline toward such things, toward such sweet delight and colors bright."[29] The word he uses for punishment (ta'zir) is a legal term, meaning punishment at the discretion of the ruler, applied to homosexual sex acts in the Hanafi school of law that prevailed among Sunni Muslims in Mughal territory.[30] If, in the throes of his love affair, he were threatened with ta'zir at the hands of the police, this would explain the urgency with which his own father chained him up. After passing these dangerous straits, he encounters despair and insanity that drives him to the wilderness.

Taking refuge at the tomb of the great Chishti master Burhan al-din Gharib is a stepping-stone to recovery. The tomb-shrine was a powerful place for Muslims in the Deccan who invested in it potent symbolic capital. It was a place of refuge for those seeking to escape the clutches of power, whether that power was political persecution, family control, or the demands of reason. It was also seen to be the spiritual center of protective power that overarched the Deccan region, leading kings to patronize it and respect it. Even Awrangzeb—despite his reputation for Islamic orthodoxy and lacking respect for dead saints—desired to be buried in Khuldabad near the tomb of Burhan al-Din, as it was seen to be a symbolic gateway to heaven.[31]

This viewpoint is made plain by the author Khaksar Sabzavari. He was a visitor to Awrangabad, or perhaps a new migrant drawn to the city by its status as the new Mughal capital. In his book *Savanih* (Life and travels), he details his tour of the city and its attractions, but he begins with praise of the tomb-shrine of Burhan al-Din Gharib, whom he considers the patron saint of the whole Deccan region, of which Awrangabad was the leading urban center. Describing the town of Khuldabad, which grew up around the hospice of Burhan al-Din Gharib and later around his tomb, he writes, "In short, the abode of the [spiritual] ruler Burhan al-Din resembles the garden of paradise. In the town and surrounding areas, one thousand and four hundred saints are laid to rest."

> How lovely that garden of tombs built on a hill
> From there prayer reaches from below to on high
> It is as if the milky-way were strewn over the earth
> That is illumined by the saints like stars in the sky
> Their much-visited tombs are as many as stars
> Though counting all of their famous names I try
> . . . .
> Their land is ever verdant with bliss and joy
> Like a garden that's never met a season cold or dry
> To record the year of my visit to this place
> I sing this couplet, this rhyming pair I versify
> Rizwan the guardian angel opened heaven's door
> When "such a pure garden" the year did signify[32]

The phrase "such a pure garden" (*rawza-ye ba safa*) has both religious meaning and numerical value. In Urdu, Persian, and Arabic, each letter has an associated number in a complex system called *abjad*. The sum of the letters in "such a pure garden" gives the number 1185, signifying the year of the author's visit according to the Islamic calendar (equivalent to 1771 CE). But the coded phrase also links the Sufi necropolis, or city of tombs, to purity and salvation. It is an earthly replica of the garden of paradise, not in any physical resemblance but in a purely symbolic significance (in contrast to the attempt of Mughal emperors to create tomb gardens that physically replicated paradise, such as Shahjahan with the Taj Mahal in Agra or Awrangzeb with his Bibi ka Maqbara in Awrangabad).

It was no accident that Siraj took refuge at the dargah of Burhan al-Din Gharib during his madness resulting from his disastrous homoerotic affair that provoked his family's opposition. Burhan al-Din was also subtly "driven out" of Delhi by his Sufi brothers and fellow-disciples of Nizam al-Din Awliya, as his enthusiasm for dancing during samaʿ was seen to be transgressive. Despite his position as an elder at the Chishti center in Delhi, he was passed over for the primary succession, which went to the more sober and scholarly Shaikh Nasir al-Din. In fact, he almost was passed over for authorization (*khilafat*) to act as a spiritual master himself. There is controversy over whether Nizam al-Din Awliya, on his deathbed, invested him with such authority. In his old age, Burhan al-Din moved to the Deccan, where, far from disgrace in Delhi, he helped spread the Chishti community in the south and reconstituted his high status.

Attitudes toward Homosexuality among Chishti Sufis

Despite his energetic dancing, Burhan al-Din Gharib used to say, "Real experience of samaʿ is lamentation and contemplation—the rest is mere temptation!"[33] His Chishti style of love mysticism certainly did have in it an element of temptation. Praising love as worship and promoting passion as a way of life might encourage what some would criticize as profligate or lustful behavior. The early Chishti masters discussed the problem of sexuality and its relation to love as well as the more controversial matter of homosexuality. They discussed it because potential for homoerotic bonding was present in samaʿ, when routine formalities of masculine behavior were loosened or dissolved; there was a fear among some that homoerotic bonding could lead to homosexual activity, a phenomenon that was difficult to discuss directly in their circles.[34]

The attitudes of early Chishti Sufi masters toward sexuality and homosexuality were subtle and complex. They provide a useful model for modern Muslims who tend to approach the subject bluntly, even brutally. In the record of Nizam al-Din Awliya's conversations and discourses, the subject came up occasionally. He did not shy away from addressing it, and Burhan al-Din Gharib was an avid conversation partner on this topic. Their basic position was that sexual activity was not sinful in itself but that it often became the conduit for sinful attitudes—like possessiveness, craving, lust, selfishness, and domination. Sexuality therefore was an obstacle toward spiritual growth and refinement, not because of the physical acts involved but because of the psychic attitudes behind them. Nizam al-Din Awliya and Burhan al-Din Gharib both renounced sexual acts and took upon themselves chastity as a spiritual practice, but they did not make this a required condition for others. But the example of Nizam al-Din Awliya certainly did mean that the Chishtis had an alternative discourse on what constituted "masculinity." They contrasted routine understanding of masculinity—equated with physical virility, sexual potency, and aggressive dominance—with their own understanding of masculinity as the power to uphold spiritual virtues and transform others for the better.

Their attitudes toward masculinity are expressed in Nizam al-Din's discourses, recorded by Amir Hasan Sijzi as *Fava'id al-Fu'ad* (Morals for the heart). The Chishti masters taught that masculinity is a spiritual quality of having a high aspiration to love God and effective attention to help others. The routine social understanding of masculinity—to be sexually potent, to sire offspring, and to provide them with wealth and power—was mistaken, they taught persistently, even against the assumptions of their followers like Amir Hasan (who asked the question and recorded the answer).[35] Sexual acts and sexuality did not make or unmake a man, in their view. A man is masculine only by his moral acts and the spiritual attitudes that underlie them. In this sense, Sufis often speak of female mystics as "men" because they partake in these moral acts and spiritual aspirations on a par with male mystics, without being prevented by their reproductive anatomy, their female gender, or their feminine socialization.[36]

If real masculinity means spiritual potency, and this is decoupled from social manifestations of masculine potency, as manifested through sexual acts, then there is room for alternative social expressions of sexuality. Most important for the early Chishtis, there was room for nonsexuality like abstinence (refraining from sexual acts), chastity (restraining sexual attraction), or asexuality (not having sexual desires). But there might also be room for homoerotic behavior or even homosexual orientation. The early Chishtis discussed these matters, which were of some controversy, because the religious tradition they inherited from Iran and Khurasan had homoerotic episodes in it, especially those involving the much revered figures of Ahmad Ghazali (died 1120–21 in Qazvin) and ʿAin al-Quzat Hamadani (died 1131 in Hamadan).

Ahmad Ghazali wrote a poetic explanation of the stages of love (titled *Savanih*) and authored a treatise defending the practice of listening to music (titled *Bavariq al-Ilmaʿ*), both of which were read avidly by Chishti Sufis. One generation younger than Ahmad Ghazali was ʿAin al-Quzat Hamadani, a brilliant intellect and gifted writer of Persian prose; he is often represented as Ahmad Ghazali's disciple in Sufism. ʿAin al-Quzat presented his philosophical assault on dry reason and scholastic theology in his masterpiece, *Tamhidat* or "Introductions," which was required reading in Chishti circles and was the first text to be translated into Deccani Urdu.[37] Both figures were beloved but controversial. Ahmad Ghazali used to practice "playing the witness" both in Sufi musical gatherings and outside its ritual space. It is said that when ʿAin al-Quzat was young, he served as a "witness" for Ahmad Ghazali, who contemplated his beauty in such an intense way that ʿAin al-Quzat's father, a theologically trained judge, grew worried and tried to keep him away.

That is the context for a discussion that happened in the company of Nizam al-Din Awliya.[38] This story reveals how Nizam al-Din Awliya taught that even a flawed person could become the channel through which God's mercy flowed into the lives of others. Withhold judgment, explained Nizam al-Din, to acknowledge your own faults rather than seek faults in others. This was the moral framework through which he addressed questions of homosexuality and propriety, which were raised by Buhan al-Din Gharib upon the mention of Ahmad Ghazali.[39] Many anecdotes tell that Ahmad Ghazali would choose younger males as his "beloved" to act as his "witness" through whom he could contemplate the beauty of God's creation. The questions are whether this attitude constituted a character flaw and whether this action involved sexual relations that were sinful.

Burhan al-Din Gharib commented that Ahmad Ghazali was affected by homosexuality. Nizam al-Din Awliya reprimanded him, saying that this comment was not correct. He countered that Ahmad Ghazali acted in this way only because he wanted to court the public's blame (*malamat*). As Nizam al-Din Awliya explained, Ahmad Ghazali played with the disjunction between what others observed about him and what his inner intention was. He was observed keeping company with younger males, admiring their beauty, and staying with them in private; this roused the suspicion that he was engaging in sexual acts out of lust and drew toward himself the bad opinion of others. But the end of the story reveals that his inner spiritual state was pure and so his actions violated no norms; Nizam al-Din Awliya concluded, "The powerful spirituality as possessed by Shaikh Ahmad was not a common thing and could be the characteristic of only a pious man of perfect abstinence."[40]

Nizam al-Din Awliya drew this story from a wide variety of anecdotes told about Ahmad Ghazali and his practice of "playing the witness." In modern terms, we would call this a "homoerotic devotional practice" in which sensual and aesthetic enjoyment of human beauty is transmuted into spiritual contemplation of God's presence in and through the created world. Through it, erotic forces were sublimated and transformed into spiritual insights. The question of whether this homoerotic devotional practice led to sexual relations between the males involved cannot be resolved by the evidence at hand. Still more difficult to address is the question of whether practitioners of "playing the witness" were homosexual in terms of their identity. The narratives told about them do not answer these questions. Rather, the narratives assert that they were pure in their practice (*pak-baz*) and not engaged in lustful activity, and they highlight the spiritual insights generated from this practice.

The renowned scholar of Persian literature and Sufi thought Nasrollah Pourjavady has analyzed these narratives about Ahmad Ghazali and illustrated how he was an exponent of "contemplating through gazing at an exemplary beauty (*nazar-baz*) and loved a young man (*shahid-dost*)."[41]

What can we conclude from this discussion of sexuality in the conversations of early Chishti masters? Nizam al-Din Awliya saw issues of sexuality as intimately related to spirituality, for both flow from the wellsprings of human life and are expressions of its power. His concern was to direct this power from crude physical dimensions, away from socially competitive dimensions, and toward spiritually refined dimensions. When issues of sexuality arose in his discussions, Nizam al-Din Awliya did not condemn sexual activity in legalistic ways but encouraged his followers to consider what attitudes gave rise to it and how it affected human relationships. He resisted the urge, so common in his patriarchal society, to use the sexuality of others as an opportunity to condemn them. Rather, he taught that one should always restrain one's egoistic urge to criticize others and see negative qualities in them, especially with issues as visceral as sex. Nizam al-Din Awliya did not say that homosexuality was legal or illegal—legality was not his concern. His concern was spirituality, and he left it to judges and politicians to argue about legal rules. He also did not say whether homosexuality was natural or unnatural.[42] Nizam al-Din was not terribly concerned about homosexual orientation, which he viewed with no more alarm than he viewed heterosexual orientation. His concern was rather about sexual activity of any kind, which he saw as leading to obsessive attachment to worldly ambitions and sensual pleasures. His personal example was that sexual desire should be sublimated—not denied through bodily austerities but redirected toward spiritual discipline.

"Playing the Witness" in the Deccan

In early Chishti conversations, alarm over homosexuality was voiced by Burhan al-Din Gharib. When Nizam al-Din commented that Ahmad Ghazali had been accused of loving young men, he stressed the accusation as the problem. But Burhan al-Din suggested that Ahmad Ghazali's homosexuality (as orientation or attraction) was the problem. Nizam al-Din Awliya gently corrected Burhan al-Din. His attitudes are important because Burhan al-Din was one of the chief exemplars of Chishti Sufism in the Deccan. Burhan al-Din acknowledged that heated engagement with love poetry and ritual music relied on an underlying current of erotic force that, in his social context, was homoerotic, and he was concerned that it might give license to homosexual behavior. But despite this concern, he remained a staunch advocate of music, poetry, and dance in a ritual context. There is evidence that homoerotic bonding was common in samaʿ sessions as they were practiced by Burhan al-Din's followers in the Deccan. The practice of "playing the witness" was also cultivated in these circles, though it is difficult to assess whether homoerotic contemplation was linked to homosexual orientation among the participants.

One later Sufi who was inspired by Burhan al-Din Gharib's teachings was Shah Bajan (died 1507), about whom we will learn more in chapter 5. In Shah Bajan's circles in Burhanpur, the practice of "playing the witness" was common. It sparked a written critique by Muhammad ibn Fazlullah, a Chishti Sufi from Burhanpur (died 1619–20). He alleged that Sufis in his city engaged in "gazing at beautiful young males" as a form of worship, which he feared would be heresy if taken to the extreme where they claimed God manifested in the bodily form of youths.[43] Clearly, Muhammad ibn Fazlullah felt that many Sufis of Burhanpur were in need of repentance. The Chishti tradition of Burhanpur moved to Awrangabad when that city was reestablished, and we can assume that the practice of "playing the witness" and critique of it also moved to Awrangabad, along with the practice of samaʿ, which was its ritual setting.

It is from the example of Burhan al-Din Gharib and his followers that Siraj Awrangabadi learned how to be a Sufi. He recovered from his love madness at the tomb of Burhan al-Din Gharib and decided to live a celibate life based on his example. Siraj imbibed the therapeutic spirit of Burhan al-Din Gharib to see his own love of beauty as spiritually potent, if possibly dangerous. At his tomb, Siraj was able to recover from his insanity, dedicate himself to Sufism, and rejoin society. He learned to see his youthful lover not as a person who spurned him but as a manifestation of God's presence, which led him through necessary lessons. This helped him to recover from the pain of the experience. More important, Siraj learned to see his captivation with beauty as a metaphor for his love for God and, like Burhan al-Din Gharib, focused his erotic energies into poetry and music during samaʿ.

Siraj may have restrained his sexual activity, but could he erase his sexual orientation? Did his orientation that led him to fall in love with another male persist in his psychology, even if he renounced sexual attachment and activity? It appears that Siraj did practice "playing the witness" in very dramatic ways, choosing to admire the beauty of younger males as a way to contemplate God's beauty, long after he renounced sexual activity. The practice is reflected in some of his most powerful ghazals, like this one that implies a male beloved:[44]

> My slim-waisted love's become kind slowly slowly
>   Perhaps my sighs affected his mind slowly slowly
> That rosy-cheeked beauty cracks a smile, speaks
>   Where love buds, fruit you'll find slowly slowly
> Circling step by step, eyes brimming wine cups
>   The saqi bewildered my mind slowly slowly
> Riding this burning heart, guided by soaring sighs
>   The abode of my lover I find slowly slowly
> My heart resolved to fly to my beloved's street
>   But wings and feathers grow defined slowly slowly
> O gentle breeze, go and speak in my lover's lane
>   The tale of my tangled emotions unwind slowly slowly
> As that flirt raises an eyebrow of objection, Siraj,
>   My heart's ups and downs get refined slowly slowly

The reader of this English translation may wonder what makes this beloved male, for the images of a slim waist, rosy cheeks, intoxicating eyes, and flirtatious eyebrow could apply to either male or female. The gender of the beloved is provided by the verb conjugation in the first couplet (*hua hai meherban vo mu-kamar* means literally "that [male] with a waist slim as a hair has become kind"), because Urdu verbs are conjugated differently for a male subject than for a female subject.

Teasing out clues about the gender of the beloved in Urdu ghazals is not easy, as the poetry thrives on ambiguity. In this case, it appears that Siraj is addressing a beloved "witness" and sees his own attraction to the witness as a way to refine his spiritual insight and stoke his love for God. As the final couplet says, "As that flirt raises an eyebrow of objection, Siraj, / My heart's ups and downs get refined slowly slowly." These ups and downs of the heart could refer to his heartbeat, beating faster in proximity to someone beautiful whom he admires; but it could also refer to the heart's ups and downs in terms of traveling the spiritual path of struggle through stages of intimacy and alienation from God's presence.

From the evidence of Siraj's poetry and biographies, it cannot be determined whether these loving bonds with other males were sexually charged or spiritual potent—or perhaps were a powerful combination of the two. Yet it is plain that these loving bonds enacted a style of masculinity, one that was sensitive, vulnerable, defined by relationships with others, and that found completion in sacrificing for the sake of others. These are values that many modern readers will identify as "feminine." Modern concepts of masculinity stress individual autonomy, aggressive competition, impressive physique, or moneyed power. These are notions of masculinity that are promoted by a culture of global capitalism and are deeply informed by Anglo-American cultural norms rooted in Protestant Christianity, as spread with great effectiveness by advertising and cinema. But were they values of the Mughal and Deccan cultures to which Siraj belonged? It could be argued that patriarchal cultures all share a concept of masculinity (as defined against femininity) that is broadly the same, even if they differ widely in language, religious norms, social organization, economic productivity, and political structure. At least, this is the thrust of feminist scholarship, which, after analyzing the common concepts in patriarchal cultures, then sheds light on the nuanced differences between them and the subtle ways that women are raised to be different from men and inferior to them.

While modern Anglo-American culture and Islamic Mughal culture can both be characterized as patriarchal, they express patriarchal values in different ways. The task of discerning differences while analyzing commonalities is made much more difficult by the fact that modern Anglo-American culture has had a profound impact upon South Asian Islamic society, at least since 1857, when the last vestiges of the Mughal Empire in Delhi were destroyed by British colonialism. Elsewhere, I have illustrated the radical shift of values that this political triumph of Victorian Britain caused among Muslims in South Asia, especially in regard to gender and sexuality.[45] The discussion here must be brief, and any generalizations will have limitations.

In general, Mughal culture promoted a warrior-patron ethos, in which the ideal man was a soldier-administrator who could mobilize brute force effectively but also had refined taste in appreciating beauty. In this sense, domination and competition were important masculine values. Yet the culture also valued personal intimacy and interconnection between males, for a man's social status was largely defined by patronage of or dependence upon other men. Typically, men operated within a largely all-male environment, while interaction with women was largely limited to three classes of women: wives or female family members, female servants, and courtesans. Of these female interactions, probably the most intensive and influential upon a man was with female family members — namely mothers and sisters. Men were certainly not defined primarily by how they complemented a wife within an isolated nuclear family unit (which is a great contrast to how modern society defines masculinity, whether in an Anglo-American context or modern Islamic contexts). This culture set the norms for elite Muslim men, and educational institutions sought to instill its values in a wider population of soldiers, clerks, artists, and religious specialists. These values were transmitted primarily through Persian language texts on ethics (*akhlaq*) that were later translated into Urdu and formed the spine of the education curriculum.

In this patriarchal system, poetry and literary sensibilities were very important qualities for men. Poetic sensitivity represented the aesthetic and emotive side of masculinity, which patriarchal Mughal culture held as necessary for dominant men in the system. It represented a crosscurrent in patriarchy that not only reinforced the system but also potentially challenged some of its harder structures. It reinforced the system by being a marker of aristocratic class, educational status, competitive intelligence, and refined taste — markers that kept many men from achieving dominance. But it potentially challenged the system, for the values expressed in poetry were those of accepting fate, embracing disaster, enduring pain, and submitting to hopeless self-sacrifice — values that would ill equip a man for social advancement, accumulation of wealth, and the apt exercise of power. In Mughal culture, poetic sensitivity was necessary for men but had to be balanced with the practical exercise of power.[46] This ideal balance is revealed visually in many portraits of noblemen who stand in profile, one hand on a sword at his waist and the other hand raising a rose to his nose.

If poetic sensitivity was a crosscurrent in the stormy sea of Mughal masculinity, then Sufism was an undercurrent. Sufis took the value of poetic sensitivity to be the very crux of a life and denounced social competitiveness, wealth accumulation, and wielding power as dangerous distractions. These activities were assertions of the ego, which kept one ensnared in worldly temptations and prevented one from cultivating love. Sufis promoted an alternative notion of masculinity, which if given a certain spin could be a critique of masculinity promoted by the dominant culture. As such, Sufis formed a "subculture" that believed that men overcome by worldly ambition were not real men but eunuchs; in contrast, real men were those with the inner strength to resist temptation of worldly gain and devote themselves to loving God alone. By and large, this subculture tapped into this cultural undercurrent while accommodating to the dominant culture. Sufis rarely challenged patriarchal values directly. Though there are some rare examples in the Mughal era when Sufis did this by flouting sexual norms or transgressing gender boundaries, they did so mainly to demonstrate with radical behavior their own personal holiness rather than in an endeavor to change patriarchal values in society.[47] Mainly, Sufis in the Chishti community cherished a countercultural notion of masculinity in their gatherings but did not assert it against the norms of the wider society, to the point that members of their community could function effectively as social agents while cherishing expressions of counter-masculinity in their poems, music, and saintly exemplars.

As an adult, Siraj trod a careful path to negotiate the demands of masculinity as defined by his Deccan society, which had inherited Mughal culture (upholding its norms even as it adapted them to local conditions). He rejected the more aggressive values of masculinity by refusing to marry a woman, take up a profession, or earn money to head a household. Yet he renounced his youthful rebellion during his homosexual romance, the time when he abandoned his family and exhibited insane behavior. Taking initiation with a Sufi master offered him a middle way between these extremes. He found a father figure who did not insist that he marry to perpetuate the family and who provided him with an alternative set of ideal values of masculinity oriented toward spiritual refinement, aesthetic sensitivity, and interdependent vulnerability. Siraj's Sufi initiation also gave him brother figures who shared these ideals of masculinity while restoring his sense of community bonds and social respectability. In addition, Sufism provided a set of rituals that defined a space in which he could demonstrate love in emotionally intense and erotically charged ways while restraining him from overtly sexual relations. The gathering of samaʿ, with its synesthetic power, was the primary ritual theater in which he could play out this drama, impressing values of loving self-sacrifice upon his consciousness while physically drawing near to his fellow devotees and thereby symbolically feeling drawn closer to intimacy with God.

In the following ghazal, Siraj comments on masculinity and expresses the qualities that he feels make a real man:[48]

> When quicksilver burns up you say it's mere dust
> When a lover dissolves you say he's a real man
> Drink of your heart's blood like a poison draught
> Where's the doctor whom you ask—will it hurt?
> What's the text, "The Light's Dawn," beside your face?[49]
> Who'll take a page of gold foil and say it's the sun?
> Like an aroma I'm saturated in each color of flower
> Take that, nightingale! Can you say "I'm the rose"?
> Though I've read the whole divan of the sun's rays
> Your beauty's in one line if I say "You're unique"[50]
> My soul plays this game: losing is exile, winning is union
> The board is sorrow, and my heart? Just say it's a pawn
> A lover's cold sigh is really fire, Siraj
> In this fire's raging heat just release a cold sigh

No words could express more succinctly Siraj's conception of masculinity than the first couplet: "When a lover dissolves you say he's a real man." The person who deserves the name "man" is a lover, and the one who is a lover is only he who dissolves in emotion, burns in suffering, and gives his soul completely to another.

Such a man gives up his soul in the love of God. He outstrips even the nightingale, the archetypal lover of the rose, for the nightingale can sing sweetly of separation but can never claim to become the rose. In contrast, the real man who has given up his soul—like Mansur Hallaj, the Sufi martyr (died 922)—can say, "I am the real" (in Arabic, *ana al-haqq*). His ego was sacrificed and his sense of self so dissolved into the moment that he could say, "I am the real," meaning "I am God." In the ghazal above, Siraj composed the phrase "I'm the rose" in Arabic (*ana al-ward*) to make this comparison subtly playful but clear. The nightingale can sing about the beauty of the rose and his longing for union with the rose but can never say, "I am the rose." The human being, however, has a greater power of love when it is fully directed toward God, for then he can realize union with God and say, "I am the real." But to achieve this state and status takes great spiritual aspiration and courage—manly virtues directed toward overcoming the ego rather than toward competing with others. One must gamble with one's very life (*jan-baz*) in a contest that by worldly standards is a sure loss: "My soul plays this game: losing is exile, winning is union / The board is sorrow, and my heart? Just say it's a pawn." To achieve this greatest victory of union, one must relegate one's own heart—its pleasure or pain and sorrow or joy—to the fluctuations of divine will and grace. One must be willing to throw down on the game board as a sacrifice anything other than God.

As he matured, Siraj pursued this ideal of spiritual masculinity.[51] It drove him to sacrifice his own desires. He first renounced sexual relations that could promise comfort and intimacy. Then he gave up writing ghazals that had earned him such social renown and appreciation. Then he seems to have sacrificed the ritual focus of his remaining erotic energy by giving up "playing the witness," which had sustained him in his mature years. We know from Siraj's own testimony how his Sufi teacher had commanded him to give up composing ghazals, and many of those poems had praised the practice of "playing the witness." While Siraj did give up composing these love lyrics that fueled the Qawwals' singing in devotional gatherings, he was not commanded to stop attending or organizing these musical sessions. Therefore, his practice of "playing the witness" could have continued to be a ritual outlet for his erotic energies, long after he had stopped composing ghazals.

His Sufi teacher was mainly concerned with how Siraj behaved in the ritual space of musical gatherings when he commanded him to cease with ghazals. Ghazals were the most powerful poetic form for Siraj, since they were short and ideally suited for singing. He was commanded to give these up, but he was not silenced entirely. Even as he stifled the erotic outlet of ghazals, Siraj continued to write epic poems and letters to his friends and followers. "The Fragrant Garden of Imagination" was written just one year before his shaikh died.[52] Perhaps it was meant as an apology for his poetry-reciting and beauty-captivated ways, which emerged in samaʿ even if he had renounced romantic attachments.

We can conjecture about what sparked Siraj to write this veiled autobiographical epic poem at the time he did, as his Sufi teacher was reaching the end of his life. Perhaps his teacher took Siraj's spiritual discipline to a new intensity and commanded him to cease "playing the witness." Perhaps with this hardship, he was preparing Siraj to take over his position as khalifa or *sajjada-nashin* once he died: khalifa means an authoritative follower who acts as a master's representative and takes his own followers, while *sajjada-nashin* refers to the follower who "sits on the master's prayer carpet," inheriting the master's position after his death. Therefore, the master may have intentionally imposed an ego-testing hardship upon Siraj. Siraj had certainly felt tension about this practice long before, as he lamented the lack of sincerity of men. There seemed to be few men who respected his homoerotic bonding and style of masculinity and who fulfilled the persona of a "witness." He voiced these tensions in this ghazal:[53]

> In this world, among friends there is no masculinity
> No shame, shyness or kindness, there is no clemency
> To your face they may call you friend, but still
> Deep in their hardened hearts there is no sincerity
> They go straight for those who squint askance for gain
> The sincere find among beauties there's no dignity
> They all choose to cozy up to those selfish thorns
> In the beauty of their rosy faces there is no subtlety
> They waste their lives, alas, with the undeserving
> Till in their hearts, for friendship there is no capacity
> They fall down at the bewitching glimpse of any idol
> There're no miracles among ascetics, there is no sagacity
> Rogues are powerful now while the purebred are ruined
> Beneath the jewelry can't they see there is no nobility?
> Don't fly, you nightingale, toward this world's garden
> In those flowers' alluring aromas there is no loyalty
> Don't befriend anyone except the real One, Siraj
> This world has no attractions, there is no intimacy

The last two couplets especially seem to hint at a future decision by Siraj to renounce "playing the witness," which was his last deep connection to other people. He speaks to his own heart as if to a nightingale, prone to fly toward any rose that blooms in beauty, but he advises his heart's bird that this garden is worldly and its flowers may have every alluring aroma—except for the rare fragrance of loyal companionship (*rifaqat*). His unspoken conclusion is that he will reserve his heart for the garden of the next world, whose blooms never fade and whose companions never grow cold. The final couplet speaks as if this conclusion has already been achieved—"Don't befriend anyone except the real One, Siraj." He should reserve his love and intimacy for God alone and must see the world as having no attractions.

This ghazal echoes the sentiments in his autobiographical masnavi. In "The Fragrant Garden of Imagination," he calls the ways of the beautiful fake and charges that their words are untrustworthy. He beseeches God to save him from the chains of their beauty and to restrain him from tasting the honey from their lips. His prayer is, "Save me from the beautiful ones so that I may see your beauty." Thus with these words of renouncing "playing the witness," Siraj concludes his epic poem:[54]

> Widely roamed my heart, intimacy with others to sample
> > But now I'm racing toward the Kaʿaba, leaving the temple
> I come toward you bearing this humble request
> > Just give me guidance, tell me which way is best
> "Never ever neglect me or each act is fruitless[55]
> > With concentration each hope comes to fullness"
> In every way I am hopeless, sunk in blame
> > I come to you, my face darkened with shame
> But you can wash this dirty face for sure
> > With the water of your grace, rinse me pure
> I wasted my life worshiping beauty's idolatry
> > I spent my days heedless in ignorant frivolity
> I want to live now lit up by awareness's beam
> > Now I have awakened from my negligent dream
> Siraj, stop seeking those whose claims are flimsy
> > For God's special friends, that goal is unworthy
> Instead, day and night, repeat this line in meditation
> > Repeat it—in God's name—with every exhalation
> "To you I entrust all that I used to clutch
> > You alone judge whether it is little or much"

If Siraj finally gave up the practice of "playing the witness"—as these poems imply—then he lost the major thread that still connected him to the world. "Playing the witness" had given him a connection of love with others, even if that love was severed from social acceptability. Despite being tenuous, it was still a form of love. Yet he gave it up in pursuit of spiritual manliness, which was to give up anything that one desired in favor of gaining intimacy with God alone. The only attachment he had to his world was to his friends, to whom he continued to send poignant letters.

Conclusion

Looking over this portrait of Siraj, with his life's spiritual and sensual dimensions so closely interwoven, can we extract a principle? As can only be expected from the life of a Sufi, it is a principle with an inherent paradox. Love is always precious love, nothing less—yet love is always imperfect love, never more. That is, love is a dynamic tension; it is always essentially love, and yet it has stages and progressions. One must be engrossed in it fully in the moment but must never be self-satisfied in it at any stage, or else it has slipped from one's grasp. Love always calls one to move beyond one's comfort into unknown depths. At the beginning of any stage of love, one feels newly awakened to heightened states of awareness, but by the end of that stage one feel numb, as if one had been in hibernation. Before the next stage of love is yet to fully manifest, one feels like one is suffering through a long, dark night to awaken anew. Siraj's writings speak of this phase of struggling and suffering, but he is silent about the joy that may have come to him when it had all passed away.

CHAPTER FIVE

Poetry as Music

Whoever wanders like a *bairagi* in a lost love's swoon
  In the concert of cool sighs finds his own *raga*'s tune
Siraj has a destiny more auspicious than Alexander's
  Facing his lover's mirror-like cheek is quite a fortune

—*verses from a ghazal by Siraj*

Many Urdu literary critics note that Siraj's poetry has a musical quality. Some of his poems invoke music through classical terms, like the couplets above alluding to the names of Indian *raga* (musical mode).¹ However, even if his couplets do not cite musical terms, they create a musical effect. His choice of words creates a strong meter, an appealing cadence, and an alliterative lilt by means of which some of his ghazals almost sound like music.² Siraj specifically wrote many of his ghazals to be sung rather than recited aloud or read off the page. The arena in which he presented his poems was not the courtly assembly or the literary salon, as was the fashion among romantic poets. It was instead the *mehfil-e samaʿ* or gathering for musical meditation. This chapter investigates how Siraj composed poems to be sung, specifically in the Qawwali style of Sufi musical devotion.

A chronicler of poets who lived in the Deccan, ʿAbd al-Jabbar Khan Malkapuri, recorded Siraj's life in his *Beloved of the Age (Mahbub al-Zaman Tazkira-ye Shuʿara-ye Dakkan)*, published around the start of the twentieth century. He notes that Siraj not only composed poetry but also set it in a musical context: "One day each week, Siraj would arrange for a session of listening to devotional music, in which most of the city's nobles and spiritual teachers would gather. Qawwals and reciters would sing his ghazals. Sometimes the listeners would break into weeping and sometimes they would fall to the ground. Some would become agitated with rapture (*vajd*) or ecstasy (*hal*), while some would sink deep into the oceans of unity (*vahdat*)."³ According to this account, Siraj organized musical assemblies when he was an acknowledged Sufi master. Singers would present Siraj's own works, and he composed specifically for Qawwali singers.

Even in his immature years, Siraj's early poetry was intensely oral and musical, designed to move listeners to a state of rapture rather than to mere appreciation. Siraj himself writes in a short autobiographical statement that

> this poor wretch was overcome with passionate love. . . . From the tumult of that intoxicated state, he brought forth from the hidden recesses of the soul to the broad expanse of the tongue Persian poetry that was enough to cause a riot and spread pain. But in accord with his immature state, he did not bother to write down that Persian poetry, though sometimes if he desired—in order to allow himself to savor their sweetness just a bit—he might write some of them down on paper. . . . If those rhyming words would be heard, the whole world would teeter on the precipice of astonishment, and would be able to picture in concrete form the whole of divine inspiration.[4]

From this statement, we learn the aim of his Persian poems: to put the spiritual experience of divine inspiration into sensory form, in terms of sounds that conjure up images, scent, tastes, and textures. This form should be not only sensory but also sensual, so that meanings encoded in them are beautiful and captivating, leading the listener further along the progress of love.

The Music of Love

Siraj values aesthetic beauty if it serves as a bridge leading from sensual delight to romantic involvement to loving devotion to spiritual experience of divine presence. He echoes the sentiment that Muslim poets have long upheld, "The metaphoric is the bridge to the ultimate" (*al-majaz qantarat li'l-haqiqa* in the Arabic proverb). By happy linguistic coincidence, in Urdu the terms for metaphor, flirtation, and supplication all rhyme (*majaz, naz,* and *niyaz*). These rhymes outline a theology of beauty, in which sensory appearances stir emotive responses that can be channeled into spiritual refinement. This is the opposite of ascetic theology, which asserts that this world is essentially ugly, dirty, and polluting, such that it must be forcefully rejected in order to achieve spiritual refinement.

Siraj upholds this theology of beauty, as he affirms in his many other ghazals, like the following:[5]

> Since for beauties arrogant flirtation is required
>   For lovers eloquent supplication is required
> If one wants to travel the path to reality
>   A path of metaphoric passion is required
> Prostrate upon the lovely idol's footprint
>   For prayer, a heart's dedication is required
> Tyrant, give the suffering what they deserve
>   Only heart-caressing titillation is required
> To perfect a party of lovers, like that of Siraj
>   Only a soul-melting lamentation is required

In the final couplet, Siraj hints that his theology of beauty has music as its primary ritual. Listening to devotional music in a ritual setting is the "prayer of lovers," according to Chishti Sufis. Siraj notes that the party of lovers (*mehfil-e 'ashiqan*) is not complete without a wail of lament that melts the soul, just as a gathering of devotional music needs not merely artful melody but an edgy cry.

Siraj upholds and amplifies the long-established traditions of the Chishti community, which dedicated itself to music and poetry in balance with ascetic rigor. The beauty of melody could spark a cry of self-abandon, as illustrated by one of the early leaders of this community, Qutb al-Din Bakhtiyar Kaki (died 1235 in Delhi). He was the paradigmatic personality who defined the furthest extreme of spiritual response to devotional music, as an early biographer of Chishti saints explains:

> Once a gathering of sama' happened at the hospice (*khanqah*) of Shaikh 'Ali Sekri. Qutb al-Din, may God have mercy upon him, was present in this assembly. A Qawwal was singing this poem — "Those slain by submission's knife / Ever from beyond find new life." This poetic line penetrated into the deepest core of Shaikh Qutb al-Din's heart. He reached home in a state of profound spiritual bewilderment (*tahayyur*) and was almost unconscious. He would say over and over, "Recite that line!" The singers would repeat that line again and again while he remained in the world of bewilderment. Despite this, whenever the call was sounded, he would make his obligatory prayer, then again call for this poetic line to be sung repeatedly. The Qawwals kept singing this line while he remained in the world of bewilderment. His spiritual state and his unself-consciousness

grew more intense. It lasted for four days and nights continuously until, on the fifth night, he expired.[6]

This narrative illustrates the supreme importance given by Chishti Sufis to the ritual of samaʿ, which could have dramatic spiritual effects. It also aptly displays the tension between formal prayer and musical contemplation. For Chishti Sufis, these two forms of worship were seen as complementary rather than conflicting. Formal prayer—with its postures, gestures, and pronouncements—engaged the outer body directly, creating the opportunity to instill spiritual values and ethical virtues into the heart. Contemplation through music engaged the inner heart directly, opening the possibility of having one's spiritual state expressed through bodily responses. Spontaneous weeping, rapt gestures, involuntary utterances, or inspired dance would all be bodily responses to a spiritual state of the heart in which egoism was disdained, denied, dissolved, or transcended.

In most instances, these responses were transient. Listeners who experienced them derived some insight from the event but returned to routine awareness. Shaikh Qutb al-Din's prolonged sojourn in the "world of bewilderment" was unusual, and its final result—a joyful but unexpected death—was extreme. Yet it reveals the power of a heart-caressing line of poetry when it is set to powerful music. As Siraj said in the poem above, "Tyrant, give the suffering what they deserve / Only heart-caressing titillation is required." The poetry's deep effect on Shaikh Qutb al-Din was possible only because of his prior "suffering" through renunciation of worldly goals, embracing poverty, and burning with love. His death was exactly what he deserved, as the ultimate bodily expression of his heart's state—being emptied of self and filled with longing for union with God.

In the narrative about Shaikh Qutb al-Din, this was the diagnosis of the doctor brought to treat him. According to traditional Islamic medicine, the doctor examined his urine to diagnose his illness. He said, "This urine is that of a man who has been ruined by the inner burning of love and longing. His liver [the seat of passionate emotions] has been completely charred."[7] The devotional music and its poetic line were not the cause of his death. Rather, they were only a skillful means or "a path of metaphoric passion." As Siraj said above, "If one wants to travel the path to reality / A path of metaphoric passion is required." Shaikh Qutb al-Din's love created in him a spiritual condition that, given the right trigger and vehicle, could manifest in bodily expression and social force.

One generation after the extreme event of Shaikh Qutb al-Din's death, his follower Nizam al-Din Awliya led the movement to systematize Qawwali. Under his direction, Qawwali became accessible to the wider public, no longer limited as a private ritual of elites within a Sufi community. Widening the audience necessitated expounding firm rules, for the performers and for the different grades of listeners. Nizam al-Din Awliya instituted a system of fines for those who broke the rules of decorum and respect. For example, he once fined Amir Khusro for rising in a state of ecstasy and dancing with his arms raised; he had not renounced worldly professions (as a court poet, he was a salaried employee of the sultan) and therefore did not have the right to raise his hands above his waist as if he received his livelihood directly from God.

Amir Khusro gave Qawwali a fixed but flexible musical form by training a troupe of young men in percussion, instruments, and singing. Amir Khusro also started the tradition of composing poetry specifically to be sung in samaʿ, and his poems remain the core repertoire of Qawwali. Another scholarly disciple, Fakhr al-Din Zarradi (died 1337), wrote a rulebook for the musical ritual and presented an Islamic theological defense against detractors.[8] These steps toward systematization made samaʿ a safe vehicle for the public and, in a perhaps unintended consequence, contained the potentially dramatic effects of samaʿ like Qutb al-Din's untimely death.

Despite this, Qutb al-Din's example remained an ideal for later generations. When Nizam al-Din Awliya, on his deathbed, was asked by his followers if there was anything in his life that he regretted, he dismissed the question as not worthy of a saint. Then he admitted that, as a young man, he was once praying and God granted him the opportunity to request his heart's desire, so he asked for steadfastness in carrying out religious duties (*istiqama*). Now near death, he acknowledged that indeed God had granted him steadfastness, but he regretted that he had not asked instead to die during musical rapture during samaʿ.

There can be no greater testament to the powerful example of Shaikh Qutb al-Din Bakhtiyar Kaki. His example traveled south into the Deccan along with Nizam al-Din's disciples, such as the poet Amir Hasan. He settled near Awrangabad and memorialized Shaikh Qutb al-Din's death in a Persian poem: "That line is a gem from a special mine, upon which that great man's life was spilled / All those by the knife of submission killed, each moment from God with new life are filled."[9] Amir Hasan was a great admirer of Amir Khusro and Burhan al-Din Gharib, both of whom were fined for dancing in samaʿ. Burhan al-Din Gharib was also fined by Nizam al-Din Awliya for crawling across the floor during a musical assembly, apparently while he was in an extended and exhausting state of ecstasy.

Of all the disciples of Nizam al-Din Awliya, it is Burhan al-Din Gharib who was most devoted to Qawwali and musical contemplation. While many moderated their practice of listening to music in response to new conditions, Burhan al-Din intensified it. He was the primary model for Chishtis who listened to devotional poems sung in ritual gatherings as communal musical meditation. Burhan al-Din emphasized the worship of God through music, which had been an authentic part of the Chishti spiritual path in the circle of Nizam al-Din Awliya and his teachers.

Some followers of Nizam al-Din chose to rein in the rapturous quality of this musical ritual, limit who could attend, and discourage emotive experiences of ecstasy. His principal successor, Nasir al-Din Chiragh-e Delhi, had an acerbic temperament and scholarly demeanor; he would rather discuss elements of Arabic grammar and comment on the Qurʾan than quote Persian love poetry and listen to music. His young protégé who moved to the Deccan, Gesu Daraz (died 1422), whose formal name was Sayyid Muhammad Husaini, similarly distrusted music as public worship. At his hospice in Gulbarga, he enforced new rules to limit instrumentation used with Qawwali and to restrict attendance to music sessions; his system became known as *band-samaʿ* or "restricted listening." In contrast, Burhan al-Din perpetuated this musical ritual in the new soil of the Deccan and amplified its importance.

The Rapturous Legacy of Burhan al-Din Gharib

Even among Chishtis, Burhan al-Din's style of musical mysticism was considered excessive. He was ardently devoted to ecstasy and dance in samaʿ. An early biographer of Chishti Sufis writes, "In samaʾ, this saint was completely extreme, experienced much ecstasy, and said the prayers of lovers. He had a distinctive style in dancing, so that the companions of this saint were called Burhanis among the lovers. Whoever was in the presence of this saint for an hour fell in love with the beauty of his saintliness, because of the ecstasy of his passionate words and the purity of his enchanting conversation." His poetic temperament and musical sensitivity attracted both Amir Khusro and Amir Hasan to him, and they were "captivated by his love, because of his graceful nature and his passion."[10]

We do not know the nature of his rapturous dance style, but it seems more systematically developed than the erratic outbursts that conventionally signal ecstatic abandon in contemporary Chishti communities. His followers adopted this style of movement in sama', indicating that it was a group activity, not just the eccentricity of one man. His followers were given the nickname "Burhanis," which indicates that other Sufis may have criticized their overenthusiasm for music and dance. Their movements might have been stylized like the spinning and turning of Mevlevi dervishes of Turkey.[11]

Burhan al-Din's admirer Amir Hasan expresses their mutual love of ecstatic Sufi practice in this Persian ghazal:

> What flirtation have you learned,
>   you archer of winking glances
>   Raze the heart, char the soul,
>   go beyond flimsy romances
> Dark as your cheek's mole,
>   I steal up to the sweetness of your lip
>   From ambush springs your gaze,
>   like Turks launching arrows, casting lances
> Never ask directions from those
>   who languish around the Ka'aba
>   Who, like me, turn only the direction
>   their idol beckons and prances
> My reason can never overpower
>   my longing for beautiful faces
>   For a feeble dove to hunt a soaring falcon
>   are there chances?
> What prayer beads in my hand,
>   which Sufi cloak on my back?
>   Why count me a renunciant,
>   this master whom beauty entrances?
> Start this gathering anew or I'll
>   burn down the house and you, too,
>   You hypocrite who meditates
>   without melodies, without dances!
> While you live, Hasan, content your heart
>   to suffer longing from afar
>   For a caged songbird, what strategy
>   the chance of escape enhances?[12]

In this poem, Amir Hasan elevates the love of beauty over the control of asceticism. What use are prayer beads for constant meditation or a cloak to symbolize initiation with a spiritual teacher if one's heart does not melt with the love of beauty? It is music that is the highest expression of harmony and beauty, in which eloquent words, driving rhythm, soaring melody, and captivating companions all combine in a synesthesia that bewilders reason and stirs the heart. For Amir Hasan, any devotion that disavows music is mere hypocrisy; it is daily fare for dried husks of ascetic preachers but poison for the real mystic. He threatens any Sufi who pretends disdain for music—"Start this gathering anew or I'll burn down the house and you, too, / You hypocrite who meditates without melodies, without dances!" Behind his poem, we can sense the presence of Burhan al-Din Gharib, the great advocate of Sufi music and dance in the Deccan.

Burhan al-Din's personality inspired Chishtis in the Deccan. Several generations after his death, Khuldabad—the town where his tomb became a shrine—came under the dominion of a new Islamic dynasty, the Faruqis of Khandesh. They built a capital city named Burhanpur, about 220 kilometers distant from Khuldabad. Burhanpur became an active site of Chishti Sufism. Although today Burhanpur is located in Madhya Pradesh, it was in medieval times the northern gateway to the Deccan; major roads from Delhi, Gujarat, and Malwa all led to Burhanpur, from where they were channeled south to Dawlatabad, Khuldabad, and more southern Deccan towns.

The Faruqi dynasty adopted Burhan al-Din Gharib as its patron saint and claimed to rule as the fruit of his blessings. Burhan al-Din set such a strong precedent that the twentieth-century author Bashir Muhammad Khan begins his massive two-volume book chronicling the Sufis of Burhanpur with the life story of Burhan al-Din, even though the saint lived and died in Khuldabad.[13] The chronicler tells that Burhan al-Din stopped on his trip south to Dawlatabad to rest at a village along the banks of the Tapti River: "He and his group of followers rested for a night at this spot. He sat on a rock by the side of the river, made his ritual washing there, and along with his followers prayed *namaz*. Then he beseeched God saying, 'O Lord, make this place into a great city!'"[14] This narrative claims that an ancestor of the founder of the Faruqi dynasty was the chief of that region and provided Burhan al-Din and his company with food, shelter, and protection. For this reason, the saint beseeched God to make the place a city and predicted that the chief's descendants would become kings.[15] In this new city and with the protection of a nascent dynasty,

Chishti Sufis in Burhanpur continued Burhan al-Din Gharib's tradition of Islamic mysticism that focused on samaʿ sessions of poetry, rhythm, and music that could lead those in attendance into states of ecstasy. These ecstatic states could erupt into dancing, gesturing, spontaneous recitation of poetry or spiritual boasts, uncontrollable sobbing, or even unconsciousness. All these various behaviors were signs of the subject's experience of self-surrender, or even selflessness.[16]

A good example of such behavior is found in a Chishti Sufi named Baha' al-Din and known popularly as "Shah Bajan" (died 1507). He was a scholar from Ahmedabad, Gujarat, who specialized in reports about the Prophet Muhammad's conduct (*hadis*). While setting out for the hajj, a vision of the Prophet commanded him to settle in Burhanpur as a spiritual guide. Returning to Ahmedabad he found that his Sufi master, Rahmatullah Mutavakkil, had died and left his cloak (*khirqa*, a symbol of spiritual authority and renunciation of worldly concerns). He took the cloak and laid it as a shroud over the tomb of his dead master; just then he heard the Qawwals nearby singing Hindi verses, "Let me meet you, Shah Rahmatullah / Without you, whose feet will I touch?"[17] From the tomb, he heard a voice address him as "Bajan" or musical one: "Go touch the feet of the Music-maker!" Hearing this, he fell into a state of rapture.

Returning to his senses, he took the cloak off the tomb and wore it, ready to accept his destiny as the successor to Rahmatullah Mutavakkil. From that day, he was known as Shah Bajan or "Master Music-Maker." Shah Bajan became an expert musician who transmitted Sufi teachings through poetry and song. He traveled to Khuldabad to visit the dargah of Burhan al-Din Gharib, who said to him in a dream, "I am indeed dead now and this territory that was under my care, namely Burhanpur, I entrust to you and I give you a written document of authority."[18] But Shah Bajan was still uncertain and may have felt the need for a living spiritual master to give him authorization to settle in the Deccan. In Bidar, he took initiation from a follower of Shaikh Masʿud Bakk, a Chishti Sufi and excellent writer in Persian who expressed the experience of ecstasy in poetry and exposited in prose the ideals of the unity of being (*vahdat al-vujud*).[19]

Shah Bajan settled at Burhanpur with patronage from the ruler of Khandesh and built a mosque and hospice (*khanqah*) for his disciples and followers. He also wrote a book about his master.[20] It records Rahmatullah Mutavakkil's oral teachings (*malfuzat*) but also contains Shah Bajan's poetry in vernacular Deccani, which makes it one of the earliest examples of Urdu poems.[21] With other Sufi poets of Burhanpur, Shah Bajan crafted a poetic language that was mixed (*rekhta*), its Hindi grammatical base spiced with expressions from Persian. They called this local language Gujari, the oldest root of what we now call Urdu. Gujari was the southern dialect of this language, spoken in Muslim-influenced quarters of Gujarat and the western Deccan (in contrast to Hindavi, the northern dialect spoken around Delhi; Shah Bajan was the first person recorded to have called the northern dialect Hindavi).[22]

Rekhta was a term applied to songs with lyrics in the vernacular mixed with expressions from Persian.[23] Such mixing happened when Hindi songs were performed in courts of Muslim kings or gatherings of Sufis.[24] Hafiz Mahmud Sherani proposes that this style of lyric gradually became popular as a vernacular language and spread outside the limits of music to become a poetic language.[25] In rekhta songs, a couplet or stanza would contain both Hindi and Persian terms used together. Shah Bajan's poetry provides many examples.[26] This is a rare glimpse into the genesis of a new language and reveals how Urdu developed in the Deccan rather than in North India.[27]

Shah Bajan uses lyric forms such as *dohra* and *geet*. Their language and meter owe little to Persian genres like ghazal or masnavi. The language is simple and direct Gujari, yet there are a few lines of Persian interlaced that restate the Gujari meaning but in a more formal tone. One can think of the Gujari words "translating" the Persian into a more easily understandable medium; or one can think of the Persian words "making significant" the Gujari by connecting it to the formal and interregional language associated with Islamic dominance. The Sufi poet connected the "local" Indian spoken idiom to the "universal" Islamic symbolic world invoked by Persian. Chishti Sufis like Shah Bajan brought Islam down to earth in their local context, making its practices meaningful in their society and "translating" its values through symbols that were easily understandable by common people.

Shah Bajan designed his poetry to be sung in Qawwali; his poems often specify the musical mode in which they are to be sung (he uses the Persian term *parda* for mode, referring to *raga*). The miracles reported about him also have to do with music. He would organize samaʿ gatherings every day between afternoon and evening prayers. If he would experience rapture, he would promise the Qawwals, "I will give you five hundred rupees, you will get a thousand rupees!" The next day, the Qawwals would claim these huge amounts from the impoverished saint.

Poetry as Music 109

Shah Bajan would tell his attendant to go and dig in a certain place and the appropriate amount of coins would be found "from the treasury of the unseen world" to distribute to the musicians.[28]

He taught his disciples that "it is the real work of a Sufi to listen to all things and attribute their voices to the real One, such that he comprehend that all things are a place of manifestation of God. If not, how can it be that a *rabab* [lute] has leather containing such rich tones and hard wood releasing such subtle cries? [He cites a poem] You must be sending divine secrets through the lute / otherwise why should I believe mere dry wood?"[29] Shah Bajan echoes the words of Nizam al-Din Awliya, who said, "I get such blessing from the empty bowl of the rabab / any dust mote experiencing it glows like the sun."[30] Shah Bajan explained this spiritual goal of resonant emptiness with a simple musical parable about the creation of a reed flute: "The flute is first a reed cut from the reed-bed, which is then hollowed out by being burned inside with fire. An iron poker laid in the fire is made red-hot and it burns deep holes into the reed. From each of these holes, the flute releases complaining notes and sounds a wail so powerful that the Sufi's heart is pierced."[31]

Shah Bajan echoes the images made famous by Jalal al-Din Rumi (died 1273 in Qonya, Turkey). Rumi's ghazals are sung in Qawwali and equate listening to music with intuiting the inner meaning of divine speech conveyed in revelation. Rumi's epic poem *Masnavi-ye Ma'navi* (The allegorical ode) begins with the song of the reed flute, through whose hollow body the breath of God blows, giving rise to a plaintive musical cry that is a common accompaniment to sama' and equates it to the voice of God speaking to Moses: "The reed, soother to all sundered lovers—its piercing modes reveal our hidden pain. . . . Welcome love! By love our earthly flesh borne to heaven are mountains made supple, moved to dance. Love moved Mount Sinai, my love, and made Moses swoon. Let me touch those harmonious lips and I, reed-like, will tell what may be told."[32] Muslims who accepted devotional music saw the essence of religion as the cultivation of love, moving from metaphorical (*majazi*) love for a human being to ultimate (*haqiqi*) love for God.[33]

Shah Bajan developed a taste for sama' after he settled in the Deccan.[34] This means his commitment to musical devotion based on the metaphor of passionate love was caused directly by his interactions with the personality of Burhan al-Din Gharib at his tomb, among his followers, and through visionary encounters with him. Chishti Sufis in the Deccan left more than spiritual teachings, for most people who admired Sufis did not necessarily aspire to live by their teachings, which are difficult and profound. Shah Bajan and his companions left a legacy in the more popular realm of language, poetry, and music. They helped craft a new vernacular language, Gujari, which would later evolve into Deccani, the southern dialect of Urdu. Though the literary sources that record their lives and teachings are in Persian, these texts contain record of their persistent use of Gujari (especially in poems and songs) to communicate their spiritual teachings in an accessible, enjoyable, and inspiring form. The wider population of the Deccan could participate with them in this arena, whether Sufi or not, whether Muslim or other.

Shah Bajan illustrates how Chishti Sufis in the Deccan combined poetry and song in order to transmit their mystical theology. Others in Burhanpur and Bijapur formed a network of innovators in language, along with Chishtis in Bijapur.[35] In spreading mystical insight and Islamic ethics through poetry and song, they helped create a new vernacular, which became the regional dialect of Deccani Urdu. Their efforts gave rise to a refined poetic language with the ghazal as its most sophisticated expression.

Burhan al-Din Gharib sowed the seeds of musical mysticism in the Deccan, and Shah Bajan ensured its perpetuation in the regional capital of Burhanpur. Likewise, Siraj embodied this Chishti tradition with particular vibrancy in the new capital of Awrangabad during the Mughal period. Siraj composed poems to be sung in Sufi gatherings and filled his poems with images of music-making. He uses musical images to illustrate the tensions of love, making allegories between the ritual of sama' and the soul's journey through mystical love. In one couplet of the ghazal below, for example, he uses images of the reed flute, as did Rumi and Shah Bajan:[36]

> The night of parting brought me calamity
>   This misery ignites fire in my chest cavity
> Parting approaches beating warning drums
>   Reed flutes sigh with double-tone intensity
> Why shouldn't Siraj, in this festival of grief
>   Take off with love in defiance of gravity?

Siraj adds a twist to conventional imagery, for the reed flute to which he refers is the *shehnai*. This is an Indian adaptation of the Persian and Turkish *shah-ney* or "royal flute," which can achieve the haunting effect of playing in two different registers—piercingly high and mournfully low—in a single breath. Used in Sufi music, it has a devastating effect of simultaneous lamentation and resignation, embodying the very essence of mystical love.

In its Indian form, the *shehnai* is a wind instrument that can play double-register tones, but it is fitted with a mouthpiece of buzzing reed (as in a Western oboe) that gives its voice a piercing quality in addition to its plaintive timbre. Coupled with kettledrums (*nawbat*), this instrument announced the arrival of royalty or a groom (who is called *naw-shah* or new king). Siraj uses these musical allegories with heartbreaking irony. The *shehnai* and drums conventionally proclaim the impending union in a marriage, but in this poem they warn of inevitable separation and painful parting.

Qawwali Promoted and Contested in Awrangabad

Siraj had a mentor in Shaikh Nizam al-Din Awrangabadi who advocated music in Islamic culture. He was the nearest living example of the tradition upheld by Burhan al-Din Gharib, Shah Bajan, and other Chishti masters in the Deccan. Nizam al-Din Awrangabadi and his circle led a Chishti florescence in Awrangabad, when the city became an imperial Mughal city and rich center of commerce. His Kalīmī branch of the Chishti order publicly upheld musical mysticism over and against competition from Naqshbandi Sufis recently ascendant in Mughal realms.

Naqshbandi Sufis claimed to have a properly Sunni style of mysticism, which disallowed vocal mediation, disavowed the use of music, and discouraged emotive devotion. Where they became strong, Naqshbandis encouraged a more chauvinistic stand against local practices, Shi'i sympathies, and accommodation with Hindus. Naqshbandis were proud of their Central Asian "Turani" roots and their recent arrival in India, imagining that this brought them a purer Islamic pedigree that local Sufis did not have, especially not the Chishtis, who acclimatized to the South Asian cultural environment. The Naqshbandis claimed affinity with the Mughal ruling family and took firm root in Awrangabad. Under the leadership of Baba Palangposh (died 1699) and his successor Baba Musafir (died 1715), the Naqshbandi community thrived among soldiers and administrators in Awrangzeb's army.[37]

The Chishti leader Nizam al-Din Awrangabadi led musical gatherings that contrasted with those of the somber Naqshbandis. Chishti and Naqshbandi communities interacted intensely in Awrangabad.

Positively, their interaction amounted to cross-pollination. The Chishtis adopted some themes and techniques from Naqshbandis, as in Nizam al-Din Awrangabadi's treatise on meditation, titled *Nizam al-Qulub*.[38] His revival of the Chishti order incorporated an initiation into the Naqshbandi lineage (along with Suhravardi, Qadiri, and Chishti lineages).[39] Negatively, their interaction led to competition, as both Sufi communities looked for patronage among the Mughal nobles of Awrangabad. Naqshbandi Sufis criticized the Chishti practice of samaʿ and listening to Qawwali. Nizam al-Din Awrangabadi reportedly moved his assemblies of samaʿ to a venue far from the Naqshbandi center called Panchakki to the Shahgunj neighborhood of Awrangabad in order to shield his community from censure.[40]

Nizam al-Din Awrangabadi perpetuated Chishti traditions but moderated them in Awrangabad. He downplayed elements that would lead to conflict between the two styles of mysticism and insisted, like his teacher in Delhi, Shaikh Kalimullah, that all the Sufi orders were authentic expressions of Muhammad's teachings. This interaction and competition between Chishtis and Naqshbandis one generation earlier may have led Siraj's Sufi teacher to become alarmed at his poetic output and its musical resonance, as we will examine in detail in the next section.

Such criticism was directed primarily against the ambiguity inherent in poetry, especially when sung in public. Ambivalent images about love could be "misinterpreted" by listeners and could excite lustful urges, leading to sinful activity and social discord (*fitna*). Ghazal poets relied on ambivalent imagery in order to create tensions between different levels of love and diverse kinds of passions. Ambiguous reference to the beloved—whether the beloved is a person, an experience, or God—creates tension between sensual and spiritual references. This tension is integral to the ghazal and gives the genre its dynamism. It is also integral to the Sufi use of poetry, for sensual responses could be harnessed by the listener and directed toward spiritual refinement. Redirecting sensual responses and erotic energies into spiritual refinement provides the fuel for dynamic motion in a mystical ascension (*miʿraj*).

Redirecting the motion of these energies does not require repudiating the sensual and erotic nature of the imagery. Its ambivalence is the very power that it holds in potential, waiting to be released in the experience of the listener. But this process, so central to musical mysticism and its use of poetry, is often criticized as being tied to sensual and erotic images. Many Sufis of an ascetic orientation have made just this criticism.

In response, some Sufis of a scholastic disposition have argued that the tension between sensual and spiritual can be resolved by asserting that the poetry is "allegorical." Allegorical poems speak in sensual images but really intend symbolic meaning. The poem is properly understood only once decoded and the real meaning, once conveyed in the clothing of symbolism, is revealed with its sensual material referent shorn away. Allegorical interpretation does not allow multiple levels of the image to coexist but rather establishes a hierarchy between them. Once the symbolic meaning of the image is understood, the material or sensual referent is eclipsed or jettisoned.

The assertion that such poetry should be understood as allegory works only when the poem is read on the page or used in a lecture. Allegorical interpretation is an intellectual exercise of citation and commentary. But poems are sung—given voice through melody and given pulse through rhythm—and when voiced as music, an allegorical interpretive strategy does not resolve the tension. Singing the poem allows all levels of the image to impact the listener at once, in real time, in the momentary beat of music that cannot be stalled or stopped in order to add a commentary. The delivery of the poem through music does not allow the sifting of images into different levels, to divert attention away from the sensual or romantic and argue the real meaning is symbolic or spiritual. This is why Siraj's poetry exerts its full force only when sung and why Siraj composed it orally, often specifically for Qawwal singers to deliver to his Sufi audience.

In their performance, Qawwals musically exploit creative ambiguity in interpreting metaphors that describe the beloved. Do such metaphors apply to all beautiful sensory perceptions, to beautifully alluring people, to a particular person to whom one is passionately attracted, to the spiritual teacher whom one loves, to the Prophet Muhammad and his family, or to God? The answer is "yes" to each and "no" to any one exclusively. Qawwali is built upon this ambiguity. Far from resolving it, Qawwali heightens it, especially in the social framework of a ritual setting. Qawwali is not an individual pursuit but happens in a sacred space defined by the presence of others. It is essentially communal (despite modern pressures to record it as music or perform it on stage). The ritual space is made sacred by the presence of a revered person, either a saint in the tomb after his death or a living spiritual guide who convenes the assembly (or most often both, with the living guide acting as representative or inheritor of the dead saint's authority). Images of a beautiful beloved person naturally have multiple valences in this setting. There is the person of the dead saint, who is beautiful in radiating spiritual energies that continue after his death. There is the person of the living representative, who is beautiful in transmitting charisma to his community of followers. There are persons in the audience, often close friends or relatives, whose are beautiful in that they are partners on the spiritual path. Finally, there is also the possibility that someone in the audience strikes a listener as particularly beautiful and captivating (*shahid*), so that contemplation of his or her face and appearance can lead to an intense focus on the beauty of God's creation. If none in the audience serves this role, an image that one carries in memory or imagination can play this function.

Listening to love poetry sung as music in a public gathering of Sufis provides all these means for meditation and contemplation. The public gathering also provides limits on potentially transgressive behavior. This is why the Chishti practice of samaʿ remained an integral part of Islamic mysticism for five centuries up to the time of Siraj. Nizam al-Din Awliya, the key figure in institutionalizing this practice, discussed the issue of interpreting the poetry's ambivalent images in ways that shaped all subsequent Chishti practice of Qawwali. He said,

> Tomorrow on the Day of Judgment, a divine voice will ask, "As you were listening to poetry did you understand its descriptions to apply to me?" I will answer, "Yes!" The voice will further ask, "These descriptions are of sensory phenomena while my essence is eternal, so how can it be that sensory descriptions apply to an eternal essence beyond sensation?" I will reply, "O God, I only applied them to you because of my intense love!" The voice will declare its judgment, "Because you loved in this way, I have forgiving compassion upon you."[41]

The ambiguity of the metaphors is designed to move the listener from one level of interpretation to the next, in a dynamic progression of love. If the metaphors were not ambiguous (if they did not describe two or more different things at the very same time with a shared image), they could not act as bridges to convey the listener to a new place. One way to clarify confusion on this point would be to ask, On which shore of the river is a bridge grounded?

As Siraj himself wrote in one of his most Sufism-infused ghazals, "Lay your head on a pillow of velvet, but don't let your eyes succumb to sleep."⁴² Laying your head on a pillow of velvet means enjoying deeply the taste (*zawq*) of love at whatever stage in whatever form one finds it manifest and allowing oneself to experience it fully, to sink deeply into it and allow oneself to be fully open to its influence. But removing all sleep from your eyes means to stay conscious that all stages of love are incomplete; they are invitations to move on to ever more refined experiences of love. Moving on will necessarily entail longing, separation, and despair, but these painful feelings hold out the promise for new stages, more profound insight, and eventually love that is more real.

This is why erotic images are central to the poetry that is sung in Qawwali in general, and to the poems of Siraj in particular. These erotic images are not necessarily sexual images. Rather, erotic images refer to the urge toward union with another and concomitant loss of egoistic boundaries. Sexual energy might be inherent in these erotic images but is not necessarily delineated graphically. In this sense, eros is not to be denied in this sung poetry but rather to be harnessed so that its deep-seated and dynamic energies can fuel the listeners' movement into greater and greater spiritual refinement. At least this is the tradition of Nizam al-Din Awliya, as perpetuated by Burhan al-Din Gharib and those Sufis in the Deccan who followed him. They practiced samaʿ that was open to the public with all its varied levels of experience and tended toward poetry that included erotic images.

Conclusion

The Qawwals sing for an audience consisting of different kinds of listeners and plan their performance accordingly. Some listeners are deeply committed Sufis who have experienced the spiritual states that Siraj's poem so vividly describes, such that singing its words brings them deeply into that state, leading to lamentation and weeping. Others are Sufis who are have very aesthetic temperaments, whom the music and lyrics can raise to new levels of inspired internal reaction that may not be observable at all to an outsider, embedded as it is in profound thought and contemplation. Others are emotionally vulnerable—perhaps Sufi beginners—whom the music drives toward ecstatic states that break the tyranny of reason and calculation. Others are just curious, simply enjoy the music, or crave a distraction from the grind of daily life. Usually the audience consists of only men, though sometimes women also join or sit within hearing range. The mixed nature of the audience leads to a danger of music and poetry arousing lustful passions among listeners. Ascetic observers could misinterpret the passions being performed in the ritual space of samaʿ, leading them to oppose it and question the Islamic credentials of its patrons. This was a danger for Siraj as it is for listeners in the present day.

While Siraj knew this danger well, he did not let it detract him from attending samaʿ gatherings and composing poetry for them. For Siraj, the purpose of life was to pursue refinement through love's burning, in an attempt to transcend the limited routines and self-centeredness of ego. For Sufi listeners, the gathering of samaʿ is a bounded ritualized space for this pursuit. They enact it in an intensified way in this limited sphere for a special time and then return to more routine activities of life, hopefully with their frame of reference altered or at least its limitations temporarily suspended. Because the ghazal is infused with the poet's own spiritual experience, it can spark similar spiritual experiences in the listeners when vitalized through being sung in a ritual context of heightened sensitivity, openness, and expectation.

Siraj exuberantly practiced samaʿ despite the controversy it provoked. However, it appears that his Sufi master perceived the danger, not the promise, of his poetic performance in this ritual space. How his poetry was turned into music is a crucial element in understanding the troublesome role of eros in his life, as a Mughal male and Muslim mystic. It is also the key to understanding why his Sufi master commanded him to stop composing poems, for they were sung in ritual and social gatherings rather than simply composed on the page.

After only seven years of composing poetry to be sung, Siraj's Sufi master commanded him to stop. Siraj complied. His aspiration was to become a Sufi master, after all, rather than a famous poet. Even after his teacher's death, about nine years later, he continued to refrain from composing poetry.[43] Yet Siraj had become famous in a very short time—in seven years of composing Urdu ghazals he was seen as a master. Younger poets sought him out as a poetry teacher. These include some of the finest poets of the eighteenth century.[44] Even after he stopped composing, his ghazals were already absorbed into the Qawwali repertoire in the Deccan. They spread as literary texts to other regions, wherever Urdu was cultivated.

Shah Siraj died on April 6, 1764 (4 Shawwal, 1177 Hijri), suffering in illness alone at the age of forty-nine, for he never married and headed no household. Many poets of his day admired him and composed "chronograms" in verse to commemorate his death. The poet Shafiq composed this quatrain:⁴⁵

> A noble, in worship sincere, in composing graceful
> From whose pen come poems worthy and beautiful
> Shafiq's saying counts the year of his passing
> "Shah Siraj turned his face toward the Merciful"

The sum of the *abjad* value of the letters in the final line is 1177, the year by Islamic reckoning in which Siraj died. The greatest scholar of Aurangabad, Azad Bilgrami—himself a poet of Arabic and Persian—composed a memorial.⁴⁶ The heavy formality and sincere sorrow of these memorial poems is lightened by some humorous ones as well. Shafiq composed the chronogram, "Woe to the heart, Siraj has become mud," which also adds up to the year of his passing.⁴⁷

This last chronogram, with its macabre humor, reminds us that even in death, life does go on. Siraj built up a small Sufi hospice called his *takiya* and wrote to his beloved friend 'Abd al-Rasul Khan, asking him, "Upon my demise, if you don't want to go away with me [to the next world] then at least come and stay with my community at the *takiya*!"⁴⁸ Yet 'Abd al-Rasul Khan was occupied in army service in Bijapur and only much later took on Sufi discipline fully to become known as Shah 'Abd al-Rasul Chishti. Siraj had many times called his closest disciple, Shah Chiragh, to come and care for him and his institution, but Shah Chiragh was busy in Ahmadnagar building up his own circle of followers. Late in his life, Siraj wrote to Shah Chiragh threatening that he would, even in his weakness and ill health, mount a horse and ride to the army in Bijapur to meet 'Abd al-Rasul Khan and personally persuade him to return.⁴⁹ But his body collapsed before he could get his foot into the stirrups.

Siraj's loyal friend Zia al-Din Parwana funded the building of a small dome over his tomb. Only then did Shah Chiragh return to Awrangabad and take up custodianship of Siraj's *takiya* and leadership of his circle of disciples. Upon Shah Chiragh's death, his son Maqbul Chiragh and grandson Roshan Chiragh inherited the position of custodian; after them it went to a khalifa of theirs, Sayyid Karim Shah, and to his descendants. As long as the nizams ruled, succession continued at the *takiya* unabated, land grants supported Sufis who renounced worldly gain, and Siraj's poetry was sung in Qawwali gatherings that they organized.⁵⁰

Thus the sun set on the northern horizon of the Deccan, as Siraj the sun died in Awrangabad. But on the southern horizon, the moon was poised to rise. Siraj lived through the city's golden age as it was briefly the capital of the Mughal Empire and then the headquarters of the nizam's Deccan kingdom. As Siraj faded into old age, the city too entered a twilight era. Less than a decade after his death, the Deccan capital shifted to Hyderabad, and there on the southern horizon of the Deccan, Mah Laqa Bai the moon was about to rise into being. But between them stretched a vast territory, not just of geographical land but also of devotional topography. The next chapter will cross that vast distance. It marks a transit between one personality and the other, between one city and another, between one Islamic sect and another.

CHAPTER SIX

Transit—When Sufis Meet Shi'is

In every way, your praise God is reciting, Mawla 'Ali
With inspired words about you, lord abiding Mawla 'Ali
You're a brother to Muhammad, keep leading Mawla 'Ali
The center of both worlds, rightly guiding Mawla 'Ali
　　Full moon glowing, Mawla 'Ali, dawn sun rising, Mawla 'Ali

—*first stanza of a poem praising 'Ali by Iman,
the teacher of Mah Laqa Bai*

Shah Siraj met some of the most eminent literary and Sufi personalities of the Deccan, but he never met Mah Laqa Bai, the courtesan dancer and Urdu poetess with whom this book compares him. Their paths never crossed. He lived in Awrangabad when it was the Deccan capital, and she lived in Hyderabad when the capital shifted there one generation later. They never met in person, but they do meet in the realm of imagination. They are comparable as poets of the Urdu ghazal and as mystics in a shared Islamic devotional continuum. More specifically, Sufi masters like Siraj did meet and collaborate with Shi'i courtesans like Mah Laqa Bai, though on the surface their sexuality and gender roles are markedly different.

At the deepest level, it is love that brings together the Sufi poet and the courtesan dancer, even though one was Sunni while the other was Shi'i. They both cultivated love in general and love for 'Ali in particular, who was known by the honorific titles Hazrat (your Honor) or Mawla (our Master). 'Ali was seen by both groups to be the embodiment of divine light and guidance that continued after his close relative, the Prophet Muhammad, passed away. This devotional fervor is portrayed in the five-line stanza from a poem by Mah Laqa Bai's poetry teacher (*ustad*) that is quoted above; in it, the sun and moon with their radiance are mere outward manifestations of the intense inner light that shines into the world through 'Ali.[1] This shared devotional ground creates a religious topography with specific ritual sites in the Deccan. The cumulative effect of this topography is to bring different sectarian communities into an unusual intimacy of shared values and close cooperation. This transit chapter aims to illustrate how the cooperation is mapped, despite nuanced differences between Shi'is and Sufis over theology.

Transit Allows a Meeting without Meeting

This chapter marks a transit and transition from Shah Siraj to Mah Laqa Bai. In premodern astrology, "transit" refers to how planets move through one astrological constellation and into the next. It describes how heavenly bodies seem to cross paths. If we imagine Shah Siraj as a constellation representing a Sufi master and poet of Awrangabad, we can imagine Mah Laqa Bai as a neighboring constellation representing a Shi'i dancer and poet of Hyderabad. As the planet of dominance passes from one constellation to another, how can we compare these two personalities? Let us enter this comparison with a vignette presented by Shah Siraj, where he imagines meeting courtesans like Mah Laqa Bai.

In his poem "The Fragrant Garden of Imagination," Siraj describes himself as being on familiar terms with courtesans. The vignette highlights the importance of gender and sexuality in their two personality types. Shah Siraj is a man who is depressed over his failed love affair with another man and has no desire for women. The courtesans are women who, beyond the constraints of marriage, entertain and sometimes discipline men. They enjoy the privilege of speaking with men boldly and openly, though their place in patriarchal society is always conditioned by reliance on patronage by male elites. In this vignette, Siraj is wallowing in despair after his male love has left him and moved to Hyderabad. He attends a gathering of music and dance in a lovely garden but can find no delight. There the courtesans try to please him and tease him—through their wit and grace—into giving up melancholy over his lost lover. Yet the artistic beauty of the courtesans only deepens his heartache. The couplets show his appreciation of and friendship with the courtesans:[2]

> If someday by chance I enter a gathering of dance
>   Sitting there to watch is arduous for me
> Each of the dancing girls is a heart-stealer
>   Each one is a courtesan of stunning beauty[3]
> They sing a tune, turn with enticing grace
>   Show off their beauty with impeccable style

Each one blossoming in her fourteen years
    Working her magic to steal away hearts
Each is superb in her finery and adornment
    In flowing gowns stitched with glimmering lace
Each of their hands stained crimson with henna
    With one glance water would boil into steam
Each with a forehead pendant of jeweled gold
    So gleaming that the sun takes from them light
The pen has no power to describe their grace
    Or to write down the beauty of their pace
Feet poised in dance, each is so stunning
    They steal the heart's beat and soul's power
Their glance's rhythmic nuance above a sly smile
    A song's enticement through *paan*-chewing lips
Is it any wonder a man's will wanes at the sight
    When a stone, seeing them, would melt into water?
Their dance complete, they gather around me
    Each asks me what's the state of my heart:

[. . . The courtesans say]
"Everyone around you is engrossed in delight
    They're overjoyed by these simple pleasures
But you! You're in a storm of grief, what's wrong?
    Your lips are dry but your eyes are wet, what's wrong?
Tell us now, why is your heart so worn down
    Why has sorrow reduced you to dust and water?
I swear, you must tell us the cause of such grief
    Whose hand has wounded you so deeply?
What fairy-faced beauty has worked magic on you
    Martyred by the blade of a lovely forehead's frown?
Over whom does such sorrow so upset your heart
    That your very life's breath has come to ruin?
Tell us now, unburden your heart, tell us all
    For it is our art, as well, to steal the heart!
For aren't we also beautiful in every way?
    Whatever you desire, we are experts in love!
So why are you holding back your heart from us?
    Why do you refuse to tell us your love-pangs?

All in vain you are letting your heart burn
    As if you find pleasure in your secret pain
Enough now, just have a small moment of fun
    Come now, just wipe the tears from your eyes!"
But what could I say? How to express my state?
    With each breath my soul is wracked with pain
In no way do I find any rest or respite
    This wildness of grief never lessens its grip

[So Siraj told the courtesans]
"Can the gathering of song and dance cheer my heart
    When sorrow has struck and destroyed my soul?"

[... Each courtesan replied]
"Oh my God, woe is me! Woe is me, O my God!
    If you say this again, I'll just die with you!
How will I ever find consolation again?
    I'm in such anguish—where can I escape?
Through the whole world, it's true what they say:
    The earth is hard and the heavens are far away!"

In the shared field of aesthetics, Sufi and courtesan meet. When poems are sung, they can evoke love that can transport one from the hardness of this earth to the heavens, even though they are far away.

It was not merely in pleasure gardens or lovelorn advice that Sufis and courtesans interacted. In the Deccan, Sufis, who were mainly Sunni, and courtesans, who were largely Shi'i, also met in the shared devotional topography of deep love for 'Ali and the wider family of the Prophet (*al-e bait*). This chapter explores this topography of shared symbols, theological commonalities, and ritual overlaps between Sufi Sunnis and Shi'is. It focuses on sites that aid in understanding the complex juxtaposition and interplay between different religious communities in the Deccan.

View from the Sama'-Khana

Love for 'Ali and his descendants forms an important element in Sufism. Illustrating this is a fascinating quatrain of Persian poetry ascribed to the founder of the Chishti Sufi community, Mu'in al-Din Chishti. It is sung in Qawwali during rituals gatherings in sites such as a *sama'-khana*, a special hall for listening to music that is often built at Sufi dargahs in the Deccan. The same poem is often inscribed in calligraphy at devotional sites such as the ʿashur-khana, devotional halls where Shiʿis gather to commemorate the martyrdom of Husain, the son of ʿAli and grandson of Muhammad, along with other members of his family.

> Husain is king and Husain is king of all other kings
> > Husain is religion and Husain preserves sacred things
> > Rather than place his hand on Yazid's, he gave his head
> > > Because of Husain "No god but God" in this world rings

This Persian quatrain extols the virtues of Husain. It pictures him as a hero who upheld Islam by sacrificing his life rather than submitting to an unjust usurper, Yazid (ruled as Umayyad king from 680 until he died in 683). Is it a poem expressing Sufi or Shiʿi ideals? It is both.

Love of ʿAli and the Prophet's family is a shared symbolic resource for Shiʿis and Sufis. Love of ʿAli also acts as a structural bridge between Shiʿis and those Sunnis who have a Sufi orientation (whom we can term Sufi Sunnis).[4] The love of ʿAli forms an important element that promoted peaceful coexistence between Sunni and Shiʿis Muslims in the Deccan. These two sectarian communities were defined briefly in chapter 1, but we will explore them in more detail as they interacted in the Deccan. Sunni and Shiʿi sectarian categories are each composed of diverse subgroups. The Sunnis call themselves *Ahl-e Sunnat o Jamaʿat* or "Those Who Follow Example and Consensus" of the early Muslim community to elect a representative from the Prophet's followers. They recognize the right to rule of the first four caliphs who succeeded the Prophet as temporal rulers, after which political authority devolved onto kings and sultans. They believe that caliphs and jurists made legal decisions that are valid and binding, and follow one of several different formalizations of these legal norms, often called a legal school (*mazhab*). The majority of Muslims worldwide are Sunnis, and the same was true in the Deccan.

While being Sunni in sectarian allegiance, one can also be Sufi in devotional orientation. The vast majority of Sunni Muslims in the Deccan were Sufi-oriented, with the Chishti and Qadiri lineages being the dominant Sufi orders (*tariqa*).[5] Scholars and journalists who assert that Sunnis and Sufis are different categories make a factual error.[6] Sufis are those who engage their religion in order to seek mystical insight and direct experience of God, and Sufi Sunnis do this from within a social sectarian allegiance to Sunni schools of law.

In South Asia, Shiʿis are a significant minority, especially so in the Deccan region where Shiʿi dynasties ruled (such as Bijapur, Ahmadnagar, and Golkonda, with its capital at Hyderabad). Shiʿis call themselves Partisans of ʿAli (Shiʿat ʿAli), a name with devotional, political, and legal implications. Shiʿis recognize only ʿAli as the political and moral leader after the Prophet Muhammad and hold that ʿAli's male heirs should rule rather than the kings and sultans who wielded actual power. In law, Shiʿis follow the example of the imams (ʿAli and his designated male heirs in the succeeding twelve generations) but not other elders of the Muslim community who have no blood ties to the Prophet. Shiʿis systematized this example into legal and ritual norms, creating their own legal school (the Jaʿfari *mazhab*).⁷ Like Sunnis, the Shiʿi community encompasses many different devotional orientations. Among Shiʿis in the Deccan, the majority were "Desi Shiʿis" with a local orientation (the term "Desi" taken from the Urdu word *des*, meaning the local land). They were mystically inclined and practiced Shiʿi rituals that were highly "Indianized." These developed under patronage of Shiʿite dynasties such as Qutb-Shahi kings, who ruled from 1518 until 1687 from their capital at Golkonda Fort and later Hyderabad city.

When addressing sectarian allegiances—Sunni and Shiʿi—one must be attentive to varieties. Rather than exaggerate the difference between them, varieties within them allow overlap, confluence, or coexistence. We can call the Sufi-oriented Sunni piety "soft Sunni" because it did not define itself antagonistically against Shiʿis or other so-called heretical movements. Rather, it defined itself positively as adherence to Sunni legal norms animated by an inner spiritual cultivation inspired by ʿAli, as the first and prototypical Sufi master and saint (*valiʾallah*). We can describe the Desi Shiʿi piety as "soft Shiʿi," as it did not define itself antagonistically against the practices of neighboring Sunnis and did not ideologically oppose Sufism. In Desi Shiʿi devotion, ʿAli was not primarily the marker of political loyalty that defined sectarian allegiance but was more specifically the focus for personal spiritual love and mystical absorption.

Having made these distinctions, we will focus on Sufi Sunnis in this section and will discuss Desi Shiʿis subsequently. The definition of Sufi Muslims is not sharply distinguished from other Sunnis but rather blurs along a devotional continuum. For instance, Chishti Sufis, who historically defined the contours of Sufi devotion in the Deccan, blended rather seamlessly with Qadiri Sufis. While Chishtis were more avid promoters of musical devotion through sama' rituals (especially in the form of Qawwali at a dargah), the local Qadiris often adopted musical and sung forms of zikr; in addition, Qawwali repertoire included devotional songs specifically in praise of Shaikh 'Abd al-Qadir Jilani (died 1166 in Baghdad). In the Deccan, the Qadiri and Chishti lineages often fused.[8]

This structural orientation to 'Ali distinguished Sufi Sunnis with Chishti and Qadiri affiliation from Sufi Sunnis of the Naqshbandi lineage, which did not venerate 'Ali. In contrast, the Naqshbandi lineage of charismatic initiation traced its origin to Abu Bakr al-Siddiq (the first caliph) rather than through 'Ali.[9] Accordingly, Naqshbandis tended to be "harder" Sunnis despite their Sufi orientation. Naqshbandis came to the Deccan late, along with the Mughal army in the seventeenth century, and they tended to define themselves as "proper" Sunnis who opposed the Shi'is. Their Sufi orientation was enfolded within a "hard" antagonistic Sunni exterior shared with Sunnis who had no Sufi orientation (such as some jurists, *hadis* experts, or preachers) and defined their community by sharp sectarian opposition against Shi'is. This defines a devotional continuum, with more Indianized Sufi Sunnis at one extreme blending into more "foreign" Sufi Sunnis in the middle and non-Sufi Sunnis at the other extreme.

The leading exponents of the Indianized Sunni Sufis were of the Chishti order. An important aspect of the Chishti community was its "Alid loyalty" or devotion to 'Ali and Husain.[10] The Chishti community traced its lineage, or *silsila*, back to the Prophet through 'Ali and venerated 'Ali as the first *vali*, the first "empowered friend." Chishti loyalty to 'Ali was not about his right to rule or the political claims of his descendants. Rather, the Chishtis concentrated on the religious teachings and mystical insights that the Prophet transmitted to 'Ali and from him to spiritual leaders both inside his family (especially to Husain) and outside his family (especially to Hasan Basri, an early moralistic theologian who died in 728). While all Muslims received the Qur'an and his public example of conduct, 'Ali received an "inner teaching" from the Prophet because of his intimacy with him. This is the symbolic meaning of the event in which 'Ali imitated the Prophet when Arab opponents in Mecca were plotting to assassinate the Prophet. 'Ali slept in the Prophet's bed that night as a decoy while the Prophet escaped to Medina. The inner meaning of this political event is that 'Ali reflected the Prophet's personality in a unique way. This reflection was elaborated upon theologically by speaking of the Prophet as light and of 'Ali as a beam of that light;

in an outer sense the beam of light is different from its source, but in essence the two are the same light. Their intimacy was sealed through 'Ali's marriage to Fatima, the Prophet Muhammad's daughter. This social union symbolized the inner intimacy that the two men already shared, which was a transmission of light, a spark of love, and the courage to sacrifice that for the inner teaching of Islam.

The message of devotion to 'Ali is made more explicit in an Urdu poem by Bedam Varsi (died 1795), a contemporary of Siraj whose poems are also sung in Qawwali. In it he praises Fatima, known as Zahra "the radiant," and her family:[11]

> In the garden of Zahra all kinds of roses bloom
> The color of 'Ali in some, in others the aroma of the Prophet
> Why shouldn't 'Ali, the Lion of God, not be the Hand of God?
> The purpose of all spiritual gifts is this — "There is no youth like 'Ali"
> Just as Muhammad is unique, nobody was, is or will be like 'Ali

The saying in Arabic "There is no youth like 'Ali" (*la fata illa 'Ali*) reminds us of Shi'i slogans based upon sayings of the Prophet in praise of 'Ali's steadfastness, heroism, and willingness to sacrifice himself in battle: "There is no youth brave as 'Ali and no sword like *zu'l-fiqar*!" For Sufis, 'Ali's two-bladed sword, called *zu'l-fiqar*, is seen to represent the power of severing one's desires from worldly goals and cutting away the ego's pretension so that one can become a vessel for divine will in this world.

Chishti Sufis mention 'Ali's name to spark spiritual insight and ethical vigor rather than to invoke 'Ali as a hero in order to raise a rebellion and establish a just political order. For Sufis, the brave youth 'Ali is seen not as a warrior in battle but as an ascetic ready to face the enemy within and quell the ego through self-abnegation. His fearless son, Husain, is seen not as a political rebel for a lost cause but as a champion of self-sacrifice who gave preference to others. Both imams are dear to Sufis for showing how to fight the greater struggle, or *jihad-e akbar*, more than for their political campaigns.[12]

Qawwali performances traditionally begin with the song "Man Kuntu Mawla," a musical setting of the famous *hadis* pronounced by the Prophet at Ghadir Khumm: after the final pilgrimage, the Prophet "took 'Ali's hand and placed him on his right side. Then he said, 'Am I the authority whom you obey?' They answered, 'We obey your directions.' Then he said, 'For whomever I am master and the authority whom he obeys, let 'Ali be his master. Oh God! Be friendly with the friends of 'Ali and oppose the enemies of 'Ali.'"¹³ Amir Khusro set the words of this *hadis* to a tune. In performance, the *hadis* in Arabic is sung followed by a Persian explication of it and often a Hindi amplification of it, concluding with a complex and ecstatic *taranna*, a pattern of rapturous syllables. This might even be one of the original tunes around which Qawwali performances were systematized. God's power is seen in Muhammad's actions, and Muhammad's character is seen in 'Ali's person, and 'Ali's essence is seen in Husain's self-sacrificing martyrdom, whose charisma is perpetuated by Sufi saints in myriad localities and routine situations. Love for 'Ali and his message of self-sacrifice was most dramatically performed in the *samaʿ-khana* during Qawwali.¹⁴

View from the ʿAshur-Khana

Let us shift focus from the *samaʿ-khana*, a Sufi institution, to a Shiʿi devotional site that also combines ritual and music, the *ʿashur-khana* or mourning hall, in order to gain a new perspective on devotion to 'Ali. As we saw in a view from the *samaʿ-khana*, where Sufi Muslims listen to devotional music, Sunnis with Sufi allegiances are not sharply distinguished from other Sunnis. Similarly, in the Deccan, Desi Shiʿis as a group are not sharply distinguished from other Shiʿis, their practices being rather blurred along a devotional continuum. The group defined above as Desi Shiʿis are not clearly differentiated from other more ideological Shiʿis who were resident in the Deccan. The element that differentiates them is whether they define their sectarian identity by antagonistic confrontation with others, namely Sunnis, and how their identity as Shiʿis is performed in ritual. One of the main ritual spaces in which their identity is performed is the *ʿashur-khana*.

Starting in the twelfth century, the Delhi sultanate established Turkic military garrisons, Persian court structures, and Sunni Islamic ritual norms in the Deccan, as sketched in chapter 1. By the fourteenth century, Deccan kingdoms became independent from Delhi and were mainly ruled by sultans of Turkic ethnicity.¹⁵ Deccan kingdoms enjoyed easy connection to Iran and Iraq from ports on the Arabian Sea. New immigrants arrived to the Deccan from the holy cities of Karbala and Najaf and other places where Shiʿi Muslims were prominent. Those who came with Persian language, court etiquette, administrative skill, and literary refinement were welcomed and given high positions. Many of these new immigrants—called *afaqi* or "foreigner from over the horizon"—were Shi'i. Initially, they had to keep their religious practices and sectarian identity secret—a practice called *taqiya* or concealment. This is an accepted practice in Shi'ism as it developed as a minority sectarian allegiance in political environments that could be hostile.

Concealment was prudent because the first independent kingdom in the Deccan, the Bahmani dynasty, maintained Sunni identity. Bahmani rulers looked to Sufis to give their kingdom symbolic justification, and they found support in the Chishti leader Muhammad Husaini Gesu Daraz, who emigrated from Delhi to the Bahmani capital of Gulbarga. Gesu Daraz was a scholarly and savvy spiritual leader who advised kings and blessed Bahmani rule. The Chishti practice of respecting 'Ali and his family intensified, encouraged by Persian immigrants who took up administrative positions and who were secretly Shi'i.[16] The confluence of Shi'i and Sufi ideals drew from the symbols that they shared. It coordinated with the political expediency of the Bahmani kings, who were willing to take up any strategy to find popular legitimacy. A new dynasty based upon loyalty to Husain and 'Ali was emerging in the Deccan, and this encouraged allegiance to Shi'i ideals.[17]

Shi'ism spread in the Deccan not as a rebellion against established rulers or in opposition to Sunni assertiveness. Rather, it spread through shared devotion to 'Ali, which was already strong in Sufi Sunni communities like the Chishti community that had gained prestige, and among dynastic overlords who looked to Chishti leaders to grant popular support. For instance, the first Bahmani congregational mosque (the *jami'a masjid* built in 1367 in the fortress at Gulbarga) bears the names of the five family members of the Prophet and lineage of the imams as well as the three names of the other khalifas, combining Sunni and Shi'i iconography.[18] The Bahmani kings built a monumental tomb for Gesu Daraz with a wooden railing set with silver teardrop-shaped medallions bearing the names of the twelve imams. The devotion to 'Ali and his family among Gesu Daraz and his followers, who largely set the tone for Sufi Sunni devotion in the Deccan, was so strong that some historians falsely report that the Chishti master was a Shi'i.[19]

By 1500, the Bahmani dynasty weakened while regional governors gained power. The realm fractured into five kingdoms ruled by former governors, and the search for political legitimacy took on new urgency. Many of the new Deccan kings adopted Shi'ism and allied with the Safavid Empire in Iran, which enforced Shi'ism as the state religion. These regional kings shaped the spiritual orientation and ritual practices of Desi Shi'is. To see how a regional dynasty patronized Desi Shi'ism, we can turn to the example of the Qutb-Shahi kings who ruled at Golkonda and established the city of Hyderabad.

Sultan Quli was the first ruler of this dynasty (ruled 1518–43). He was a Turkoman soldier serving the Bahmani sultan. His name meant "slave of the ruler." As military chief, he was given the title Qutb al-Mulk or "Pillar of the Realm." He was appointed governor of Telangana with its rich diamond mines, prosperous trade route to the Bay of Bengal, and impregnable fort-city of Golkonda. As Bahmani power weakened, he took on the royal title Qutb-Shah. Influenced by the Safavid dynasty, Sultan Quli Qutb-Shah made Shi'ism the state religion of Golkonda by having the communal sermon (*khutba*) read in the name of the twelve imams. Under Shi'i aegis, the Qutb-Shahi court promoted certain "syncretic" practices to create a single culture that highlighted common cultural and religious traits among its very heterogeneous subjects. Qutb-Shahi rulers built 'ashur-khanas, devotional halls in which they erected '*alams* or battle standards representing the martyred imams and members of the Prophet's family. '*Alams* were constructed of precious metals of exquisite craftsmanship and were laden with symbols reminding the viewer of personalities from the Prophet's family (*al-e bait*). These ritual objects were venerated by devotees who came to the 'ashur-khana during the holy days of Muharram, the Islamic month during which the battle of Karbala took place and Husain and his many supporters were martyred.[20]

Devotees could touch the '*alam* just like one might touch the body of a spiritual master for blessing. One could present offerings like parched rice, palm sugar (in Urdu, *ghur*), and coconut in the same gesture as one would present offerings to a Hindu deity.

> The Qutb-Shahs adopted a unique method for creating a common cultural ethos among the people by following a broad based liberal policy in religious observance. The love of common *pirs* and the devotion to 'ashur-khanas was common both in the Muslims and the Hindus. . . . The purely religious part of the Muharram ceremonies were meant for Muslims, more so for the Shi'is, and they did remain so. But the sacredness of the '*alams* at 'ashur-khanas, the presentation of *nazar*, and *langar* [offerings] were all universalized. The 'ashur-khanas thus became a meeting place of people of all religions and castes. . . . Most of these ceremonies were "Indianized" and coincided with the ceremonies current among the people of the

region. . . . ʿAshur-khanas thus served as a platform for the people of a diversified society to meet in a brotherly atmosphere.²¹

In ʿashur-khanas, commemoration ceremonies for Muharram were held and poems called marsiyas mourned the martyred imams. Qutb-Shahi kings and court poets composed in Deccani Urdu to further ground their Shiʿi devotion in the local idiom and replace or supplement earlier Persian marsiyas composed in Iran.

Though Qutb-Shahi rulers adopted Shiʿi doctrine from Iranian sources, they actively adapted it to the Deccan Indian environment. Karen Ruffle calls this process "vernacularization," meaning the cultural translation of Shiʿi heroes, heroines, texts, and rituals into a distinctively South Asian idiom.²² She uses the term "translation" to mean much more than a mere change of language. Persian texts from Iran were translated into Deccani Urdu, beginning with the influential tale of martyrdom in Karbala, *Rawzat al-Shuhada* (composed in Persian around 1501 by Mulla Husain Vaʾiz Kashifi). Such texts were integrally linked to oral performances, like Shiʿi sermons or orations of mourning (*rawza-khwani*) for the unjust suffering of the Prophet's family. Toby Howarth traced the development of this oral tradition of preaching based on Persian texts composed in Iran but transformed into popular rituals starting in the Qutb-Shahi period.²³ Textual translation became subsumed into a wider and deeper process of "vernacularization" as Shiʿi texts (written in Iran in Persian) were linked to oral performances, religious rituals, and local customs in the Deccan.

Mir Muhammad Muʾmin from Astarabad played a pivotal role in this process. This Iranian immigrant-scholar rose to become chief minister (*peshva-ye sultanat*) and established the new city of Hyderabad, which he designed to be a "New Isfahan." He advanced this process of vernacularization: "Mir Muhammad Muʾmin founded many villages as centers of Shiʿi and Islamic life. In them, he constructed reservoirs, mosques, caravanserais and ʿashur-khanas. The mosques and ʿashur-khanas brought the Hindu villagers into contact with the Islamic and Shiʿi way of life. The ʿalams and other symbols of the tragedy of Karbala were introduced by Mir Muʾmin into these villages where they aroused Hindu curiosity and helped to convert them to Shiʿism."²⁴ Popularization of Shiʿi rituals "converted" them into a local idiom that appealed to the environment in linguistic, cultural, and aesthetic ways.

Vernacularization is thus an apt term for this two-way process: it lowered Shi'i beliefs, texts, and rituals toward the understanding of common people in a new environment while simultaneously raising new populations into the sphere of influence of these beliefs, texts, and rituals. This study uses the term "Desi" rather than "vernacular," but the meaning is the same. While this process could lead to gradual conversion of Hindus and tribals to Shi'i Islam, it had a wider impact by encouraging Hindus to incorporate Shi'i figures or practices into their local Hindu practice. Muharram rituals attracted participation from non-Muslims in the Deccan without conversion being an issue at all; Hindu poets composed marsiyas in honor of Shi'i heroines and heroes, and Muslims who identified as Sunni participated in Muharram rituals.[25] Such a cultural movement is seen in the Charminar, the architectural monument that Mir Mu'min designed to anchor Hyderabad as capital of the Qutb-Shahi realm, for this monument manages to be Islamic, specifically Shi'i, and also significant for local Hindus.[26]

Qutb-Shahi rulers encouraged the local acculturation of a continual stream of immigrants who came as traders, soldiers, scholars, and administrators to the Deccan from Persianate lands (Iran, Tajikistan, Uzbekistan, Azarbaijan, Afghanistan, Turkmenistan, and outlying zones). The policy worked also in reverse, bringing diverse Hindu groups (like Marathas, Telugus, Rajputs, and Gujars along with various tribal groups) with different languages, cultures, and religious practices into a common culture under the umbrella of Islamic rule.[27] The policy allowed the Qutb-Shahi dynasty to rule for 170 years with little internal dissent, sectarian violence, or open revolt. However, some emigrants from Persianate lands, especially from Safavid strongholds, resisted the Desi trend toward adopting specifically Deccani idioms: "The rise of the Safavid state, which made Shi'ism the official creed of Iran in 1502, intensified sectarian recrimination; coupled with Safavid warfare against the surrounding Sunni empires—the Ottoman and Uzbek—and diplomatic tussles with the Mughals, . . . any suggestion of a Sunni-Shi'i dialogue, still less of a conciliation, could be no more than wishful thinking."[28] Thus some immigrants to the Deccan from Safavid realms maintained a cultural and religious chauvinism that saw Persian language as superior to and Safavid-style Shi'ism as purer than the local hybrid of the Qutb-Shahi realm.

Such Iranian chauvinists were sometimes jurists or religious scholars whose textual orientation led them to disparage the popular rituals that constituted the heart of Desi Shi'i devotion. If chauvinists spoke too strongly against local practices or antagonized Sunnis, they were criticized as agitators who undermined the local cultural consensus upon which peace in the realm rested. Many Shi'i theologians and jurists were patronized by the Qutb-Shahi dynasty, but Shi'ism did not spread through Persian books written by Iranian immigrants. It spread rather through popular rituals that accommodated to the local landscape and ritual expectations of the Deccan population, a process of making a Desi Shi'ism in a South Asian vernacular idiom.[29]

View from the Hilltop Shrine

Sunni and Shi'i Muslims lived side by side in the Deccan. The region was shaped politically and religiously by dynasties that emphasized the symbolic elements that Sunnis and Shi'is shared. Their prosperity and rule depended upon finding legitimacy in symbols, beliefs, and personas that were respected by both Shi'is and Sunnis. Was this situation mere coexistence, or did it go deeper to constitute *convivencia* or an ethos of mutual prosperity? To answer this question, we must shift our focus to sites where different communities shared a sacred place and overlapped in their devotional rituals.

One site where mutual devotion to 'Ali played out was the hilltop shrine of Mawla 'Ali. This was a sacred site in the Qutb-Shahi region where mutual devotion to 'Ali was intense. The shrine, called Koh-e Mawla 'Ali, consists of a bare rocky hillock about ten miles north of Hyderabad. It is one of the most important Shi'i shrines of the region. The site is the result of a vision experienced by a eunuch who served in the Qutb-Shahi court (*khawaja sara*). This eunuch, named Yaqut, left the city of Golkonda during a plague to stay at a village called Lalaguda.[30] There Yaqut saw in a dream an Arab dressed in green who said that 'Ali was calling. In the dream, Yaqut rose and followed the green-clad Arab to a hillock and saw 'Ali sitting on a high rock upon which he rested his right hand. Yaqut paid respects to 'Ali, but before the eunuch could speak, the vision ended.

Yaqut woke and later recognized a nearby hill as that which appeared in his dream. Climbing the hill the eunuch found the high rock with the impression of 'Ali's right hand. Yaqut ordered stonecutters to carve into the rock along these traces and create a deeper recess in the shape of 'Ali's hand. The eunuch placed this rock in an archway (*rivaq*) built on the hill and returned to court to inform the king of this miraculous trace of 'Ali's visit. Sultan Ibrahim Qutb-Shah (ruled 1550–80) believed this vision.

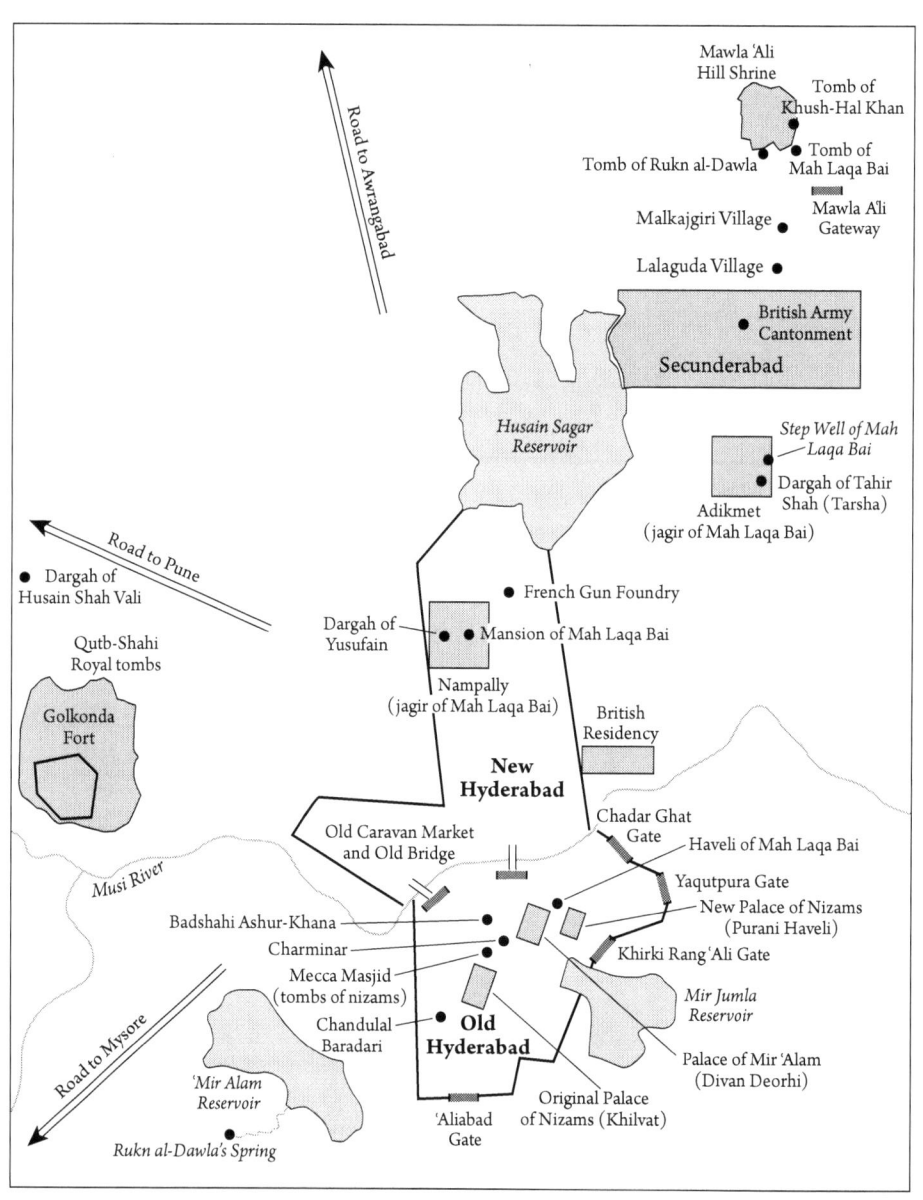

Hyderabad City in the early nineteenth century

He traveled to the hill to venerate the handprint, initiating an annual pilgrimage that continues today.[31] He ordered buildings established around the site and devoted the revenue of lands for its upkeep and ʿurs celebration. For many centuries the site continued to grow with devotional buildings, pilgrim rest houses, ʿashur-khanas, and graveyards springing up on the top of the hill, midway in the long climb, and around the base of the hillock. It became a sign of royal prestige to patronize building at the shrine, with kings, nobles, courtiers, and courtesans—whether Shiʿi, Sunni, or Hindu—dedicating funds for such projects. The shrine is not simply an ʿashur-khana, though it functions as one during Muharram. It is more accurately a dargah, a shrine housing a holy person's body or relic, which in this case is the handprint of ʿAli. It is a place of pilgrimage all year round rather than a building for venerating ʿalams and hosting majlis for mourning during Muharram alone.

The pilgrimage is intense during the mawlid celebrating the birthday of ʿAli (on 13 Rajab) and the ʿurs celebrating the discovery of his relic (on 17 Rajab). The later celebration contains many rituals that Sufi Sunnis practice during the ʿurs rituals to venerate the bodily relic—primarily the tomb—of revered saints, especially the processions in which devotees bring drapery cloth (chadar), offerings of incense and precious substances (sandal), sweets, and other offerings most closely associated with wedding rituals. A major difference is that a Sufi ʿurs commemorates the death anniversary of the saint, whereas this ʿurs celebrates the moment when the site of ʿAli's handprint was discovered.[32]

Qawwali singing is performed at the tombs of Sunni Sufi masters, but it is also presented during the ʿurs of Mawla ʿAli. Qawwali is sung during the processions of the offerings through Hyderabad before they are taken up to the hilltop dargah of Mawla ʿAli (though it is unclear whether Qawwali is a recent addition to the ritual or was always present).[33] The ʿurs of Mawla ʿAli illustrates the success of "Desi" Shiʿi devotion to overlap creatively with both Sufi-Sunni devotion and Hindu devotion. This shrine was the pivot point for a syncretic religious culture that characterized Hyderabad and the wider Deccan region in premodern times. Desi Shiʿism and Sufism were expressions of "popular religion" among Muslims. At the level of formal theology as expressed in texts and sermons, there were stark differences between Sunnis and Shiʿis; when theologians, jurists, and sectarian leaders of the two communities spoke to each other, it was in terms of debate and tones of denunciation. But while acknowledging that differences were real, we must not overstate their impact. At the level of ritual, devotional performance, and celebration, the two communities could share so much that the boundary between them blurred or even dissolved.

View of Sunni and Shi'i Identities from a Mughal Garrison

At the shrine of Mawla 'Ali, Shi'is and Sunnis with a Sufi orientation came together in mutual camaraderie around their shared devotion to 'Ali and Husain. The shrine was both a physical site and a symbolic beacon, reminding residents of Hyderabad that 'Ali's blessing was wider than any sectarian cup held out to receive it. But in 1686 that sacred and political order was upset by Mughal invasion. That year, many Hyderabadis climbed up to the shrine of Mawla 'Ali to seek refuge. Mughal power pushed southward from Awrangabad while the Qutb-Shahi kings fended them off through alliances, bribes, and occasional military duels. However, these strategies ultimately failed. After Mughal conquest, the Shi'i character of Hyderabad was thrown into crisis. Although earlier Mughal emperors tried to develop a secular dynastic ethos (in which Hindu Rajput warriors and Shi'i Iranian statesmen could rise in rank as courtiers), later Mughal emperors drifted toward a harder Sunni identity. The chauvinist trend peaked under Awrangzeb, who conquered the Deccan.

Awrangzeb justified his conquest by attacking the morality, sectarian loyalty, and political allegiances of the Qutb-Shahi king Abu'l-Hasan Tana Shah (died 1688 in a Mughal prison). Awrangzeb's official historian wrote,

> Abu'l-Hasan, the ruler of Hyderabad, was stupid and sunk in sinful lust; misled by his evil fortune, he shut his eyes to the sins punishable in the next world, and made the vagabond Hindus the managers and administrators of the affairs of his State, and gave currency to the rites of that accursed race. And, those travelers in the wrong path of futile wondering and ignorance, those carrion-eating demons of the wilderness, namely the Persians [Shi'is], with the support of that worthless sect [Hindus], began to practice there publicly all kinds of shameful sins.[34]

In reality, Awrangzeb invaded Golkonda because of Abu'l-Hasan Tana Shah's policy of covertly supporting Maratha chieftains' in raiding Mughal domains. This was elaborately obscured by a Sunni sectarian explanation: the Qutb-Shahi king was a Shi'i, which corrupted his morality, allowed him to promote Hindus over Muslims, made him welcome emigrants from Shiʿi Iran, and led him to have the sermons during Friday prayers read in the name of the Safavid monarch.

Mughal forces pillaged Hyderabad while a protracted siege of the Golkonda fort lasted eight months. Awrangzeb's forces set up a command camp (a location now called Fateh Maidan or Field of Conquest) near the Husain Sagar reservoir and established a garrison inside the walled city (a neighborhood now called Mughalpura). Finally Abuʾl-Hasan Tana Shah surrendered: Hyderabad was absorbed into the Mughal Deccan province, and the last Qutb-Shahi king died in a Mughal prison and was buried in Khuldabad. Awrangzeb's historian described the state of destruction of Hyderabad, saying, "Of the men of Hyderabad, not a soul remained alive. Houses, river and plain became filled with the dead. . . . The survivors did not hesitate to eat the carrion of men and animals. Mile after mile, the eye fell on only mounds of corpses. The incessant rain melted away the flesh and the skin. . . . After some months when the rains ceased, the white ridges of bones looked from a distance like hillocks of snow."[35]

For almost a century, Hyderabad languished. The buildings of Shiʿi rulers of Hyderabad were largely destroyed; palaces were demolished and the ʿashur-khanas were looted of their ritual objects. Awrangzeb used as a prison house the Badshahi ʿAshur-Khana, or royal mourning hall that was built beside the royal palace in Hyderabad.[36] Its ʿalams had been forged of gold, studded with jewels, and wrapped in gold brocade cloth (*zarbafti*) with Qurʾanic verses woven into them. Awrangabad flourished with a renaissance of religious life, civic building, and literary ferment the effervescence of which Siraj witnessed and drew upon for his Sufi poetry. In contrast, Hyderabad suffered with a huge loss of population, a deep decay of civic structures, and closure of many religious sites and rituals. Mughal governors tightly controlled Shiʿi public rituals and let the city decline as a punishment for the resistance of Qutb-Shahi rulers. Many Mughal nobles had been injured or killed in the siege of Golkonda, including family members of Nizam al-Mulk Asaf-Jah (ruled 1724–48), the first nizam of the Deccan.[37]

Hyderabad weathered a hard century from 1686 until 1763. The fourth son of Nizam al-Mulk took the title of Asaf-Jah the Second and ruled from 1762 until 1803. This ruler, Nizam ʿAli Khan, shifted the capital from Awrangabad to Hyderabad soon after he came to power. There, Shiʿi devotional sites again received royal patronage, this time by a post-Mughal Sunni ruler who tailored his dynastic ethos to expectations of the local population, including an influential Shi'i population. The nizam had new *'alams* erected in the Badshahi 'Ashur-Khana.³⁸ During his rule, Mah Laqa Bai and her circle were active in building up the hilltop shrine of Mawla 'Ali on a grand scale. Female courtesans played a conspicuous role in reaffirming Shi'i devotion in Hyderabad, even though political power had passed into Sunni hands in the post-Mughal dispensation. In the military crisis of Mughal invasion, sectarian division between Shi'i and Sunni was exaggerated, yet the shared culture of 'Alid loyalty that thrived in the Deccan before Mughal rule persisted. Comparison between Shah Siraj and Mah Laqa Bai reveals that this shared culture not only survived beneath official rhetoric but reasserted itself once the Deccan region became independent under the nizams.

Even in Awrangabad, the center of Mughal power in the Deccan, we find signs of the resilience of this shared religious culture of reverence for 'Ali, Husain, and the imams. One such sign we find in Shah Siraj. At the climax of his love epic "The Fragrant Garden of Imagination," Siraj invokes the holy persons of the Prophet's family as revered in Shi'i devotion. To strengthen his resolve to renounce sexual and romantic attachments, he swears by each name of the "Fourteen Pure Ones" (*chahar-deh ma'sumin*) to whom the Shi'is swear loyalty: the Prophet; his daughter Fatima; her husband, 'Ali; and his eleven male descendants, who are the imams.³⁹ He even swears on the name of the *mahdi*, the last imam, who has disappeared from view without dying in order to give hope and guidance to those who suffer and who promises to come in the last days to reassert justice.

Shah Siraj and Mah Laqa Bai never met. Yet Sufis, especially those devoted to Qawwali, as was Siraj, did encounter and befriend Shi'i courtesans, who were dancers like Mah Laqa Bai. Her mother enjoyed the company of the Sufi artist Tajalli 'Ali Shah (1731–1800), while Mah Laqa Bai herself grew up under the tutelage of a singer whose repertoire included Qawwali, Khush-hal Khan (died 1822–23).⁴⁰ So the moon reflects the light of the sun. Siraj, in his autobiographical saga of lost love, "The Fragrant Garden of Imagination," depicts himself steeped in sorrow when he meets a troupe of courtesan dancers who try to ease his pain. So the sun shares its light with the moon.

In his Sufi love poetry, Shah Siraj expressed reverence for the imams. In her Desi Shi'i artistic life, Mah Laqa Bai expressed devotion to the imams through the conventions of love poetry. Though they never met, we can imagine them crossing paths. Would Siraj in pride recite his couplet, "Were the crescent moon polite, on seeing your brow / It would bow day or night when you meet with *salams*"?[41] Or would he hide in shame, reciting his couplet, "Looking at that moon faced beauty, Siraj, like a candle / I'm hiding shyly behind my own dripping beads of sweat"?[42] If the man who wrote as Siraj "the sun" would meet the woman who wrote as Chanda "the moon," they would contrast outwardly as implied by their poetic names. He was an ascetic and she a courtesan. His devotional heat and passion would contrast with her reverent coolness and grace. His earnest unself-consciousness would contrast with her polished artistry. His ecstatic gestures in gatherings of Qawwali at Sufi tombs would contrast with her sumptuous choreography in performances of dance in royal courts. Yet beneath these contrasts in appearance lie profound commonalities, as both struggled to express love through words and to embody love in deeds.

SECOND ORBIT

Mah Laqa the Moon

> He saw my moon-face lover and retreated in shame
> Give a saffron smear to the renunciant brow of the sun
> Since long I've given up my heart and soul for you
> Give my lips just a kiss, it's the least you could've done
>
> —*two couplets from a ghazal by Mah Laqa Bai*

This section of the book will focus on the life and personality, poetry, and dance of Mah Laqa Bai. Her given name was Chanda Bibi, but she is best known by her court title, Mah Laqa.[1] She wrote Urdu poetry under the pen name "Chanda." She was born in Hyderabad in 1768 and died there in 1824–25.[2] This half of the book—called the Second Orbit—observes the movements of this woman named after the moon. As her poem quoted above taunts, sometimes the moon eclipses the sun in beauty.[3] Thus this section leaves Shah Siraj to focus on the unique character and productive artistic life of Mah Laqa Bai. Its five chapters offer translations into English of her poetry. Urdu literature experts note her importance as one of the first women anywhere to compose a full divan of ghazals, but her poems are little known outside the Deccan. Few of her poems have been previously translated into English or analyzed in detail.

Histories of Urdu literature usually mention Mah Laqa Bai only as a female poet and then refer to her high social status and political savvy as a courtesan before moving on quickly to famous male poets. Few of them pause to consider how she deftly combined romantic and mystical themes in her love poems or why they almost always end with a gesture of loving devotion to ʿAli or Husain. As a Shiʿi poetess who blended mystical and devotional tones in Urdu love poems, Mah Laqa Bai is important enough to command more attention.[4]

There were many Shi'i poets in Urdu literature, but few of them so consistently spiced ghazals with devotional images. Rather, most Urdu poets who were Shi'is (and some who were Sunnis) wrote devotional poetry in the genre of marsiya or masnavi if they desired to pay honor to 'Ali, Husain, and other revered figures from the Prophet's family. Mah Laqa Bai challenges this split between genres. She also challenges received notions of women's roles in Islamic society, for she not only composed poetry and published it but also was a highly public personality in Hyderabad's courtly and religious life. Her love poems give us glimpses into her public roles as dance performer, adviser in politics, and patron of the arts. Mah Laqa Bai nudges us gracefully to keep our focus on the Deccan region, raising the question of whether women were given creative outlets and public roles in Islamic societies in the Deccan that may have been denied them elsewhere.

In the ghazal that opens her divan, Mah Laqa Bai professes to fall silent before the majesty of God, Muhammad, and the imams who perpetuate the Prophet's charismatic leadership. Yet she speaks eloquently about her inability to speak:[5]

> Who has the power to praise God, should a tongue try to speak
> > It's as if this world were nothing but silent and weak
> To tell Muhammad's virtue, who needs a poets' glittering gathering?
> > Keep the tongue from babbling, like a candle's glowing wick
> Take the path of praise, but you'll never step foot at its end
> > Though both youth and sage head out in this vastness to seek
> How can elegant thought arrive anywhere but its own incapacity?
> > So close your mouth, let eloquent tears roll down your cheek
> Who except the true One could express the beauty of the imams?
> > Such a hidden point, like Chanda the moon, stays at heaven's peak

Did her ardent love for the imams and adherence to Shi'i piety limit her public role as a woman and artist? This question of what constraints affected Muslim women becomes more urgent when we consider that another woman vied with her for the honor of being the "first female poet to compile a divan of Urdu ghazal," Lutf al-Nisa Imtiyaz from Awrangabad (died after 1798).[6] Together, these women poets force us to consider the Deccan as a site for women's creativity.

Mah Laqa Bai has an intriguing and rare personality as a courtesan, being a woman dedicated to love who never married. She offers a rich example of how a woman constrained by patriarchal demands of femininity manipulated them to achieve her artistic and spiritual goals. Courtesans rivaled men in the fields of wit, satire, fashion, and the arts, in South Asia as well as in other regions. Walter Andrews and Mehmet Kalpaklı argue that "the skills of the courtesan were many and varied—music, literature, rhetoric, and witty conversation. The courtesan was the public face of women engaged in the social arts of men."[7] It might surprise modern feminists to find that Mah Laqa Bai did not always speak in the voice of a woman; she mainly wrote poetry from the gendered voice of a man pursuing a beloved, though there are moments in her poems where this voice is reversed. Yet in each closing couplet she returns to a female person as "Ali's servant-girl." How to make sense of this bewildering exchange of gendered voices and roles? This requires a sustained look at her poetry and personality in the next five chapters.

Urdu poetry has given this Shi'i woman a uniquely powerful and subtle voice, when most of her fellow women "were nothing but silent and weak"—at least by their absence from historical narratives. Mah Laqa Bai, though, was in no way a typical woman of her time, her city, or her religious community. She emerged from an obscure family of marginalized outsiders to achieve a high position in the court of the second and third nizams in Hyderabad at the peak of its prosperity. She was an adept at music and dance as a courtesan, yet she upheld Shi'i piety in a kingdom that had recently been conquered by Sunni overlords.

Chapters 7 through 11 examine the paradox of a courtesan's combination of Shi'i piety, Urdu poetry, and seductive power. Mah Laqa Bai helped to create a dignified place for Shi'i devotion in a Sunni court through her poetry, patronage, and personality. These chapters translate and interpret her ghazals with their praise of Imam 'Ali, their allegiance

Mah Laqa Bai portrait, oil painting from the mid-nineteenth century, housed at the Archaeology Museum in Public Gardens, Hyderabad (photo by G. Shashidhar Reddy)

to the Sunni nizams, and their seductive power over leading men. Mah Laqa Bai's multidimensional life demands from us a multidisciplinary approach, drawing from the tools of religious studies, literary criticism, art history, and gender and sexuality studies.

Various material resources will aid in achieving this ambitious aim. First, there is Mah Laqa Bai's divan of love poems that has been published several times. Our ability to interpret the poems is deepened because an early manuscript exists (possibly written by her own hand) that she presented to a representative of the East India Company in Hyderabad; this edition of her divan was copied while she was still working on the collection and reveals an earlier version of some poems.[8] Thus we get a rare glance into her poet's workshop, see the growth of some poems, and acquire evidence of the evolution of Urdu.

The chapters that follow also examine texts written about Mah Laqa Bai during her lifetime and after her death. She herself commissioned the *Mah-nama* or "Moon Chronicle," which includes her detailed family history as part of the history of Hyderabad.[9] This was rendered from Persian into Urdu in 1894 as a biography, *Hayat-e Mah Laqa* or "The Life of Mah Laqa."[10] Modern scholars in Urdu have also written about her as an influential personality in Hyderabad's history with differing degrees of reformist zeal or feminist critique.[11] Descriptions of her personality were written by admirers, including the most powerfully placed, highly educated, and creative literati in the realm. In addition to literary, religious, and historical texts, we possess an artistic legacy of paintings that depict her and the buildings, both religious and secular, that she established. The most important of these buildings are religious structures at the hilltop shrine of Mawla ʿAli and her tomb garden at its base.[12]

Her other buildings include a manor house, a palace used to train female musicians and dancers, water wells, and other secular edifices, many of which have been destroyed or marred in Hyderabad's urban growth. Surveying this state of affairs, Mah Laqa Bai would wink with sly understanding and maybe sing her own verse, "Brokenness gets the highest honor on judgment day's seat." After all, she prayed for a splendid life in this world and salvation in the next, not immortality. As we begin to explore this elegant, articulate, and unconventional Islamic personality, let us listen to her whole ghazal:[13]

> When I heard word of his restlessness, my heart skipped a beat
>> My soul's tranquillity will return the moment our eyes meet
> My heart hardly believes the promise to one day meet my love
>> I'll just stroll rapt on blooming paths till that promise is complete
> It's been ages I've been sitting with this moon-rivaling beauty
>> But I've never had the chance for embraces firm or kisses sweet
> On the path of love, the heart is exhausted and run-down
>> Such brokenness gets the highest honor on judgment day's seat
> Oh 'Ali, in your magnanimity may you grant to Chanda
>> An empowered rank — in both worlds — one with dignity replete

CHAPTER SEVEN

Mah Laqa Bai's Radiance

Oh Ali, keep Chanda glowing with a ray of your brilliance
   As the sun is illumined each day as your radiance pours out
—*final couplet of a ghazal by Mah Laqa Bai*

The best way to start this chapter of Mah Laqa Bai is to watch a performance. Her dance performances at the turn of the nineteenth century were impossible to record. Yet Indian filmmakers have recreated the visual impact of courtesan dance. In films like *Mandi* and *Umrao Jaan*, vivid dance sequences are set against the tense ambivalence with which South Asian society has viewed courtesans.

Set in Hyderabad, *Mandi* (directed by Shyam Benegal in 1983) is about a brothel beset by modern changes. Rukmini Bai (played by Shabana Azmi) is the madam of a *kotha* (a "store house" signifying a brothel), which passed from control of a Muslim courtesan as madam to a Hindu courtesan with no change in character. Rukmini Bai raises the former madam's daughter, Zeenat (played by Smita Patel), as her own and trains her in singing. Other young women live there as dancers and prostitutes, along with an elderly lady, several children, and a drunk male attendant. The young women entertain men both artistically and sexually, but times are changing fast. Their new landlord wants to develop a shopping mall, and a feminist politician—Shanti Devi, the head of Nari Niketan or the Women's Advancement Society—is leading a moral crusade against them.

In one scene, Shanti Devi leads a political procession, chanting, "Prostitutes out of town!" In front of the kotha, she stands on a chair to give a speech: "Will we allow women to sell themselves in the market? We will never allow that! Never. I haven't come here today to give lectures. We will face this problem head on. We will go inside the brothel and make our sisters understand they have to leave this dirty work!" The activists enter the kotha and Shanti Devi announces, "You will have to shut down your business." Rukmini Bai answers, "Business? We are artists. It is in our very breath. Can we stop breathing if you ask us to?" The courtesans trick the activists and Rukmini Bai bids them farewell, promising to send a monetary donation to their reform association. She says to herself, "We are here because society is there. If you care so much, then go and keep the men indoors! If men were not buying, would women be selling themselves? Everyone blames only the women, but it is men who deceive."

In the next scene, Zeenat performs at an engagement party with Shanti Devi in the audience. Zeenat sings a ghazal with graceful movements and facial expressions (*abhinaya*) from dance theater. Rukmini Bai addresses the audience, "We are honored to have been invited tonight. We are fortunate to have been given this opportunity to perform our art before such respected citizens of our city. Unfortunately, some irresponsible persons are giving a bad name to our art. But we will keep our traditional art alive at any cost. Your encouragement is our inspiration! But some reckless people are trying to drive us from our very own city. I pity them because they don't understand music, rhythm, and melody."

Rumkini Bai's victory is only temporary, as social forces are working against her. The madam and her girls are faced with eviction, and they threaten to go to court. When their landlord offers Rukmini Bai a big sum to move, she reacts with passion: "Do you really value everything only with money? You value our art and tradition only with rupees? We, who remove the dirt from this society, only because of us are human relations preserved! We take away the loneliness of men every day. We give shelter to helpless women. And instead of helping us, you insult us by throwing money in our faces! Enemies are better than friends like you." The landlord persuades her to accept the money and move to an abandoned mansion outside of town, near the Mawla 'Ali shrine. At the foot of the sacred hill, Rukmini Bai discovers the abandoned tomb of a Sufi. She reveres him, and he blesses their endeavors. Soon the place is bustling with visitors. The tomb throngs with pilgrims and grows into a dargah with Qawwali ringing across the hills. In the film's music score, the Warsi Brothers — a famous Qawwali troupe based in Hyderabad — sing lyrics by Amir Khusro. The film's message is that modern changes and commercialization of human relationships have driven courtesans to become mere prostitutes, but they still symbolize the fertility and vivacity of society as a whole, even from their position as exiles.

Mandi is closely related to an earlier film, *Umrao Jaan* (directed by Muzaffar Ali in 1981). *Umrao Jaan* reflects similar issues through the lens of an earlier generation.[1] Set in the mid-nineteenth century, the film depicts the life of courtesans in Lucknow, which enjoyed cultural florescence before it was invaded by the British army in 1856. Its story is based on an Urdu novel by Mirza Hadi Rusva (died 1931).[2] A girl, kidnapped and sold to a brothel madam (played by Shaukat Azmi), is raised as Umrao Jaan (played by Rekha). She becomes famous for singing, dancing, and composing poetry. The director contrasts the aesthetically rich atmosphere of the brothel with the limitations of autonomy for the women involved; despite the rigorous grace in which the courtesans perfect their arts, the limits to their autonomy are enforced by convention and violence.

In one scene the madam of the kotha, who lives in aristocratic splendor, has just purchased the frightened girl, who is sitting next to her. The madam says to her elderly aid, Husaini, "I would say 250 Rupees for this girl is not so expensive. . . . Her face is quite innocent. God only knows from where these fellows get such girls. They have no fear of God at all. Husaini, I'm completely innocent in this! These sleazy brutes are the ones who commit a sin. Why should we concern ourselves? If not here, she would have been sold to somewhere else." Husaini consoles her, "She will lead a sublime life here. . . . Give this girl to me and I'll bring her up. She will belong to you, but I'll nurture her." Under the umbrella of royal patronage, the commercial side of their entertaining is not contradictory to the artistic side, as it appears to be in *Mandi*.

The girl's name is changed to Umrao Jan, a name befitting a courtesan. She learns singing with an *ustad* (master musician) and studies religion with a *mawlvi* (Shi'i religious teacher) who stays at the kotha. Her *mawlvi* guides her to compose poetry and teaches her the ghazal of Siraj that initiated chapter 2: "Hear news of love's bewilderment: no beauty remains, no feverish madness / No you remains, no I remains—all that remains is unself-consciousness." The *mawlvi* uses this poem to teach her about love, both romantic and spiritual.

The film shows Umrao Jan's budding encounters with love of all varieties: commercial, romantic, and sexual. It explores the cultural tension between prostitute and performer in the life of a nineteenth-century courtesan. In one scene, Umrao Jan is in a room of the kotha, lounging with a client who has become her lover, Navvab Sultan. While she sings to him a poem that she has set to music, a soldier enters brusquely and demands, "Keep singing, why have you stopped? Don't consider me a stranger. . . . I've come to hear you sing. . . . The brothel of a harlot is a public place. It is not the right of any one man." The courtesan's caretaker argues, "The brothel of a harlot belongs to anyone who can spend lavishly enough!" The soldier retorts, "Does that mean I'm reluctant to spend?" and begins to insult the caretaker and Umrao Jan.

To defend her honor, Navvab Sultan kills the soldier and takes shelter at a friend's home, to which he calls Umrao Jan. But the ladies of the house confront her, resenting her presence. An older female servant asks, "Madam, who is this girl?" The mistress's daughter replies, "What has it to do with you?" The servant retorts, "As if I don't know who she is! Who doesn't know her?" Umrao Jan asks sarcastically, "Why ask if you already know who I am?" The older servant says, "Hey lady, was I talking to you? I was speaking to the mistress of this, my house. Who am I to speak to one such as you? You're such a lofty person!" The mistress's daughter responds to the servant's insults, "Are you going to leave now or do you want me to whack you with my slipper?" Umrao Jan intervenes, "Dear lady, never mind her—she has no manners." The servant then attacks the courtesan verbally, "You harlot, how dare you speak to me! I'll grab your braid and strangle you to death!"

As the mistress's daughter beats the servant with her slipper, the mistress asks what the commotion is about. The old servant wails, "This slut got her to beat me!" The mistress's daughter thinks her mother will take her side and reprimand the servant, but instead the mistress says, "My daughter, you beat up this wretched old soul for no reason at all, and that too for the sake of a courtesan?" The old servant wails, "That is just what I was saying! Such women are never to be trusted! Better to avoid even their shadows." The mistress takes sides with the old servant woman who called the courtesan a harlot (*randi*) rather than the more cultured term for courtesan (*tava'if*). She asserts that courtesans should not enter respectable homes; they are a threat to married women and work against their interests.

These films reveal an enduring truth about courtesans in premodern South Asia. Courtesans struggled to live in the ambiguous space between performer and prostitute. From their own viewpoint and that of their supporters, they were artistic performers first and foremost, and in premodern times this view prevailed. But at the same time, from the viewpoint of conventional women and many male clients, the courtesans were considered prostitutes who, even if they did not sell their bodies for sex, still displayed their bodies through performing dance in ways that were considered immoral. In modern times, this view has predominated, though there are some who mourn the decline of the artistic tradition of poetry, song, and dance that the courtesans upheld.[3]

In these films, both women could be both pious from a spiritual point of view and suspect from a social point of view. The courtesan, even as she was accused of prostitution or loose morals, was a recognized social role and played a part in the religious life of the community. In *Mandi*, the courtesans and prostitutes respect holy persons and places, and the pilgrims who come there accept them as an integral part of the social landscape. In *Umrao Jaan*, the courtesans mix freely with respected *mawlvis*, religious teachers and literary scholars. They are recognized as having artistic talent and spiritual merit beyond financial or sexual dealings, and they deferentially cease entertaining during the holy months of Muharram and Ramazan. Even earlier than Umrao Jan, we have the life of Mah Laqa Bai, the grandest example of a courtesan living up to her full potential. She lived at a time before colonial occupation and its imposition of Victorian values of prudery, utilitarianism, and social reform. In those times, a courtesan could be at one and the same time a performer, a sexually available woman, and a spiritual agent.

Mah Laqa Bai's Traces

Courtesans continue to live in the vivid colors of Indian cinema. However, that medium distorts their persons with the prejudices of modern filmmakers and audiences. To search for the real Mah Laqa Bai, we can turn to actual material remains. Mah Laqa Bai's religious aspirations and public persona are reflected in her buildings on Mawla ʿAli hill, the best place to begin looking for Mah Laqa Bai's traces. Mawla ʿAli hill is integral to her birth and also to her death; at the shrine atop the hill she worshipped and in a garden at the foot of the hill she built a monumental tomb for her mother and herself.

Mah Laqa Bai and her circle, including her adopted courtesan daughter, Husn Laqa Bai, and her music professor, Khush-hal Khan, patronized a burst of building activity on the hill.[4] On the east side of the hill, where stairs are cut out of the rock, is a ceremonial archway build by Khush-hal Khan. Its inscription reads

> To decorate the lofty shrine, with pure intent and sincerity
> He built a mosque, an ʿashur-khana and grand archway
> What a good fate that Khush-hal Khan has built
> On this noble hill with good planning and sacrificial soul[5]

The last line of this quatrain gives in *abjad* notation the date of construction: AH 1238, equivalent to 1822.⁶

At the shrine on the hill, Mah Laqa Bai extended in stone masonry a covered hall (*dalan*) that had originally been built in timber by the third nizam, Sikandar Jah (ruled 1803–29), and his uncle Nasir al-Dawla. Mah Laqa Bai's daughter, Husn Laqa Bai, built a reservoir for cool drinking water (*abdar-khana*) midway up the stairs. While Mah Laqa Bai was still alive in 1803–4, she constructed an elaborate well and reservoir along the route that pilgrims traveled to reach Mawla ʿAli from Hyderabad. The description of this structure makes clear its devotional intent:

> Another of the inventions of this leader of beauties is a reservoir called "For the Path of God." It is located on the path taken by pilgrims heading to visit that hill that is the splendor of the heavens, which belongs to the Wine-Pourer of paradise, The Leader of humans and spirits, the Fearless Lion of skillful means, the Heir of the Prophet, namely ʿAli—upon him be blessings and peace. The reservoir is filled to overflowing with a constant flow of water that is so pure . . . that it expresses the meaning of the verse, *This one that is sweet that subdues thirst by its purity* (Qurʾan 25:53). By the continual play of its ripples, one can understand the verse, *They shall drink from a spring that is called salsabil* (Q 76:18). Those whose lips drink its waters call out *Indeed we have created all living things of water* (Q 21:30). With ecstatic joy they lift their cups according to the verse, *They may drink of a pure wine sealed with a sealing fragrant as musk* (Q 83:25).⁷

These Qurʾanic citations picture those who enjoy salvation drinking from the springs of paradise, which flow with sweet water and fragrant wine. ʿAli pours cups of this drink for those entering into paradise. Mah Laqa Bai weaves these scriptural associations together in one of her ghazals:⁸

> Saqi is busy pouring but without potency is the wine
>   Without my lover's gaze what joy is there in wine
> On whose murder are you intent as you send out today
>   Youth's vigorous beauty mounted on cantering wine
> Let one glance of your forgiveness fall on a criminal
>   Who has drunk to the dregs uncountable cups of wine
> Oh saqi, just for a moment meet the eyes of one
>   Who desires again and again nothing but wine
> At resurrection time, Oh ʿAli, won't you give Chanda
>   A sip from paradise's pure delightful wine?

This delightful wine is *ab-e kawsar*, which flows from the spring of paradise. It is a wine that is easy to digest (*khush-guvar*) and leaves no hangover, instead refreshing and reviving the soul with each draught.[9] With rich symbolic association, shared by Shi'is and Sufis, the reservoir that Mah Laqa Bai built added sacred power to the holy shrine.

Mah Laqa Bai's Persona

Though most courtesans were Shi'is, Mah Laqa Bai had an especially intense devotion to 'Ali as the charismatic lord of Mawla 'Ali hill, evident in her buildings on and around the shrine. Her intense devotion was due to her mother's influence and the circumstances of her birth. Her mother was born in Gujarat, the daughter of an administrative officer under the Mughal governor of Ahmedabad. Chapter 9 will explore their turbulent family history; here it is enough to note that she along with her mother and two sisters were abandoned by their father, fell into poverty, fled Ahmedabad, and were adopted by a roving band with whom they wandered south into the Deccan. In one of her poems, Mah Laqa Bai mentions such desert nomads, like the gypsy-like *bhagat* minstrels from whom her family learned to sing and dance:[10]

> When into the tavern with jug in hand my moon-faced lover comes
> > How strange that even to ascetics the yearning to sip wine comes
> If this crazed nomad leaves the desert to head in toward town
> > Each urbanite who's lost in frenzy suddenly to his senses comes
> So deep have I suppressed my love for that veiled beauty
> > I fear my heart's sigh into her range of hearing never comes
> Her face bright as a mirror is adorning our party after so long
> > If any pious preacher knocks, tell him "Each in silence comes"
> I'll toss the record of Chanda's deeds into passion's churning waves
> > If 'Ali, the forgiver of my sins, with a wine-cup my way comes

The girls learned music and dance from the wandering minstrels (*bhagatiyan*) and headed back to the cities. They joined the army of Nizam al-Mulk Asaf-Jah, the first nizam of Hyderabad. Among its nobles, they achieved fame for their beauty, grace, and artistry, rising to the status of star courtesans.

Mah Laqa Bai's mother was named Raj Kanvar Bai (died 1792–93). She settled in Hyderabad and married a nobleman at advanced age, around fifty years. She became pregnant, though it appears that her husband died or disappeared before Mah Laqa Bai was born. Her mother almost died in this pregnancy, and her miraculous survival attests to her family's strong links to Shiʿism and to the persistence of local Desi Shiʿi devotion in Hyderabad despite the ostensibly Sunni rule of the nizams after the Mughal conquest:

> During the time when Raj Kanvar Bai was pregnant with Mah Laqa Bai, she went to the hill of Mawla ʿAli for *ziyarat* to Amir al-Muʾminin [ʿAli]. She was with Shah Tajalli ʿAli, the author of *Tuzuk-e Asafiyya* or "Pomp and Order of the Asaf-Jahi Dynasty," an illustrated history that describes the restoration of Hyderabad. Tajalli ʿAli Shah was a scholar and sage, calligrapher and painter, who was unique in his era for wit and wisdom—who was riding along with her because of his relation to her as depending on her patronage. Suddenly, the signs of an impending miscarriage came over Raj Kanvar Bai, and she began to bleed. Tajalli ʿAli Shah immediately rushed into the holy court of Murtaza [ʿAli]. He took from there pieces of string and burning incense. He came out and tied the string around Raj Kanvar Bai's waist and wafted the incense toward her. By these simple actions, there occurred a miraculous intervention by ʿAli, the conquering lion of God, may peace be upon him. The blood stopped flowing and the fetus stayed firmly in place.[11]

Shah Tajalli ʿAli, who wrote *Tuzuk-e Asafiyya*, was a noted poet, calligrapher, and painter in the court of the second nizam. Their crisis at Mawla ʿAli illustrates the persistence of an overlapping Desi Shiʿi and Sufi Sunni devotional life in Hyderabad. Tajalli ʿAli was ostensibly a Sunni but, as a Chishti Sufi, he was deeply devoted to ʿAli as a charismatic leader and spiritual guide.[12] He accompanied Raj Kanvar Bai, a Shiʿi courtesan turned wife of a Mughal noble. As friends, they could make the pilgrimage together to the shrine of Mawla ʿAli, where sectarian differences were muted in the radiance of ʿAli's spiritual presence in the local landscape.

Thanks to the miraculous intervention of ʿAli and the healing touch of a Sufi friend, Raj Kanvar Bai survived her miscarriage crisis. Thus on April 4, 1768 (20 Ẓuʾl-Qaʾda, AH 1181), a girl was born and named Chanda Bibi.[13] Her mother gave the girl to be raised by her eldest daughter, Mahtab Kanvar Bai. Mahtab Kanvar Bai was a courtesan who used her seductive grace to maximum advantage by entering the household of a Shiʿi nobleman as a secondary wife; she was his constant companion even in public spectacles of hunting or war. This nobleman, Rukn al-

Dawla, served as prime minister for a decade until he was assassinated in 1775. After this, Mahtab Kanvar Bai lived in his estate in wealthy luxury, yet she had no children of her own.

Mah Laqa Bai's mother knew that Mahtab Kanvar Bai could provide a richer and securer home for her baby than she herself could. Perhaps she gave the girl away in order to retire from worldly cares, as she was already an elderly woman and wished to pursue religious devotions. The sources are ambiguous on the exact reasons:

> Raj Kanvar Bai dedicated herself to worship and invoking God. Although . . . Raj Kanvar Bai has had her name recorded in the register of professional earners (*kasabi*), she always retained the good judgment and moral refinement of her pure pedigree. As long as she lived, she kept the five-times daily prayers, and continually engaged in litanies, recitations, glorifications and praises for God. She was a devoted follower of pious sages and learned scholars. In the end, her companionship with pious ascetics (*ahl-e suluk*) and mystics (*ahl-e batin*) rubbed off on her. She took on their qualities such that most of her time was spent in the hard work of intuitive understanding, contemplation and mystical imagination. She would stay up to the end of the night reciting her litany (*vazifa*) and would speak with nobody.[14]

With her mother retired from the world and focused on God, Mah Laqa Bai was raised in the household of the nizam's prime minister under the care of her half sister, Mahtab Kanvar Bai, who was more like her aunt in age. We do not know whether Mah Laqa ever met her mother again until she died in 1792 or 1793, when Mah Laqa Bai was around twenty-four years old.

Mah Laqa Bai honored her mother by building a highly decorative mausoleum, in a *barah-dari* or open square pavilion with three arches on each side (in which her own tomb was later added). She had the tomb designed with no stone covering but only a body-sized rectangle of dirt exposed, along with a dedication plaque. This design was typical for courtesans, whose status after death was revealed, as it was in life, by their being left uncovered. The mausoleum was surrounded by gardens, with a gateway leading into the compound, symmetrical pleasure pavilions on the right and left, and a small reservoir of water and a jewel-like small mosque behind the tomb. Poetic inscriptions give the date of the mausoleum as 1793–94 CE, but the grand gateway was built in 1824–25,

Pavilion housing the tomb of Mah Laqa Bai and her mother, Raj Kanvar Bai, located at the foot of Mawla 'Ali Hill outside Hyderabad (photo by Scott Kugle)

just after Mah Laqa Bai's death.[15] She had Persian couplets inscribed over the gate, memorializing the year of her mother's death:

> Raj Kanvar, the slave-girl of 'Ali, King of men
>   Was in generosity and morals better than the next . . .
> If one says this, the year of her death is fixed
>   "Come now, that helpless old woman God nixed."

As a chronogram, this final couplet must provide — by adding up the numerical value, according to the *abjad* system, of each letter in the line — the date of death of her mother.

Beyond the simple information that Mah Laqa Bai had her mother's tomb complex built and in which year she died, this poem reveals two characteristics of Mah Laqa Bai's personality that she learned from the women who shaped her early life. The first characteristic is a flirtatious pride in her beauty and grace; this she must have learned from her half sister who raised her, Mahtab Kanvar Bai, who had known her two aunts who were experts in music, dance, and seduction. The second characteristic is a spiritual piety that is devoted to 'Ali; this devotion she learned from her mother, who gave her away in infancy to pursue mystical insight and draw closer to God through love for 'Ali. Passionate devotion to 'Ali is an element of all Shi'i devotion, but for the courtesans it seems to have been especially intense.

Mah Laqa Bai's Voice

Though Mah Laqa Bai was only one of throngs who came to Mawla ʿAli to express their love and distress, she expressed more eloquently than most the ambivalent emotions of one who loved ʿAli. This is because she did so from the position of a courtesan and dancer in the actual royal court. This gave her voice a particular articulateness, since she was raised in the highly aesthetic climate of the royal courtesans. It also gave her voice a specific strength, because her words were amplified by her wealth and status as a court noble. Finally, it gave her words a unique intensity, as she composed poetry expressing her love of ʿAli as a perpetually single woman, beyond the routine roles patriarchy assigned to women as daughter, wife, mother, and widow.

Mah Laqa Bai's elder half sister raised her in a mansion called Zenana Devrhi or Women's Manor, where she must have received the best aesthetic education that money and prestige could buy. She was taught Persian, wrote poetry in Urdu, learned dance, and studied classical music under her instructor, Khush-hal Khan, a Shiʿi musician who was an exponent of Dhrupad and Khayal styles of singing (*kalavant*). She also associated with her mother's old friend Tajalli ʿAli Shah, the poet, historian, and illustrator.

As she matured, Chanda Bibi entered aristocratic circles as a courtesan and dancer, attracting the fond attention of the second Asaf-Jahi nizam, who took her as a confidante and companion. She was introduced into the intimate circle of the nizam by the new prime minister, Aristu Jah (died 1804), a Shiʿi nobleman originally named Ghulam Sayyid Khan whose title means "Like Aristotle in Magnificence" and who had been present at the celebrations of Chanda Bibi's birth.[16] These included her *chhati shab* (on the sixth day after birth, when the house is cleaned, the mother and child are bathed, the midwife is given gifts, and the baby is named) and her *ʿaqiqa* ceremony (when an infant's hair is first cut and the baby is initiated into Islam).[17] The nobleman took an interest in her as her earliest biography records: "With the attention and dedication and generous patronage of the Deccan prince and his prime minister, the radiance of Chanda Bibi grew more intense, like the light of a waxing moon."[18] This suggests that Aristu Jah, the Shiʿi prime minister, was grooming Mah Laqa Bai to get close to the nizam, a Sunni ruler. Perhaps his political strategy was to influence a ruler through female companions.

During the Nawroz celebration of the Persian New Year in 1802 (AH 1217), when Mah Laqa Bai was about thirty-five years old, a celebration was held to honor soldiers and courtiers with gifts, titles, and grants after the nizam returned from a campaign. Nawroz was one of the most important festivals. Since Qutb-Shahi times it had been an occasion for rulers to show off their wealth and prestige in the spring season. At this occasion, Chanda Bibi was the star performer. After her dance, the nizam gave her the formal court title Mah Laqa Bai or "Madam Moon Cheek." Aristu Jah, who had been promoting her, suggested her new title as an appropriate amplification of her given name, Chanda Bibi or "Miss Moon-Light." Along with a title, she was given extensive land grants (*jagir*) both within the city and in the countryside, which made her independently wealthy. She became a courtier (*navvab*) with signs of royal authority, such as an honorary guard and kettledrums to clear the road before her palanquin.[19] Mah Laqa Bai owed her fate to the patronage of Aristu Jah, but she also paid homage to the nizam who shifted the capital of the Deccan province to Hyderabad, away from Awrangabad and its closeness to Mughal rule.

Though Nizam ʿAli Khan never declared independence from the Mughal Empire, he reigned as de facto king. At the new court in Hyderabad, the second Asaf-Jah began to hold sumptuous festivities in the style of independent kings. He reintroduced many of the local Deccan celebrations that had been hallmarks of the Qutb-Shahi reign, including specifically Shiʿite festivals like ʿAshura and the ʿurs of Mawla ʿAli. They also included Hindu festivals, like Basant, the spring festival. Although they were Sunni rulers, the nizams gradually restored the composite religious culture that had been torn by Awrangzeb's invasion, as described in chapter 6.

In one Basant celebration, Mah Laqa Bai perhaps danced in honor of the nizam and used the occasion to present her own ghazal:[20]

> Spring is here, with wine's arousal and waves of blossoms kissing
> With God's bounty, of luxury, rapture and bliss nothing's missing
> Great God in heaven, how should I describe his dwelling place?
> He whose party has been ordained tonight by fate's impressing
> He fulfills whatever desires anyone's heart may harbor
> In this era, the generosity of none is more promising
> The savior of us all, nizam of the realm, called Asaf-Jah
> May he live long as Khizr, with the twelve imams' blessing

> Chanda always hopes you'll give from your platter of bounty
> She asks only to never turn to another in moments distressing

She praises the nizam as the savior (*masih*) who, like Jesus, can blow a life-reviving breath into a corpse. The second Asaf-Jahi ruler, Nizam ʿAli Khan, did restore Hyderabad after its long recovery from Mughal destruction. He did so by bringing back court rituals and religious festivities that depended so heavily on music, dance, spectacle, and poetry.

Mah Laqa Bai praises the nizam with religious imagery that hints at the profound revival of the composite culture of the Deccan. She cites Khizr, the mysterious visionary figure who represented to Sufis the eternal wisdom of inspiration that enlivens all the saints. She asks that the nizam may live as long as Khizr, who was granted eternal life to appear in new guises in each age. Though Khizr appears in the Qurʾan, and thus is acknowledged by all Muslims, his personality is most central to Sufis, and their literature develops his character most fully.[21] After this bow to Sufis, who are mainly Sunni, Mah Laqa Bai immediately invokes the twelve imams of Shiʿism, asking that the nizam's long life be made into just rule with their blessings. Both Sufi and Shiʿi images grace a poem whose opening line places it in a celebration of Basant, a holiday dedicated to Saraswati, the Hindu goddess of arts and music.

Despite this rhetorical praise of a composite religious culture, there was most likely subtle tension between a Sunni ruler and Shiʿi courtiers around him. In these poems, which were probably presented publicly in court, Mah Laqa Bai does not praise ʿAli as spiritual king prominently in the last couplet, as she otherwise does. It was part of her greater role, above her art and sexuality, to help maintain this delicate balance between Shiʿi and Sunni in the kingdom. With Shiʿis as a minority recently displaced from power by a Sunni dynasty, her community's survival depended on a counterpoint of self-assertion and self-restraint, not unlike her dances.

Mah Laqa Bai's Role

As a courtesan, Mah Laqa Bai's role at court was multidimensional. She was a dancer, musician, wit, adviser, and patron in both religious and artistic pursuits. She was also extremely adept in court politics.[22] Her poetry reflects these many roles, and her ghazals integrate Shiʿi spirituality into the seemingly secular activities of courtly life, dance, and romantic love. She chose to write only in the ghazal form. Each of her ghazals consists of only five couplets, reflecting the five members of the holy family: the Prophet; his daughter Fatima; her husband, 'Ali; and their two sons, Husain and Hasan (died 670). With the exception of a few overtly political poems offered to her patrons, the fifth and final couplet of each poem is devoted to praising 'Ali. The final couplet shows its author, Mah Laqa Bai with the pen name Chanda, in a posture of intimacy with 'Ali as his servant, supplicant, extoller, or loyal partisan.

Parts of Mah Laqa Bai's personality are revealed through her poems, even though ghazals are not in general autobiographical. Much contemporary Urdu literary criticism disparages the use of ghazals for building a biographical sketch of the poet. Yet Walter Andrews and Mehmet Kalpaklı note that ghazals are more utilitarian than often acknowledged. These poems had a "double nature" in being both aesthetic creation and social currency:

> They are produced both for idealistic, aesthetic purposes and for the most mundane of goals—to make a living, to attract a patron, to ask for a job, to write a letter, to celebrate an occasion, to seduce a beloved, to impress a friend.... This is precisely what we want to suggest about Ottoman poetry: that the divan represents an illusion (that the techniques of poetry are universal, ideal, and eternal) and that Ottoman poetry is most interesting and, in a sense, universal when it is embedded and understood in the context of the raw complexity of Ottoman life.[23]

Although Walters and Kalpaklı discuss Ottoman-era poetry in Turkish, their insights hold also for Mughal-era poetry in Urdu.

The dynamic is the same, and pursuing this comparison in the Deccan, we find that this idea that poetry has dual uses (social reflection and imaginative construction) applies to Urdu literature in eighteenth-century South Asia just as it does to Turkish literature in sixteenth-century Ottoman realms. Mah Laqa Bai's ghazals also have this dual nature—they function both as formal creations (of rhyme, rhythm, and imagery) and as social interaction (of shared discourse, social competition, and bids for admiration).

Her poems are most interesting when seen as embedded in the raw complexity of post-Mughal life in the Deccan. One can see Mah Laqa Bai's experience as a dancer in this poem:[24]

> Cups of crimson wine are circling in rounds of dance
>   If the beloved is glimpsed, this party abounds in dance
> God has made this beloved peerless in my view
>   Everything before my eyes resounds with dance
> You captivate beasts and birds along with people low and high
>   Each in its way obeys your command in bounds of dance
> Leave the party of my rivals and come over to mine
>   I'll show you a star whose very name sounds like dance
> Why shouldn't Chanda be proud, O 'Ali, in both worlds?
>   At home with you she eternally astounds with dance

As a dancer, Mah Laqa Bai crafted a public role for herself in Hyderabad. She gained access to the court through dance and became intimate with various powerful nobles. In this poem, she alludes to her own role as court dancer in many different ways. In a secular setting, she entertained drinking parties: "Cups of crimson wine are circling in rounds of dance."

Dance at court was not merely entertainment; it was a political spectacle. The beauty and grace of performers reflected the wealth, power, and dominance of patrons; in this poem, the king on the throne is the center of a vast dance where all are subject to his control—"You captivate beasts and birds along with people low and high / Each in its way obeys your command in bounds of dance." The ruler is compared to the archetypal Islamic sovereign, the Prophet Sulaiman (King Solomon), whose command subjected even birds, beasts, and forces of nature. Charming opponents into cooperation through aesthetic display was just as important as forcing them into submission through military power. The second Asaf-Jah, Nizam 'Ali Khan, understood this perfectly. His court historian, the poet and illustrator Tajalli 'Ali Shah, recorded many incidents in which crucial diplomacy was conducted through the "Music Tent" (*muzrib khiyam*). He sent his prime minister, Rukn al-Dawla, to negotiate with their staunch enemies, the Marathas. Rukn al-Dawla made an alliance with Madho Rao, the new Maratha chieftain (ruled 1774–95), in his pleasure pavilions along a riverbank illuminated with glittering lamps that reflected in the water. He hosted many nights of dance, and Tajalli 'Ali records that this tent "was the envy of those who dwelled in the city [Pune]." Tajalli 'Ali included in his official history beautifully painted miniatures showing the dancers, and he writes, "Wherever one turned one's eyes there was nothing but the sparkle of lamps. Wherever one turned one's ears there was nothing but heart-delighting melodies. His lordship [Rukn al-Dawla] took the Maratha chieftain, Madho Rao, with him into a boat for a pleasure cruise and gave him many gifts [a royal robe and jewels] and gold coins."[25] Rulers used dancers to extend their power, but the dancer also had her own agenda: to charm and seduce powerful men. Mah Laqa Bai teases, "Leave the party of my rivals and come over to mine." Finally, Mah Laqa Bai ends on a spiritual note, addressing the apparent contradiction between humility required before Imam 'Ali and the proud display needed for a dancer. She achieves a resolution by attributing her every success, even in public performance, to her intimacy with 'Ali—"At home with you she eternally astounds with dance."

Dance was an integral part of court ceremony to mark victory celebrations after war, the Nawroz festival that was celebrated with pomp, and court gatherings to impress visiting diplomats or conduct negotiations with rivals. The paintings in Tajalli 'Ali Shah's *Tuzuk-e Asafiyya* show female dancers and musicians accompanying the nizam in affairs of war, trips for hunting, diplomatic envoys, and other state events.[26] One image shows the nizam and his courtiers, including Aristu Jah the prime minister, ready to enjoy a dance by Mah Laqa Bai on the banks of the Husain Sagar reservoir in Hyderabad, after a hunting expedition with royal women.[27]

Her art as a dancer thus gave Mah Laqa Bai a public role in warfare. She accompanied the second nizam on various campaigns and is reported to have ridden with him on his elephant. When not fighting against the state's enemies, the nizam and his courtiers were fighting against animals in the wilderness to prove their armed expertise. He took her with him, as she was an expert archer as well. Hunting was a prime metaphor for romantic pursuits, in which Mah Laqa Bai also excelled, as witnessed by this poem:[28]

> In a flash I'd release from captivity each prey
>   If I could hunt my hunter, O God, for just a day
> News of spring's arrival comes to me in my cage
>   Not a feather is left intact in my excited fray
> What net of curls could capture such a clever heart?
>   Its fated hour comes, it gets caught without delay
> Except for you, no other has ever caught my eye
>   Yet you captured this gazelle, my heart, from far away
> Let Chanda be ever your captive, not that of her enemies
>   Mawla 'Ali, for only this in all the world does Chanda pray

Between hunting for gazelles and being hunted by lovers, Mah Laq Bai's poetry unfolds. In this particular ghazal, she takes the point of view of the captive victim of a skillful hunter. The speaker in the poem imagines wistfully how to change the ways of the world "if I could hunt my hunter, O God, for just a day." But later, the speaker revels in being caught and reveals that her lover's glance is the most skillful weapon to capture a heart. Finally, as always, she rises to a spiritual register and prays to be the prey of 'Ali, that valiant warrior and marksman. If so, then all others who hunt her will miss their mark.

Mah Laqa Bai had reason to mention enemies, for succeeding at court was not just a matter of dancing but also depended upon outmaneuvering enemies, rivals, and detractors. As a court noble, she was subject to the intrigues and jealousies of rivals. As a courtesan, she could fully trust no man as a patron or protector, and there is evidence in her witticisms that have been preserved that she had to parry derision and criticism in court and in public, aimed at her vulnerability as a single woman and public performer.[29] The only male figure she could rely upon was 'Ali, her spiritual patron and the essence of masculinity in her view, as reflected in this poem:[30]

> If my sigh would just have an effect on you, my hunter
>   There'd remain in the heart no trace of your injustice, my hunter
> It was I myself who got caught up in your net, because
>   When have you ever thought of catching me, my hunter?
> Since forever my fluttering heart desired only your snare
>   Won't you forget your neglect and pass this way, my hunter?
> With an exhilarating shudder, your quarry now gives up the soul
>   Another breath might come when you take notice, my hunter
> This is all I ask of you, O 'Ali, so just let this moment be
>   Dawn for Chanda and sunset for her enemies, my hunter

Hunting is a dangerous game, just like politics. These poems display the overtly political aspects of Mah Laqa Bai's life at court. She petitions 'Ali for protection and for victory over her rivals in the very same poems in which she speaks of romance and intimacy between lover and beloved.

As a courtesan, her love games with men were always a veiled form of manipulating them so that she could get wealth, status, and power. Another ghazal shows how well she realized that the play of seduction was also the play of politics:[31]

> Why make a drama of reaching for your sword?
>> My head is a bubble on the rippling current of your sword
> Don't summon her healing glance to salve my heart's wound
>> Her saber tongue makes incisions as sharp as any sword
> I stood strong, leading the corps of your lovers
>> Till my head fell at your feet as if before a double sword
> To those half-gone in throes of love a breath of life remains
>> Have mercy, glance their way as a coup de grâce's sword
> O 'Ali, grant prestige to those who wish Chanda well
>> Those who show her ill will, guide their heads to the sword

This poem not only shows her knowledge of martial affairs at court and in the army but also reveals that she had enemies in court as well as patrons. She beseeches 'Ali not only to reward her patrons and well-wishers but to degrade and destroy her enemies and those who regard her with ill-will. With powerful patrons at court—like Aristu Jah—she would not have to face open threats, but due to her status as a single woman, performer, and courtesan, she had much to fear from those who attacked her reputation through sexuality, back-biting, and gossip.

Conclusion

Mah Laqa Bai's multifaceted personality added radiance to the court life of the second and third nizams of Hyderabad. She was a poet who also patronized other writers. She was a singer and dancer who turned her skills to not only devotional but also political aims. An astute politician and adviser to the nizams, her presence helped to balance out potential conflict between Sunni and Shi'i forces in the Deccan kingdom. She enacted all these roles from her social position as a courtesan who, by all accounts, was considered the most beautiful woman of her age in Hyderabad.

There is no firm count of how many powerful men Mah Laqa Bai charmed or seduced. Among them are two prime ministers of Iranian immigrant ancestry in the court of the second nizam. The next chapter will explore her relationship with male patrons, showing how she drew them close to her. She polished her appearance in order to increase her brilliance. In retrospect, her biographers noted that she radiated beauty from her very birth: "On a Monday when the sun was at its zenith . . . a girl as beautiful as a heavenly maid clothed in moonlight was born.

Astrologers gave her the name Chanda Bibi. Historians have recorded that, at the moment of her birth, there was such a bright light that the whole room was illumined. All those present for the birth witnessed this and were amazed."[32] This was no doubt a hagiographic embellishment to make seem inevitable her eventual greatness. However, her beauty's radiant light drew men close to her much like a candle's glow will draws moths, to their delight and peril. Did men use her, or did she use men? That is a question that will occupy us in the coming chapter.

CHAPTER EIGHT

Mah Laqa Bai's Men

> Because it is said a rose grows in this valley of love
>   The traveler's foot continues to search for its thorn
> Mawla 'Ali, give from your treasure of generosity enough
>   To keep Chanda from searching for another patron
>
> —*two verses from a ghazal by Mah Laqa Bai*

Mah Laqa Bai achieved fame through her arsenal of talent, but talent is worthless without an audience to reward it. The audience for her talents was entirely male. She accrued power by securing patronage through intimacy with powerful men, as she alludes to in this poem quoted above.[1] She relied upon male patronage despite the fact that her family and household consisted almost entirely of women. This chapter explores her relationship with men—men of both sword and pen—before the book later describes her intricate family history shaped by male absence and her devotional life driven by love of an ideal man, Imam 'Ali.

The Appeal for Patrons

Many dimensions of her personality were important in Mah Laqa Bai's rise to fame. Her dancing talent was central, and her beauty amplified her skill. But it was her ability to compose poetry that played a crucial role in court life. If a noble were to rise in power, he or she had to be quickwitted and eloquent, able to versify impromptu at any occasion. Poems of praise and flattery were important at the court of the nizams.

Mah Laqa Bai includes several poems in her divan that are ghazals in form, yet they function as a *qasida* praising a ruler or hero. These ghazals highlight her relationship with Aristu Jah and Nizam 'Ali Khan, her early patrons. In poems dedicated to Aristu Jah, she invokes 'Ali and the imams to protect him, hinting at their shared Shi'ite faith:[2]

> With Nawroz mirth and springtime passion is the way it goes
>> With your kind glance, the world's garden blooms with rose
> Don't ask if any can rival in this age such luxury and bliss
>> From his generosity alone in each house ruby wine flows
> For his auspicious ancestry, Aristu Jah is famous far and wide
>> His love of learning and kind patronage everyone knows
> Let her soul be sacrificed for the imams, this slave prays
>> That Mawla 'Ali protect him with shade wherever he goes
> Like the sun in the heavens, that's no exaggeration, it is clear
>> Only because of your kindness does Chanda enjoy repose

Aristu Jah held his own court as prime minister, and it was there where Mah Laqa Bai honed her talents. She would recite such poems impromptu at lavish celebrations like Nawroz. Later, she wrote them into her growing divan.

Spring festivals were important occasions with public displays of praise and gratitude for patrons like Aristu Jah. The following ghazal was likely presented as part of a dance performance or *mujra* in which the dancers offered *salam* or salutations to the ruler. *Mujra* has come in Urdu to denote a dance of courtesans, but it originally comes from an Arabic phrase *salam ma-jara*, meaning "greetings of praise that have been offered." Mah Laqa Bai would present this poem on the occasion of Basant (the Indian spring festival celebrated with yellow color):[3]

> When among the garden's roses strolls that prince so grand
>> From all sides nightingales call *salam* like a dancing band
> Hearing their lovely cry, my heart says, "Let's go
>> Take a look wearing springtime yellow! Come on, stand!"
> I reached that party more glorious than Faridun's reign
>> I saw that honored prince on a throne parasolled and fanned
> Facing him, Hatim al-Ta'i would fear being called generous
>> For he rivals Cyrus the great in magnanimous command
> From Aristu Jah, just one little thing does Chanda ask
>> You've already given gold and elephants, so add a grant of land?

These poems are unusual for her, for they focus less on Imam 'Ali and shine the spotlight on male patrons. Rather than end with a devotional invocation of the Shi'i imam, she concludes with a request for gifts from her actual patron. Aristu Jah had given her elephants and gold, so she

Prime Minister Aristu Jah (left) and the second nizam (right), miniature painting housed at the Archaeology Museum in Public Gardens, Hyderabad (photo by G. Shashidhar Reddy)

now requests a land grant (*jagir*) that would be a wealth base for her in perpetuity. He should give so generously not because the poet deserves it—though the poem must be eloquent to get a hearing—but rather because it is the virtue of the hearer to give. The patron is more generous than the mythic figure of Hatim al-Ta'i, the Arabian prince who willingly sacrificed his riding camel in order to provide meat to host visitors. His celebrations are more lavish than those of the legendary Iranian king Faridun, whose spring festivities lasted for nine full days. This poem, then, is in the form of a ghazal but functions as a qasida full of praise in hope of making a request at the end.

Another ghazal compares the nizam's Nawroz celebration to the festivities of Jamshed, the mythic pre-Islamic Iranian king honored by both Sunnis and Shi'is:[4]

> In your reign is such magnificent luxury, O king of kings
>   For Nawroz fests, did Jamshed gather such glittering things?
> Tell me, in pomp and splendor is anyone your match?
>   Byzantium and China's emperors serve you as underlings
> What need have I to tell you of my desperate need
>   The generous sun gives dust motes their glimmerings
> It's well-known the world wide from princes to beggars
>   No one is turned away from your hospitality's blessings
> Let Chanda always care for thousands, but it's the nizam
>   Our Deccan king, our Rustom, to whose hem she clings

These ghazals take on the quality of a qasida praising the ruler's might and generosity to win his favor and repay his patronage. Such poems that do not mention ʿAli or the imams are rare in her output.[5] These more secular poems were designed for very specific occasions to elicit the patronage of powerful men. As a courtesan, Mah Laqa Bai had to attract the male gaze, seize it, captivate through it, and manipulate it so that her vulnerable position as an unmarried but sexually available woman translated into an empowered position with protection by aristocratic men, their money, and the status they conveyed.

Mah Laqa Bai and the Prime Ministers

Mah Laqa Bai's first patron, Aristu Jah, was instrumental in advancing her career. He prompted her to collect her poetry into a divan in 1798 toward the end of his long, ambitious, and adventurous political life.[6] Aristu Jah began his career as a fortress administrator in Awrangabad but was appointed prime minister in the place of Rukn al-Dawla in 1775. With his reputation for wisdom and wiles, Aristu Jah's position at court grew so powerful as to breed jealousy, and others conspired against him. His crisis occurred at the battle of Khardla in March 1795. Aristu Jah had convinced the second nizam that his forces could face and defeat the feared Marathas. This departed from prior policy of diplomatic engagement with the Marathas to avoid war. The nizam with his army rode to the borderlands—ostensibly on an extended hunting trip—and faced the Maratha army. Maratha leaders bribed several of the nizam's generals and courtiers to desert, including Mir ʿAlam, who had been Aristu Jah's protégé. In the ensuing battle, the Marathas routed the nizam, and he was forced to pay a huge indemnity and cede land and forts. Aristu Jah was taken as a hostage in Pune, and in his absence his position in Hyderabad began to be taken over by Mir ʿAlam (died 1808).

After two years, Aristu Jah managed to free himself. He cleverly manipulated factions within the Maratha leadership such that the nizam's indemnity of the Treaty of Khardla was rescinded. Aristu Jah returned to Hyderabad a hero, just as the nizam was about to dismiss British troops quartered at Hyderabad, throw his lot with French regiments, and enter into an alliance with Tipu Sultan of Mysore (died 1799). Aristu Jah urged the nizam to reverse course, reinstate the British, and disband French troops under the command of Michel Joachim Marie Raymond, better known as Monsieur Raymond; in turn, the British drew up a new defense treaty pledging to defend the nizam's forces against the Marathas.[7] Rumors circulated that the French forces were engineering a coup, possibly backing one of the nizam's sons against their aging father. In 1798 amid such rumors, the commander of the French garrison, Raymond, died at the height of his powers; most likely Aristu Jah crafted his assassination by poison.

Aristu Jah secured power by intertwining his family with the nizam's family. Nizam ʿAli Khan gave one of his sons to Aristu Jah to rear as his own when the prime minister's son died (though this son was subsequently killed in the Khardla campaign). Aristu Jah later arranged his granddaughter's marriage to Nizam ʿAli Khan's son and successor, Sikandar Jah. The wily minister Aristu Jah patronized Mah Laqa Bai with hopes of getting her into the harem of the second nizam as a wife or concubine; having a loyal ally in the female quarters of the nizam's household would give Aristu Jah a firmer hold upon the ruler's policies. It would have fulfilled the dreams of Mah Laqa Bai's mother and half sister who raised her. Her mother had married an official and her half sister had married the previous prime minister, so the next step was for a woman from their family to get intimate with the nizam himself. Aristu Jah would have profited by fulfilling their wishes. He introduced Mah Laqa Bai in court, had her perform for the nizam, and let her win his favor. At the age of fifteen, she gained intimate access to the nizam and accompanied him on various military campaigns and hunting expeditions, enjoying the honor of riding with him on the royal elephant.[8] But despite enjoying her company and admiring her beauty, the second nizam did not take Mah Laqa Bai into his palace as a wife or concubine. That was likely resisted by his official wife and other women of the household who wielded enormous sway over the ruler.

This leaves open the question of whether Mah Laqa Bai became the mistress of Aristu Jah or whether their relationship remained one of patronage and appreciation. Sources say that Aristu Jah enjoyed her "intimate companionship" or *musahibat*, a Persian-Urdu word that is deliciously ambiguous. It could mean avid companionship, close friendship, or physical intimacy. This range of meanings presents a vagueness useful for a courtesan but frustrating for a historian. What we can say for sure is that Aristu Jah played the role of patron in court, which was the most formative of Mah Laqa Bai's relationships with men and without which she could not have achieved the fame that she did.

Aristu Jah was so closely tied to the second nizam that the ruler's death signaled the beginning of the end for his wily prime minister. Nizam 'Ali Khan died of natural causes on August 6, 1803. His only surviving son was Sikandar Jah; the nizam's eldest son had rebelled against his father as had his son-in-law, so both were eliminated. Thus Sikander Jah ascended the throne unopposed as the third Asaf-Jahi nizam. Aristu Jah died on May 9, 1804—ostensibly of sudden fever but likely by poison after protection of the second nizam ceased. When Aristu Jah died, Mir 'Alam became prime minister. He was Aristu Jah's protégé turned nemesis who had conspired against him when he was imprisoned by the Marathas.

The third nizam, Sikandar Jah, appointed Mir 'Alam on July 13, 1804. The new prime minister persecuted Aristu Jah's widow, family, and associates in revenge for Aristu Jah's having had him disgraced and exiled four years earlier. Like the deceased prime minister, Mir 'Alam was from an Iranian Shi'i family. But unlike his predecessor, Mir 'Alam was an Anglophile who rose to power as the East India Company's representative (*wakil*) to Hyderabad. Mir 'Alam supported British colonial interests in South India as a way of maintaining the nizam's independent rule and his own position of power within its competing factions.

Mah Laqa Bai escaped the new prime minister's vendetta against the former supporters of Aristu Jah. To the contrary, she had long before caught his gaze. He was infatuated with her, and she drew him closer now that he was in a position of unassailable power. Mir 'Alam admired her beauty and her literary skill, such that he desired her companionship, but did that mean that she became Mir 'Alam's mistress? Did his admiration for her translate into a sexual relationship? The Persian and Urdu sources obfuscate this point. In his travelogue written in 1802, titled *Tuhfat al-'Alam*, Mir 'Alam's uncle 'Abd al-Latif Shushtari reports that Mir 'Alam met Mah Laqa Bai while he was a young professor at a madrassa.

He "immediately fell in love with this moon-faced beauty" so fully that he could think only of poetry, left his studies and teaching, and soon fell out with an illness that lasted for three months.⁹ Jawhar represents their relationship as one of teacher and student, with Mir ʿAlam as the master of Persian letters who guided Mah Laqa Bai in poetic composition; he writes that "Mir ʿAlam used to say, 'I have never seen a student with such deep understanding, intelligent nature and rich disposition as Mah Laqa Bai.' Since he described her with such virtue, endowment and profundity, Mir ʿAlam chose her for companionship (*musahibat*) and intimacy (*ham-dami*). Though companionship with this bloom in the rose-garden of beauty, he sowed the seed of his enjoyment in the fertile soil of tranquil bliss."¹⁰

Jawhar uses at least three different terms to describe the relationship between Mir ʿAlam and Mah Laqa Bai. The first is friendship (*mujalisat*), meaning that their personalities were in accord so that they enjoyed sitting together; true to this meaning, Jawhar pictures the two as engaged in literary discourse, learned discussion, and poetic composition. The second term, companionship (*musahibat*), is more ambiguous, since it is related to the term for master and mistress; it is companionship of a closeness that goes beyond shared interests to a level of mingled personalities. But it does not necessarily mean sexual relations, for indeed Mah Laqa Bai is described as "companion" also to the second nizam and to Aristu Jah. Jawhar uses a third term, intimacy (*ham-dami*), that is more direct; it literally means "of the same breath," implying that two people are so close that their breathing mingles. It is impossible to be so close to someone as to breathe the same breath without becoming sensually intimate. Jawhar politely shies away from stating the obvious when he conjures up images of Mir ʿAlam planting the seeds of his enjoyment in Mah Laqa Bai's fertile soil. Mir ʿAlam's biographer in the 1920s, Muhammad Siraj al-Din Talib, cites these quotations about the closeness of Mah Laqa Bai and Mir ʿAlam to show how he knew poetry and valued poets; but the biographer completely ignores the issue of their sexual intimacy, as if it were not worth discussing. William Dalrymple asserts that Mah Laqa Bai was Mir ʿAlam's mistress, based on comments in the papers of the British Resident at Hyderabad.¹¹

The main account of Mir ʿAlam's love for Mah Laqa Bai comes from his own pen. He wrote an epic poem in Persian to describe her beauty from top to bottom—a masnavi titled "A Head to Foot Description of

Mah Laqa" (*Sarapa-ye Mah Laqa*). Its first twelve lines address her with images of her beauty as reflected in Mir ʿAlam's longing gaze.[12]

> O Moon who shares the heavens' intimacy
>   Head to foot you're a heart-captivating fantasy
> You are a person whose very eye is passion
>   From top to toe you are a charm of affection
> Your whole form with the heart's pen is presented
>   Your body with the soul's essence is fermented

The circumstances under which Mir ʿAlam wrote the poem are not known. It reads almost like a plea for intimacy. It could have been written in his youthful passion or perhaps was sent to Mah Laqa Bai once Aristu Jah died as an indication that he, the new prime minister, would take up her patronage just as his predecessor did.

However, his relationship with Mah Laqa Bai appears to be more erotic. It is possible that he lusted for her while Aristu Jah was alive but could not get near her because of that elder statesman's proprietary relationship with her. He uses market imagery of the bazar to imply that Mah Laqa Bai is open to new bidders: "You who sell a glimpse and buy a life / In flirtation's market, your wink is rife."[13] There is deep irony in his using this term "bazar" in relation to her reputation as a courtesan, a figure sometimes ridiculed as a prostitute or "woman of the market" (*bazari*). From the description of her tall stature and graceful gait, the poem moves down her body cataloging the ravishing loveliness of each and every part:[14]

> O cheek like the moon, clothed in moonlight
>   Your brow is like moonbeams, silvery is your sight
> I'll summarize the whole album of your lovely grace
>   By choosing one page with just your forehead's trace

In these lines, Mir ʿAlam dwells on her court title, Mah Laqa or "Moon Cheek." Her profile, her forehead, and her temples sum up her beauty as radiant and subtle as silvery moonlight. From her face, the description moves from her hair to her eyes and still lower.

When Mir ʿAlam's head-to-foot description reaches her mouth and tongue, he praises her eloquence as well as her beauty.[15] He cannot describe her mouth without petitioning for a kiss.[16] Yet he attributes the temptation and seduction (*fitna*) to the object of his desire rather than to himself.[17] As the poet's lusty gaze moves down her body, his poem makes gestures toward modesty. His couplets play between concealing and revealing as he arrives at her neck, bosom, belly, navel, lower back, and beyond:[18]

> Jealousy of your face holds sun and moon in its scope
>> Your bosom is the dawning place of eternal hope
> From shoulder to breast ripples of purity shimmer
>> Your bosom's dawn reflects in the heart's silver mirror

As he recreates her beautiful body in a poetic striptease, he blames her as a mistress of coquetry. Mir ʿAlam invokes modesty yet revels in its opposite—wanton self-display—as his description moves down from the expressive zone of the face to the more erotic zone of the torso:[19]

> Attracted to your navel, the glance sinks from timidity
>> It drowns—have mercy!—in that deep well of modesty
> No word is there that your waist defines
>> To apprehend it one reads between the lines
> ....
> With all this beauty is a secret unspeakable
>> No one is privy to it without silence respectable
> None can know of this hidden secret's depth
>> Except one lost in passion embracing his death
> So that I might not spoil the secret's appeal
>> The pen in my hand slips now to your heel

Just as he is about to uncover with description the "hidden secret's depth" of her most private realms, he feigns modesty and the speechlessness of passion. His descriptive gaze slips down to her feet.

After her feet, the end of the physical journey down her body's beauty, the poem goes on to describe her cultural cultivation. Thus retreating from the embodied and erotic, Mir ʿAlam admits how lovesick he is for her:[20]

> Listen to my woes with your heart's ears
>> Bear eye-witness to the secret of my tears
> Go now to her and tell this story secretly
>> Just a short tale to that moon who's so lovely

With this appeal for compassion and intimacy, Mir ʿAlam completes his long masnavi. This translation provides only a sample of the poem's 224 couplets to indicate its tone and trajectory. It reveals the immodesty of Mir ʿAlam's gaze and the erotic intensity of his appreciation, though veiled behind polite language in florid description.

His poem is an invitation to sexual intimacy under the cover of unrequited love that has made him sick with longing. Writing a poem to supplicate a loved one or to praise an admired one is an act of vulnerability. It reveals one's dependence upon another who is of a higher station. The poet's mastery of words is her or his only compensation for being at the mercy of circumstance, which has placed her or him in the control of another. Thus we find that, in the beginning of her career, Mah Laqa Bai wrote poems in praise of men like Aristu Jah and Nizam ʿAli Khan; but at the peak of her powers, men on the rise wrote poems to her. Mir ʿAlam had replaced his rival, Aristu Jah, as prime minister and perhaps was responsible for his death, but to truly secure his position he needed to win the approval and intimacy of Mah Laqa Bai. Such was her powerful position at court, especially under the rule of a new nizam who had to prove his worthiness as a beauty-loving and art-appreciating patron. To win her favor, Mir ʿAlam composed this lengthy poem on her beauty and seductive powers. It appears likely, in the reflected glow of this head-to-foot description, that Mir ʿAlam did enjoy sexual intimacy and romantic attachment with Mah Laqa Bai. If they were sexually intimate, it commends Mah Laqa Bai's wiles and political acumen, for Mir ʿAlam's power was in the ascendant.

Even before the death of Aristu Jah, Mir ʿAlam scented new currents of power that were going to affect life at the nizam's court. He acted as the nizam's representative to the East India Company based in Calcutta. From 1787, he spent three years in Calcutta, learning about British military and administrative policies and befriending many influential officers. Based on his familiarity with the British, he engineered his rise to power in Hyderabad. Mir ʿAlam's fame increased after he led the combined Deccan and British forces to defeat Tipu Sultan of Mysore and loot his treasury at Srirangapatnam. He conspired with top British officials to mastermind the war against Tipu Sultan and felt he had the backing of the British once he returned to Hyderabad. He aspired to displace his rival, Aristu Jah, and acted with new arrogance.

On his return from triumph against Tipu Sultan, Mir ʿAlam organized a huge party on October 18, 1799, at his mansion, where Mah Laqa Bai was the star performer. During this celebration, she had a private audience with Sir John Malcolm, the assistant British Resident in Hyderabad, who had grown close to Mir 'Alam's family during the campaign against Tipu Sultan. In this private audience, Mah Laqa Bai presented a copy of her divan to the British official as a gift.[21] We must speculate about what this episode meant for Mah Laqa Bai. Was this a romantically motivated liaison or a politically motivated spy mission? In these years, tension grew between Mir 'Alam and Aristu Jah while debates raged behind the formality of court life about whether the British troops in Hyderabad could be trusted to protect the interests of the nizam. It would not be the first time a woman was deputed to seduce a powerful man in order to get information from him or leverage over him.

Only one year before, in 1798, a young female relative of Mir 'Alam was encouraged to get close to the British Resident in Hyderabad, James Kirkpatrick; he served as the ambassador of the East India Company to the nizam from 1797 until 1805. Kirkpatrick eventually took this young lady, named Khair al-Nisa, into his household as a concubine or wife. The affair eventually caused the British Resident to be recalled from Hyderabad in disgrace and led Mir 'Alam to be banished, as documented in vivid detail by William Dalrymple in *White Mughals*. However, in the beginning, the affair was a sign of the political closeness of Mir 'Alam's family to the British, mirroring his own political rise as the most Anglophile of the nizam's advisers. With Mir 'Alam's family planting its beautiful female members in the household of the British Resident, it may have been Aristu Jah's countermove to encourage Mah Laqa Bai to get close to the British Resident's assistant, John Malcolm. By using Mah Laqa Bai, Aristu Jah could get an information channel directly from the British administration and make Mir 'Alam seethe with jealousy.

Mah Laqa Bai had close relations with two prime ministers and a British diplomat, but she also was intimate with one of the leading Hindu nobles of the nizam's regime, Rambha Rao Jayawant. The second Asaf-Jah Nizam 'Ali Khan promoted Maratha warrior chiefs like Rambha Rao to high position (he was given the titles raja and bahadur), since the nizam's major rival for power was the Maratha ruler of Pune. Rambha Rao was counted as a stalwart warrior and cultivated gentleman who had once saved the nizam's life when a rampaging buffalo charged into court.[22] Rambha Rao descended from the Nimbalkar family of Maratha warriors who were related by marriage to the clan of Shivaji Bhonsle (died 1680) that ruled from Pune. It is a persistent stereotype that Shivaji's family were Hindu kings who opposed Muslim rule. Rambha Rao and his clan offer a counterexample to dispel this stereotype. His family was fully integrated into the structure of Muslim rule, as had been Shivaji's own father and grandfather before his experiment in Maratha independence.

According to their family legends, Rambha Rao's grandfather had served the raja of Sagnapur (near Nanded), who was an ally of the Mughals in Maratha country. His grandfather was a strong warrior, but rivals conspired to have the Mughal emperor Bahadur Shah imprison him. From prison in the Red Fort in Delhi, the unfortunate Maratha warrior could see an 'ashur-khana where 'alams were installed. Seeing these symbols of perseverance despite persecution and bravery in the face of oppression, the Maratha vowed that if released from prison he would celebrate Muharram. The next day, the emperor freed him and restored him to favor. In thanks, he observed Muharram with fervor though remaining Hindu.[23]

That Maratha warrior's son became attached to the first Asaf-Jah, Nizam al-Mulk, in Delhi and accompanied him to the Deccan. In turn, his son also served the nizams. The son was originally named Baji Rao but became known as Rambha Rao. He served the second nizam, who honored him with the title raja or ruler. Raja Rambha Rao continued the tradition of his grandfather, commemorating Muharram with no contradiction between upholding Maratha warrior heritage, worshipping as a Hindu, and commemorating Muharram. As he grew close to Mah Laqa Bai, she may have encouraged him to invest in buildings at the Mawla 'Ali shrine. A *barah-dari* or open square pavilion built on the sacred hill is attributed to him.

Rambha Rao was one of Mah Laqa Bai's early admirers. He may have been the first to provide her a salary as entertainer in his private court; it is unclear whether he or Aristu Jah was the first to promote her.[24] Sources report that Rambha Rao was enraptured by her beauty and grace, and they shared a common appreciation of fine stallions. On a diplomatic mission to the rival court of the Marathas at Pune, Mah Laqa Bai amazed their chief minister Nana Phadnavis (died 1800) when she displayed her thorough knowledge of Arabian horses and bought many to take back to Hyderabad. When they asked her what business she had with horses, she replied that she was purchasing the stallions for her friend, Raja Rambha Rao, who admired them greatly.[25] Thus Mah Laqa Bai thumbed her nose at the Maratha chiefs, reminding them that the nizam of Hyderabad's court included Maratha warriors, too. However, by the end of the eighteenth century, the nature of the nizam's rule was changing. Allying with the British East India Company, the nizam was able to broker a stalemate with the Marathas of Pune and to defeat his rival, Tipu Sultan of Mysore. Yet in doing so he also sold out military defense of Hyderabad to English troops and became indebted to the East India Company to support its barracks. Loyal soldiers like Rambha Rao became relics of the past. The regime was supported more by bankers than by warriors.

A new class of Hindu nobles rose to power after the death of the second nizam in 1803. The third nizam appointed Maharaja Chandulal, whose family had served as clerks and accountants in the customs department, to be the treasury minister (*divan*). He helped to transfer lands from the nizam's control to the East India Company to help pay for the upkeep of British troops. The troops were housed in a British district north of Hyderabad, called Secunderabad Cantonment after the new nizam, Sikandar Jah (whose name the British transcribed as "Secunder"). Maharaja Chandulal was "very well educated both as a scholar and as a public officer," wrote the British Resident Henry Russell (served 1811 until 20). "His understanding is sound, his talents quick, his memory retentive, his industry indefatigable and he has great experience and aptitude for all kinds of business from the highest branches to the most minute detail."[26] Shrewd, stingy, and clever, the finance minister Maharaja Chandulal was almost the opposite personality from the military nobles who had formerly held power. Loyal, fierce, and generous nobles like Raja Rambha Rao were going out of style. Flowing with the change of times, Mah Laqa Bai shifted her favors to Maharaja Chandulal and was the star performer in his personal court.

Mah Laqa Bai's Poetic Companions

Mah Laqa Bai's allure was not just sexual but also artistic. She won the admiration of Maharaja Chandulal, the treasury minister, during the time when Mir 'Alam was prime minister. Chandulal was not merely the finance minister and most powerful Hindu noble in the early nineteenth century; he was also an Urdu poet with the pen name "Shadan." Mah Laqa Bai enjoyed his company and his patronage. There are several ghazals in her divan that match the meter and rhyme of Chandulal's poems exactly.[27] It appears that they were admiring competitors in poetry recitals (*musha'ira*), in which the rhyme and meter would be announced in advance and all participating poets had to compose in the same format to see who could best mine the limitations for creative possibilities.

Mah Laqa Bai frequented the gatherings sponsored by Chandulal, and she performed at the *barah-dari* that he had specially built to entertain the third nizam.[28] Entertainment for the nizam was an important part of his strategy to win favor, for his relationship with the nizam was turbulent. Chandulal won Mah Laqa Bai's acceptance not with love poems and romantic dalliance but with patronage. She in turn supported him by gracing his gatherings with her presence and conferring upon him prestige of connoisseurship, which was the symbol of political power at court. However, after her death, Chandulal prompted the nizam to reclaim her *jagir* (enforcing the Mughal tradition of not allowing heirs to inherit property given as court grants); he gave her adopted daughter (or daughters) stipends instead, keeping them dependent on male largesse.

Mah Laqa Bai's relationship to other poets was crucial to her development. During the reign of the second nizam, poets found royal patronage in Awrangabad and Hyderabad.[29] One of them, Tajalli 'Ali Shah, was an intimate friend of Mah Laqa Bai's mother who saved the fetal Mah Laqa Bai from miscarriage. He helped Mah Laqa Bai refine her poetic eloquence, perhaps directly in her youth and indirectly in her maturity, through the agency of his primary student, Muhammad Sher Khan "Iman" (died 1806). Iman became Mah Laqa Bai's poetry teacher and was counted among her admirers. He was born in Hyderabad and took Tajalli 'Ali as his poetry teacher (*ustad*).[30] In his masterpiece *Tuzuk-e Asafiyya*, Tajalli 'Ali made special mention of Iman and boasted of the eloquence of his student. After his father's death, Iman took over his position as royal historian. Aristu Jah recognized his talent and promoted him. Iman wrote several qasida poems praising Aristu Jah on his birthday celebration and composed a special poem for his granddaughter Jahan-Parvar Begum (who was married to the heir apparent Sikandar Jah, son of the second nizam).[31]

Iman rose to fame attending poetry recitals organized by Aristu Jah and other patrons, from which he emerged as a master poet of his age; in Hyderabad, no *musha'ira* would begin until Iman deigned to show up.[32] Aspiring poets looked to him for guidance, including Mah Laqa Bai. Nasir al-Din Hashmi, historian of female writers in Urdu, says, "In addition to being a poet herself, Mah Laqa Bai was an excellent judge of other poets. Around her was always an active enterprise for poetry and poets, and she ceaselessly encouraged and enabled other poets to practice their art. . . . In total, Mah Laqa Bai took part in advancing the cause of Urdu language not only through her poetry, but also through supporting other poets and writers. In poetry, she was the disciple of Sher Muhammad Khan Iman."[33] His students were numerous, though Mah Laqa Bai ranks as one of the most accomplished. Another who achieved fame with her is Iman's nephew Muhammad Sadiq "Qais" (died 1815). Qais found favor along with Mah Laqa Bai in the gatherings of Maharaja Chandulal, who declared Qais to be his *ustad*.[34] Qais was renowned for his qasidas and ghazals but also gained notoriety for rekhti that imitated the diction of women.[35] Most rekhti poets imitated the saucy language of the courtesans, and we are left to imagine Qais's interactions with Mah Laqa Bai.[36]

All these students of Iman achieved fame in different styles, but Mah Laqa Bai was the only one to inspire the teacher to compose a poem in her honor. Iman was charmed by her and wrote her a long poem in supplication and praise. In this poem of six-lined stanzas (*musaddas*), he boasts that her beauty has made him lovesick.[37] But unlike the jilted lover of the ghazal, Iman's poem ends happily. His beloved recognizes his desire, respects his supplication, and inclines toward him to grant him intimacy: "Thank God, these days she acknowledges my predicament / Together we sit, we drink, we share secrets, in full agreement."[38] It is not clear whether this convivial companionship is about sharing friendship through poetry or about quenching desire with physical intimacy—Iman leaves that tantalizingly ambiguous. A translation of several of this poem's nineteen stanzas is offered below.[39]

> Your beauty's fame lights the world to the brink
> Shining from earth to the seventh heaven's canopy
> Can fairies or celestial virgins match your beauty
> Never, as each dust speck can witness in a wink
> > Sun shining in a mirror it will break its face
> > Except if sun first sees you and knows its place
>
> On one who for a moment enjoys your embrace
> My lover, your passion's imprint will always endure
> Doctors give up on him, as he's beyond cure
> As long as he lives, his heart's gone with no trace
> > If for once he's fallen for your seductive trick
> > Even the Jesus of his age would be left sick

Just as the sun is jealous of her beauty, the moon, too, pales before her face. He writes that "hyacinth falls to pieces troubled by your curl's shade / Crescent moon is all cut up seeing your brow's blade."[40] Mah Laqa Bai outshines the sun and the moon, and in her presence Venus begins to sing. Roses bend their heads to serve her, hyacinth wilts away compared to her hair, and the great female beloveds of the Islamic tradition—like Shirin and Laila—step back in deference to her:[41]

> Ever since I'm embroiled in her beauty and gone gaga
> My heart's empty quarter is finer than where fairies dine
> Since long, I am drunk on boundless passion's wine
> On the world's lips I'm an epic subject, an endless saga
>> When word of my passion reaches the wilderness
>> Majnun leaps into a bewildered romp of happiness
> . . . .
> Since the moment I saw her face from a distance
> I feel passion only for her in my mind and deep feelings
> With heavenly virgins or earthly beauties I have no dealings
> It's a simple fact—I don't say it from any arrogance
>> In describing roses and jasmine I don't waste my powers
>> I'm no breeze spreading intoxication among the flowers

Although Iman lauds Mah Laqa Bai's beauty in this poem, he ends up praising himself. Real men are those whose souls are burned by the fires of passion, for their crude natures are thereby purified by love's heat. In the final stanza, the poet addresses himself, "Iman, the only good man is one who smiles when pained / Only he who endures love's burning is a true man refined."[42] Iman professes his love but does not hope for intimacy with her, a hope more ardently displayed by Mir 'Alam's solicitation.

Why would Mah Laqa Bai's poetry master write her a love poem? Do we conclude that Iman was Mah Laqa Bai's lover, as we did with Mir 'Alam? No, for the poem's tone is very different and we have no other evidence of such a relationship. This should serve as a reminder to us of limits of biographical data in Urdu poetry—as pointed out by Shamsur Rahman Faruqi, who lampoons the idea that "poetry reflects biography or biography is mirrored in the poetry."[43] This book maintains that there is a correspondence between the poetry about Mah Laqa Bai and the relationships she enjoyed with men, yet Faruqi advises a cautious approach to making such connections. Iman's poem declares his love for Mah Laqa Bai, but this could simply be an offer of friendship rather than an indication of sexual relations between them. Love is of many kinds. The love between poets and courtesans could be more like romantic friendship and literary camaraderie.

Such is the case with another masnavi written by Ghulam Husain Jawhar in praise of Mah Laqa Bai's beauty. He was a poet and historian from Bidar who depended on her for his livelihood, and she commissioned him to write a history of Hyderabad. Jawhar included in its introduction a masnavi in Persian titled "Head-to-Foot Description of Mah Laqa Bai."[44]

He begins with a toast to Imam ʿAli and requests the wine of love, which he gets from the form of Mah Laqa Bai. "O saqi who pours for pleasure's assembly / a goblet of love's wine filled up the brim // Come, give Jawhar just one sip as a toast / to ʿAli's reign, who pours the wine of paradise."[45] Jawhar is not her lover in a romantic sense but rather her employee benefiting from her patronage. He does admire her beauty, highlighting how her body reflected her virtues of generosity and kindness. He frames the portrait with the ideal that admiration of physical beauty through "metaphoric love" leads to contemplation of spiritual beauty in "ultimate love":[46]

> Give me that wine, in secret or in open
>   That God allows and leaves no pain
> That wine which is like a Canaan moon
>   Making one smile in Babylon's prison
> It's the wine of love, care and intimacy
>   From which all of creation emerged
> Nothing tops it, like metaphorical love
>   Through which one reaches ultimate love
> Listen, eloquent saqi, to what I say
>   Accept this proposal of humble Jawhar
> Give me a cupful of the wine of love
>   Full of passion, brimming with virtue
> I yearn for a goblet of spiritual wine
>   My nature's sea is churning for this
> Bliss-bearing wine turns my negligence
>   Into a character of pearl-strewing eloquence
> So I may describe the beauty of Mah Laqa
>   In case you don't have fortune to meet her
> Though metaphorical is her description
>   It subtly and slowly takes its effect

> If you gingerly step toward such beauty
> You might ultimately ascend to heaven
> Reflected beauty of a human beloved
> Manifests divine grace and God's light

Jawhar proceeds to describe her beauty, part by part, from her head to her toes, in a familiar pattern. He urges himself on, saying, "Take the pen to string words like pearls / to describe that ocean of lovely intelligence // Take the blank paper like a pure mirror / to reflect her beauty from head to foot."[47]

Yet his description sharply differs from that of Mir ʿAlam. Though both use similar images, Mir ʿAlam casts his in a lusty, even lascivious, catalog of her erotic power. Jawhar, in contrast, takes a more allegorical and less anatomical approach. Through her beauty, Jawhar sees the beauty of the creator; by means of her loveliness, Jawhar approaches the grace of God. Indeed, he appealed to her virtues of generosity and found in her a benefactor who rescued his family from poverty. Though Jawhar's masnavi begins like an ode to a beautiful wine-pourer (*saqi-nama*), in the end it takes on the tone of a qasida to petition for a favor. In her youth, she had met this litterateur when he was called to attend the marriage of the second nizam's son, and many years later when he had fallen into poverty, Mah Laqa Bai offered him support—a salary and workshop in her library. In the end, he humbly offers to forgo gifts of money and is satisfied that his name, Jawhar or "Pearl," be associated through time with Mah Laqa Bai's embodiment of the "Moon."

Jawhar's *Tarikh-e Dil-Afroz*, or "Heart Dazzling History," documents the reign of the nizams of Hyderabad. He dedicated his history to Mah Laqa Bai and gave it the nickname by which it is still famous, *Mah-nama* or "Moon Chronicle." Of course, Jawhar also received coins, but he claimed that fame by association was enough. His humility probably won him more coins. Such is the strategy of sublimation that he uses in this composition. If there is sexual desire in his gazing at Mah Laqa Bai's beauty, he sublimates it into rarefied appreciation and channels it into allegory that deflects his gaze upward to more spiritual pursuits.

Conclusion

The men around Mah Laqa Bai savored her beauty and composed poems about her, but they saw in her a reflection of their own desires. The prime minister Aristu Jah saw in her ambition and raised her to be a powerful political personality to protect Shi'i interests (and his own) in a Sunni nizam's court. His rival for prime ministerial power, Mir 'Alam, saw in her passion and drew close to her in erotic titillation. The finance minister Maharaja Chandulal saw in her connoisseurship and displayed her at his dance parties and poetic recitations to impress the nizam. The poet Muhammad Sher Khan Iman saw in her eloquence and craved from her literary camaraderie. The historian Ghulam Husain Jawhar saw in her discernment and desired her to patronize his literary work.

These men expressed their appreciation of her physical beauty and feminine grace. The questions remain whether any of them saw her for herself—not as a seductress or politician or poet or patron but as a woman—and whether Mah Laqa Bai expected such full appreciation of her humanity from these men. In her poetry, she seems to desire the appreciation only of Imam 'Ali, whom she praises in most ghazals as the ideal man and her spiritual lover. That devotional love and intimacy we will explore in more detail in chapter 11. Yet in her actual life, she seems to have maintained cautious autonomy from the powerful men who surrounded her, likely as the result of the failure of actual men in her family life to provide the security and protection that was their duty according to patriarchal norms. The next chapter will examine her family history, to answer how she came to be in Hyderabad, how she became a courtesan, how she became an independently wealthy unmarried woman, and how her view of men was shaped.

CHAPTER NINE

Mah Laqa Bai's Shame

As the rays of your beauty cause sweat drops to drip
   Shamed, the moist sun hides behind a hem of clouds
Chanda has no fear of dark omens, for her protector
   Is 'Ali who brightens the sun in this world and the next

— *two verses from a ghazal by Mah Laqa Bai*

Among South Asian Muslims, the concept of "shame" has both positive and negative dimensions. Shame as *haya* is considered a virtue equivalent to how English speakers consider "modesty," describing not just dress and etiquette but also attitude. But shame as *sharm* has a negative meaning, as it is used in the poem cited above.[1] Shame means the loss of public respect when virtues are abandoned, especially in the sphere of sexual reputation. There is much tension in the story of Mah Laqa Bai about the quality of shame that most Muslims consider essential for a proper woman. While she had social respect and personified dignity, Mah Laqa Bai also cultivated a courtesan's pride in displaying her seductive beauty, which violated routine Islamic notions of shame. This chapter investigates tensions inherent in her role as a courtesan. To understand that role fully, it explores the fascinating history of her female-dominated family that teetered on the boundary between dignity and shame.

The Courtesan's Role

As described in chapter 1, courtesans were elevated personalities in premodern South Asia. They were subtly different from concubines or mere prostitutes, although these boundaries were porous. It was their artistic acumen and relative autonomy from marriage that distinguished courtesans from other unmarried women. However, successful courtesans might opt for marriage to noblemen (likely former patrons) when they grew more mature; Mah Laqa Bai's mother and half sister who raised her provide examples of this career trajectory. Mah Laqa Bai herself was so supremely successful as a courtesan that she did not need to marry later in life for security. She received a noble title, land grants, political authority, and inestimable wealth that allowed her not only to remain an unmarried performer but also to establish a household of female performers and their male support staff of musicians, artists, and scholars.

However, it was a complicated process that brought Mah Laqa Bai to this lofty position, involving a family history of female agency over several generations. The women of her family endured dire poverty, played to the baser desires of men for support, and withstood accusations of impropriety before they reached the respected position of courtesans. Her family history reveals that all was not rosy on the path to becoming a courtesan, even if Mah Laqa Bai enjoyed security and esteem in this position. She half-sarcastically writes of herself in a ghazal that even on her bed of roses, life is not without its bitterness and suffering: "Even as I rest on a bed of roses sleep won't come my way / Only if my head lies on your feet does sleep come to stay."[2] Among those courtesans who performed before the public, more danced upon thorns than found a bed of roses.

At the root of courtesans' stories, there is violence by men outside the family or failure of men inside the family to fulfill their obligations. This is true even of women who became successful courtesans, who were far fewer in number than those who were merely exploited. Only successful courtesans got their stories told, and even then storytellers often covered over their struggles and suffering. A courtesan who told her own stories tended to focus on the roses and to hide the thorns in her family's experiences. This chapter explores Mah Laqa Bai's family history, paying close attention to the tensions found in a woman's role as a courtesan, concubine, or prostitute.

These roles are not clearly defined, despite the protestations of those who have recorded Mah Laqa Bai's biography. Typical is the entry about her in Nasir al-Din Hashmi's account, written in the 1930s, of women's contributions to Urdu literature. He notes, "Mah Laqa Bai Chanda was an expert in the art of music and was a royal courtesan (*shahi tava'if*). But her condition was totally different from that of today's women who are professional courtesans (*pesha-war tava'ifan*)."[3] By "professional" he means that they are commercial and charge money for sexual acts. While Mah Laqa Bai was certainly not so crass as to be a commercial prostitute, the black and white distinction between earners and artists drawn by Hashmi was far more ambiguous in reality. For example, Mah Laqa Bai's mother, the courtesan Raj Kanvar Bai, was always troubled by rumors that accused her of being a wage earner (*kasabi*) rather than purely a performer.⁴ Such rumors hurt her chances of getting married into nobility and may have caused her later in life to adopt repentant piety.

While Mah Laqa Bai was not accessible to the general public for a fee, she was also not celibate. In this sense, Mah Laqa Bai offers a contrast to other aristocratic women. A Mughal princess named Jahan Ara Begum (died 1681), a sister of Awrangzeb, exercised influence in politics by remaining unmarried and celibate.⁵ But Mah Laqa Bai, as a courtesan, danced a fine line between being aesthetically provocative and being sexually profligate. Despite her great success in securing respect, erudition, wealth, and public prestige, Mah Laqa Bai's position was fraught with ambiguity. She faced criticism, which is recorded in the form of jokes.

Her biographies do not document opposition to her at court. However, they do record occasions where Mah Laqa Bai was the butt of jokes and was forced into clever repartee to defuse implicit criticism. "Mah Laqa Bai was the greatest in her age at making jokes and witty replies," her earliest Urdu biographer explains, noting that her jokes were so keen that Hyderabadis still recounted them in the late nineteenth century, when he was writing.⁶ He records some of her humorous episodes, like this one, at the end of his biography:

> It is told that once Mah Laqa Bai was arriving at the royal court wearing a *lai* [a shawl five yards long embroidered with silver or gold thread, worn over a full pleated skirt]. Somebody's shoe had caught in the edging of her shawl and was dragging along the ground after her. One sly prince present at court observed this and said, "Respected madam, your spouse seems to stick with you everywhere you go!" Without hesitation, Mah Laqa Bai gave this reply, "True, we poor people always stay with our spouses—but rich royals like you leave your spouses home in the embrace of servants!"⁷

The joke depends upon a play of words between *juta* (shoe) and *jora* (spouse), which sound similar and are linked in meaning "one of a pair." The joke is intensified by the South Asian understanding of shoes: they are highly inauspicious and are associated with humility, dirt, and disgrace. Mah Laqa Bai's entrance into court with a shoe dragging along, hanging from her shawl, is not just an embarrassing wardrobe malfunction; it is an opportunity for her to be humiliated. To "wear a garland of shoes" is an Urdu expression meaning to suffer public disgrace. The quick-witted courtier exploits this opportunity by indirectly but forcefully pointing out Mah Laqa Bai's vulnerable status as a courtesan. He disguises his barb behind a velvet cloth of politeness, addressing her as Respected Madam (*Bai Ji Sahiba*). He jokes that she has brought her "spouse" with her to court, referring to the dirty, disreputable shoe that trails along after her. The joke is that Mah Laqa Bai has no husband, for she is a courtesan. The courtier implies that if one removed all the glitter and finesse from her, she is just a disrespectable woman whom no husband would claim as a wife, except maybe someone as degraded as a shoe.

How did Mah Laqa Bai escape this public humiliation? Her wit turns the tables on her male accuser. She dodges a thrust at her gender vulnerability and engages in repartee against his class arrogance. She ingenuously accepts his accusation of being of lowly origin only to counter by saying yes, we poor women stay close to our husbands, while you rich men leave your wives imprisoned in palaces where they are left to fornicate with servants. Poor people cannot afford palaces and separate quarters for females (*parda*), but at least they can keep their spouses faithful through sincere companionship! Her riposte is delightfully double-edged. Is she criticizing the rich prince or his pampered and shackled wife? At first it seems like an attack on the wife, who takes comfort in adulterous affairs with servants while her husband is out on royal business; such a wife is, despite her rich clothes, stained by the hands of the poor who are her servants as she happily tosses aside her husband's honor to fulfill her lusts. At least with Mah Laqa Bai, the dirty shoe is visible from the outside, hanging from her shawl—not like the rich courtier's wife, whose dirty shoe is hidden from view under her skirt! Or her reply could be aimed not at the insulting courtier's wife but rather at the courtier himself. After all, it is his class arrogance and patriarchal privilege that led him to leave his home and wife to engage in aristocratic pursuits, the classiest of which was being charmed by courtesans like Mah Laqa Bai herself. The courtesans' allure makes him carelessly leave his wife at home to writhe in unfulfilled desires and to consort with servants.

The courtier humiliates her by calling her a fallen woman, but Mah Laqa Bai lambastes him for not being a faithful man. If she is not able to find respectability in a husband, he is not able to find happiness in a wife! In the end, her joke pokes fun at both the rich, roaming husband and the pampered, lusty wife. Even more pointedly, she criticizes the system of married respectability behind which both take refuge. Marriage was designed to maintain wealth, privilege, and dynasty rather than to promote sincere happiness and satisfaction. That system would crumble were it not for the unmarried women — whether courtesans or prostitutes — who were outside of its respectable facade.

In another joke, Mah Laqa Bai had to face criticism for being childless: "Once, Mah Laqa Bai's party was riding by near Charminar. Suddenly, a small ornamental canister of lime [for making *paan*] fell from inside her palanquin and rolled to the ground. Some smart aleck nearby commented, 'Madam's just laid an egg!' In a flash, Mah Laqa turned and replied, 'How amazing, the egg just got laid and already the cock has begun to crow!'"[8] *Paan* was an integral part of royal life in South Asia: it is a digestive chew made from betel leaf and smeared lime and wrapped around slivers of areca nuts mixed with spices and condiments. The lime was made from powdered eggshells or coral (or sometimes pearls) mixed with water to make a paste. Lime was stored in small round canisters of finely crafted metal like silver, often the size of a chicken's egg.

This joke is built on the connection between the lime canister and an egg, which have a physical resemblance and a relationship of calcium-rich materials. The joke's bite depends on deeper issues raise by eggs, namely fertility and fecundity. Mah Laqa Bai had no children, so she was an infertile woman who laid no eggs. Rather, she adopted girls to train in performing and seductive arts. Her *haveli* or manor house was filled with girls, the best of whom were her "daughters" who would run the courtesan lineage after her demise, the others of whom were her "servants" who learned the trade.

Mah Laqa Bai's wit reverses the insult in a flash. Who was it that called out this insult on the road? Perhaps the egg that fell from her palanquin had already hatched into a brash and strutting cock, now calling out to make his presence known, but just a moment before he was some insignificant thing, silent and inert. Her tone suggests that it would be better for everyone if he remained silent. In this record, we are not told who made the joke, but if it had been a man with religious authority, like a *mawlvi* or jurist, her reply would have been even sharper. This is because in Urdu, the expression for a man shouting the call to prayer (*bang dene lagna*) is the same expression as for a cock crowing. Her repartee would be especially cutting if the wit who insulted her were a young but pious man who claimed religious authority to look down upon a courtesan.

Mah Laqa Bai was vulnerable to taunts despite her noble title, artistic expertise, and independent wealth. Nevertheless, she was well equipped to parry them and even score against those who challenged her. This vulnerability is an important starting point for investigating the situation of courtesans and the accusation that they were prostitutes. If Mah Laqa Bai, after all her success, still had to face such social stigma, then what did other courtesans have to suffer? Her family story reveals this suffering and also shows women's intelligence and cunning in overcoming it.

Mah Laqa Bai's Life in History

As a courtesan, Mah Laqa Bai was not just an artist but also a patron of arts. An avid reader of history, she commissioned a historian to write the narrative of her city. Under her patronage and with her library, Ghulam Husain Jawhar wrote *Tarikh-e Dil-Afroz* or "Heart Dazzling History" in 1814. The book is also known as *Tajalliyat-e Mah Laqa* or "Manifestations of the Moon Cheek" or simply *Mah-nama* or "Moon Chronicle," hinting that the history of the city is a frame for Mah Laqa Bai's own place in it. Mah Laqa Bai's multifaceted personality allows biographers and historians to highlight some facets of which they approve and downplay others that challenge their preconceptions. Was Mah Laqa Bai the courtesan a sensual dancer or a noble artist? Was she a pious woman or a public spectacle? Was she a woman of dubious origin or a devoted Shi'i? These are the tensions inherent in her story, and each retelling shifts the emphasis, depending on the audience.

The history she commissioned rooted her in Hyderabad's sacred geography and its Shi'i nobility. Yet beneath the veneer of nobility lay the reality of mobility. Her family's mobility was born of desperation, the desperation of women left defenseless by unfaithful men. Her history gives her biography and genealogy and tells of her family's mobility both geographically (from Gujarat to Hyderabad) and socially (from paupers to nobles). This chapter explores her self-presentation in Persian and traces how it became distorted by later biographers in Urdu, who were uncomfortable with the tension between the roles of pious Shi'i woman and courtesan dancer. Her skill as a courtesan allowed her to cultivate literary, scholarly, and artistic talents to secure the status of nobility. However, reaching this lofty position involved a complicated family history over several generations. This chapter presents Mah Laqa Bai's story in detail, discussing controversial points to tease out the subtle truth from beneath polite lies. It will compare the narratives of different sources, with special attention to the differences between the original Persian

Tombs of Mah Laqa Bai (*left*) and her mother, Raj Kanvar Bai (*center*) (photo by Scott Kugle)

history of her family and later Urdu biographies that retell her story for modern audiences.

Mah Laqa Bai's mother, named Mida Bibi or "Miss Chaste," was born in Gujarat as the youngest of three sisters and two brothers. Her father was a Mughal noble and Sayyid who held an administrative office under the governor of Ahmedabad during the reign of Emperor Muhammad Shah (ruled 1719–48).[9] Her father wasted money entrusted to him by the governor, and, facing arrest, he fled. He left behind his wife, who was also from a Sayyid family.[10] Their home and possessions were confiscated and she, reduced to utter poverty, left Ahmedabad. With her three daughters and two sons, she struggled on the open road until they were picked up by a roving band—probably Hindu minstrels of a gypsy character (called *bhagat* in Urdu and Hindi)—who sang and danced for a living, presenting devotional songs for popular entertainment.[11] For years, the family wandered through Rajasthan and south into the Deccan along with these

Mah Laqa Bai's Shame

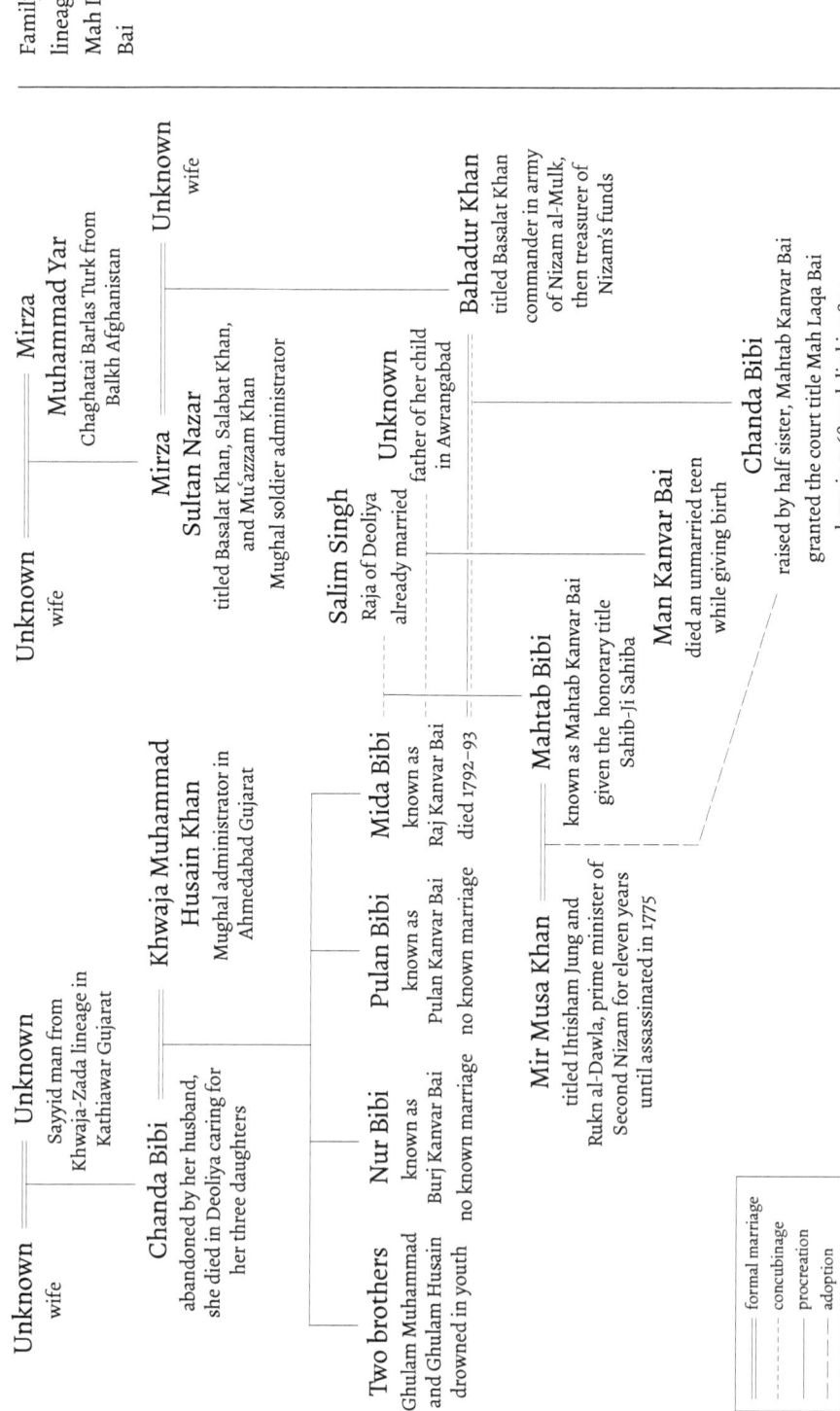

Family lineage of Mah Laqa Bai

minstrels. The girls learned music and dance from the minstrels who protected them, but on the way, their mother died and their brothers disappeared.

The three sisters supported themselves by dancing and singing, though the sources display reticence in admitting this. Some sources state that the two eldest daughters danced and sang in public so that the youngest sister, Mida Bibi, could remain in *parda* as was the custom of her Sayyid ancestors. Perhaps she was being held in reserve to be given to a powerful man who might pull the family out of poverty. Eventually, this youngest sister was given as a concubine to a local Rajput prince (Raja Salim Singh of Deoliya). She bore him a daughter, but the prince's first wife—enraged by jealousy—drove the family out. They fled with the minstrel troop. Farther south at Burhanpur—the gateway city to the Deccan—the sisters met the Mughal army of Nizam al-Mulk. They traveled with the army to Awrangabad as dancers entertaining the soldiers; along the way Mida Bibi became pregnant and gave birth to a second daughter. By the time they reached Awrangabad, the whole family of females changed their names, adopting stage names befitting royal courtesans. It is this new role as courtesans that generates such controversy among historians and biographers of Mah Laqa Bai. Vexing questions include these: How did they become courtesans? What did this entail in terms of sexuality? Did their becoming courtesans represent a shameful step down or a profitable step up?

There are several controversial episodes in the life story of Mah Laqa Bai's family that are crucial for understanding how Mah Laqa Bai became a courtesan with rich patronage, refined education, and artistic prowess. These episodes are controversial because they involve female sexuality and gender roles. Examining the earliest source will tease out how Mah Laqa Bai became a courtesan, what dangers that role entailed, and what benefits it may have provided women in the early modern Deccan. The earliest source is *Tajalliyat-e Mah* by Jawhar, a history in Persian (which exists as an unpublished manuscript). Mah Laqa Bai commissioned this history that recorded events as she wanted them remembered for posterity. It is the prime source upon which later works about Mah Laqa Bai's life are based, such as *Hayat-e Mah Laqa*, written by Maulvi Ghulam Samdani Gawhar in 1894. This booklet translates Jawhar's Persian account into Urdu and frames it as a biography. Upon it Samina Shawkat based her modern biography, written in 1959 and no longer in print.[12] In the present, the account that circulates is an Urdu biography published in 1998, *Mah Laqa—Halat-e Zindagi*, by Rahat ʿAzmi, who is well known in Hyderabad as an Urdu poet recognized for Shiʿi piety.[13] He is a popular historian who sifted through sources to clarify uncertainty about her birth and death, important buildings, songs, and poetry.

All these biographers admire Mah Laqa Bai, though modern ones hedge around her life as a courtesan. The original recorder of her story, Jawhar, assumed that her wealth, social status, and royalty shielded her from patriarchal Islamic norms; he told her life story upholding Islamic morality in general while accepting that courtesans, like kings, were exceptions to the rule. In contrast, ʿAzmi is uncomfortable with the sexuality of Mah Laqa Bai, and his puritan approach denies controversial points about her gender and sexuality. As the introduction of ʿAzmi's biography asserts, "Mah Laqa Bai was preserved by her family's nobility—she was not a courtesan but rather a pure expert in the arts and scholarship!"[14] ʿAzmi argues that Mah Laqa Bai was not a courtesan (*tavaʾif*) but rather a female scholar and artist (*ʿilm o fann ki mahira*) whose personality was chaste (*pakiza nafs*).[15] This verdict is given scholarly approval by Dr. Ashraf Rafiʿ, former head of the Department of Urdu at Osmania University, who explains that Mah Laqa Bai was called a courtesan by all of her biographers in Persian and Urdu, but that does not mean that she was actually a courtesan; rather, that label was ascribed to her during her lifetime by detractors, who felt that women who sang or danced in public were debased. She writes, "In those times, women singing and dancing in public was considered shameful (*maʿyub*); for this reason Chanda [Mah Laqa Bai] was branded as a courtesan because she was a passionate and perfect artist and not because she was a commercial prostitute (*kasabi*) or professional entertainer (*pesha-var*)."[16]

Each biographer has a different understanding of what "courtesan" means in relation to the label "prostitute." Based on these divergent understandings, some deny that "courtesan" applies to her, while others accept that it applies with reservations and clarifications. All insist that Mah Laqa Bai was talented, but they differ in their assessment of her status as an unmarried female public performer. All the sources share the idea that genealogy intimately affects one's morality (they all quote the Arabic proverb "All things return to their origin" to express how one's family background determines one's personal qualities).[17] And all hold that Mah Laqa Bai was noble and generous because of her Sayyid lineage and her mother's saintliness. The earliest source allows that her mother, Mida Bibi, was a courtesan and dancer in her youth yet became a saint in her maturity; her dancing and mingling with men did not negate her inner piety. But Islamic mores grew more conservative by the late twentieth century, to the point that 'Azmi denies that Mida Bibi was a dancer and ignores facts in the sources he quotes at length.

Rise to Fame or Descent into Shame?

Controversial episodes in the life story of Mah Laqa Bai's family are crucial to understanding how she became a courtesan. How did Mah Laqa Bai's mother along with her two aunts learn music and dance? Did her mother and aunts perform in public, and if so, in what context? Did her mother conceive children as a married woman or as a concubine? Did her mother teach her daughters to be courtesans? How did Mah Laqa Bai's first half sister marry, and how did her second half sister die in childbirth without having been married? To resolve these controversies, it is important to return to the original source for her life, the Persian history by Jawhar. It is more honest and straightforward about female sexuality and a courtesan's status, since it is free of the modern reformist agendas that affect biographies written in the twentieth century.

Consider the episode when Chanda Bibi (the maternal grandmother of Mah Laqa Bai) and her three daughters (Nur Bibi, Pulan Bibi, and Mida Bibi, the mother of Mah Laqa Bai) left their home in Ahmedabad and settled with the bhagat minstrels who sang and danced for a living. The earliest source, Jawhar, records,

> After Chanda Bibi headed out into the desert of alienation, divine bounty provided a guide—for it is the principle of the divine to extend a helping hand to the fallen and fulfill the wishes of those in need. Chanda Bibi and her three daughters found a place to stay in the quarters where a tribe of dancers lived. When they observed the poverty and helplessness of this woman they brought food to her as charity. They urged her to come to their home to learn dancing and singing, saying that "you should let us teach your daughters, who are real beauties, both singing and dancing, and let your good name and family reputation be forgotten; take up this profession (*pesha*) for there is no other means to earn a livelihood and overcome your cares other than earning (*iktisab*) in this way."[18]

After an initial refusal, the mother realized that the bhagat minstrels were right and allowed her daughters to learn music and dance. In this

Persian narrative, the bhagats are not blamed for turning the girls toward dance. Rather, they are presented as generous in their own limited way; divine providence sent them to lead the family out of poverty. In the twentieth century, 'Azmi found this narrative disturbing and strove to prove that Mah Laqa Bai's mother did not perform in front of male audiences. In his mind, that would preclude her from having an authentic Islamic spirituality and would cast a shadow of immorality over Mah Laqa Bai.[19]

After settling with the bhagats, the mother and her daughters became acquainted with the Rajput prince who ruled this area. This led to deeper artistic and sexual entanglements.

> In the days when Chanda Bibi along with her three daughters came to Deoliya (or Devlia), they lived in the neighborhood of the bhagats. Under coercion from the bhagats, she overcame her steadfast refusal to all her three daughters to learn singing. Mida Bibi [the mother of Mah Laqa Bai] was chosen to be the bed-companion of Raja Salim Singh. As was the policy of rulers of the time, the Raja maintained a house for learning music where many beautiful women and worshippers of beauty came to serve the masters of music and benefit from learning musical modes. They came to take instruction in singing and dancing from the bhagats, bringing their eyes that work miracles, their bodies that exude beauty, and their black tresses that waft perfume. Her older sister, Nur Bibi, who was characterized by a nimble nature and upright intelligence, used to spend most of her time at the house of music along with other girls with rosy cheeks and agile feet. From the bhagats she got intimate knowledge of the scales of music, then desired to hear the melodies from the masters of music who were experts at expounding the thirty-six notes. In the shortest possible time, she became an expert in music. Each time she came back home, she would teach Pulan Bibi—but not Mida Bibi—the modes of singing, the postures of dancing, and the principles of melodies. During this period, her sister became conversant in all the principles and practices of music.[20]

The original Persian source narrates a subtle story. At first, the mother thought it was demeaning for her daughters to learn music, but after she got her youngest daughter, Mida Bibi, to join the household of a local Rajput king, she relented. Mida Bibi apparently became a concubine of the Rajput king, for the king already had a wife, called the queen (*rani*).

The source does not call Mida Bibi a second wife but rather describes her as the king's bedmate (*ham-bistari*).

This arrangement gave the sisters access to music education in the high-status royal tradition rather than in the low-status bhagat style of street theater. The source suggests that the eldest sister, Nur Bibi, enthusiastically left the house to study music and dance and then returned home to teach her younger sister, Pulan Bibi. It is implied that the youngest sister, Mida Bibi, did not learn music and dance but stayed in *parda* as the concubine of the king. The Persian source hints that learning music was a sign of the sisters' intelligence rather than a lessening of their morality. It was a mark of royal honor to know music and dance, not a brand of debauchery.

When the family settled among the bhagat folk in Deoliya, the local ruler was a Rajput named Salim Singh, son of Pratab Singh, who may have been an independent ruler or a vassal of the Mughal Empire, as were many Rajput kings. He appointed provisions for the family, arranged housing, and sent valuable gifts, eventually asking for the youngest daughter, Mida Bibi, to join his household. What kind of invitation was this? The raja was a Hindu prince who had a formal wife titled *rani*, though we do not know whether they had any children. Was he asking for Mida Bibi as a concubine for pleasure or to produce an heir? The sources do not specify his motive, but it is clear that this was no formal marriage.

The Persian chronicle by Jawhar clearly says that Mida Bibi's mother "sent that tender sprout of beauty's garden to be the bed-mate (*ham-bistari*) and enjoy the embrace (*ham-aghosh*) of Raja Salim Singh."[21] Jawhar says that the mother was reluctant at first but accepted when she witnessed how the Raja upheld their dignity and treated them with respect; his depiction stresses how the family benefited from allowing the youngest daughter to become a concubine: "In the period that Mida Bibi was the bedmate of the Raja, she lived in luxury and pleasure and style and grace. The branch of her existence blossomed and bore fruit. Drops of rain from the fertile clouds of the Raja fell into the open oyster of her hopes, and a priceless pearl began to form."[22] The florid passages in Persian are certainly ornate, but they provide subtle allusions to the state of mind of the characters.

In this passage, the handsome Rajput prince is compared to a dark rain cloud, scattering his drops of fertilizing liquid. The beautiful Muslim concubine is compared to an oyster, eagerly opening in hopes of catching a drop and producing a pearl. Beneath the florid imagery and its sexual allusions, this passage gives insight into the characters' motives. The prince is like a spring rain cloud scattering drops—he acts as princes do, taking sensual pleasure wherever he can get it, for a cloud does not discriminate where it sheds its load of spring rain. The concubine is like an oyster that wishes to produce a sparkling pearl—she pleases her master in hopes of getting pregnant, which will raise her status and give her a secure place in the palace. Such allusions are often ironed flat by modern translators and biographers. In the Persian narrative, neither mother nor daughter appears resolutely reluctant to enter this arrangement, for it offered their family security. Mida Bibi would enjoy luxury inside the palace, her mother would receive provision, and the two older sisters would gain access to the royal house of music, where they would learn the arts.

Mida Bibi's status as a concubine is a crucial element in the answer to the question of whether or not she sang and danced in public. Jawhar writes that the mother allowed her daughters to learn singing and dancing, implying that all three studied these performing arts. Later, he specifies that only the older two sisters learned at this point because the youngest, Mida Bibi, served as the bedmate of the Rajput prince.[23] In this earliest version of her story, Mida Bibi did not avoid learning music and dance because she found this demeaning but rather because she was already occupied with being a concubine. She provided her family access to the royal house of music, where her older sisters could learn singing and dancing, but Mida Bibi herself was otherwise engaged in directly entertaining the king.

The modern biographer 'Azmi claims that Mida Bibi observed *parda* with her mother, refusing to leave the house while her two sisters learned music to perform in order to earn income.[24] If Mida Bibi had not been performing publicly, how did the Rajput prince meet and solicit her? If she were piously observing *parda*, how did the prince fall in love and propose that she join him as a concubine? The early Persian narrative reports that the Rajput prince met Mida Bibi, fell in love, sent precious gifts, and proposed to her mother that Mida Bibi come to live in his palace as his intimate companion. It appears that his gifts and leverage persuaded the impoverished mother to part with Mida Bibi. The earlier sources do not say that the Rajput prince saw Mida Bibi dance, but neither do they assert that Mida Bibi was keeping seclusion. It is difficult to establish for certain when Mida Bidi took up dancing and singing.

After she gave birth to a girl, Mida Bibi incurred the envy of the Rajput's wife, who tried to poison her. She survived, but her mother died of grief. During this period of anxiety and confusion, the bhagat minstrels took advantage of the daughters' skills. Jawhar writes,

> When Mida Bibi fell victim to the Raja's wife who invoked spells of sorcerers and enmity of the envious, they were almost ruined. For this reason, both sisters [Nur Bibi and Pulan Bibi] sought ways to preserve their lives. At this moment, a group of bhagats, who were seen as masters because of their training in singing and dance, decided to take advantage of the opportunity afforded by the death of their mother, Chanda Bibi. So they urged Mida Bibi and the others to flee the royal house, though they knew that Raja Salim Singh did not want her to leave. They saw this as the moment of opportunity, and took all three sisters along with them and fled along the road to Malwa and by crossing the Narmada River headed for the Deccan.[25]

The bhagat minstrels saw their opportunity to take the girls, now more valuable because of their musical skills. They helped all three sisters (with their two young brothers and Mida Bibi's infant daughter) flee Deoliya, but in the confusion both brothers were lost. The original Persian source suggests that they drowned while the family was frantically crossing the Narmada River to escape the raja's dominion and reach the Deccan. Most likely, Mida Bibi began to perform in public in the Deccan. ʿAzmi denies that she ever performed in public because, in his modern reformist view, that would be unsuitable for a pious Shiʿi woman of pure ancestry. But earlier sources report that when the women reached Awrangabad, the girls' dance there earned them fame throughout the city. With this fame, they changed their names. Nur Bibi became known as Burj Kanvar Bai, Pulan Bibi became Pulan Kanvar Bai, Mida Bibi became Raj Kanvar Bai, and Mida Bibi's little daughter, Mahtab Bibi, became known as Mahtab Kanvar Bai.

All three sisters changed their names to stage names suitable for courtesan performers, even Mida Bibi and her young daughter. The Persian source notes the close relationship that Raj Kanvar Bai enjoyed with the aristocracy of the Asaf-Jahi dynasty.[26] This was the case even though Raj Kanvar Bai, the mother of Mah Laqa, stayed home to care for her young daughter, Mahtab Kanvar Bai (the older half sister of Mah Laqa). The modern biographer ʿAzmi selectively writes that Mida Bibi, now known as Raj Kanvar Bai, stayed at home and did not go out to dance like her elder two sisters, as if she refused to learn music and disdained dancing out of pious virtue.²⁷ In contrast, the original Persian source by Jawhar specifies that she performed in the "music tent" (*muzrib khiyam*) that traveled along with the army:²⁸ "In that time, all three sisters—namely Raj Kanvar Bai, Pulan Kanvar Bai and Burj Kanvar Bai—performed among the nizam's army in glittering gatherings that spread rapture and joy.... Most of the Asaf-Jahi nobles became especially fond of Raj Kanvar Bai, inviting her to spent intimate time (*mu'anasat*) with them."²⁹

Further events confirm that all the women of this family danced before male audiences. Mida Bibi, now called Raj Kanvar Bai, conceived a second child during the years that she and her sisters stayed with the Asaf-Jahi army in Awrangabad. All the sources are silent about this. None mentions who the father was of this girl-child named Man Kanvar Bai. The original Persian source blithely attributes her pregnancy to divine providence: "During the period that Raj Kanvar Bai was staying in Awrangabad, by the will of the divine creator, there was brought forth from the womb of Raj Kanvar Bai a daughter as beautiful as a fairy princess who stepped gracefully onto the carpet of this world."³⁰ This suggests that Raj Kanvar Bai was a courtesan in the army camp, performing for male audiences (of soldiers, many of whom were nobles) and entertaining them intimately—so intimately that she could become pregnant.

The question of how Mah Laqa Bai's mother gave birth to her three daughters complicates the discussion of her sexuality and gender. She gave birth to her first daughter when she was Mida Bibi, the concubine of a Rajput ruler. All the sources agree that this first child, Mahtab Bibi, was fathered by the Rajput prince and that Mida Bibi delivered her while living in his palace.³¹ We also know that Mida Bibi, by then called Raj Kanvar Bai, joined the Asaf-Jahi army in Burhanpur and moved with it to Awrangabad. She and her sisters stayed for some time, and she gave birth to her second daughter there.³²

The Persian source does not say that the Rajput prince fathered this second daughter, Man Kanvar Bai. If Raj Kanvar Bai had been pregnant when she fled the Rajput's palace, the earlier sources would have mentioned that the Rajput prince was the father. The Persian source attributes the pregnancy to divine providence, but 'Azmi's modern biography insists that Raj Kanvar Bai's second daughter must have been fathered by the Rajput prince.³³ 'Azmi interprets the earlier sources' silence as proof that Raj Kanvar Bai bore a second child with the Rajput prince. But this assertion covers the reality that she bore an illegitimate daughter, for she was sexually intimate with other men while acting as a courtesan. It must have taken more than nine months for the family to flee Deoliya, find a position with the army in Burhanpur, and move to Awrangabad. By the time they arrived, her first daughter, Mahtab Kanvar Bai, who was born before they fled Deoliya, was reaching marriageable age.

The original Persian narrative suggests that Raj Kanvar Bai reveled in the birth of her second daughter. Courtesans welcomed the birth of daughters, and Raj Kanvar Bai raised her daughters to be courtesans after her. Was this adoption of a courtesan's career a step up or a step down for the sisters? 'Azmi says explicitly that it was a step down: "For these sisters, the day they decided to earn their livelihood by means of dance and music was a day of shame and regret. First and foremost, they changed their name, thereby losing the honor and respect of their family lineage. Besides this loss, it is clear how much they were disgusted by their own choice to perform in this way. How hard the pressure of dire circumstances must have been to make them do this!"[34] On the contrary, the sisters' performing music and dance appears to have been a step up.

The women of this family were on the upward ascent to social prestige and power. When they joined the Asaf-Jahi army, they all chose names that would grant them respect as musician-dancer-seducers. They dropped the domestic endearment "Bibi" (meaning "Miss") and added to it the royal appellation "Kanvar" (meaning "prince") and the polite feminine address "Bai" (meaning "madam"). They changed their names once they became famous for singing and dancing.[35] Their stage names would both hide their personal origins and amplify their appeal to the public. Their public was noblemen, so the names they chose included a title that smacked of royalty. Pulan Bibi retained her given name (which has no special meaning) in her new person—Pulan Kanvar Bai. Nur Bibi, meaning "Miss Light," adopted Burj Kanvar Bai, meaning "Madam Starry Prince." She retained a reference to illumination but got rid of the more pious name "Nur" (meaning light) and replaced it with the more romantic term "Burj" (meaning a constellation of stars determining one's good fortune). Mida Bibi changed her name radically. She completely discarded Mida Bibi (meaning "Miss Chaste") and replaced it with Raj Kanvar Bai, meaning "Madam King's Prince." Her new name spelled out her ambition to receive patronage from kings. The appellation "Bai" was added as a term of respect for a high-status woman. It was originally a Rajput term for "foster-sister" or a woman who had suckled from the same mother's breast (*ham-shir*); in a metaphorical extension, it was applied to women of high status who dealt with men in court or in public.

Muslims in Rajputana and Deccan regions also adopted the title with the same signification. Men would call an empowered woman "Bai," which both gave them respect and created a fictive filial bond, making the royal men their protectors as if they were a foster-sister.

Why did the sisters alter their names and choose these particular new names? ʿAzmi asserts that shame was the cause. They had lost their family honor, so they changed their names to hide their shameful situation, choosing names linked to nobility that would hint at their hidden pedigree. In ʿAzmi's narrative, the sisters adopted new names to hide their family's fall in status, recover lost dignity, and remind the public that they were of noble birth.[36] But the earlier Persian narrative suggests that the name change was not out of shame but rather ambition. Their new names gave the sisters a public persona as performers, linked to their noble audience. They were the "foster-sisters" of noblemen, empowered to circulate in public among male strangers, perform for them, and possibly seduce them in exchange for patronage, privilege, and power.

These three sisters adopted stage names that would shield them from expectations imposed on ordinary women and give them entrance to the highest circles of power. After changing their names and discarding pretense to female piety, their access to aristocratic men was limited only by their powers of seduction, their skill in performing, and their sensual appeal. Mah Laqa Bai's mother also changed the name of her eldest daughter to Mahtab Kanvar Bai, "Madam Moonlight Prince," showing that she intended to raise her as a courtesan. There would be little other opportunity for her, as the illegitimate Muslim daughter of a Hindu Rajput ruler. She named her younger daughter Man Kanvar Bai, "Madam Honor Prince," though she was the illegitimate daughter.

Mida Bibi's sisters performed in public while she reared her daughters and trained them in singing and dance at home.[37] She was grooming them not to be simple prostitutes or merely public performers but rather to perform for a select noble audience in hopes of their establishing attachment and maybe marriage. Her eldest daughter, Mahtab Kanvar Bai, achieved the dream of many a courtesan: she got a powerful nobleman, Rukn al-Dawla, the prime minister of the nizam, to fall in love with her and also marry her.[38]

Mida Bibi's second daughter, Man Kanvar Bai, was headed in the same direction. Despite her illegitimate birth, Mida Bibi raised the girl and reveled in her beauty as she grew. She was courted by nobles at a very young age. The early Persian narrative states, "She [Man Kanvar Bai] was so beautiful that, while she was still a young maiden, her loveliness attracted Navvab Shuja' al-Mulk, named Mir Muhammad Sharif Khan and also titled Basalat Jang, who was the brother of Mir Nizam al-Mulk 'Ali Khan Bahadur [the second nizam of the Asaf-Jahi dynasty]. He fell deeply and madly in love with her unmatchable beauty that he carried her to his own palace and kept her there."[39] Being carried to a nobleman's palace is a euphemism for being made a concubine. The sexual nature of being carried off is made clear by the fact that Man Kanvar Bai died young while giving birth to her first child.[40] The original Persian source states that she attracted many of the highest noblemen but unfortunately got pregnant at too early an age and died in childbirth. It appears that she entered the public arena of male desire too early, before she had the cleverness to act as a courtesan and ability to manipulate men's desire into women's profit. Her attractiveness was not leavened with calculating skill, and she was taken as a concubine or simply raped by a high-ranking noble and died giving birth, too young to bear it.

This whole episode implies that her mother, Mida Bibi, learned music and dance along with her sisters and later performed with the stage name Raj Kanvar Bai to gain patronage from noblemen; she encouraged her daughters to do the same. In Burhanpur or Awrangabad, she must have performed dance and seduced high-status men, impelling them to support her and her family. The early sources use very abstract terms derived from Arabic to describe Raj Kanvar Bai's "interaction (*ikhtilat*) and close relation (*irtibat*)" with Asaf-Jahi nobles.[41] *Ikhtilat* as "interaction" implies social mixing, especially with those outside one's immediate and secure family network, and *irtibat* as "relation" implies developing ties that are physically intimate and emotionally deep, beyond simple social visits. Her interaction and relation with the nobility of Awrangabad was in fact an artistic and sexual adventure. As a result, she became pregnant with her second child in Awrangabad, a child whose fate was to die at too young an age.

The mother and elder sister fared much better. They channeled their beauty and skill into capturing the attention of powerful male clients. They manipulated them into offering their hands in marriage. This was a great success for this family, whose ultimate goal was not to remain courtesans but to become wives of nobility with the luxury and stability that this would provide. Mahtab Kanvar Bai scored the ultimate prize and joined the household of the prime minister, Rukn al-Dawla. The original Persian source specifies that this was a valid and legal contact of marriage

(ʿaqd-e nikah-e sahih o sharʿi), in contrast to the family's earlier bonds of concubinage and informal patronage. But she was not the prime minister's first and primary wife. With the protection and support of Rukn al-Dawla, the family of courtesans moved to Hyderabad when the capital shifted there in 1763.

Mah Laqa Bai's mother also got a nobleman to legally marry her. At around the age of fifty, she married the treasurer of the nizam's personal funds (bakhshi-yi sarf-e khass) who bore the title Basalat Khan. This noble had fallen in love with her when she was younger, when the sisters had first joined the nizam's army. Yet he did not marry her until decades later, when he was convinced of her good character and family honor.[42] The original Persian source tells that they entered into a "contract of companionship" (ʿaqd-e musahibat). This mostly likely refers to *mutʿa* or informal marriage, which was legal and binding under Shiʿi customary law (in the Jaʿfari school of jurisprudence).[43] This was an informal oral contract of marriage for a temporary period, designed to allow partners to enjoy each other's company and sexual intimacy more than to create a permanent bond for raising children or building a household. Yet children born in a *mutʿa* marriage legitimately inherited their father's name and status.

When Raj Kanvar Bai gave birth to her youngest daughter, the baby was considered the legitimate child of a nobleman. The girl did not need Kanvar or "Prince" in her name. She was simply named Chanda Bibi, or "Miss Moon," the same name as her maternal grandmother. Chanda Bibi would grow up to become Mah Laqa Bai and had noble status through her father; she received a wealthy upbringing through her elder half sister's husband, the prime minister. By adopting the title "Prince" in their new stage names, the sisters and their daughters aimed to obtain access to real princes. Through the stages of performance, seduction, love, and marriage, they moved from noble in fictitious name only to noble in real wealth and power.

Evaluating a Courtesan's Progress

Mah Laqa Bai's mother traversed the whole range of life options for women in her time. To pull her family out of desperate poverty, she became the concubine of a local ruler. She fled and became a courtesan performer, even as she raised her daughters as a single mother. In midlife, she transcended the social stigma attached to female performers or unwed mothers and became a legal wife. At the end of her life, she gave away her youngest child and became a holy ascetic. The earliest Persian source sees no contradictions in this multitude of roles for one woman's adventurous life. But the modern biography of 'Azmi goes to great lengths to clean up the story, depicting Mah Laqa Bai's mother as a pious Shi'i noblewoman who had fallen on hard times but maintained her morality by observing *parda*; this caricature is possible only if 'Azmi denies some facts and obscures many tensions.

This chapter has presented the original Persian source as the most authentic and honest account of these women's journey through the life of courtesans. It has compared this account with 'Azmi's contemporary biography to illustrate how modern sensibilities have distorted their character. But between the eighteenth-century Persian account and the late twentieth-century biography, there is another version of the story: the first Urdu biography stands between them both in time and in attitude. It was written in 1894 by Ghulam Samdani Gawhar. He recorded the witty repartee of Mah Laqa Bai but agonized over how Mah Laqa Bai's mother could have been both a dancer and also a pious woman.[44] In Gawhar's view, Mah Laqa Bai's mother danced in public once the family joined up with the Asaf-Jahi army camp in Burhanpur.[45] Yet this did not diminish her noble virtues or her Shi'i piety, even if she "earned money" by performing for Asaf-Jahi nobles and soldiers.

Gawhar argues that Mah Laqa Bai's mother turned disrepute and disgrace to her advantage, through a subtle pun on the word *nam*, which in Urdu means both "name" and "reputation." Gawhar writes, "Although Mida Bibi—also known now as Raj Kanvar Bai—has had her name recorded in the register of professional earners [*kasabi*], she always retained the good judgment and moral refinement of her pure pedigree. As long as she lived, she kept the five-times daily prayers, and continually engaged in litanies, recitations, glorifications and praises for God."[46] A female earner is the antithesis of the noble pious lady living in *parda*. In fact, the term "earner" for a woman is just one step above the derogatory *bazari* who sells her body. Out of modesty, Gawhar does not state how she earned or in what profession she went public. He saw courtesans as artistic performers and educated aesthetes rather than considered whether they earned money through sensual or sexual means.

In Gawhar's view, Mah Laqa Bai's mother engaged in activities that undermined feminine norms—stepping out of *parda*, working among men in public, dancing and singing, having children out of wedlock, and perhaps even prostitution—but this did not negate her Islamic spiritual potential or her devotional authenticity. For ʿAzmi, one century later, these are irreconcilable contradictions. But in the late nineteenth century, Gawhar accepted that a courtesan could be a performer or prostitute while still retaining her dignity as a Muslim of high status, intellectual vigor, and cultural refinement. This is because his perspective was informed by living examples of courtesans who were respected members of his society. Gawhar wrote during the reign of the sixth nizam, when the courtesan culture still thrived among the courtesan descendants of Mah Laqa Bai's community.[47]

These women were known as Mah Laqa Bai's "slave girls" (*kanizak*). The distinction between owning the girls and training the girls as apprentices in music and dance is not made by the sources. It is hard to judge whether the young women in her palace were artists in training, refugees with no family protection who were "adopted" into her household, servants who worked for her, or slaves who had been purchased. In any case, Mah Laqa Bai put them to rigorous training in the musical arts. Gawhar describes how her days were filled with religious devotions, business dealings, and literary discussions, while her nights were dedicated to music and dance training: "When the sun begins to set, [Mah Laqa Bai] says her evening and night-time prayers together. After that, masters of musical arts would come to her, and there would be lessons in singing and dancing. The slave-girls of great beauty would be learning how to play drums [*mridang*], instruments [*sazang*], zither [*qanun*] and water chimes [*jaltarang*], along with lovely melodies on the three-stringed lute [*rabab*] and seven-stringed lute [*chang*]."[48] This legacy of training in music and dance continued long after Mah Laqa Bai herself passed away. Gawhar knew courtesans who still played, sang, danced, and taught in their mansions, supported by the nizam's system of stipends and land grants. Gawhar's biography was written when some courtesans who had trained with Mah Laqa Bai's adopted daughter were still alive.

Sources written before the twentieth century accept that a courtesan could be a devoted Shiʿi, renowned artist, and sexually active woman outside the bounds of marriage. Mah Laqa Bai was an exception to the rules that governed routine women. She lived by her own community's set of rules, which included intense Islamic spirituality: for example, Mah Laqa Bai composed and performed many songs that praise the Shiʿi imams, set to melodic mode (*raga*) and rhythm cycle (*tala*) of Hindustani classical music.[49] The next two chapters will explore her lyrics and spirituality more fully. The courtesans' Islamic spirituality was intense and meaningful even if it did not fully conform to the *shariʿa* as pronounced by jurists. However, in their society, the king and court also lived by their own rules, which did not conform fully to the *shariʿa*. For both these groups, Islam was not defined by the *shariʿa* as pronounced by jurists — it was wider and more inclusive than that and allowed for compromises and exceptions. Courtesans thrived in the ambiguity that this social system allowed.

As this section concludes, readers may wonder what is real in the story of Mah Laqa Bai and her family. What elements of their narrative are verifiable as being beyond exaggeration or distortion or invention? Mah Laqa Bai herself, the kernel of the story, is certainly real. Miniature paintings depict her dancing in court, poems describe her beauty and grace from the pens of notables, and architectural remains are inscribed with her name as patron. These material traces document her mature position of fame and wealth. Yet we also know that despite her greatness, she suffered from vulnerability.

Jokes circulated about her showing that she was not above ridicule. The fact that she had to use her wit to deflect oblique criticism reveals that her position in Hyderabad was not above reproach. This reproach had to do with her family background and suspicions that her female relatives had risen to nobility from murky origins through the arts as courtesans. Her female relatives are also verifiable personalities, as her elder sister and mother were married to known nobles in Hyderabad whose remains exist in Shiʿi graveyards at Mawla ʿAli.

These female relatives' marriages reveal a tension in their status: they were highly desirable but not completely respectable. So the story of their journey from Ahmedabad to the Deccan is their story of upward mobility through female seductiveness and artistic ingenuity. Their story before they joined the nizam's army is unverifiable, as it comes before their acquaintance with known noblemen and marriage with them. Their own story reveals this as an intrinsic break, by admitting that each member of the all-female family changed her name in order to become courtesans. Whatever came before their name change is speculative. Their ties to the local Rajput ruler of Deoliya and their learning music and dance from the bhagat minstrels are probable but not verifiable. The women must have learned music and dance somewhere, and this part of the narrative explains how they acquired these skills. Their parents' noble status in Gujarat, their strong Shiʿi allegiance, and their Sayyid genealogy (on both maternal and paternal sides) is much less probable and is certainly not verifiable. The usefulness of these elements of the story for Mah Laqa

Bai to secure her status in Hyderabad outweighs their probable truthfulness.

We know of these elements of the story of her female relatives only because of the oral narrative provided by Mah Laqa Bai herself. She supplied the story to the historian Jawhar, meaning that it is open to falsification and elaboration like any oral narrative. It was impossible for Jawhar to confirm or refute the facts presented to him about her family's adventures before they arrived in the Deccan. It is also difficult for modern historians to verify this information: its broad outlines conform to historical facts, while its crucial details are not traceable. For instance, we know that Sayyids from Barhah rose to important positions in the Mughal administration, but did Mah Laqa Bai's ancestors belong to this family? We know that there are several villages called Deoliya in Rajputana between Ahmedabad and Ujjain, but was one ruled by a prince named Salim Singh who patronized a house of music and took in concubines? Such details will never be confirmed. Jawhar integrated this oral tradition into his Persian history of Hyderabad, and all modern biographers inherit it from him. One has to rely on the words of Mah Laqa Bai herself to assess her family, personality, and position.

Conclusion

The story of Mah Laqa Bai's mother, aunts, and sisters presents a strange and colorful history of an all-female family. Yet all history is a blend of fact and fantasy. It must make sense of material and textual evidence, but to make sense of facts historians weave a narrative with a plot, characters, metaphors, and morals. In a plot, some details are highlighted while others are elided; some characters are raised to the foreground while others are left in the background. In a narrative, certain words, phrases, and metaphors are chosen to give mere facts meaning and relevance to an audience.[50] History is much like literature, in that both consist of narratives, yet history is a narrative that must be answerable to evidence and reason.

This realization of the historian's limitations raises a vexing question. When oral narratives are integrated into textual histories, can we confirm their truth? Mah Laqa Bai triumphed because her own narrative of her family's rise to prominence was preserved as history. Her brilliance blinded her contemporaries—especially the historian Jawhar, who wrote down her story—to any shame in her rise to fame. Jawhar penned a chronogram in Persian when he finished writing his history: "As bright as dawn is the brilliance of Mah Laqa's beauty."[51] Yet her triumph is subject to later revisions, for the prejudices of later authors can distort the morality of the subject. In the case of the most recent biography, 'Azmi went to lengths to reform his subject, to the point of denying that she was a courtesan.

Such interpretations fuel this exercise in textual archaeology. This chapter has attempted to establish the truth behind various textual retellings of her family origins. Even if the ultimate truth cannot be established, we can attempt a deeper understanding of the subject, maybe even an empathetic leap, by revealing how historians and biographers have misrecognized her. This leap of empathy is the very goal of writing, whether history or literary prose or poetry. According to Ruth Vanita, a poet and feminist cultural critic who notes how poets have long been the intimates and supporters of courtesans, this is because the act of writing "aspires to evoke imaginative sympathy in readers for those who are in predicaments very different from their own."[52]

CHAPTER TEN

The Performance of Gender

> If I stop him along his way, angry at me he remains
> Still desire for your alleyway in my heart remains
> Look here, they call Chanda the slave of 'Ali
> Can it be no other man of faith in Hyderabad remains?
>
> —*two verses from a ghazal by Mah Laqa Bai*

The previous chapter focused on female sexuality as an inherent part of the courtesan's social power. The courtesan Mah Laqa Bai used her charms—both bodily and artistic—to win the favor of men and earn power for herself. This fact leads us to two different but related questions in this chapter. As a powerful woman, did she use her resources for the empowerment of women in general? That is, was Mah Laqa Bai a feminist before the political movement in modern times called feminism?

Many literary historians look to Mah Laqa Bai to play a feminist role, but whether she does or not invites our exploration. If she was an early feminist, then her feminist voice should be found in her artistic legacy. But we must keep in mind that one's actual gender may not be the same as the gender roles portrayed in one's poems. This chapter's focus on the two questions asked above will lead us to a deeper appreciation of gender roles (both masculine and feminine) in Islamic society in the Deccan and of how gender is portrayed in Urdu poetry. It is helpful in both cases to analyze "gender" as a kind of performance and to see Mah Laqa Bai as a consummate performer.

Let us address the second question first, because it is more concrete and we have direct evidence of Mah Laqa Bai's poems before us, such as the one quoted above.[1] In it, she refers to herself as a slave of 'Ali who may be female but surpasses all the men of her city in faith. She competes with men, but does she do so as a woman? Does she write as a woman? Surely she is one of the first women to compile a collection of Urdu ghazals, but can we characterize her poetic voice as feminine? Such issues must be addressed before we turn to the question of whether her persona was feminist.

Speaking Poems like a Woman

Urdu poetry from its very origins was innovative in terms of gender. Urdu grew organically out of the meeting and mixing of Persian and Indic literary sensibilities. The poetic language of Urdu was known as rekhta (mixed language) with a vernacular Indian grammar base embellished with Persianate expressions. Although rekhta adopted its poetic genres and imagery from Persian poetry, its Indic grammar base was structured with a dichotomy between male and female gender (to describe things as well as persons). Persian has no such dichotomy. Those who wrote ghazals in Urdu were forced to depict gendered roles for the lover and beloved in ways that poets in Persian did not.

The result was that Urdu poetry itself became a gendered genre—its poetic language was called rekhta if the speaker's voice was masculine but was called rekhti if the speaker's voice was feminine. In rekhta poetry, the speaker in the poem—usually the lover—is male, and he beseeches or berates his beloved (who could be female or male). In rekhti poetry, the speaker is a female lover who seduces or titillates a beloved (who could be female or male). It is ironic that the male speaker in rekhta poetry usually takes on submissive postures as a smitten lover, in contrast to the conventional masculine ethos in social and political interactions. Inversely, the female speaker in rekhti poetry often takes on very ribald and aggressive postures as a lover whose enjoyment of love can be lusty.[2] Because the lover in rekhta poetry seldom gets to see his beloved (let alone touch her or him), this male-voiced poetry slips easily into registers of metaphoric or spiritual love. But because the lover in rekhti is bolder and embodied, this female-voiced lover dips easily into playful and raunchy sensuality.

These ironic reversals are deepened by the fact that male poets composed rekhti lyrics. The actual gender of the poet did not determine the gender of the poetry's lover persona. In essence, men sometimes took the voices of women as their protagonist, playing with women's dialect and expressions that, in a culture that practiced female seclusion, could differ from the dialect of men. One might even call rekhti "transvestite poetry" in which men dress up in the linguistic clothing of women for comic or erotic effect. Eighteenth-century men could find freedom from the conventions of respectability in taking on a woman's voice, conventions that otherwise tightly bound them in polite society. Rekhti poetry was an outlet for sensuality and audacious eroticism. Often male poets depicted a female lover rapt with desire for another woman, in a kind of voyeuristic imagining of lesbian love. Those who reformed the canon of Urdu literature in the late nineteenth century relegated the whole genre to the realm of "obscene." One century later, adventurous scholars like Carla Petievich and Ruth Vanita have revived interest in rekhti poetry as literature rather than just titillation. Vanita writes about rekhti to recover women's intimate experiences, while Petievich asks whether rekhti written by men can tell us anything at all about actual women's lives.

The insights gleaned from their new analyses of rekhti poetry can help us better understand rekhta as well. Male poets could write in the female voice by adopting the manner of rekhti. Yet could a female poet, admittedly a more rare phenomenon in that era, write in the male voice by adopting the manner of rekhta? Put more simply, does Mah Laqa Bai write her ghazal poems in rekhta or rekhti? Does she depict a lover who speaks in a male voice or in a female voice? The question is easy to ask but difficult to answer because she writes in both but commits to neither.

Examples of pure rekhti are hard to find in the collection of Mah Laqa Bai.[3] Below is one ghazal where the beloved is clearly male. The lover speaking keeps asking him if he will do various actions, all of which are conjugated for a male actor who is familiar to the speaker. The lover's gender is never specified, but by implication it is an imploring female lover who speaks.[4]

> Will you keep inventing new oppressions every day?
>   You will ruin countless lovers' hearts in this way
> Will you release me from your net? But then
>   You will make someone else your captive prey
> Will you truly think only of me, even if
>   You will entertain other lovers for display?
> Will you ever make a heart happy? It seems
>   You will keep aloof, letting hearts in sorrow stay
> Will you accept, O master 'Ali, a hundred lives like Chanda's?
>   You will help her sacrifice, for this alone she'll pray

Although the lover speaking in the poem could well be a woman addressing a male beloved, the speaker's gender is not clearly delineated. Her statements are not distinctly feminine, nor are the experiences of being in love about which she speaks. Mah Laqa Bai in general refused to write poetry that spoke in a typically female voice or was situated in specifically female positions.

Could Mah Laqa Bai, as a woman poet, write in the voice of a female lover? Yes, she could have chosen to write in rekhti, for that style had developed in the Deccan. A court poet of Bijapur, Hashimi Bijapuri (died 1697), is credited with inventing the genre of ghazals that speak in the voice of a woman. Because this poet was blind, he was allowed access to women's quarters of the palace and aristocratic homes. He listened acutely and picked up the dialect, idioms, and themes that women used among themselves.[5] The genre spread from Bijapur to Burhanpur at the Deccan's northern edge. Later, it flowered in Delhi and Lucknow but was seen as a "lesser" genre, fit for obscene humor and the bodily pleasures of love. The women it depicts as lovers are not powerful social actors. It was not an apt genre for a woman who was trying to make it in a man's world, for it tended to reduce its female lovers to displays of concupiscence.

Therefore, it is not surprising that Mah Laqa Bai mainly chose to write love poems in which the lover speaks in a male idiom. This ghazal is an example of her style in writing through the male voice, addressing a female beloved pictured as having long black hair in a braid dangling down her back:[6]

> Look out, shoulders, don't get tangled up with her braid
>   The poison bite of black snakes should keep you afraid
> I spent all night with you, but this lover's hope is unfulfilled
>   This dawn of parting is like judgment day before me arrayed
> My heart still craves an arch from her eyebrow
>   That dark eye which has countless happy marriages frayed
> How can this innocent heart ever understand your power?
>   All who meet you, O cruel one, suffer a painful raid
> No heart's state is kept from you, 'Ali, who knows all things
>   You give the sun light, so keep safe Chanda, your maid

In this ghazal, verbs are conjugated in such a way as to keep the speaking subject's gender ambiguous. Yet the beloved is described by her braid, which is like a long black snake whose bite is so dangerous that the lover not only warns himself to stay away but also calls out to the beloved's shoulders to beware. That image determined the gender of the lover and beloved in this translation, though they are otherwise ambiguous.

Modern readers might interpret the image of long hair as a sign that the beloved is female, but in premodern Urdu poetry this is not always the case. Long snaking curls are not the provenance of women alone. A male beloved could also be described with wreathing and coiling locks, if they are described as a tangled nest rather than as two snake-like braids. This image provides one of Mah Laqa Bai's ghazals with its rhyme word, the unusual choice of "snakes":[7]

> In writhing coils, your locks of hair are like snakes
>   No one, even in dreams, has seen such black snakes
> If I glimpse in my sleep your perfumed curls
>   All night my tearful eyes see nothing but snakes
> Is it a stray hair clinging to my love's moist cheek?
>   No, dewdrops in moonlight are licked by shy snakes
> Give my mind rest, O wine-pourer, so hand me the goblet
>   Stay close, let me see reflected your brow wreathed in snakes
> Blow a breath of reverence, Chanda, for Najaf's noble king
>   It'll make shudder and fall the threatening hood of any snakes

In contrast to the previous poem, these coiling black locks belong to a beloved whose gender remains ambiguous throughout. Only in the fourth couplet is there a suggestion that the long black hair might belong to a male beloved; the lover refers to him as wine-pourer (*saqi*), a role traditionally played by handsome young men in royal gatherings. Still, in the intimacy of a private meeting between lover and beloved, a woman might pour wine, and some miniature paintings do depict young beautiful women carrying flasks. In the final couplet, the speaker addresses Chanda directly, reminding her to confront any threat, such as a rearing black snake like a cobra, by taking with reverence the name of 'Ali—"Najaf's noble king." Here a masculine/feminine dyad is created, but it is projected between Chanda and Imam 'Ali and leaves the speaker's gender still ambiguous.

If it is difficult to assign a gender to the beloved even when his or her physical features are described, and if poems were often composed in such a way as to keep ambiguous the speaker's gender, then how can we say that Mah Laqa Bai composed her poems in rekhta? In some of her poems, the speaker's gender is more directly identified. In the following poem's first couplet, the verb is conjugated in the masculine gender—"I stare away"—which reveals that the speaker is a male:[8]

> My heart sighs as my memories explore a certain someone
>> Night and day I stare away waiting for a certain someone
> Your desire will always be for others, but still
>> In my heart all others pale before a certain someone
> If someone begs a kiss, just give for kindness's sake
>> You might cause pain if you ignore a certain someone
> How can I explain the distress that grips my heart?
>> He never listens however might implore a certain someone
> By God, Chanda's love is true, I assure each and every one
>> Except for Najaf's king, could she adore a certain someone?

The lover is male in the first couplet, announcing the composition as a rekhta poem and implying a female beloved as the lover stays awake "waiting for a certain someone." Yet the astute reader will notice that the gender of lover and beloved are not stable.

In the ghazal, the speaker's voice can shift in gender from couplet to couplet. The integrity of the poem comes with the constant rhythm and insistent rhyme rather than by offering a single speaker's voice. The ghazal is not a personal confession but rather offers a snapshot of lover and beloved in different postures of love. This creative ambiguity is very much present in Mah Laqa Bai's collection of ghazals, both within any single poem and across the collection as a whole. In general, Mah Laqa Bai writes love poems in which the speaker is male—in general but not always, and that ambiguity is very important. Yet even if the speaker is male in her poems, does that mean women are absent or subsidiary? Not at all—the woman is the dominant force in the relationship, as the object of a male lover's desire, even if the poem does not speak in her voice. Indeed, her silence displays a position of strength, for in the ghazal the lover speaks out of weakness, need, and desperation! Silence is the prerogative of a beloved who is aloof, independent, and happy without the forlorn lover.

As a woman poet, Mah Laqa Bai wrote about her own experiences, even if the lover who speaks in her ghazals is male. Mah Laqa Bai can write about herself as an object of love, for she certainly spent much of her energy making herself an object of male desire. The following poem implies that the beloved is a woman, suggesting that a man is gazing with love upon her. The beloved's fingertips are dyed bright with henna (*mehndi*) in the style of a dancer, so red that they outshine the gems that encrust her bracelet. This image provides this ghazal with its unusual rhyming word—*yaqut* or ruby:[9]

> How could a ruby face her lip's radiant red?
>   Just hearing her name, a ruby's luster pales
> Chewing *paan*, that tormenter permitted a kiss, but her lips
>   Were caressed by only her fortunate betel nut's ruby veil
> Frowning, she turned to insult her poor lover
>   Whose color faded like an ill-omened blue ruby
> When your jeweled bangle slides down your wrist
>   Your henna-dyed fingertips outshine its pendant ruby
> O 'Ali, in paradise grant Chanda a simple gift
>   A mansion of crimson jewels with a door of ruby

This poem depicts the beloved not only as a woman but as a courtesan. Her henna-stained hands beckon, her *paan*-reddened lips entice, and her choice insults keep admirers in supplication; these are the signs of a courtesan. Shah Siraj used these same signals to describe courtesans who comforted him in his youthful lovesickness: the henna on their hands so red that they turn water to steam, the gold pendant on their foreheads so bright that they give light to the sun, the witticisms they unleash through *paan*-chewing lips so seductive that they could melt stones into water.[10] In poems like the one above, Mah Laqa Bai takes on the persona of a male lover in order to describe in delicious detail a female beloved who is at once charming and formidable. This gives us a hint as to why she, as a woman poet, often writes in a male voice. As a courtesan, she is adept at changing personas and seeing herself through the eyes of another. She must, after all, behave not just as it pleases her to behave but as it pleases the male audience that she must hold rapt.

This is characteristic of women in patriarchal environments, but it is more exaggerated for a courtesan for it defines her profession. She sees herself through the male gaze as it sees her. She must imagine herself in the way the man who lusts after her does, in order to anticipate his lust, draw it out, play with it, capture it, and ultimately use it to her own advantage. She must do so with such ease and grace as to make him feel privileged to be so used. The following ghazal is a typical example of her love poems written in the voice of a male lover speaking to a female beloved, who is addressed as Venus:[11]

> I survived exile's night, now to meet my love comes the day
> God has shown us once more that spring comes one day
> Since you upped and left my side, O moon-faced beauty,
> Don't ask why such restlessness comes to me each day
> I swear by the goblet's lip, my saqi, give me more wine!
> The night is for drunkenness—the hangover comes by day
> O Venus, your night brings a wounded heart no rest
> Only sighing, complaining and crying becomes his day
> Only if Chanda passes each breath remembering 'Ali's name
> Does her life count and the passing time becomes a day

The necessity of teasing and pleasing men helps explain why Mah Laqa Bai wrote in the voice of a male lover. When in the second couplet she has her male lover address his beloved as "moon-faced beauty" (*mah-ru*), she is not only using a classic image from Persian and Urdu poetry but also making a secret gesture toward herself, for she is also named after the moon and in miniature paintings is depicted with a crescent moon beaming over her brow. Even if she wrote in the voice of a male lover, this persona gave her the opportunity to describe the feminine allure that she embodied in her actual social context as a performer.

A Woman Speaking Poems

Mah Laqa Bai wrote poetry in which the gendered voices are ambiguous, shifting, and full of parody. But these poems also insist, by mentioning her own name, Chanda, in each closing couplet, that the author is a woman. She did not always write in the voice of a woman, but it was as a woman that she wrote. So what did it mean for Mah Laqa Bai—socially, politically, or artistically—to write poems as a woman in public view? Did this challenge patriarchy? Was she a feminist before the name existed to describe her?

The scholar Carla Petievich asks why female poets often adopted a normative, masculine voice in composing ghazals—that is, why did they write in rekhta? She explains, "We see clearly that women who composed lyric poetry chose to speak in a masculine voice. Surely, they did so because they understood the deep conventions of the poetic system in which they were participating, valued the system, and wished to participate fully in it. To adopt the voice of rekhti would not have effected full participation."[12] According to Petievich, women poets desired to participate in the social activity of writing and reciting ghazal poetry and did so according to that genre's own internal conventions. Equal participation in the genre was more important to women poets like Mah Laqa Bai than writing "confessional poetry" that expressed their experiences as women. The ghazal's convention is for the lover's voice to be male, no matter the gender of his beloved or the gender of the actual poet.

That was simply a product of the patriarchal environment in which ghazal writing evolved. This patriarchal environment allowed men flexibility to invert conventions that was not allowed to female poets. Male poets who wrote rekhti in the voice of a female lover participated fully in the poetic tradition. A good example of this is Qais from Hyderabad, a contemporary of Mah Laqa Bai who was respected as a ghazal poet even while he occasionally wrote raunchy rekhti verses.[13] Men had the option of adopting a feminine persona in their poetic voice (for the purpose of writing ribald or comic or lascivious poetry) without sacrificing their public position as authors. But women, coming from a much more tentative position as public authors, did not have that choice. Petievich shows that women poets had to prove their worth among male poets by adopting the normative gendered voice of the ghazal, which is male.

For formal and literary purposes, female poets like Mah Laqa Bai chose to write in a predominantly male voice. Accepting this means that her poetry, her most eloquent legacy for the present, may not provide much insight for feminist scholars who comb the archives of literature and history to find examples of women's empowerment in the past.[14] In that project, Mah Laqa Bai has attracted a great deal of contemporary attention, as journalists and feminist scholars have connected her personality to modern projects of women's education, expression, and empowerment. They do this through looking at her land grants and her buildings rather than at her poetry. Journalists and scholars in Hyderabad have commented that the lands of Mah Laqa Bai's mansion in Nampally had evolved, long after her death, into a college for women.[15]

Contemporary journalists and heritage admirers might retell Mah Laqa Bai's life story by dressing her in the guise of a female activist. Though she was certainly generous and made a spiritual practice out of distributing her wealth to the poor and pious, she did not specifically give away her wealth to poor women or promote public education. Her educational endeavors focused on training young girls to become dancers, musicians, and courtesans like herself. She may have purchased many of them as slaves (in her biographical sources, such a girl was called "young servant" or *kanizak*), as was customary and legal in her era. She does not appear to be a feminist in the modern sense of the word: she was not a social and political activist struggling to change the power structures of society so that ordinary women could enjoy more autonomy.[16]

In asking whether Mah Laqa Bai was a feminist, we have to acknowledge that this label is anachronistic. With more subtlety, we can ask whether there are elements in her personality and position that can be turned to a feminist agenda. She was not a feminist in the sense of upholding women's dignity independent from men, despite her leading a life free of the conventional restraints of marriage and child-rearing. She took for granted that women, like men, exist in a chain of dependence. Her goal was to activate this chain to her own benefit, by intensifying her dependence on male figures at the top of the chain and exerting her control over men lower down. She politically associated with the most powerful men at court while staying aloof from other men (or charming them into submission) through art. She religiously directed her love and admiration toward male figures like the imams in general and ʿAli in particular. Being dependent on ʿAli as slave, servant, devotee, and lover meant gaining the power to stay aloof from other men. This expressed an ideal not of autonomy but rather of elevated dependence. One could argue that this is the only form that "feminism" could take in a premodern environment (with no framework of individual liberties, constitutional rights, or public access to education regardless of class or gender). For women in this environment, the only form of independence from patriarchal structures was manipulation of sacred symbols and adherence to religious ideals, which gave them only conditional independence from men's control.

Some contemporary South Asian feminists allege that Mah Laqa Bai's poems do not speak with an authentic feminist voice about the struggles of real women to achieve freedom and independence from male supremacy. Rather, the courtesan's voice and poetry could be seen as a by-product of male dominance. Raising up courtesans as the epitome of beauty and refinement was a male strategy to keep real women down. According to this feminist interpretation of literary history, the courtesan's femininity was just another performance to fulfill male desire.

This style of political feminism views courtesans as females who betray womankind by decorating themselves in the luster of crumbs tossed to them from the banquet table of male dominance. Rather than held up as examples of women's creativity, artistry, and autonomy, in this view courtesans are denounced as a golden rung in the chain that restrains authentic women from achieving their true potential, and along with prostitutes they require social reform rather than literary praise. A less politicized view might appreciate the fact that female authors do not want their writing acknowledged solely because they are women, but rather they aspire to participate as equals—and maybe as rivals—of male authors. They desire to be taken seriously as contributors to their respective genres (from the novel with its modern foundation to the ghazal with its medieval pedigree) and therefore do not write exclusively as women or about women's experiences, as Carla Petievich maintains.

However, very few women were able to participate in literary production at that level before the advent of modern reform movements. Of the small number who composed ghazals before the twentieth century, most were courtesans or queens, and they certainly did not represent the experiences of the vast majority of women in their literary output. Often they did not even write in anything that can be identified as a recognizably "female" voice. So Mah Laqa Bai's place in the canon of Urdu literature continues to be ambiguous.

Language in Which Female Poets Speak

Mah Laqa Bai is controversial in terms of women's empowerment as literary experts. Likewise, she is controversial in terms of her use of language in the development of Urdu. In Hyderabad, the question of language is fraught with political consequence because the city is not only a center of modern Urdu literary production but also a center of a distinct regional dialect called Deccani. The role of Deccani dialect in the development of modern Urdu is controversial. For scholars from Hyderabad, it is a sore point; their local dialect is often viewed condescendingly as an "impure" form of the language that is befouled with loan words from Marathi, Telugu and Kanada, muddied with contracted mispronunciations and weighted down with archaic expressions.

The Urdu literary canon was mainly constructed by literary figures who were mostly male and mainly from Northern India. These figures upheld their own "refined" Urdu, which was heavily inflected by Persian vocabulary and expression, as the standard Urdu for literary expression. Although most scholars admit that the Deccan was an early crucible for the development of Urdu and was the origin of the Urdu ghazal as a genre, they usually give the region's authors short shrift. They focus on the "mature flowering" of Urdu poetry in Delhi and Lucknow in the period after Vali Deccani brought the practice of composing ghazals in Urdu to the north. In most histories of Urdu, Vali is revered, Siraj is mentioned, and then the baton of excellence is passed to poets in North India, picturing later poets in the Deccan as obscure or third-rate.

For scholars and literary critics resident in the Deccan region, this conception of "chaste Urdu" is condescending. It aggravates political scars of the past. It covers up the devastation of the Mughal invasion and erases the ideological violence inflicted upon the Deccan kingdoms. Some scholars and critics have responded by upholding their southern region's contributions to Urdu and extolling the literary qualities of its Deccani dialect. This movement of regional pride coincides with debates about gender and feminism.

One poet and women's rights activist in Hyderabad is Jameela Nishat, the general secretary of Shaheen Women's Resource and Welfare Association. She asserts that women and their expressions largely fueled the development of Deccani Urdu. She claims that Deccani can be called an "aesthetically feminine" dialect that is uniquely equipped to express women's experiences, to the point that male writers adopted the voice and persona of heroines. She equates the influence of Persian on Urdu with male dominance and Mughal imperialism: "In our opinion, therefore, the empowerment of the North Indian masculine Urdu on the aesthetically feminine Dakhini [Deccani] Urdu ... gradually led to the educated people of the Deccan being alienated from their roots."[17]

To Nishat's gendered history of Urdu, the poetry of Mah Laqa Bai is troubling. Residents of the Deccan being "alienated from their roots" linguistically and culturally came from their having been conquered by the Mughal armies of Awrangzeb. Following the Mughals, the nizams' military and administrative aristocracy came from Northern India and brought to the Deccan a dialect of Urdu that was more heavily influenced by Persian in vocabulary, pronunciation, and poetic imagery; it became known as the language of the lofty camp of the Mughal army (*zaban-i urdu-i muʿalla*), which became shortened to Urdu. Under the rule of the nizams, this "Persianized" Urdu came into fashion in court and among poets whom the court patronized.

One of the earliest poets patronized by the nizam's court was Mah Laqa Bai. For this reason, Nishat scrutinizes her poetic voice and the language she uses. Nishat judges that Mah Laqa Bai betrayed her gender as a female poet by participating in the "false purification of the Dakhini [Deccani] language" that was advocated by late Mughal-era poets. Nishat contends that this movement "intended to remove local and indigenous elements in the existing spoken and written language of the times and gradually led to its Persianization."[18] What was the nature of this change in poetic language? Was it a "masculinization" of the Urdu language that stole away the potential for women to express themselves in its literature, as Nishat asserts?

The poetic language of Urdu did change rapidly after the Mughal conquest. Poets imported more Persianized vocabulary while distinctively Deccani words and grammatical constructions were avoided. Mah Laqa Bai's collection of ghazals gives vivid evidence of this process. Fortunately, archives have preserved different manuscript copies of her divan, which were copied at different times in her life. This means we have multiple windows into her editing and revising of any single poem, for it was the custom for Urdu poets not just to add new poems to their collection with the passage of time but also to edit existing poems.

In particular, we are indebted to Sir John Malcolm, assistant to the British Resident in Hyderabad in his youth (died 1833). With gusto he attended dance performances by Mah Laqa Bai. At one private performance on October 18, 1799, when she was thirty-one years old and at her zenith, Mah Laqa Bai presented to him a copy of her ghazals, which he kept in his personal effects when he left Hyderabad for other diplomatic postings. This collection containing 118 ghazals made its way to the British Library in London. After this tryst and exchange of gifts, Mah Laqa Bai continued to refine her ghazals for a decade or more. Near the end of her life, she sponsored the historian and poet Jawhar to write a history of Hyderabad that highlighted her achievements; when Jawhar finished this history in 1818, he appended to it her divan, which consisted at that time of 123 ghazals.[19] About a century later, Mah Laqa Bai's divan was published in Hyderabad, at which time it contained 125 ghazals. We can conclude that Mah Laqa Bai continued to write poems, though these earlier manuscripts contain smaller versions of her collection. She added new poems and revised older ones. The manuscripts contain earlier versions of some of the same ghazals found in the published edition, allowing us to trace at least two moments in her revision process.

Using these archival resources, we can compare earlier and later versions. It is clear that Mah Laqa Bai revised her ghazals to remove grammatical constructions that are distinctly Deccani. She often replaced them with modes of expression that are closer to the northern dialect of Urdu, which has since become "standard" literary Urdu. She probably made such changes under the advice of her teacher, the poet Iman, who was influenced by the northern dialect of Urdu. In their era, Hyderabad received an influx of poets and writers from North India, as Delhi became unstable due to weak leadership among later Mughal emperors, infighting among their ministers, and raids by the Marathas. Mah Laqa Bai adjusted her style to conform to the taste of her patrons, the nizams, who had a deep attachment to the northern cultural zone. She revised her poems not only in language but also in imagery. Sometimes she clarified a couplet that contained obscure or complex expressions, and other times she eliminated a couplet altogether to replace it with a different one. This evidence allows us to address Jameela Nishat's contention that this process of revision and linguistic alteration imposed masculinist and Persianizing norms onto Deccani Urdu. Did Mah Laqa Bai help undermine a feminine mode of expression and advocate a masculine one? Did she betray feminine expression in Urdu literature, despite her position as one of the earliest women to excel in the Urdu ghazal?

In the Deccan, the Urdu idiom used in poetry began to change with the advent of Mughal rule. In the eighteenth century, ghazals became the most popular form of poetry. Ghazals displaced the *geet* for singing sentiments of love and rivaled the Shi'i-oriented marsiya for expressing devotional beliefs; both genres had been popular before the Mughal conquest. The pace of change quickened after Hyderabad became the nizam's capital in 1763. Nishat admires Mah Laqa Bai as the "first woman poet known to us [in the Deccan]" but also positions her as a traitor to the feminist cause and Deccan pride. Nishat notes with alarm how Mah Laqa Bai wrote ghazals that were "talking in a masculine tone," how her writing helped empower the Persianized dialect of North Indian masculine Urdu, and how she furthered the cultural trend through which Deccani "became the language of ridicule and mockery."[20] But was Mah Laqa Bai conscious of altering the poetic language of Deccani Urdu? Did she see herself as a representative of Deccani language and culture at all?

Mah Laqa Bai was not beholden to the prior literature of Deccani dialect. Her family migrated from Gujarat to the Deccan only one generation before her birth, and their ancestry was from Northern India. The women of her family acculturated to the Deccan through interaction with the Mughal army of the Deccan (in Burhanpur and later in Awrangabad). Their dialect was adapted to life among the soldiers, scholars, and

The Performance of Gender 223

merchants who accompanied the nizam's army. This was precisely the social space in which northern influences were mixing with local Deccani styles of expression. Mah Laqa Bai's family moved to Hyderabad because the capital shifted there. Her loyalty was to the nizam and his courtiers rather than to any notion of Deccan soil and identity.

However, Mah Laqa Bai did identify with some aspects of the Deccani idiom and the region's distinct history. This is particularly true in terms of her religious identity as a Shi'i woman. The Deccan had long been a stronghold of Shi'i devotion, and the city of Hyderabad held a special place in the hearts of Shi'i believers. The hilltop shrine of Mawla 'Ali gave the women of her family an entry point into the spiritual heart of the city; as noted earlier, Mah Laqa Bai was devoted to the shrine's rituals and helped build its institutions. She patronized religious festivals and rituals of the Deccan, which had a strong Shi'i orientation, as we will explore in the next chapter. Along with Shi'i courtiers of Iranian background, she encouraged the Sunni nizams to adopt some Qutb-Shahi royal symbols and rites that were strongly inflected by Shi'ism as a sign that the nizams' rule was in continuity with the past glory of Hyderabad rather than imposed by conquest. Her Shi'i faith allowed her to adopt and perpetuate certain aspects of Deccan custom, though she was not a Deccan chauvinist in language or politics.

To conclude this section on political controversies over women writing poems in Urdu, we return to the image of Mah Laqa Bai revising her ghazals. Her revisions illustrate the change in poetic diction and spoken dialect that was occurring around her, as Mughal norms and Persianized styles took hold in the Deccan. But as she revised her poems, was Mah Laqa Bai conscious of eliminating Deccani idioms and imposing a standard Urdu from the north? She was aware of "refining" her style, but she probably did not perceive this as having political or ideological motives. Rather, she revised her poems to adopt a more Persianized style out of a courtesan's desire to entertain and entice. Her ghazals, after all, were part of her performance. They were not the private expressions of her inner identity, either as a Deccan resident or as a woman. They were to be sung, accompanied by dance, in court and in the private parties of patrons. Her revisions were to make the songs clearer and more musically appealing to her audience. Her audience consisted mainly of the second nizam's family and followers from the north and his prime ministers from Iran, all of whom favored a more heavily Persianized diction. Their aesthetic set the tone for her songs, and they were the targets of enticement and seduction during her performances.

Gender as Performance

This chapter explores the manifestations of gender expressed in Mah Laqa Bai's writing. Her poems contain many gender ambiguities. They speak mainly in the voice of a masculine lover, which place them squarely in the dominant mode of ghazal writing. The speak sometimes to a female beloved, though most often the gender of the beloved is not indicated or is deliberately obscured, which is also characteristic of Urdu ghazals. That she spoke in the voice of a masculine lover may surprise contemporary readers, especially those who expect a female poet to be a feminist or to express experiences unique to women. Mah Laqa Bai frustrates those expectations, which are imposed upon her by the needs and hopes of contemporary readers in our own political environment. Today's readers who expect Mah Laqa Bai's poems to take a political stand representing womankind or Deccani nativism are left feeling bewildered when her poems do not dance to these contemporary tunes. Bewilderment can deepen into a sense of betrayal, especially considering the crucial place that Mah Laqa Bai occupies, as one of the earliest female ghazal writers.

Viewing her in retrospect, we tend to see her mainly as a female poet, but this facet of Mah Laqa Bai's identity was subsumed by her being a performer. Poetry was part and parcel of her being a courtesan. Being a performer was the primary element of her identity, over and above her being a woman, a Deccan resident, a pious Shi'i, or an Urdu poet. All other characteristics of her personality were inflected to increase her popularity as a performer. So performance is the activity that allows us to comprehend her complex position as a woman writing ghazals, poems written in a voice that is mainly male, speaking of passionate love for woman or a man. By highlighting her role as a courtesan, we can understand her poems' complex interplay between male persona gazing upon, pursuing, or being subdued by a female beloved.

It is a strange paradox that as a courtesan who was dedicated to crafting a self to attract the gaze of men, Mah Laqa Bai and others like her were able to live relatively independent from men. Chapter 8 presented biographical details of her interactions with powerful men at the nizam's court, upon whom she depended for patronage and through whom she came to have the wealth and status that gave her autonomy—probably more autonomy than any other woman in her society. Later in life, she invested her hope in other women rather than in men. In her mansion, called Khassa Rang Mahal, she trained hundreds of girls in the arts of music and dance. She adopted the best as her daughter, raised her to be a courtesan, and gave her the name Husn Laqa Bai or "Madam Beauty Cheek." Mah Laqa Bai designated her to be madam of the household after her. Her nineteenth-century biography recalls that after Mah Laqa Bai passed away, "her adopted daughter Husn Laqa Bai became the owner of her entire estate. . . . Husn Laqa Bai was raised in impeccable manners, cultivated and educated, a good judge of culture and a font of generosity. Her grand manor house and garden is still existent on Nampally road and she had a second garden in Lingampally. As long as Husn Laqa Bai remained alive, the courtesans' way of life continued in good order."[21] In 1894 when this was written, the courtesans' houses were supported by financial grants from the nizams. The nizams continued in power until 1948 as the largest "princely state" in India. Thus the tradition of courtesans continued longer in Hyderabad than in other areas where British Victorian values were more influential. By the mid-twentieth century, Mah Laqa Bai's mansion had been transformed into a girls' school, which still exists in the Nampally neighborhood.

Yet it is notable that in 1894, Mah Laqa Bai's followers were known as "dancing girls" rather than as courtesan artists. Despite the nizam's patronage, the social ethos was changing. Dancing girls or prostitutes had no possibility to be—like Mah Laqa Bai had been before—a social leader, influential politician, or respected artist whose spiritual aspiration earned her widespread acclaim. These dancing girls' position in society became steadily degraded, as documented by Karen Leonard, who analyzed court cases from Hyderabad in the late nineteenth century. Leonard demonstrates that younger courtesans were leaving their institutions by eloping to marry men or running away with the jewelry they were allowed to wear, jewelry that belonged to the madams who sued to get them back.[22] Such court cases demonstrate that the courtesan's way of life was under strain as the twentieth century approached. Yet even if they were merely "dancing girls" or prostitutes, their very existence reminds us of the persistence of women-dominated spaces and their largely independent social lives.

Courtesans enjoyed autonomy that most women of their society did not, yet they were not independent of men. The male lover's speaking voice in Mah Laqa Bai's poems reminds us of the persistent gaze and demands of men, even in the life of such an autonomous and enabled woman as Mah Laqa Bai. In order to turn her wealth, status, and power to her own advantage, a courtesan had to constantly perform her gender before men. She had to present the persona of a desirable, seductive, but rarely accessible woman, a persona that appealed to all the senses. It was through dance that her manipulation of the senses found its consummate and most powerful form. Mah Laqa Bai's position as a female dancer gives her adoption of a male voice in her poetry a complex depth. That she writes as a man gazing in love or lust upon a woman is not "covering up" her own gender; rather, through this device she plays with her own gender as a performer habitualized to displaying her body artfully to capture the gaze of men.

We can say that Mah Laqa Bai was born to perform. Her birth celebrations were a grand spectacle in the theatrics of power. Her family history goes into detail about the occasion, which Mah Laqa Bai must have heard about again and again from her mother, elder half sister, and other supporters who helped raise her. On the sixth day after her birth, her relatives hosted the celebration of Chhati Shab. It was a royal affair to show off the pomp of her family, for her elder half sister had married Rukn al-Dawla, who became the prime minister only four years before Mah Laqa Bai's birth, and her half sister celebrated this birth as if it were her own child.

Rukn al-Dawla was appointed prime minister around the time when the second nizam moved his capital to Hyderabad. In Hyderabad, the nobility took over grand mansions. Rukn al-Dawla was assigned a palace while Basalat Khan, the father of Mah Laqa Bai, purchased the mansion of Rustom Dil Khan.[23] For the celebration of her birth, that mansion was extravagantly decorated and powerful nobles attended. Jawhar, Mah Laqa Bai's historian, describes the event:

> On the order of a prince, this Chhati Shab celebration was held in the palace of Rustom Dil Khan [which had been purchased by Basalat Khan]. . . . Rukn al-Dawla, the prime minister of the Asaf-Jahi dynasty, came to that palace and took great pains to have it lavishly decorated. . . . Nobles came along with royal soldiers to give their respects in full regalia and to take the *kicheri* of the celebration with their own hands and give the customary congratulations.[24]

Kicheri, a fortifying dish of rice with lentils, was an integral part of the celebration. The dish circled through the city on a royal elephant from noble's mansion to courtier's palace until it was delivered at the house where the birth took place. It transmitted the blessings of the whole city, whose people turned out to participate in the procession, to the house in which the infant was born. For the Chhati Shab celebration, the house held many visitors:

> An assembly of music and dance was organized, with camphor candles and crystal chandeliers that roused the envy of all others. The joyful and beautiful voices of the celebration reached the heights of heaven. To come pay their respects and dispense their blessings, master musicians and adept performers of Hindustan and the Deccan came and gathered in the house of this beautiful new-born. There came a troop of handsome men strutting like peacocks in finery and female dancers with blandishing eyes and alluring gestures, each of whom was a world of seductive fascination. Turn after turn, they came to the house of Raj Kanvar Bai, that abode of spreading music and dance, to offer felicitations and perform their arts of song and dance.[25]

As Jawhar describes this scene, the musical imagery grows so intense that he abandons prose and slip into a masnavi with its own musical rhythm:

> Once again, you've stirred up waves on music's sea
>   The ear of the heavens hears the call of your melody
> Your song is like that of Venus in her celestial spheres
>   In so many hues in harmony with the tones of the lute
> With viol and harp, lute pluck and tambourine play
>   You strike up a chord all night and throughout the day
> Dressed in golden suits that glitter like sun's rays
>   Shimmering in silver gowns lustrous as moonshine
> Another in clothes as colorful as tulips and roses
>   Inspires brigades of nightingales to call out in song
> Each in the troop in vibrant clothes and scintillating
>   Hues which set the surrounding onlookers palpitating
> Each one's costume wafts perfume and ambergris
>   The world's nostrils begin to flare with their aroma
> Thus the gathering was filled with glowing beauties
>   And glimmered like a string of multihued jewels

Jawhar's description conjures up the vision of these female dancers and the aesthetic delight for all senses that their performance creates.

Such aesthetics were not just an example of fine art but also an indispensable part of power politics in the premodern Deccan. A performance showed off the wealth of its sponsor and created social capital in terms of respect that demanded deference from others. In an era when holding public office—as Rukn al-Dawla held as prime minister—depended more on personality than on merit, sponsoring such performances gave public witness to a man's cultural refinement, aesthetic taste, and ability to delight others, which bolstered his respect in the eyes of other powerful men.

What about the performers themselves? What kind of dance did the *tava'if* of Hyderabad and the Deccan present in the late eighteenth century when Mah Laqa Bai learned her art? The existent sources—poems that describe their dances or miniature paintings that depict them—do not specify which dance form they practiced. Most likely their dance form resembled kathak, cultivated by courtesan dancers of Northern India. Such dancers in Lucknow, like those of the late eighteenth-century Deccan, were known by the term collective noun *tava'if*, which came into both northern and Deccani Urdu from Persian, meaning "a group of circling dancers."[26] The fact that the same term was applied to courtesans in the Deccan and Lucknow suggests that their dance form might also have been similar. However, the term kathak was first used to describe a dance form in North India in the late nineteenth century, making it difficult to ascertain that courtesans in both places practiced the same dance form that we now call kathak.[27]

The term *tava'if* invokes the image of a circle of dancers and also an individual dancer who moves in rapid circles. These two images describe a theory of the evolution of kathak dance. The dance form evolved from folk dances that were used by some communities of bhakti devotees to depict the playful devotion between Krishna and the cowherding women of Brindaban. In such rituals, a troupe of female dancers formed a circle to rejoice in the intimacy of Krishna: each would feel that only she were dancing with Krishna; each would express longing or rapture with individual extemporaneous movements. This dance with folk roots and Hindu devotional applications was taken into a new environment when dancing girls from Malwa or Rajputana were brought to the Mughal court for entertainment of aristocracy. Mughal sources refer to such dancing girls, but their art of movement was simply called *raqs* (generic "dance" in

Persian and Arabic) rather than kathak. Urdu texts on music report that at the Mughal court of Akbar, dancers who performed in a "Braj style" of folk dance that expresses devotional love for Krishna were trained in Persian styles of dance that had been more common in Islamic courts. These dancers were slave girls sent from regions like Malwa or Gujarat to serve and entertain in Mughal centers of power. The result could have been a form of dance that is recognized today as kathak, with its characteristic elements of erect stance, fast spins, dramatic expression (*abhinaya*), stylized walking in circles (*gat*), and a costume consisting of a flowing skirt with a head or shoulder scarf (*dupatta*).

Once taken out of its folk environment and divested of bhakti ritual significance, this genre could be transformed from a group dance into an individual performance. Individual performance was more suitable for courtesans, since it could be adapted to public settings in court or to private settings in a home or kotha. In later Mughal times, European travelers to India enthusiastically watched such dance and described the performers as simply "nautch-girls," derived from the Urdu and Hindi term *natch* (from Sanskrit *natya* or "dance").[28] As performed by courtesans, the dance form could express the modes of love—from impending union or painful separation—in a universal grammar, even if the songs (mainly *thumri*) that accompanied the dance retained the bhakti imagery describing the love of Radha for the dark-skin seducer, Krishna. In Islamic environments this imagery could be easily interpreted as ʿishq or passionate love of a type recognizable in ghazal poetry, devoid of its origins in Krishna worship. This dance style is a dynamic and vivid expression of a "composite culture" that developed in Mughal times, in which Hindu and Muslim could both take part on their own terms. Similar artistic and devotional confluence between these two communities shaped other performing arts, such as Qawwali. Such confluence developed slowly over the centuries in an environment where there was mutual overlap and interplay between Sufi-oriented Islam and bhakti-oriented Hinduism.

Claiming that kathak developed out of the courtesans' dance form and positing that it matured in an environment of Hindu-Muslim synthesis goes against the posture of some modern exponents of kathak. After the fall of Avadh to British colonialism and the exile of king Vajid ʿAli Shah from Lucknow in 1856, kathak found patrons in mainly Hindu environments in Banares, Jaipur, and Calcutta. In the twentieth century, training and performance of kathak was affected by the Hindu revivalist movement; its leading exponents began to argue that kathak was an ancient Hindu form of dance whose roots were in Sanskrit texts like the *Natyashastra* and whose poses were depicted in temple sculptures long before Muslim rule. This theory sought to cleanse the tradition of any previous association with Islamic society or Mughal courts; it denied that kathak was the dance form of courtesans, whom they disparaged as mere prostitutes or dancing girls. Once the reality of patronage by Muslim rulers had disappeared and religious nationalism began to unravel the composite culture that brought Hindus and Muslims together into shared devotional and artistic endeavors, an ancient Hindu pedigree for the dance form had to be created. Thus modern scholarship on kathak obscures the role courtesans played in cultivating it, denying that it was an all-female tradition passed down from artist to apprentice over generations of courtesans and asserting instead that kathak was perfected by male master teachers.[29] Recently, some revisionist scholars have questioned this and affirmed the positive role played by "nautch-girls" and courtesans.[30] Some bold scholars, like Pallabi Chakravorty, even argue that the dance form cannot be appreciated without acknowledging its roots in Islamic culture and, more specifically, in Sufi concepts of ecstasy and rapture.[31]

Conclusion

We conclude in a speculative mode that Mah Laqa Bai performed a dance style similar to what is known as kathak. We can say with certainty that Mah Laqa Bai's style of performance was integral to her activities as a woman composing poetry. Her poems were meant to be sung, and couplets from her ghazals were probably sung to accompany her dance. This is certainly the style of courtesan performance that was, several generations later, written about by authors such as Mirza Hadi Rusva in his novel about a Lucknow courtesan, Umrao Jan Ada.

Because her poems were written to be performed in dance and were informed by the experiences of a female performer, Mah Laqa Bai's ghazals speak of feminine sensuality more boldly than many of those written by males. However, they speak of this from the point of view of a male who is rapt in love, rather than from the point of view of a female who expresses her existential situation in a confessional poetic mode. This chapter concludes by offering two examples of ghazals that present a female beloved poised as only a performer can be. The first poem is written from a man's point of view, amazed at how deeply he is affected by a woman's artful display:[32]

> Her ostentatious grace emerged, all decked out just like that
>   I caught a glimpse—she stole my heart and soul just like that
> Shirin certainly oppressed Farhad in his love for her
>   But you've done me worse, and I'm depressed just like that
> When will that moon-faced beauty appear in my dreams?
>   My heart stays awake all night wondering just like that
> Thousands are cruel beloveds and thousands suffer in love
>   But the world has never seen one ruthless just like that
> It's no false praise for Chanda to call Hyder a pouncing lion
>   Present or absent, he helps me in need just like that

This poem focuses on the beloved's behavior—her ruthlessness, cruelty, and aloofness that complement her beauty.

In contrast, the poem below presents the female beloved as more embodied, with her pale silvery bosom, her radiant gaze like moonlight, and her sweetened lips. Her grace affects the male lover so deeply that it ironically inverts the reality of social power. The man declares that he is her slave and she is his lord, whereas in reality the dancer who might perform these couplets was raised as a slave girl and elevated, by her skill and artistry, into a courtesan. Aptly, this ghazal is structured around the rhyming word *mahzuz*, rendered in the following translation as variations on the word "pleasure":[33]

> From my rival, that silver-bosomed beauty gets pleasure
>   My distant sighs, though, seem to incite her displeasure
> O cruel one, never avert your generous gaze from me
>   One glimpse of you grants me everlasting pleasure
> I should never eat sweetmeats one after the other
>   If I kiss your lips just once, I'm sated with pleasure
> I'm searching for an apt demonstration of your lordship
>   Show your slave just a mere kindness, at your pleasure
> This alone Chanda requests, O 'Ali, God's bosom friend
>   Night and day let me bask in the glow of your pleasure

These two poems are representative of the dominant tone and imagery of most of Mah Laqa Bai's verse. They reveal how her poems are expressed in the voice of a lover who is mainly a man, speaking in admiration and despair about a beloved who is mainly a woman.

This gendered dynamic is not a betrayal of feminist obligation that a female poet write verses that express women's aspirations for empowerment. It may appear that way to modern feminist readers, but this gendered dynamic was imposed by the genre of the ghazal and by the poetic conventions of Mah Laqa Bai's aristocratic milieu. For her to compete and excel in this artistic environment, she had to adopt the rules of its game. These rules were set by male poets in a patriarchal system. Mah Laqa Bai, both in her personality and her poetry, did not challenge that system but rather sought to find a dignified place within it.

This gender dynamic arose rather organically from Mah Laqa Bai's social role as a courtesan dancer. Her role as a female performer for an overwhelmingly male audience gave her poetic voice deep insight into imagining how a male lover would be seduced and suffer for a proud female beloved. She spent her whole life cultivating this role, and her success depended on performing its dynamics publicly. In the end, we can conclude that gender for Mah Laqa Bai was a performance. Through dance and performance, she was able to turn her vulnerable position as a woman—and more acutely as an unmarried woman—into a platform for accruing status, power, and wealth.

For her, gender was not determined by anatomy or by conventions like marriage sanctified by religious custom. Rather, gender was a play of positions—of watcher and watched, of audience and performer, of desirer and desired. The most base level of this play of positions might be feelings of lust rooted in anatomical organs, but it could be elevated through artful performance into a more refined realm of psychological tensions and spiritual potentials. Her performance took base lust and raised it to sublime heights: man's desire for a woman's body might compel him to sit before her performance, but by its end he could be transformed into a lover, his longing to dominate and sate being transmuted into his love characterized by submission and sacrifice.

Mah Laqa Bai's performance of gender roles, in both her dance and its verbal representation in her poetry, proclaims that the only way to be a real man was to be a lover. Yet in her ghazals, it is she who claims that status in the final couplet of each poem, when she declares her loving submission to ʿAli and the Shiʿi imams. Most likely, in performances these final couplets were not sung and their meter did not provide the rhythm for dance. Rather, the final couplets were a more private gesture of poems that she included in her written collection. In these final couplets, Mah Laqa Bai trumps her male admirers, for she claims that she uniquely displays the qualities of a sincere lover of ʿAli and the imams; she is distinctively empowered by their protection and spiritual charisma. Her male audience, while watching her dance, may have succeeded as men in turning mere lust into love, but she herself was the consummate lover of a higher power, of Imam ʿAli, a man who was more than a mere man. The next chapter will fully explore her spirituality as a Shiʿi woman.

CHAPTER ELEVEN

Mah Laqa Bai's True Love

Could trials force Chanda to say, no matter how bad it be
   Except for you, O 'Ali, some other helper has she?
—*final couplet from a ghazal by Mah Laqa Bai*

In each final couplet of her ghazals, Mah Laqa Bai declares her loving submission to 'Ali and the Shi'i imams in innovative, charming, and audacious ways. These couplets are a characteristic feature of her poetry that indicate that she was not merely a courtesan but also a devoted Shi'i woman. Her ghazals have an element of spirituality and mysticism, despite her secular profession that might seem lascivious. The previous chapter argued that the male gaze helped create Mah Laqa Bai's personality; she both was formed by it and manipulated it to her own advantage. This is true in her poetry, which speaks in the voice of a male lover, and also in her life, in which male patrons were attracted to her and promoted her. But the male gaze of lust and love that framed Mah Laqa Bai did not fully capture her. Even as a courtesan she could be spiritual. This chapter explores her religiosity as an unmarried Shi'i woman by elucidating the devotional elements in her poems and practices.

As a courtesan, Mah Laqa Bai performed for men, manipulating them to get wealth, status, and power. The one exception to this rule of relations with men was her spiritual relationship with 'Ali—a relationship of pure love and unalloyed sincerity. The poem whose closing couplet was quoted at the head of this chapter demonstrates the contrast in how she portrays men. Her poem's female beloved is so beautifully aloof as to slay male soldiers with a mere glance, but in the final couplet, she herself—called by her own name, Chanda—becomes a female lover of 'Ali. She submits to him, supplicates him, recites his name in every breath, and calls upon him for support in every endeavor:[1]

> Black infidel eyes she has and a bloodthirsty wink has she
>   To slay any soldier, yes, a brow like a saber has she

> Whose heart will still distinguish between Islam and idolatry
>   No matter if he has prayer beads or a holy thread has he
> He burns in passion though meeting you gives tranquillity
>   Wherever there's a rose, my dear, a thorn there has to be
> My heart, try to understand—hers is just some flattery
>   Don't let her kindness fool you for cruelty also has she
> Could trials force Chanda to say, no matter how bad it may be
>   Except for you, Oh 'Ali, some other helper has she?

This poem invokes the contrast between faithful submission (*islam*) and egoistic infidelity (*kufr*), which is the terrain of Islamic mysticism. The devotee of love cannot distinguish between markers of ritual Islam and the inner reality of idolatry; to her eyes, the string of prayer beads of Muslim worshippers and the holy thread of the Brahmins are rendered equal and equally useless. The devotee of love discards empty rituals and sectarian chauvinism, knowing that real Islam means submitting to the beloved within one's heart. It blinds one to distinctions of self and other, me and you, us and them.

In Islam, deep currents of mysticism fuel passionate love that breaks the constraints of asceticism and law. Mysticism finds expression under different names: called *tasawwuf* or Sufism in Sunni communities and *'irfan* (intuitive knowledge or "gnosis") in Shi'i communities. For Shi'i mystics, *'irfan* is a mystical quest to encounter God directly rather than rely on rational belief, proper ritual, and legal conduct to ensure a later meeting postponed until judgment day. This quest is to understand with the heart's intuition that there is one true God and one authentic prophet to follow, namely Muhammad, and after that prophet there is one charismatic "friend," a helper who is 'Ali. Love of 'Ali is the doorway to ascending steps of wisdom, as 'Ali is seen to continue the charisma of the Prophet in another body and as the Prophet Muhammad is seen to radiate the light of God in a human body. Love allows the boundaries erected by reason to dissolve, bringing a seemingly distant God close into intimacy and loving care.

Shi'i Belief in Mah Laqa Bai's Poetry

Mah Laqa Bai's poetry expresses this quest, but before we can understand her poems' mystical imagery, we have to appreciate the role of 'Ali in Shi'i devotion. Shi'i Muslims believe that the Qur'an contains God's praise of ʿAli and hints at the necessity of pledging allegiance to him. For instance, the Qurʾan recites: *Verily your master is only God, and God's messenger and those among the believers who establish worship and pay the poor due while they are bowing down in prayer* (Q 5:55). The Qurʾan insists that Muslims take as their master God alone but follows immediately with the command to also take as master Muhammad, God's messenger, and after him to take as master "those among the believers" who establish worship and virtue. For Shiʿi Muslims, this is a command to follow ʿAli as the best among the believers after the Prophet, for he was the closest male blood relative to Muhammad. He was raised by the Prophet almost as a son, was chosen to marry the Prophet's eldest daughter, Fatima, and exhibited many of the virtuous qualities of the Prophet himself.

Shiʿi poets cite ʿAli's virtues and heroic deeds that border on the miraculous rather than search scripture for reference to his rule. It was ʿAli, the fierce warrior and heroic youth, whom Muhammad deputed to destroy the idols that filled the Kaʿba. Poets frequently refer to him by his nickname Abu Turab or "Man of Dust," given to him by the Prophet himself, for when ʿAli quarreled with Fatima, he restrained his anger and left to throw dust over his head.[2] ʿAli is most well known as a fearless warrior: he defended Muhammad wielding the two-bladed sword *zuʾl-fiqar* at the Battle of Uhud when the Muslims faced defeat. In praise of his bravery in a moment of grave danger, it was later said, "There is no brave youth but ʿAli and there is no sword but *zuʾl-fiqar*!"[3] ʿAli is often praised as the "Fearless Lion" (Haider-e Karrar) whom the Prophet had nicknamed "the Lion of God" (Asadallah). This hints at ʿAli's role in establishing and maintaining the Prophet Muhammad's authority, therefore being his designated heir and perpetuator of his charisma.

In arguing this point, Shiʿi scholars point out the controversial report known as "Hadis al-Manzila." In 630, near the end of his life, the Prophet Muhammad led an expedition enjoining ʿAli to stay back and safeguard Medina. When ʿAli complained that he, the ablest warrior, was left behind with the women and children, Muhammad said, "Are you not pleased to have the position [*manzila*] in relation to me as that Aaron to Moses, with the only difference that there will be no other prophet after me?"[4] The Qurʾan mentions Moses having assigned Aaron as his successor (Q 7:142) and asking God to make Aaron his partner in power (Q 20:25–32). Shiʿi theologians assert that just as Moses was given a partner in prophecy from his own family, so Muhammad was given ʿAli as partner in his prophetic career. Just as Aaron strengthened Moses and shared in his prophetic mission, so Muhammad relied upon ʿAli. Therefore, they argue, ʿAli should be granted allegiance as the rightful leader of all Muslims after the Prophet Muhammad, in whose prophetic light ʿAli shares.

In outer form the Prophet Muhammad and ʿAli are a pair, yet in inner spiritual essence they are one. They propagate one charismatic mission, share one virtuous character, and radiate God's light into the world. The fundamental credo of Shiʿi belief is the union of purpose and presence between Muhammad and ʿAli. This belief forms the basis for Shiʿis to follow the lineage of imams through ʿAli's male progeny. The Shiʿi community reveres their personalities, mourns their sacrifices, and hopes for a future restoration of justice. These themes are taken for granted by Mah Laqa Bai when she includes praise of ʿAli and the imams in her ghazals, and the theological background they provide must be grasped to fully understand her poems.

One poem of Mah Laqa Bai's that praises ʿAli is a ghazal whose *radif* refers to Najaf, the pilgrimage place in Iraq where ʿAli is buried. With this place-name as the rhyme of each couplet, the ghazal expresses extended praise of Imam ʿAli:[5]

> Why should my heart not cry like a nightingale of Najaf
>   When before my eyes spreads the rose-studded court of Najaf?
> The fortune of both worlds is gained in just a moment
>   When I stand at attention in the throne hall of Najaf
> What slave-girl would ever desire the garden of paradise
>   If she would, with heart and soul, yearn just once for Najaf
> All creatures' desires are fulfilled by that one single essence
>   There is none who doesn't stand in need of the ruler of Najaf
> Though you are sunk head to foot in a fearful sea of sin
>   Oh Chanda, you are guarded by the chivalrous knight of Najaf

This poem ends on a hopeful supplication. Though Mah Laqa Bai is "sunk head to foot in a fearful sea of sin," she can still hope for protection from ʿAli. She asks for intercession on judgment day from that "chivalrous knight of Najaf." Shiʿi Muslims believe that the Prophet Muhammad's mission to intercede with believers on judgment day extends to his closest family members: ʿAli, Fatima, and Husain. Those who pledge their allegiance to them and love them win their intercession.

Having a place-name like Najaf as the rhyming phrase is unusual in a ghazal, and this poem is unique in Mah Laqa Bai's collection for its extended focus on ʿAli. In contrast, the bulk of Mah Laqa Bai's poetry praises ʿAli in quite different ways, as she invokes his name in each ghazal interlaced with more secular love themes. Each ghazal mentions ʿAli or the imams in its final couplet, just as Shiʿi believers invoke his name before sleep. Mah Laqa Bai's major stylistic innovation is to praise Ali and the Shiʿi imams in love poetry like the ghazal rather than in genres of praise (*qasida*) or mourning (*marsiya*). Does this mark Mah Laqa Bai's poetic approach to ʿAli as particularly feminine? Mah Laqa Bai emphasizes her personal relationship with ʿAli over abstract theological statements. She approaches him as a lover, not as a believer. Of course, a lover has to believe in the beloved's unique qualities and unmatchable beauty, but she emphasizes emotion over mind and passion over assertion.

Typical of Mah Laqa Bai's praise of ʿAli in her ghazals is the following poem. In Urdu, its rhyme is *matlab*, meaning having a certain intent or wanting something from someone. In the English translation, it was not rendered into an explicit rhyme but rather enfolded within the meaning of each couplet.[6]

> I have no desire for roses, from the garden I want nothing
>   My gaze is for the dew, which reflects only its lover
> My heart renounced, rushed on, and in a gaze lies ensnared
>   By God, how will it escape your blood-shedding intent?
> Except for my God, I expect nothing from another
>   But still, from the people of this world I want love
> My love, you never understood me despite my soul sacrifice
>   You'll learn your lesson, you fool, from someone more clever
> Chanda longs not for heaven and has no fear of hell
>   In both worlds she wants just Haider, a lion of bold assault

This is typical of Mah Laqa Bai's ghazals. In its final couplet, she disavows any aim (*matlab*) other than desiring intimacy with ʿAli, called here by his nickname Haider-e Karrar, the "Fearless Lion." She neither desires heaven nor fears hell if she has the nearness of ʿAli. This closing gesture of loving submission is a petition for protection by a great warrior and of intercession by a spiritual authority. Longing for God is cultivated in the form of love for ʿAli, and the waxing of love eclipses all other religious concerns like earning merit, following rules, or fearing punishment. Yet love mysticism focused upon the person of ʿAli does not stand alone as the sole meaning of the ghazal. Rather, it is interwoven with the other couplets that depict many modes and levels of love, most of them clearly romantic and oriented toward a very human beloved.

For Mah Laqa Bai, love poetry is the vehicle for expressing her mysticism oriented by Shi'i belief. All Shi'i devotees admire Ali's power, harbor hope for his help in this world, and yearn for his family members' intercession in the next world. Mah Laqa Bai's Shi'i belief is deepened by love mysticism. Rather than be content with belief, she seeks to evoke love in herself and her listeners, leading to a transformation of the heart. As a female Shi'i poet, her poems do not focus exclusively on 'Ali but also mention his family members, especially Fatima, Hasan, and Husain. 'Ali is important not only as an individual but also as the center of a holy family. His charisma is powerful because it is passed down to later generations through his male heirs, as Shi'i Muslims believe, through twelve generations. Therefore, a portrait of Mah Laqa Bai as a Shi'i woman poet is not complete without examining how she depicts the other members of 'Ali's family.

'Ali's wife, Bibi Fatima, is central to Shi'i theology and is a fascinating figure because of ambiguous Shi'i attitudes toward her femininity. Her womb establishes the direct bloodline back to the Prophet through which the imams claim their unique legitimacy. But her sexuality causes a problem for Shi'i theologians, for women were popularly believed to be impure and less pious because of their menstrual bleeding. Though it is integral to women's fertility, menstruation was seen as preventing them from impeccably performing their worship obligations to God. Male Shi'i theologians confronted this problem by insisting that Fatima was a unique woman: she was not only pious and chaste but was also a virginal mother (much like Mary in Christian theology). If her children were holy and charismatic from birth, they could not have been born from the ambiguous bodily fluid and menstrual blood of an ordinary woman. So Fatima is said to be perpetually a virgin, even though she gave birth to male children who continue the line of imams after 'Ali. Some theologians insist that she gave birth from her thigh rather than from her genitalia. In any case, she is revered as Fatima al-Batul, the perpetual virgin.

Though Fatima's female sexuality is suspect, her feminine presence is affirmed. She is believed to be present in every Shi'i gathering to mourn the martyrdom of her descendants, the imams. She collects the tears of those who weep for them and redeems them on judgment day with her intercession to ensure God's mercy and compassion. In this way, Fatima's womb (*rahim*) becomes symbolic for God's compassion (*rahma*). Mah Laqa Bai includes in her ghazal collection certain poems that single out

Fatima for praise. In the following poem, she invokes Fatima as the archetypal mourner who watched her beloved family members sacrifice and fall and who therefore redeems the suffering and mourning of all common believers in the next world:[7]

> Even as I rest on a bed of roses, sleep won't come my way
> > Only if my head lies on your feet does sleep come to stay
> I can't seem to ever gaze upon you eye to eye
> > Bashful as narcissus, sleep waits for you, your face to display
> Since my eyelashes have humbly been sweeping your doorstep
> > Each time I face sleep it eludes me and slips away
> I get no peace, O storyteller, from your rosy description of his cheek
> > But if the breeze carries his aroma sleep will dispel gloom's gray
> O Chanda, just as Fatima lamented 'Ali's brave pain
> > All humanity's eyes are weeping sleepless night and day

In this poem, Fatima is called Qurrat al-'Ayn or "coolness of my eye," an endearing nickname given to her by Muhammad.[8] Citing her nickname in the final couplet is built up to by imagery of eyes in various states of restlessness and burning, for the poem's rhyme word is sleep (*nind*), which never seems to come.

In another ghazal, Fatima is invoked indirectly along with her family, Muhammad, 'Ali, Hasan, and Husain. Despite the overt importance of the male members, they are defined by their relationships to Fatima. As daughter, wife, or mother, she is the foundation of their single family that transmits charisma. The poem in Urdu simply calls them "the family of the cloak" (*al-e 'aba*). This refers to the incident in which the Prophet reportedly spread his cloak over the heads of these four members of his immediate family and declared them to be one. Shi'i Muslims refer to them as *panj-tan-e pak* or five bodies of one pure being. For the purpose of simplicity and directness, this English translation simply calls them Fatima's family. The ghazal's final couplet is, "Chanda's love for Fatima's family is boiling over and how / However much she thought a lot, she thinks too little now."[9]

Occasionally Mah Laqa Bai invokes Fatima in place of the usual praise of 'Ali—is this a feminist gesture? Many scholars of Shi'ism find feminist empowerment in frequent and reverent invocations of Fatima, her daughter Zainab (died 682), and other female members of the imams' families. Some argue that these female figures are cast as exemplary heroines for Shi'i Muslims—both female and male—giving Shi'ism a deeper resource for feminist understandings of the religion than other sectarian groups, in particular more than Sunnis. But in the case of Mah Laqa Bai's poetry, there does not appear to be a feminist agenda behind her invocation of Fatima. Fatima is praised in two ghazals in her collection, while Zainab and other female examples are never cited. Most of her poems refer directly to ʿAli. Mah Laqa Bai relates more easily to the male imams than she does to Fatima with her miraculous chastity.

When Mah Laqa Bai cites charismatic personalities other than ʿAli, she turns to his two sons Hasan and Husain. Unlike her indirect reference to Fatima, Mah Laqa Bai takes these sons' names directly. See for instance this ghazal with its highly musical lyrics that repeat in its rhyme word "give":[10]

> Give me more ruby wine, saqi, intoxication's just begun
>   Give me the whole jug, don't leave this thirst half-done
> He saw my moon-face lover and retreated in shame
>   Give a saffron smear to the renunciant brow of the sun
> Why complain of her negligence, she who occupies my heart
>   Give your life for love, but has it ever a lover's praise won?
> Since long I've given up my heart and soul for you
>   Give my lips just a kiss, it's the least you could've done
> O empowered ʿAli, who always grants Chanda's every wish
>   Give her the chance to sacrifice all for Husain and Hasan

These references to members of the holy family of the imams show the breadth of Mah Laqa Bai's Shiʿi piety, but its depth is revealed by her references to ʿAli.

Far more typical than invocations of other members of the holy family are the poems of Mah Laqa Bai that directly cite ʿAli. They praise his valor, cite his spiritual potency, or extol his beauty. They take his name like an incantation to ward off obstacles or attract blessings. This one, for instance, ends by beseeching ʿAli to keep Chanda's beauty at its spring-rivaling peak forever:[11]

> Anxiety over you ravaged my heart—it's merely a charred black thing
>   Who imagines from such turmoil that blazing tulip beds spring?
> How long will I stay behind this veil, prevented from reaching you
>   While amorous embraces and passionate kisses are all I'm desiring?
> Saqi, fetch a jug of wine chilled with ice, but still
>   I desire only your eyes where intoxication's heat is lingering

> Not one day have you come on the evening of your promise
>   How well you've mastered the fine art of disappointing
> O ʿAli, keep Chanda in the limelight just like this forever,
>   Her youthful vigor's worth a hundred times an earthly spring

This ghazal ends with an audaciously humble request: Mah Laqa Bai wants to be young and beautiful forever. She is sure that with ʿAli's support, what is impossible by her own means is possible by his.

Such a request seems secular and practical—especially coming from a courtesan who lives by her beauty; she takes ʿAli's name only for worldly benefit, as if it were a magical charm. To counterbalance this impression, we should consider another poem at the opposite end of the spectrum. Mah Laqa Bai has ironically structured the following ghazal around the rhyming word *taʿviz* or "magic charm." Many Muslims wear a *taʿviz* as a small piece of paper upon which are written verses from the Qurʾan, certain names of God, or numbers that represent such holy words; the paper is rolled or folded into a metal tube or leather pouch and attached to a string that is worn around the neck or high on the arm.[12] Mah Laqa Bai's poem plays with this convention and teases the listener with the question of how a charm can work without sincere intention of heart: "I don't want astrology's amulets, Chanda, or any magic spells / Love for ʿAli is the ultimate charm for my heart."[13] Mah Laqa Bai declares that she needs no amulet, whether given by a learned astrologer or by a wise sage. She insists that she does not repeat the name of ʿAli for practical gain, as if it were a magic spell. Rather, she invokes his name because love for him animates her heart. She turns to him out of sincere desire for his attention, not for some other goal that he can secure for her.

In Urdu literature, it is unusual for a poet to use ghazals so persistently for praising a religious leader. The qasida was used for praise or the masnavi for telling heroic narratives. Yet Mah Laqa Bai is not alone in this practice. Other courtesan poets also use ghazals to praise ʿAli and other members of the Prophet's family. In fact, this practice results in a confluence of two disparate trends: the trend for courtesans to specialize in writing only ghazals (rather than other poetic forms) and the tendency for courtesans to be Shiʿi. To illustrate how Mah Laqa Bai is like other courtesan poets of her era, we can compare her poetry to that of her contemporary Lutf al-Nisa.

Lutf al-Nisa wrote with the pen name "Imtiyaz" or Excellence, and she was also a Shiʿi courtesan of the Deccan. We do not possess sources to document her biography, but it appears that she was born and raised in Awrangabad and then later moved to Hyderabad.¹⁴ Lutf al-Nisa rivaled Mah Laqa Bai in circulating a divan of ghazals at about the same time; there is scholarly disagreement over who was the first woman to disseminate a full divan of Urdu ghazals. Yet what is more remarkable than who came first is that both women circulated their groundbreaking divans in the same year.¹⁵ Lutf al-Nisa praises the rule of the second nizam, who brought stability to the Deccan.¹⁶ These similarities show that Mah Laqa Bai was not unique but was one of a class of Shi'i courtesan poets who rose to prominence in her era. Yet Mah Laqa Bai's poems have a mystical depth and complex spiritual imagery that is largely absent in those poems of Lutf al-Nisa and other courtesan poets. Mah Laqa Bai's mystical love of 'Ali is a distinguishing feature.

Mystical Love of 'Ali

Love of 'Ali was Mah Laqa Bai's ultimate goal, and intensification of that love was reward in itself; in this way, her Shi'i devotion expressed a mystical quest. Her love for 'Ali would transform her and transport her. Her Shi'i devotion verged on mysticism, as the devotee's love affair with 'Ali. Her devotion to 'Ali was not simply about finding strength to face the vicissitudes of court power. It was a way of courting 'Ali through love, which might grant her power in more worldly realms as a reflection of her self-abnegating devotion to 'Ali.

For Mah Laqa Bai and other Shi'i believers, *valayat*—the act of supporting the status of 'Ali as *vali*—was more than mere sectarian partisanship. It was love that had mystical elements, causing the ego to dissolve in the overwhelming presence of the loved one, in this case 'Ali, as anchor for the chain of the imams. Henri Corbin, a scholar of Shi'ism and mysticism, explains that "Shi'ism is the religion of the *walaya* [in Arabic, or *valayat* in Persian].... The Shi'a were fully aware through the teaching of their Imams that their Shi'ism was basically a devotion of love.... Moreover, the profession of this love, of this *walaya*, takes precedence over all the obligations of the shari'a, not only in the sense that it alone authenticates the performance of these obligations but also because it can compensate for failure to meet them."¹⁷ Corbin does not distinguish between allegiance (*valayat*) and intimacy (*vilayat*), two terms from Arabic that are so close as to be interchangeable. Shi'i devotion is not just about sectarian allegiance to the imams' leadership and following a code of law based upon the imams' teachings; rather, these two elements are based upon a deeper love for the imams, love that can lead one to self-sacrifice. Mah Laqa Bai's insight is that love of any kind is of one essence, such that love for another person in a romantic or passionate mode is analogous to love for the imams in a devotional mode and love for God in a mystical mode. All these loves form a continuous chain and constitute a path of spiritual cultivation by which the soul moves from selfish preoccupation to divine illumination.

That is why the ghazal—as a love poem—can bridge seamlessly with a poem of longing for a charismatic religious leader and yearning for mystical absorption in God. Such bridging of romantic love into mystical love is depicted in this poem of Mah Laqa Bai's:[18]

> Go pass by her alley and deliver this, my messenger
>   Just a sigh from me to show what's amiss, my messenger
> I wrote for him a colorful account with my heart's blood
>   But how can one effect a heart so merciless, my messenger?
> How will these "noble scribes" learn the state of my heart?
>   How can others get my news before I dismiss my messenger?
> He laughs as he asks how I am in this lonely exile
>   Present an eye's mist and cool sigh's kiss, my messenger
> On behalf of Chanda's plea, "O King of Najaf!" quickly
>   Bow your head and his noble doorstep kiss, my messenger

The first two couplets present images from romantic love poetry. The alienated lover tries to overcome distance by sending a messenger—often the cool spring breeze—to send news of her suffering and perseverance. The third couplet shifts focus to mystical love and refers to the "noble scribes" (*kiraman katibin*), angels who record one's good and bad deeds (Q 82:11). But how can they judge her actions without knowing the state of her heart? When her love is concealed deep in her heart, so deep that she herself cannot fathom it, how can others learn of her state, even if the others are angels? The fourth couplet expresses this mystical insight with devotional fervor—the only acceptable demonstration of love is sighing and weeping. Her poems reveal Shi'i devotion based on the centrality of love: its outer demonstration is zealous loyalty to 'Ali and his political cause, while its inner dimension is absorption in the light of the imams through which one achieves union with God.

Shi'i devotion is centered upon love and thus has a common language with Sufism as cultivated in a Sunni environment. The stations of love mark the stages in spiritual refinement and mystical ascension, as displayed in this poem:[19]

> My sleepless night's accompanied by rising fortune's star thus far
>   From his house toward mine, my lover's come just thus far
> Nothing but Moses' miracle-working staff could ever
>   Raise up your self-intoxicated narcissus eyes just thus far
> You've left me with heart broken and gut torn, but I still hope
>   You cruel beloved, you'll come again my way just thus far
> Why should seeing the dewdrops fill my eyes with hope?
>   My tears have kept the whole bed of roses fresh thus far
> On hearing his name, Chanda's mind flies to the heavens, but still
>   Search for 'Ali persists no matter how high one has come thus far

In love, self-preoccupation is extinguished (*fana'*) and union with the other is sustained (*baqa'*). The fluctuation of these two spiritual states marks ascension—a rising up through refinement of mystical perception, which brings one ever closer to union with God. This is the case whether the mysticism is in a Shi'i environment or a Sufi environment.

Mystical love has both negative and positive expressions. In its negative sense, love marks an urgent goal not yet reached, and its metaphors are separation (*firaq*) and lonely yearning (*ishtiyaq*). In its positive sense, love conjures up an alluring experience that is present, and its metaphors are union and intoxication. This positive expression of love is displayed in this following poem, which addresses 'Ali by his nickname Abu Turab or "Man of Dust":[20]

> Since the heart sipped someone's glance like wine from love's urn
>   Abandoned wanders the heart, drunk and sunk in love's no-return
> The wine-pourer's visage can't hold a match to your flaming gaze
>   Whose hot cheek gave my heart passion's light and love's burn
> For what purpose have I offered my own head as a gift
>   If you still keep your heart veiled and my love spurn?
> Since my eye lingered on your sigh-inspiring cheek
>   My soul is upset and my heart flutters with love's yearn
> In both worlds, Chanda's only plea is this, Abu Turab
>   Keep me by your side at each twist of love's turn

This poem expresses Shi'i mysticism, which has many parallels with Sufi mysticism as cultivated in a Sunni environment. The poem's rhyming phrase ends with the word "heart" (*dil*); this series of words marks the stations of love or, in Mah Laqa Bai's words, "each twist of love's turn." The stations of love start with the call to self-abandonment and move to suffering from passion's heat, to lamenting alienation, to persisting despite agitation, to finally ending up in the dust—but with the hope of union with a divine lover, like ʿAli, who will come to the rescue.

Representing Shiʿi devotion as love mysticism in a language that had many elements in common with Sufism was not just an expression of the essence of Shiʿism; it was also an astute strategy for Shiʿis in the court of a post-Mughal Sunni ruler. In court, Mah Laqa Bai may have had to veil her veneration of ʿAli to not antagonize Sunni nobility. Yet she rightly praised the ruler who, despite being Sunni, provided the stability and peace of a reign that allowed rank and status for loyal nobles regardless of their sect or creed. In fact, prime ministers and noble families who were Shiʿi could rise to the peak of power and influence; key examples of this were the prime ministers who were her patrons, Aristu Jah and Mir ʿAlam. They saw the reign of the Sunni nizams as one that allowed justice for the common man, prosperity for the diligent, and patronage of Shiʿi shrines without persecution. During this era it was not just Shiʿi nobles, like Mah Laqa Bai and her circle, who patronized building projects on the hilltop shrine of Mawla ʿAli. The nizams, despite their Sunni creed, also had buildings constructed there for pilgrims, as did their Hindu nobles.

Shiʿi and Sufi Rituals in Honor of ʿAli

Mah Laqa Bai's mystical devotion to ʿAli as the perfect man was not mere rhetoric. It was encoded in the words of her poems and enacted in the works of her hands. Mah Laqa Bai was one of the richest women in the wealthiest realm in South Asia at the time. She had financial clout, symbolic status, and political power, which she mobilized in projects of artistic and ritual patronage. In her ritual patronage, she made her love for ʿAli concrete and displayed it lavishly for the public to enjoy and admire. Her most durable patronage was in the form of building up the shrine to Mawla ʿAli on the hillock outside of Hyderabad. In less tangible ways, she also promoted the love of ʿAli, the Shiʿi imams, and Sufi sages whose teachings of love mysticism rhymed with her own.

The annual ʿurs that celebrated the discovery of ʿAli's traces on the hillock was the theater in which Mah Laqa Bai acted out her devotion with full public spectacle. Her own historian, Jawhar, records the generosity and grandeur that Mah Laqa Bai lavished on this celebration. This in turn has been faithfully recorded in her Urdu biography by Gawhar:

> There are the traces of 'Ali's presence full of greatness and might upon the hill outside of Hyderabad.... Hundreds of thousands of men and women, noble and lowly, rich and poor, young and old, great and small, all come from the city of Hyderabad and its surrounding regions and gather on the mountain of heavenly majesty.... During the 'urs of Maula 'Ali, Mah Laqa Bai would go up to the noble hill. Each group of ascetics and sages would gather together for this celebration. For four days continuously at two appointed times, all kinds of food would be brought from Mah Laqa Bai's kitchen for them to eat. At their time of parting, each ascetic would be given one rupee in coin or some would get — according to their rank — five rupees each. Some would get fifty and others one hundred rupees in the name of God and for God's sake alone. To those devotees living at and serving the dargah, she would give rupees or clothes or other goods.[21]

This celebration of 'Ali's spiritual presence at Hyderabad was one of the biggest religious rituals of the year. From the time of the second nizam, the ostensibly Sunni rulers would participate in the procession.[22]

This celebration brought together Sunni and Shi'i in a shared ritual of devotion. The 'urs of Mawla 'Ali commemorated the anniversary of the discovery of 'Ali's handprint on the stone at the top of the hill, marking his perpetual charismatic presence with the people of Hyderabad. This spiritual presence cannot be compartmentalized into sectarian quarters, for Shi'i Muslims revere 'Ali as the first imam while Sufi-oriented Sunnis revere him as the first saint. Accordingly, holy people of both Shi'i and Sufi persuasion participate in the 'urs of Mawla 'Ali. Mah Laqa Bai lavished gifts upon the representatives of Sayyid families (descended genealogically from 'Ali) and also the ascetics and sages who upheld 'Ali's spiritual teachings, even if they were Sunnis.

This coming together of Shi'i and Sufi believers also occurred in another celebration. A different ritual would be held a few days earlier, on the thirteenth day of Rajab, to celebrate the birthday of 'Ali. This was called the Jashn-e Haideri. Gawhar records that "each year on the 13th of Rajab, the committee for the Jashn-e Haideri would convene. In this, the virtues of the king of saints would be recited and all kinds of food and drink would be provided."[23] In this celebration, 'Ali was referred to as the king of saints (*shah-e awliya*). This celebrates his role as the fountainhead of charismatic initiations in Sufi orders, in addition to his role as the first imam for Shi'i believers. Mah Laqa Bai would provide the financial support for feeding those who attended the celebration. Tajalli 'Ali Shah included a vivid illustration of such devotional gatherings, which the nizam attended with Sufi masters and renunciant holy men of all persuasions. The illustration shows the king sitting in their midst while they all listen to the music of Qawwali singers and Kalavants who performed Dhrupad compositions with lyrics praising 'Ali and members of the Prophet's holy family.[24]

Mah Laqa Bai devoted special attention to the rituals of Muharram, an unambiguously Shi'i commemoration in which Sunnis and Hindus also participated to revere the memory of Imam Husain's valor and self-sacrifice: "When the month of Muharram would come, Mah Laqa Bai would abstain from delicious and rich food out of sorrow for Imam Husain's sacrifice. In all the 'ashur-khanas of the land, which are numerous beyond counting, she would give every scholar an amount from one to five rupees, in accord with their status, as an offering to God. To the descendants of the Prophet and lovers of the family of the Prophet she would give thousands of rupees, depending upon their station and status."[25] At Mah Laqa Bai's grand mansion, she trained girls in singing, dancing, and the courtesan's arts, but in the days of Muharram this joyful activity would be curtailed. As if to balance the sensual with the spiritual, she had a devotional complex facing her mansion.

> Out of respect for 'Ali, she built facing it a separate palace for religious scholars. In front of the 'ashur-khana she erected a raised hall for the beating of kettledrums (*naqqar-khana*). When the new moon of Muharram appeared, she had the 'ashur-khana decorated with all kinds of sculpted images ('*alams*).... For giving sermons, a raised pulpit hung in black would be erected. There, events from the *Rawzat al-Shuhada* would be recited. For lighting up the 'ashur-khana, torches were set.... From the beginning of Muharram until the tenth day of 'Ashura, it would remain brightly lit from sundown until dawn. Every evening, poems of lamentation (*marsiya*) would be recited. In beautiful melodies, women's lamentation songs (*soz*) would be sung. After this, poems telling the events of martyrdom (*rawzakhwan*) would be recited, in accordance with the Prophet's saying, "I grant heaven to any who weep for Husain, or are made to weep or make others weep." After this, replicas of the martyr's tomb (*ta'ziya*) are carried in pro-

cession and mourners beat their chests in grief as if the Day of Judgment had actually come.[26]

Mah Laqa Bai sponsored these rituals and paid for multicourse meals to be prepared for the exhausted mourners for ten nights. She provided rosewater to sprinkle over anyone who fell unconscious while carrying floats representing the tomb of Husain.

As a counterbalance to the thoroughly Shi'i rituals of Muharram, Mah Laqa Bai patronized festivals of others sects and religions. She supported a devotional celebration deeply Sufi in orientation called the Offering on the Holy Eleventh Day (*Gyarwin Sharif* in Urdu, *Yazdehum-e Sharif* in Persian). It celebrated the continuing spiritual presence among devotees of the great Sufi master 'Abd al-Qadir Jilani, after whom the Qadiri Sufi order is named. This *hadis* scholar and Hanbali jurist in Baghdad was also a popular preacher. After his death, his family and followers spread through the Islamic world, carrying stories of their ancestor as a charismatic Sufi master and miracle worker who could help any in need of healing or protection.[27] Because he was a Sayyid (descended from Imam Hasan on his paternal side and from Imam Husain on his maternal side), 'Abd al-Qadir was also seen as a charismatic extension of the Prophet Muhammad's own personality, much like an imam in Shi'i thought. 'Abd al-Qadir Jilani became popular in Hyderabad, where shrines to him often feature pictures of a tiger or lion, linking him to Imam 'Ali, who was known as the "Lion of God."

'Abd al-Qadir Jilani was a Sufi personality, yet Mah Laqa Bai patronized grand celebrations of his death anniversary: "Each year on the eleventh day of Rabi' al-Thani, the offering of the Holy Eleventh would be celebrated in honor of his majesty, Sayyid 'Abd al-Qadir Jilani—may God sanctify his heart. Varieties of delicacies would be prepared and fed to the poor and needy. In addition, to ascetics and the pious poor, coins or clothes would be distributed."[28] She perceived this celebration as commemorating the piety and holiness of a Sayyid who, though he was not an imam as recognized by the Shi'is, was a descendant of the imams. Popular veneration of 'Abd al-Qadir Jilani made him into a simulacrum of Imam 'Ali in a guise that Sunnis could embrace.

'Abd al-Qadir Jilani is an almost mythic figure, but Mah Laqa Bai also showered her generosity on more quotidian Sufis. She built a shrine for one lowly Sufi who lived on her land near the step-well she built:

At Adikmet along the road to Mawla Ali—which now lies behind Osmania University's Arts College building—there lived a Sufi mendicant (*darvesh*) by the name of Tahir Shah. While traveling to Mawla 'Ali and back to Hyderabad, Mah Laqa Bai would see him sitting in the open, whether in blazing sun or pouring rain. Eventually, she found that he had no shelter, so for this Sufi begger she sanctioned a building with her own personal funds. Today this building is known locally as the "Pavilion of Tar-Shah" (*Tarh Shah ki Baradari*).[29]

This incident illustrates the wide embrace of her generosity and the tolerant sympathy of her Shi'i belief.

It was not just Sufis who benefited from Mah Laqa Bai's patronage. She supported an ecumenical fair honoring wise holy men of every religious community:

> Each year there would be a fair known by the name Mela Khat-Darsan. In its first day, the fair would begin with the prayers of the ascetics both young and old of both Hindustan and the Deccan, along with eloquent reciters of the Qur'an, and sages who live for knowledge. Sweets would be sent to the households of all the sages and saints (*masha'ikh*) in the land. If a sage had a household full of children and brothers, even up to twenty persons, each one by name would be given a *ser* [about two pounds] or more of sweets. The same amount would be sent to each Qur'an reciter. On the second day, all of the Sufi ascetics would gather, those free of any order along with those in the Madari, Qadiri, Chishti and others of the fourteen Sufi lineages.... For each and every one, food and drink would be prepared, along with sweets and other delicacies that would be humbly placed before them. Acres of ascetics would be seated together. On the third day, a group of about seventy thousand impoverished, needy, handicapped and diseased would gather. Each and every one of these people would receive a half *ser* of sweets. On the fourth day, the ascetics (*jogi*) and Hindu holy men (*bairagi*) would gather. For them the best kind of fried sweet would be prepared.[30]

In this fair honoring the ascetics of many religions, Mah Laqa Bai would fund the preparation of the copious costly sweets that would be distributed as a social recognition of their renunciation and spiritual prowess. Each day of the four-day fair would honor a different type of holy person: Islamic scholars, Sufi leaders, Hindu ascetics, the indigent and vulnerable. Each was honored by being offered sweets, with no discrimination on the basis of religion or sect in a potent display of Deccan *convivencia*.

According to her Shiʿi spirituality, those who took upon themselves suffering and privation proved their holiness and earned a devotee's love, and such love inspired her to selflessly give of what blessings she had in life. Her biographer Gawhar concludes by noting, "By all accounts, Mah Laqa Bai was a wondrous, high-minded woman from whose flood of generosity no community or group was excluded."[31] While theologically she was staunchly Shiʿi, when it came to ritual and celebration she was quite ecumenical. Though she personally cultivated her love mysticism by focusing on ʿAli and his family and descendants, Mah Laqa Bai allowed her love mysticism to spread widely and embrace any who sacrificed for the sake of love.

Conclusion

Mah Laqa Bai's true love was for ʿAli. Despite her lyric poetry, her expressions of Shiʿi devotion, and her avid love of building, Mah Laqa Bai was first and foremost a courtesan and dancer. As a courtesan, it was her profession and her art to seduce men, enchant them, entertain them, and cajole from them financial and political support. But in all these love games, she could never be caught up in love with a man, for that would have spelled the end of her powerful allure that was based on haughty independence. In compensation, it was ʿAli whom she could truly love. From other men, one could expect appreciation and patronage, then infidelity and separation. But from ʿAli, one could expect constant loyalty and eternal generosity.

Mah Laqa Bai remained ambivalent toward actual men but remained ardent in her love of ʿAli, the ideal man. It is as if she always remembered her family history of women being betrayed by men. Her grandmother suffered from her husband's wayward spending and abandonment. Her mother suffered as a concubine in her early life and had to raise her two eldest daughters with no male support. Mah Laqa Bai was spared such trauma while growing up in luxury and educated refinement, but she always knew she was being raised to be a courtesan, not a wife.

Because of her experience as a female dancer and courtesan, she could express love for ʿAli more deeply than other Shiʿi devotees, whether male or female. Her training as a courtesan attuned her to all the nuances of love, passion, and seduction, which she could perform publicly while other women were restrained. Mah Laqa Bai focused these erotic skills into both her rhetoric and her devotional life. In rhetoric, she produced ghazals that combine themes of romantic and spiritual love with a passionate focus on 'Ali. In her devotional life, she engaged in numerous rituals of commemoration and celebration in which her Shi'i devotion diffused into honoring the sages and holy leaders of other religious communities. Both in ritual and in rhetoric, Mah Laqa Bai displayed a mystical approach to religion without abandoning her zealous Shi'i allegiance.

Conjunction — When Sun Meets Moon

People ask, "When is this day of resurrection?"
When sight is dazed when the moon disappears
When sun and moon are made to meet

—*Qur'an, Surat al-Qiyama (75:6–8)*

The Qur'an warns that a sign of the day of resurrection is that the sun will be made to meet the moon. Opposites will be joined and routines shattered. Our distractions will be pulled aside. Our real situation will be there, blindingly bright, before our dazed sight. Before the end comes, this world constitutes a tense standoff between mind-numbing routine and miraculous moments. Most people travel well-worn paths of routine to avoid inquiring deeply into their own fragile condition; however, the two personalities compared in this study, Shah Siraj and Mah Laqa Bai, were not afraid to step outside routine. They courted the miraculous, lived beyond the norms of their society, and left vivid accounts of their journey in literary legacy and biographical records.

Like the sun and moon, Shah Siraj never met Mah Laqa Bai in this world. Rather, they meet in the realm of imagination. This concluding chapter will explicate important points that emerge from the comparison between Shah Siraj and Mah Laqa Bai, whose personalities overlap even if they never met.

Meeting through Gender

Shah Siraj and Mah Laqa Bai meet in the ambiguities of gender relations. Gender identity and the equivocal relationships it sets into play are an integral part of poetry, performance, and mysticism. Shah Siraj and Mah Laqa Bah both performed gender outside of heteronormative regulations. Both avoided marriage but for different reasons, reasons determined by their respective gender identities.

Shah Siraj avoided marriage because of his sexual orientation. He was a male attracted to other males who, after a disastrous youthful love affair, vowed to never fall in love again. Instead he sublimated sexual desires into transcendental love for God, through submission to his Sufi master in the Chishti order. Yet his erotic longing and powerful imagination found expression in love poetry that he set to Qawwali music, until his master ordered him to stop composing love poems. Shah Siraj never questioned his male gender, but he did interrogate the responsibilities of masculinity in his patriarchal society and firmly rejected the obligation to marry, procreate, and run a household. Sufism provided him an alternative structure and community, one in which homosocial bonding was the norm. Within this framework, Shah Siraj found a way to negotiate his homosexual feelings while living a life respected by others.

In contrast, Mah Laqa Bai accepted the heterosexual norms of her society even as she contested many aspects of female gender roles. She exaggerated the characteristics that her society assigned to the feminine gender in order to avoid female gender obligations. She accentuated the aspects of beauty, grace, charm, and seductiveness, yet turned these into perpetual pleasures and professional pursuits instead of upholding them as means toward the goal of attracting a mate for marriage, procreation, and child-rearing. She adopted a girl-child to inherit her wealth and continue her artistic lineage, but she avoided marriage and pregnancy, which would have made her dependent upon men. Rather, she negotiated with powerful men at court through the arts. In this sense, her behavior both embraced feminine gender characteristics through song and dance and transcended them through her cultivation of education, literacy, and poetic competitiveness. She competed with men in these domains as an equal in ways that only courtesans could. While female members of aristocratic households—as wives and daughters—could pursue learning and literature, they could not compete with men or court men in public gatherings as could courtesans. For this reason, courtesans earn the admiration of some modern feminists while bearing the condemnation of others. The social power they wielded as courtesans did not uplift all women in their society but rather marked them as the exceptions that reinforced the rules.

Beyond the specificity of these two personalities and the class of people they represented—Shah Siraj representing Sufis and Mah Laqa Bai representing courtesans—the comparison between them raises issues about gender in their society. The comparison suggests that we must look at gender identities beyond the male-female binary that structured their society. We must not be fooled by the ubiquity of the male-female binary, whether we are examining the Deccan, South Asia, or Islamic societies globally. Within the structure of the male-female binary, there are many important variations, the boundaries of which are relative rather than absolute. Within the male gender category are many ambiguities and alternative masculinities to be lived out; these include asexual men, homosexual men, or men who value homosocial bonding. As Amanullah De Sondy has argued, analysis of gender in Islam should consider plural models of masculinity to be the norm: "The plural term masculinities is then a word that goes against the grain but requires serious consideration in the study of Islam and Muslims."[1] Within the female gender category, there are many ambiguities and alternative femininities that some adopted; these include asexual women who renounced sexual relationships and those who avoided marriage to live as courtesans. There were also women forced to be concubines, bound by their sexual availability to a man but without the legitimacy of being a wife or the status of being a courtesan.

No account of society, its religious practices, and its arts will be complete without including these variations in gender performance. The very firmness of the male-female binary for the majority depends upon the existence of alternative avenues available to sexual and gender minorities.[2] Shah Siraj and Mah Laqa Bai belong to the few who explored these alternative roles in their performance of gender. Contemporary gender studies as an intellectual discipline has moved toward analyzing gender as a performance. Gender roles are performed in ways that structure relations of power in society; they are not natural categories of being that are systematized by anatomy, sex roles, or procreative functions. Mah Laqa Bai and Shah Siraj are eloquent examples of how gender is performative—from an early modern era before "gender" existed as an analytic term.

Both Mah Laqa Bai and Shah Siraj took considerable risks to achieve success through their alternative gender performance. We will never understand fully the psychological pain Shah Siraj suffered when he experienced insanity and social alienation in his adolescence. We will never know for certain the physical pain that Mah Laqa Bai endured to excel in dance or to avoid pregnancy. Neither personality recorded these trying events in a clinical way, though they must have been the very foundation for both artists' later success. The vivid literary record that both poets left transforms these trials into triumphs.

Meeting through the Arts

Shah Siraj and Mah Laqa Bai meet on the stage of the arts. The social roles that they represent overlap profoundly because Sufis and courtesans interacted through the arts. Music, dance, and literature are boundary-blurring activities that Islamic social history must address. Such activities are complex because they are rich with nuance: they aim at artistic achievements that heighten emotional response to religious ideals even as they transcend the routine boundaries of religious communities. In the Deccan, artistic activities invited participation by members of diverse communities, leading to complex interactions between Sunnis and Shi'is and between Muslims, Hindus, and others. Muslim participation in the arts had important social repercussions as well as religious significance. Music, dance, and poetry had great importance to Sufis and courtesans and created an arena of interaction that would otherwise be denied them by competition between sectarian or communal allegiances. Of course, both Shah Siraj and Mah Laqa Bai were poets, and their mutual contribution to the Urdu ghazal genre forms the very substance of this book. But for them, poetry was inextricably connected to music and dance.

Shah Siraj was a Chishti Sufi. Members of this Sufi order recited poetry, cultivated music with performative ecstasy, and expressed an ethic of love. They set the cultural paradigm for Sufis in South Asia and oriented it toward musical arts. Shah Siraj was both a Sufi master and an expert in Hindustani music, not as a performer but rather as a listener, patron, and connoisseur (*rasika*). In this sense, he was typical of many Sufis in South Asia, especially the Chishtis, who elevated the ritual of listening to music (both Qawwali and more courtly classical genres) to the level of meditative worship.

As musicians, Sufis often interacted with courtesans. Their largest field of common interest was music, but Sufis and courtesans also shared a limited overlap in dance. Courtesans like Mah Laqa Bai were exponents of kathak dance, performed in royal courts or aesthetic gatherings. Sufis did not ordinarily attend such dance performances. But they did engage in a kind of ritualized dance of their own, though "dance" in this context was not rigorously practiced art to express theater or embody myth.

Rather it was spontaneous movement to express mystical ecstasy and loss of self-consciousness.[3] In this field of expressive motion, Sufis and courtesans shared a common culture, though their practices were quite different.

In Sufism, dance-like practice occurred as part of the ritual of listening to mystical poems set to music.[4] Some Muslim jurists and ascetics denounced Sufi uses of music as un-Islamic or debauched.[5] Sufi scholars countered with spirited defenses and cited *hadis* reports to defend not just music but dance as allowed or encouraged by the Prophet. One such report quotes 'Ali as saying, "I visited the Prophet with Ja'far [ibn Abi Talib] and Zayd [ibn Haritha]. The Prophet said to Zayd: 'You are a servant in my care,' whereupon Zayd began to hop on one leg around the Prophet. The Prophet then said to Ja'far, 'You resemble me in my humanity and virtue,' whereupon Ja'far began to hop behind Zayd. The Prophet then said to me ['Ali], 'You are of me and I am of you,' whereupon I began to hop behind Ja'far."[6] In this report, the Prophet Muhammad's most stalwart companions hop around him to express their overwhelming joy at hearing him verbally express their intimate relation with him. Words from a beloved spiritual master invoked in them elements of dance.

This hopping—being suspended between earth and heaven—is a good description of Sufi ecstatic dance practiced by Chishti Sufis. The movements are largely circular: pivoting on one foot or shuffling in circles, often with one arm raised upward pointing to the singular power of God's pure being that has overwhelmed the subject and effaced his or her consciousness. Sufi manuals sometimes specify that both feet of a dancing Sufi should not leave the ground at once so that the gestures are humble rather than artfully manipulative or sensuously erotic. Among Chishti Sufis, Amir Khusro sometimes danced rapt during devotional music, though Nizam al-Din Awliya disapproved if Amir Khusro raised his hands above his waist since he had not renounced the world and earned money as a court poet.[7] Burhan al-Din Gharib once danced for eleven days consecutively, forcing musicians to repeat variations of the phrase that sent him into ecstasy until he came down from the experience.[8]

In modern ethnomusicology, this is often analyzed as "trance." Ecstatic movements during sama' are not a self-conscious and practiced art of movement and might be more aptly described as "gesture" rather than dance.[9] Hagiographical sources record stories of Sufis engaging in dance movements borrowed from the art of courtly dance like that of the courtesans in which erotic enticement is foremost. Sufis might use it to express supplication and longing for intimacy or favor from a powerful figure, as illustrated by a popular anecdote about Amir Khusro. To cheer Nizam al-Din Awliya, who was inconsolable when his favorite nephew died, Khusro dressed in women's clothing and danced before his spiritual guide.[10] His transvestite performance had the comic and erotic power to break his master's sadness. By surrendering patriarchal masculinity through courtly dance, he performed his supplication of intimacy toward a spiritual superior. A later Chishti Sufi, Musa Sada Sohag (died 1449 in Ahmedabad), followed Amir Khusro's example to dress as a woman and dance at Nizam al-Din Awliya's tomb, audaciously deciding to never remove women's dress and bangles. He became a saintly guide of courtesans and hijras and founder of the "Sada Sohagi" order of Sufis who danced and sang in public, mimicking courtesans in a transvestite performance to cement their renunciation of worldly ambition. Some of them lived in Awrangabad and others settled near where Mah Laqa Bai lived in Hyderabad's old city.[11]

The examples above show that some Sufis cultivated dance as a devotional art, but they were very few in number. Most Sufis limited their movement repertoire to ecstatic gestures or a circling shuffle to show self-abandon. In contrast, most courtesans cultivated dance or assisted in its associated performance arts. Courtesans helped develop the dance style we know as kathak, which adopted gestures from the archive of Islamic symbolism. The dance of courtesans and the gestures of Sufis are distinct, yet they share symbolic elements. Many Muslim jurists denounce dance as libertine or sensual, and because it is unacceptable to the pious, dance is symbolically powerful in Islamic cultures. Both Sufis and courtesans exploited this. Courtesans used dance to heighten their allure with the fragrance of danger and disrepute. Some Sufis used it to serve as a symbol of rejecting worldly ambition and to express nonconformist sincerity in poetry and song.

Meeting through the Love of ʿAli

Shah Siraj with Mah Laqa Bai meet through the love of Hazrat ʿAli or *vilayat*. Sufis and courtesans interacted through the shared symbolism of love for ʿAli and the "family of the Prophet." Comparing Mah Laqa Bai and Shah Siraj helps us to understand the divergence and convergence between Sufi and Shiʾi communities. The concepts of *vilayat* and charisma bring these two communities into a shared symbolic space, even if they differ over ritual and theology.

Shi'is and Sunnis share many elements often ignored, as dramatic conflict overshadows quiet cooperation. In the Deccan region, Muslim communities are predominantly Sufi Sunni and Desi Shi'i communities, which share a common element of devotion to 'Ali. Both see 'Ali as the closest follower to the Prophet Muhammad, such that 'Ali represents a continuation of the essential presence of the Prophet. Both groups see love of 'Ali as a necessary precondition for love of Muhammad. This emphasis on love of 'Ali defines the cultural concept of *vilayat*, which is central to both Sufi and Shi'i theology. The Iranian American scholar Seyyed Hossein Nasr explains that this intimate connection involves "common parentage" in 'Ali, "shared sources" of inspiration, and "mutual interactions" in their medieval elaboration.[12] This book focuses on this third arena of commonality in the early-modern interactions between Sufis and Shi'is in the Deccan. This interaction points backward in time to 'Ali's persona as genesis and inspiration for both communities.

Both Shi'is and Sufis defined their spiritual practice as absorbing the qualities of 'Ali, who personifies the ideal human being and most powerful charismatic channel for divine presence in Islamic society. Their positive approach to 'Ali, as a spiritual figure whom one emulates or loves, meant that they did not highlight a negative approach through 'Ali, as a political figure to whom one submits or gains power. Shi'i belief is based upon the assertion that 'Ali is the only rightful leader of Muslims after the Prophet Muhammad died, yet this political claim has theological and mystical elements to it as well.

Sufis share this devotion to 'Ali and belief in his preeminence among all the followers of the Prophet. Sufis of the Chishti and Qadiri orders believe that 'Ali was the closest follower of the Prophet. In theological debates, they were known as "Tafzili Sunnis" because they upheld the preeminence (*tafzil*) of 'Ali. Sufis also feel that the Prophet Muhammad's charisma must be perpetuated in the Muslim community and see 'Ali as the key figure in its perpetuation. However, Sufis understand 'Ali as a saint rather than as a ruler. They perceive his preeminence to be in spiritual potency rather than in political rightfulness. They recognize the followers of 'Ali to be saints trained in mysticism rather than rulers in a lineage of imams.

Both Shi'is and Sufis extol 'Ali as *vali*, literally the "Friend of God." He was the *vali* because he possessed the quality of *vilayat*, a concept that comes very close to the English term "charisma." *Vilayat* means closeness to or intimacy with a source of authority, which in turn grants one power over others: one who is intimate with God is granted power by God to execute divine will in the world.[13] Shi'i and Sufi communities adopted the same terms but developed subtly different interpretations of their meaning.

Both Sufis and Shi'is emphasize the necessity of charisma. Shi'is see 'Ali as the rightful leader of the Islamic community, who was an inspired and inerrant follower of the Prophet, his charisma vouchsafed by his family relationship with the Prophet. Sufis see 'Ali as a saintly exemplar, who was an inspired and intuitive follower of the Prophet, his charisma received through a mystical initiation with the Prophet. For Shi'is, allegiance to 'Ali is political but also involves loving devotion to him and his descendants of an intensity that can be mystical. For Sufis, devotion to 'Ali is spiritual but also involves emulating his example in practical ethics, such as standing up to abusive power or embracing poverty.[14] Accepting poverty or denouncing power can have important political impact, even if these actions are motivated by essentially spiritual goals.

The difference between Shi'i and Sufi understandings of 'Ali is one of degree along a continuum; it is not one of binary opposition. Several forces brought Sufis and Shi'is closer to each other within this continuum. The first is Neoplatonic philosophy, which both Shi'i thinkers and Sufi sages avidly embraced during medieval times. In this philosophy, the cosmos is understood to emanate from God's being such that humans can regain a lost knowledge that the soul is not separate from God and can begin an "ascent" from the fetters of material existence through stages of spiritual enlightenment until one attains intimacy with God, imagined as pure being.[15] Another force that brought Shi'is and Sufis together was love mysticism, which is a particular expression of Neoplatonic philosophy. God is not merely pure being but is radiant beauty such that God's emanation that creates the cosmos is an expression of love. In turn, human beings can ascend to intimacy with God not through intellectual understanding but rather through the cultivation of love and selfless devotion. Another force that brought Shi'is and Sufis together was Persian poetry, a vehicle that expressed in a highly emotional and refined manner this fusion of Neoplatonic philosophy and love mysticism.

With these forces effective during medieval centuries in Persian-speaking lands including South Asia, Sufis and Shi'is found more in common than in difference. There was little opportunity for overtly political

Shi'ism, which nudged Shi'is to cultivate a more mystical, devotional, and literary practice of their faith; this dovetailed quite neatly with Sufi activities in the same region. The growth of orders like the Chishtis and Qadiris, which traced their teachings back to 'Ali, meant that figures held as imams by Shi'is were seen as saints and exemplars of love mysticism.[16] This Persianate cultural legacy infused the Islamic societies of South Asia in general and the Deccan in particular. In sixteenth-century Iran, this confluence between Shi'i and Sufi expressions of devotion was ruptured. The Safavid dynasty took power, declared Shi'ism to be the state religion, and suppressed Sufi orders as sites of possible Sunni subversion. Since then in Iran, Sufi poetry and music have been cherished as classical arts, but Sufi orders were largely driven underground.

In the Deccan, the Qutb-Shahi sultans in Hyderabad did not enforce a sectarian policy of suppressing Sunnis or discouraging Sufis. The continuum of commonality between Shi'is and Sufis prevailed in the Deccan long after it collapsed in Iran, which had nourished it for so long in Persian writings. In the Deccan, this tradition was transposed into Urdu literature with Shah Siraj and Mah Laqa Bai as literary examples of this Desi Shi'i and Sufi Sunni continuity. At the broadest level, comparison of their lives and poetry is meaningful because it highlights how Sufis and Shi'is could meet on common ground in love mysticism.

In Shi'i mysticism as reflected in the Urdu poetry of Mah Laqa Bai, 'Ali is not merely one among the saintly "Friends of God" but rather is first among them and their source. In loving him and drawing close to him with self-surrender, a devotee appeals for aid and intercession with God. Sufis also revere saints with this combination of devotional qualities, but they acknowledge that all saints derive from the original spiritual power of 'Ali. This spiritual effulgence of 'Ali spills over into others and empowers them to become saints in his model; in Islamic theology it is known as *faiz* or outpouring. It is the crucial term that links love mysticism, with its intense focus on a beloved person, with Neoplatonic philosophy, with its more intellectual yearning for abstract union with pure being. Mah Laqa Bai composes a whole ghazal that rhymes in the word *faiz*.[17] In one couplet, she writes, "Please, just for me, illumine this world and the next / It's possible with the outpouring of just one glance from you."

Love for an ideal person becomes fuel for ascent into love of God, especially if that person is a helping "Friend of God" who can intercede with God and bring one into greater intimacy with God. Just like in romantic love, one can approach a saintly Friend of God only with self-surrender.

In this goal, both Shi'is and Sufis can participate. For both Shi'is and Sufis, the prime models of self-sacrifice are 'Ali and Husain. They were martyrs, but the example they set for others is ethical self-sacrifice in love, not merely dying for a cause. Shah Siraj wrote in one of his ghazals, "Oh Siraj, to repeat 'Ali's name you must strive / Keep fresh in your mind Hyder's passionate love."[18] From a Sufi perspective, true lovers sacrifice themselves for others. The martial heroism and religious zealotry of 'Ali and Husain are rarefied into a love mysticism that sees the lover and beloved as interpenetrating, to the point of sharing one essence.[19] This is a bewilderment that gives rise to love so powerful that one could sacrifice oneself, an act of generosity to which pious reason would never acquiesce. Shah Siraj illustrates this in his poetry when he writes,

> He forgets anxieties of both worlds who drinks from love's bottle
> He forgets the investigations of Jamshed and delusions of Aristotle
> Examine any being deeply you'll see it's a manifestation of God's light
> Siraj forgets the idol and ponders the eternal with his insight subtle[20]

Thus, 'Ali and his family are crucial characters in the Sufi view of perpetual charisma. Through them, Sufis witness the power of God to manifest through anyone anywhere, without deferring to the expectations and rules of human society. From this point of confluence, Sufis and Shi'is diverge in the social form that their love for 'Ali's charisma might take. Sufi orders try to domesticate this charisma, channel it into interpersonal relationships, and build devotional institutions around it. A Sufi takes initiation with a spiritual guide who claims a chain of Sufi initiations leading back to renowned saints, originating with 'Ali. This network of initiations from the past into the present, from a teacher to his disciples through which blessings and devotional practices are transmitted, constitutes the Sufi order. When one joins a Sufi order, one creates a family without blood ties as a liminal community that is vibrant and meaningful but is outside the mainstream institutions of social order. Taking such an initiation allowed Shah Siraj to emerge from his youthful madness and lovelorn depression to fulfill his destiny as a poet and spiritual teacher.

In a different form, Shi'is also try to domesticate the charisma of 'Ali by insisting that it manifests through a genealogical bloodline. In each generation, one male from 'Ali's descendants is designated as the imam to whom Muslims should owe allegiance, yet most Muslims do not recognize the imam. So Shi'is advocate an alternate society based on an ideal of justice that is not currently possible, channeling 'Ali's charisma to form a marginal community rather than a liminal community. The marginal community is defined by ritual and doctrine, which in the present time aims for a future restitution. Holding allegiance to this vision allowed Mah Laqa Bai to grow from a position of vulnerability as an unmarried woman into a courtesan who exerted great power and lived an exemplary ethical life.

Both of these communities perpetuate the Prophet's charisma through 'Ali, though the two communities seek to channel it, domesticate it, and institutionalize it in different ways. The result is two Muslim communities—Sufi Sunni and Desi Shi'i—that are distinct yet share many common elements. This allows them to both cooperate and compete, depending upon the social conditions. We can think of Sufis and Shi'is as forming two communities based on divergent responses to a crisis of charisma; these two communities diverged in their formative era, but they converged again in the particular cultural zone of the Deccan. Allowing us to understand this convergence is the broadest significance of a comparison between Shah Siraj and Mah Laqa Bai.

Comparing Mah Laqa Bai and Shah Siraj in the Present

In contemporary times, we witness increasing tension and competition between politicized representatives of these sectarian groups, as national rivalry between Iran and the Saudi kingdom plays out in proxy struggles in Lebanon, Syria, Iraq, and the Gulf Emirates. Similar dynamics are at play farther afield across South Asia and in the Deccan. In Hyderabad since the 1990s, for instance, tension between Sunni and Shi'i Muslims has been on the rise, mirroring the increase in tension between Muslims in general and their Hindu neighbors. Making a comparison between Shah Siraj and Mah Laqa Bai in this context points to resources in the past that can address urgent concerns in the present. Shi'i and Sunni communities have not always defined themselves against each other; they can—under the right circumstances and cultural frameworks—orient themselves toward values and persons whom they revere in common.

The early-modern Deccan provides a vivid example of this. Its example of a Desi Shi'i and Sufi Sunni *convivencia* is long-lived in the region and persists in many ways as a bulwark against extremism and the ideological polarization of religious communities. It is beyond the scope of this book to link the Deccan example to other regional occurrences of Sunni-Shi'i *convivencia* and cooperation. Yet if readers look for potential commonalities that are actualized in social practices—whether devotional, artistic, or gendered—then future research will surely increase the documentation of such sites and situations in which continuum and ambiguity, rather than ideologically sharp polarity, are the norm. Until then, the comparison between Shah Siraj and Mah Laqa Bai can stand as a shining example of how the past refuses to conform to prejudices of the present.

NOTES

Introduction

1. Quotations from the Qurʾan are set in italics to distinguish them from quotations from other sources. Translation from the Qurʾan are by the author. I am grateful to Michael Sells for his keen insights on gender in Arabic and his forceful translations of the Qurʾan.
2. Sells, *Approaching the Qurʾan*, 84–85.
3. Andrews and Kalpaklı, *Age of Beloveds*, 37.
4. Ibid., 38.

Chapter 1

1. Tradition relates that this happened in Medina at Masjid al-Fażīkh (or Masjid al-Nakhla), known after a date palm that grew there.
2. Rulers eventually dropped the title "king" (*mālik*, literally "owner" of the world, one of the names of God in the Qurʾan) and adopted "strongman" (*sulṭān*, literally "power" who supports the titular *khalīfa*).
3. For Twelver Shiʿis (Iṡnā ʿAsharī), the line of charismatic leaders ended when the twelfth imam disappeared into "occultation" (present in the world but unseen) as a boy in 873. Theologian-jurists act as spokesmen of the disappeared imam until he will return in "the last days" as the promised *mahdī* or rightly guided savior.
4. These basic beliefs of the Twelver Shiʿi community are shared by other Shiʿi groups, including a smaller community called the "Sevener" group (Ismāʿīlī). They believe that leadership passed from the sixth imam (died 765) to his eldest son, Ismaʿil, and from him to a line of his male descendants into the present. Ismaʿil died before his father, and thus Twelver Shiʿis do not accept Ismaʿil as leader and claim that his younger brother, Musa al-Kazim (died 799), became imam.
5. ʿAlī Aṣghar ibn ʿAlī Akbar's *ʿAqāʾid al-Shīʿa* [Beliefs of the Shiʿis], a popular creed written in Iran, asserts that the imams are also miraculously born circumcised, as discussed in Browne, *Literary History of Persia*, 4:391–95.
6. The Sevener Shiʿi community gave rise to revolutionary groups like the Qarmāṭī movement and the Fāṭimī movement, which led a successful insurrection conquering North Africa and parts of South Asia, announcing its leader as a counter caliph

against the "illegitimate" Sunni leader in Baghdad. This political crisis caused many Sufi leaders to oppose radical Shiʻi thought and uphold Sunni loyalty.

7. Lawrence, *Morals for the Heart*. On the life and writing of this book's author, Amir Hasan Sijzi, see Borah, "Life and Works of Amir Hasan Dihlavi."

8. Siddiqi, "Origin and Development of the Chishti Order."

9. Khaliq Ahmad Nizami, "Sufi Movement in the Deccan," in Sherwani and Joshi, *History of Medieval Deccan*, 2:173–99.

10. A concubine is a slave whose labor was providing sexual pleasure. Jurists permitted sex with slaves, but this created legal tension around conditions of ownership, consequences if a child were born from sexual intercourse with a female slave, whether women owners of male slaves were permitted to enjoy sex with them, and whether same-sex intercourse with a male slave was allowed by virtue of his being a slave.

11. Kecia Ali, "Slavery and Sexual Ethics in Islam," in Brooten, *Beyond Slavery*, 107–24.

12. The Shiʻi community argued that its early imams took temporary wives and this was not forbidden by the Prophet, though Sunni jurists argued that this was banned as prostitution by the second caliph, ʻUmar ibn al-Khattab.

13. Ali, "Courtesans in the Living Room."

14. Sells, *Approaching the Qurʾan*, 7.

15. Plato, *Ion: A Dialogue with Socrates*, in *The Essential Plato*, 1128.

16. The Qurʾan reassured Muhammad directly: *Surely this is a revelation from the Lord of the universe. The faithful spirit has brought it down upon your heart so that you may be a warner in clear Arabic language. Surely this message is the same as the previous scriptures.... It is not brought down by evil spirits, they are not worthy of it, are unable to bear it, and are far from hearing and transmitting it* (Q 26:192–96 and 210–12).

17. Persian was written in script adapted from Arabic, and it adopted many Arabic loanwords. Arabic influence changed the language such that Persian before Islamic conquest became known as Pāhlavī while after Islamic conquest it is Fārsī.

18. Pollock, *Literary Cultures in History*, 153, discusses Amir Khusro and Amir Hasan. Sharib, *Khwaja Ghareeb Nawaz*, 63–64, cites the tradition of Saʻdi visiting Delhi and Chishti Sufis enjoying his verse.

19. Sultan Muhammad II (ruled 1378–97) of the Bahmani dynasty invited Hafiz to move to the Deccan capital at Bidar; see Eaton, *Social History of the Deccan*, 61; and Browne, *Literary History of Persia*, 3:285–89. Browne notes Hafiz's son migrated to the Deccan and is buried at Burhanpur.

20. The ghazal symbolizes Indo-Persian culture like haiku can be said to stand for premodern Japanese culture or the sonnet for Renaissance European culture.

21. The ghazal by Amir Hasan is reproduced in Fārūqī, *Naghmāt-e Samāʻ*, 25–26; it begins, "ay māh-e khūbān yek shabī bā khwēsh mehmān kun mā-rā."

22. Abraham, God's bosom friend, was thrown into a furnace by a pagan tyrant,

but the blaze turned into a cool garden, as narrated in the Qurʾan (21:68–70) and Judaic traditions.

23. Scott Kugle, "Dancing with Khusro: Gender Ambiguity and Spiritual Power at a Chishti Dargah in Delhi," in Martin and Ernst, *Rethinking Islamic Studies*, 245–65.

24. Schimmel, *Mystical Dimensions of Islam*, 370, and *Islam in the Indian Subcontinent*, 59.

25. Harun Khan Sherwani, "The Qutb Shahis of Golkonda-Hyderabad," in Sherwani and Joshi, *History of Medieval Deccan*, 1:465.

First Orbit

1. *Sirāj* in Arabic means a source of light, but the Qurʾan uses it to indicate the sun. It often refers to the lamps that are lit in mosques, which are also sources of light. It is very similar to the Persian word *chirāgh* (lamp) and the Hindi word *sūraj* (sun).

2. Sirāj, *Kulliyāt-e Sirāj*, 467. Ghazal 10 in radīf *mīm*, last two couplets. Its first couplet is: "jā bōl ay ṣabā dō dilārām kōñ salām / mērī ṭaraf sēñ dil-bar-e gul-fām kōñ salām."

3. Shafīq, *Gul-e Raʿnā*, mss., 507–10. The author of this memorial of poets in Awrangabad died in 1809 and was a disciple of Azad Bilgrami (died 1786), the scholar who nurtured a cultural revival in Awrangabad, whose circle included Sirāj.

4. Qāqshāl, *Tuḥfat al-Shuʿarā*, mss. Hyderabad: Salar Jung, 35–42.

5. Sabzāvarī, *Savāniḥ*, mss.

6. The tomb of Siraj is a small domed shrine in the center of the Pānch-Kūʾāñ graveyard, in the space between two gateways called Nawbat Darvāza and Kālā Darvāza.

7. Sharib, *Khwaja Gharib Nawaz*, 140.

8. Sirāj, *Kulliyāt-e Sirāj*, 559. Ghazal 5 in radīf *yē*. Its first couplet is: "rāh-e khudā-parastī avval hai khūd-parastī / hastī meiñ nistī hai awr nistī meiñ hastī."

Chapter 2

1. Sirāj, *Kulliyāt-e Sirāj*, 667. Ghazal 151 in radīf *yē*. Its first line is: "khabar-e taḥayyur-e ʿishq sun na junūn rahā na parī rahī / na tō tū rahā na tō maiñ rahā jō rahī sō bē-khabarī rahī."

2. Kalīmullāh, *Kashkūl-e Kalīmī*, 11–12; Kugle, *Sufi Meditation and Contemplation*.

3. Sells, *Mystical Languages of Unsaying*, 90–115.

4. Schimmel, *And Muhammad Is His Messenger*, 62, 245.

5. Green, *Indian Sufism since the Seventeenth Century* and "Stories of Saints and Sultans."

6. Schimmel, *Mystical Dimensions of Islam*, 362.

7. Ibid.

8. Malkāpūrī, *Maḥbūb żūʾl-Minan*, 2:1051.

9. Ibid., 2:779. Shah Murtaza Qadiri was born in Gujarat, moved to Bijapur, and is buried near the tomb of the ʿAdil-Shahi minister, Ikhlas Khan.

10. Ibid., 1:297–300. His given name was Sayyid Hasan, and he migrated from ʿIraq to Delhi, where he became a disciple of Sarmad Shahid, and hence wandered naked to Golkonda at the end of Qutb-Shahi reign.

11. Heer, *Precious Pearl*.

12. Sirāj, *Kulliyāt-e Sirāj*, 720. Ghazal 4 in his series of *tarjiʿa-band* ghazals; its first couplet is: "us kī khāk-e qadam jō pātā hūñ / chashm meiñ surma kar lagātā hūñ."

Chapter 3

1. Sirāj, *Kulliyāt-e Sirāj*, 273. Last three lines of a narrative epic titled *Ḥamd-e Bāri Taʿālā* (Praise for the exalted creator).

2. Awrangzēb means "He Who Adorns the Throne" and Awrangābād means "Abode of the Throne."

3. Sabzāvarī, *Savāniḥ*, mss., folio 25v.

4. Schimmel, *Islam in the Indian Subcontinent*, 59.

5. On Deccan gardens, see M. A. Nayeem, "Qutub Shahi Gardens in Golconda and Hyderabad," and Oudesh Rani Bawa, "Petals like Beautiful Tongues: Gardens of the 16th Century in Deccani Urdu Poetry," in *Deccan Studies Journal* 5, no. 2 (2007).

6. Jaʿfar, "Valī—Insān-dōst awr Vatan-parast Shāʿir [Vali: A humanist and nationalist poet]," in Narang, *Valī Dakkanī*, 38.

7. Mir mentions this new poetic language when he acknowledged his debt to Vali, saying, "It's no surprise I became a minstrel of rekhta verse / For my beloved sweetheart was a resident of the Deccan"; see Kanda, *Masterpieces of Urdu Ghazal*, 18.

8. Qāqshāl, *Tuḥfat al-Shuʿarāʾ*, mss., is the first detailed account of Sirāj's life, as discussed in Sirāj, *Kulliyāt-e Sirāj*, 29–32.

9. ʿAbd al-Rahman Chishti of Awrangabad is a relatively unknown personality; Green, *Indian Sufism since the Seventeenth Century*, 21, asserts that he was a follower of Nizam al-Din Awrangabadi and was named ʿAbd al-Rahman son of ʿAbd al-Rahim. This is confirmed by M. A. Mirza, an expert in Awrangabad's literary history writing a book on Siraj, who informs that ʿAbd al-Rahman is buried at Ellichpur (now known as Achalpur in Maharashtra), where he went to care for his sick mother.

10. Fārūqī, *Naghmāt-e Samāʿ*, 218. This Persian ghazal is preserved in the oral tradition of Qawwali repertoire. Its first couplet is: "faẓl-e raḥmān rah-numā-ye o peshvā-ye mā tūʾī / bar guzīda-ye bargāh-e khāliq-e yaktā tūʾī."

11. Sirāj, *Kulliyāt-e Sirāj*, 455. Ghazal number 8 in radīf *lām*, first and last couplet; its first couplet is: "hūñ parēshāñ yār kī zulf-e parēshāñ kē ṭufail / chāh-e gham meiñ hūñ maiñ us chāh-e zanakhdāñ kē ṭufail."

12. Ibid., 555. Ghazal number 10 in radīf *hē*, first, third, and last couplets; its first couplet is: "gham-e āhista-rūʾiyāñ rafta rafta / kiyā hai mujh kōñ ḥairāñ rafta rafta." The final couplet alludes to God's consoling us that *Indeed in every difficulty there is ease, in every difficulty there is ease* (Q 94:5–6).

13. Siraj mainly wrote ghazals but also several long *masnavī* epics and other forms like *rubāʿī* quatrain, *qaṣīda* ode, *mukhammas* quintupled verse, *tarjīʿ-band* ghazals-in-

series linked by a refrain, and *mustazād* ghazals augmented by additional metrical phrases that rhyme. The death date of ʿAbd al-Rasul Khan, who collected his poems, is unknown.

14. Sirāj, *Kulliyāt-e Sirāj*, 40.

15. Qāqshāl, *Tuḥfat al-Shuʿarā*, mss., 35–36. Qaqshal's date of death is unknown, but he lived in the mid-eighteenth century. Siraj's Persian ghazals are rare and were considered lost, so I translated two of them in another article; see Kugle, "Making Passion Popular: Sung Poetry in Urdu and Its Social Effects in South Asia" (forthcoming).

16. Qāqshāl, *Tuḥfat al-Shuʿarā*, mss., 35–36. Only a single couplet is preserved that reads: "tohmat ālūdīm o asrār nā-haqq ʿālim ast / bā vujūd-e pākī-dāman cheh rusvā-īm mā."

17. Shafīq, *Gul-e Raʿnā*, mss., 508.

18. Ibid.

19. Sirāj, *Kulliyāt-e Sirāj*, 279. Ghazal 1 in radīf *alif*. Its first couplet is: "nām tērā maṭlaʿ-ye fihrist hai dīvān kā / hai zabān kā vird khāṣa awr vazīfa jān kā."

20. Schimmel, *And Muhammad Is His Messenger*, 116–17.

21. Shafīq, *Gul-e Raʿnā*, mss., 508.

22. The Arabic saying is "faqrī fakhrī." See Schimmel, *And Muhammad Is His Messenger*, 48.

23. Green, *Indian Sufism since the Seventeenth Century*, 21.

24. Sirāj, *Kulliyāt-e Sirāj*, 462. Ghazal 4 in radīf *mīm*. Its first couplet is: "kiyā hai lashkar-e gham nē hamārē dil peh hujūm / ʿajab nahīñ hai agar fawj-e ʿaish huē maʿdūm." This ghazal was translated with the rhyme "no wonder" starting the second line of each couplet rather than ending the second line of each couplet, in a stylistic variation of the translation strategy.

25. Ernst, *Shambhala Guide to Sufism*, 24.

26. Sirāj, *Kulliyāt-e Sirāj*, 679. Ghazal 170 in radīf *yē*. Its first couplet is: "jis kōñ tērē naina kī mastī hai / roz o shab shughul-e mai-parastī hai." This ghazal was translated with no English rhyme scheme, in another stylistic variation of the translation strategy; it does not always work to render the ghazal's end rhyme into an English end rhyme.

27. Weir, "Whoso Knoweth Himself…"

28. Sirāj, *Kulliyāt-e Sirāj*, 575. Ghazal 25 in radīf *yē*. Its first couplet is: "hijr kī āg meiñ ʿażāb na dē / miṣl-e sīmāb iẓṭirāb na dē." This ghazal was translated with the rhyming phrase "don't give" embedded within the second line of each couplet rather than ending the second line of each couplet, in a stylistic variation of the translation strategy.

29. Ibid., 695. *Mustazād* 5 titled "Bāz-gasht." Its first couplet is: "jān bi-lab hūñ hai kahāñ voh dilbar-e jādū laqab / dilbar-e jādū laqab kē hijr meiñ hūñ jān bi-lab."

30. Ibid., 342. Ghazal 81 in radīf *alif*. Its first couplet is: "dō rangī khūb nahīn ēk rang hō jā / sarāpā mūm hō yā sang hō jā." The translation skips the fourth couplet filled with word plays on musical instruments.

31. Lawrence, "Honoring Women through Sexual Abstinence."
32. Nizami, *Life and Times of Shaykh Nasir-u'd-Din*, 27.
33. For discussion of mind-body dichotomy, see Kugle, *Sufis and Saints' Bodies*, 10–26.
34. Sirāj, *Kulliyāt-e Sirāj*, 352. Ghazal 3 in radīf *bē*. Its first couplet is: "majlis-e ʿaish garam huē yā rabb / yār agar huē shamaʿ-ye bazm ṭarab."
35. Austin, *Ibn al-ʿArabi*, 56.

Chapter 4

1. Sirāj, *Kulliyāt-e Sirāj*, 317. Ghazal 48 in radīf *alif*, first and second couplets. Its first couplet reads: "jis nē tujh ḥusn par nigāh kiyā / nūr-e khurshīd farsh-e rāh kiyā."
2. Foucault, *History of Sexuality*.
3. Halperin, *One Hundred Years of Homosexuality*; Massad, *Desiring Arabs*.
4. Boswell, *Christianity, Social Tolerance and Homosexuality*; Brooten, *Love between Women*.
5. Halperin, *How to Do the History of Homosexuality*, 105–37.
6. El-Rouayheb, *Before Homosexuality in the Arab-Islamic World*.
7. Vanita and Kidwai, *Same-Sex Love in India*.
8. This volatile intellectual field is well summarized by Bayaban and Najmabadi, *Islamicate Sexualities*, vii–xiv; in the context of South Asia, it is well summarized by Vanita, *Love's Rite*, 49–63.
9. De Sondy, *Crisis of Islamic Masculinities*, 144–47.
10. Walter Penrose, "Colliding Cultures: Masculinity and Homoeroticism in Mughal and Early Colonial South Asia," in O'Donnell and O'Rourke, *Queer Masculinities*, 144–65.
11. Digby, *Sufis and Soldiers in Awrangzeb's Deccan*, 80–81.
12. Gijs Kruijtzer, "Book Review of Nile Green, *Indian Sufism since the Seventeenth Century*," *Journal of Economic and Social History of the Orient* 51 (2008): 689–91.
13. De Sondy, *Crisis of Islamic Masculinities*, 139–43; De Sondy notes the importance of men's relations with courtesans and with younger males as shaping not just their erotic sensibilities but their social ethos and, in the case of poets, also their literary acumen.
14. Shafīq, *Gul-e Raʿnā*, mss., 507.
15. For example, the Persian *masnavī* by Ghanimat titled *Nairang-e ʿIshq* (written during the reign of Awrangzeb) tells the story of a merchant, ʿAziz, who fell in love with a young man named Shahid. See Vanita and Kidwai, *Same-Sex Love in India*, 159–60; and Muzaffar Alam and Sanjay Subramanyam, "Afterlife of a Mughal Masnavi," in Hansen and Lelyveld, *Wilderness of Possibilities*, 61.
16. Qāqshāl, *Tuḥfat al-Shuʿara*, mss., Hyderabad: AP State Oriental Manuscript and Research Library. See a discussion of different versions of this text in Sirāj, *Kulliyāt-e Sirāj*, 31.
17. Ibid., mss., Hyderabad: Salar Jung, 35–42.

18. Sirāj, *Kulliyāt-e Sirāj*, 31–32.

19. Ibid., 31.

20. Khan, *Pearl in Wine*, 308–11, gives a biography of Fakhr al-Din Awrangabadi, known as Muḥibb al-Nabī or The One Who Loves the Prophet.

21. Examples are Baba Palangposh and Baba Musafir (in the Naqshbandi community) in Awrangabad, and Yusuf and Sharif al-Din in Hyderabad (who belonged to the Kalīmi branch of the Chishti community, as did Siraj).

22. Sirāj, *Kulliyāt-e Sirāj*, 33.

23. His father was named Lala-ji, but the young man's own name is not given. Siraj calls him "Mohan," which means beautiful and is a title of the Hindu deity Krishna. It is uncertain whether this common given name was the young man's actual name, though Siraj did compose a ghazal that repeats the word *mohan* in each line—Sirāj, *Kulliyāt-e Sirāj*, 493, ghazal 23 in radīf *nūn*. For a summary of the affair see Azhar, *Urdū Meiñ Shāhid-Bāzī*, 99–104; and Vanita and Kidwai, *Same-Sex Love in India*, 169–72.

24. Katherine Butler Brown, "If Music Be the Food of Love: Masculinity and Eroticism in the Mughal *Mehfil*," in Orsini, *Love in South Asia*; and Penrose, "Colliding Cultures."

25. Sirāj, *Kulliyāt-e Sirāj*, 127.

26. Vanita and Kidwai, *Same-Sex Love in India*, 169.

27. Ibid., 171.

28. Ibid., 172.

29. Sirāj, *Kulliyāt-e Sirāj*, 242—*Būstān-e Khayāl*, lines 1115–19. Translation by Scott Kugle.

30. See Kugle, *Sufis and Saints' Bodies*, chapter 4, on homoerotic attraction among South Asian Sufis and *taʿzīr*, the *sharīʿa* term applied.

31. The emperor's viscera were buried in Ahmadnagar, where he died, and his body was transported to Khuldabad for burial—against orthodox Islamic tenets. See Green, *Indian Sufism since the Seventeenth Century*, 47.

32. Sabzāvarī, *Savāniḥ*, mss., folio 3, narrates how Awrangzeb established the city, describes its monuments, and lavishes attention on the city's Sufi shrines.

33. Malkāpūrī, *Maḥbūb żū'l-Minan*, 1:157. This saying in Arabic is "al-samāʿ damʿa wa fikra—al-bāqī fitna."

34. This discussion is treated in greater detail in Scott Kugle, "Sufi Attitudes toward Homosexuality: Case of the Chishti Order in South Asia," in Aquil, *Literary and Religious Practices in South Asian Sufism*, 31–59.

35. Sijzī, *Favāʾid al-Fuʾād*, 117–18, part 1, majlis 30.

36. Chishti Sufis often look up to Bibi Fatima (the mother of Nizam al-Din Awliya) and Bibi Hafiza (the daughter of Muʿin al-Din Chishti) as such women. If many women are prevented from pursuing Sufi cultivation along with men, it is also true that some women have overcome these obstacles; see Shaikh, *Sufi Narratives of Intimacy*; and R. Cornell, *Early Sufi Women*.

37. Safi, *Politics of Knowledge in Premodern Iran*, 169.
38. Sijzī, *Favā'id al-Fu'ād*, 194–95, part 2, majlis 33.
39. Ibid., 195.
40. Ibid., 196.
41. Nasrollah Pourjavady, "The Witness Play of Ahmad Ghazali," in Lawson, *Reason and Inspiration in Islam*, 203.
42. The translator of his discourses raises that issue, though we can infer from Nizam al-Din Awliya's language that he saw nothing unnatural about erotic attraction between men, as it was a common theme in the stories and poetry of esteemed poets, scholars, and Sufis.
43. Burhānpūrī, *Taḥẕīr al-Ṭālibīn*, mss.
44. Sirāj, *Kulliyāt-e Sirāj*, 551. Ghazal 4 in radīf *hē*. Its first couplet is: "huā hai meherbāñ vō mū-kamar āhista āhista / kiyā mujh āh nē shāyad aśar āhista āhista."
45. Scott Kugle, "Sultan Mahmud's Make-Over," in Vanita, *Queering India*, 30–46.
46. Under British colonialism, many Muslim intellectuals attacked their own literary tradition, especially the Urdu ghazal, denouncing it as effeminate, fatalistic, affected, artificial, and sometimes "homosexual." They championed poetry that expressed Victorian values in the guise of reformed Islamic values. See Pritchett, *Nets of Awareness*.
47. Examples include Shah Husain, Sarmad Shahid, and Musa Sada Sohag; on the latter, see Kugle, "Dancing with Khusro."
48. Sirāj, *Kulliyāt-e Sirāj*, 583. Ghazal 36 in radīf *yē*. Its first couplet is: "sīmāb jal gayā tō us sē gard bōliyē / 'āshiq fanā huā tō us sē mard bōliyē."
49. "The Light's Dawn" refers to a romantic *maśnavī* by Khusro titled *Maṭlaʿ al-Anvār*.
50. Unique (*fard*) means both a personal quality and also a one-line segment of poetry (the first half of a couplet). Sirāj makes a play of words to say, "The description of your beauty is such that, if one starts a couplet with one line, there is no other line to complete it—your beauty's description is beyond anyone to complete." Collections of Urdu poetry include at the very end *fard* lines whose full couplet was never completed.
51. Sirāj called this aim masculinity because in his patriarchal social order, manhood was the highest goal. In reality, his spiritual aim was a set of ideals that are ultimately beyond gender binary differences, but his expression of these ideals in his society and language was limited by patriarchal realities.
52. The next-to-last couplet explains that the masnavi was written in AH 1160 (1747 CE), which is exactly the number of couplets in the poem.
53. Sirāj, *Kulliyāt-e Sirāj*, 650–51. Ghazal 129 in radīf *yē*. Its first couplet is: "'ālam kē dōstōñ meiñ muruvvat nahīñ rahī / sharm o ḥayā o meher o shafqat nahīñ rahī."
54. Ibid., 244, couplets 1140–47 and 1154–56.
55. Fruitless (*abtar*) means impotent or unable to bear children to continue one's

family line. This is an Arabic word adopted into Urdu, which resounds with the Qurʾan's statement *The one who spurns you is surely fruitless* (Q 108:3), a divine response to a pagan Arab who scoffed at the Prophet Muhammad whose two sons died in infancy.

Chapter 5

1. Sirāj, *Kulliyāt-e Sirāj*, 675. Ghazal 124 in radīf *yē*, first and final couplet. Its first couplet reads: "jis kōñ piyū kē hijr kā bairāg hai / āh kā majlis meiñ us kī rāg hai."
2. Ibid., 123–24, discusses the musical quality of Siraj's poetry.
3. Malkapuri is quoted in Sirāj, *Kulliyāt-e Sirāj*, 54.
4. Shafīq, *Gul-e Raʿnā*, mss., 507–8, where Siraj describes himself in the third person.
5. Sirāj, *Kulliyāt-e Sirāj*, 604. Ghazal 24 in radīf *yē*. Its first couplet is: "chūñ keh khūbōñ kōñ nāz lāzim hai / ʿāshiqōñ kōñ niyāz lāzim hai."
6. Amīr Khūrd, *Siyār al-Awliyā*, 64, with translation by Ernst, *Shambhala Guide to Sufism*, 186. The poem is by Ahmad-e Jam (died 1141), and the crucial lines read: "kushtagān-e khanjar-e taslīm rā / har zamān az ghaib jān-e dīgar ast."
7. Ibid., 66.
8. Ernst and Lawrence, *Sufi Martyrs of Love*, 37.
9. In Persian this couplet is "jān bar īn yek bait dāda ast ān buzūrg, arrē īn gawhar ze kān-e dīgar ast / kushtagān-e khanjar-e taslīm rā, har zamān az ghaib jān-e dīgar ast." Translation by Scott Kugle based on an English version by Lawrence, *Morals for the Heart*, 72.
10. Ernst, *Eternal Garden*, 120, quoting Amīr Khūrd, *Siyār al-Awliyā*.
11. They are followers of Mawlana Rumi, who took dance as a means of ecstatic meditation rather than just a sign of involuntary ecstasy.
12. Thackston, *Millennium of Classical Persian Poetry*, 53. Translation by Scott Kugle.
13. Khān, *Tārīkh-e Awliyā-ye Kirām-e Burhānpūr*, 19–33.
14. Ibid., 23, quoting *Waqīʿāt-e Mamlakat-e Burhānpūr*.
15. Ibid., 23, quoting *Gulzār-e Abrār*.
16. Lawrence, "Early Chishti Approach to Samaʿ."
17. In Gujari it reads, "Shāh Raḥmatullāh munjh peh milāō / tum bāj lagūñ kis kē pāō."
18. Khān, *Tārīkh-e Awliyā-ye Kirām-e Burhānpūr*, 78.
19. Ernst, "From Hagiography to Martyrology," 308–27. Masʿud Bakk was the first Chishti Sufi to explicitly mention the name of Ibn ʿArabi and the philosophy of *vaḥdat al-vujūd* or "oneness of being" that is associated with him.
20. Shāh Bājan, *Khazāʾin-e Raḥmat*, mss. For more detail, see Kugle, "Burhan al-Din Gharib," 91–97, and "Movement from Persian to Urdu in the Deccan."
21. Madanī, *Sukhanvarān-e Gujarāt*, 47–50 and 65–69.
22. Parvēz, *Shāh Bājan*, 32–47. Mutālā, *Mashāʾikh-e Aḥmadābād*, 1:78, claims that the first examples of written Urdu come from Gujarat in this dialect called Gujarī.

23. Imre Bangha, "Rekhta: Poetry in Mixed Language," in Orsini, *Before the Divide*, 24–26.

24. Rahman, *From Hindi to Urdu*, 29.

25. Khān, *Tārīkh-e Awliyā-ye Kirām-e Burhānpūr*, 49.

26. Ibid., 87, and Parvēz, *Shāh Bājan*, 157, both record the rekhta lyric of Shah Bajan.

27. Mixed Hindi-Persian songs attributed to Amir Khusro—such as the verses sung in Qawwali, "Ze ḥāl-e miskīn ma-kun taghāful, durāyē naina banāyē batiyāṅ" (Do not ignore my pitiful state, winking your eyes and weaving your tales)—are not included in his written collection of poems, so the authenticity of attribution to Khusro is doubtful. Therefore it is likely that rekhta poems did not originate in the early fourteenth century with Khusro, but rather at least a century later with less known Sufi poets like Shah Bajan.

28. Khān, *Tārīkh-e Awliyā-ye Kirām-e Burhānpūr*, 79.

29. Ibid., 83. The poem in Persian is "asrār-e haqq tū-st keh mī-khīzad az rebāb / varna ze chūb-e khashk mā-rā gumān na-bud."

30. The poem in Persian is "az kansa-ye rabāb mā-rā niʿmatī rasīd / shūd aftāb har keh az-ū żarra chashīd."

31. Khān, *Tārīkh-e Awliyā-ye Kirām-e Burhānpūr*, 84.

32. Lewis, *Rumi Past and Present*, 363–64.

33. Omid Safi, "The Sufi Path of Love in Iran and India," in Khan, *Pearl in Wine*, 221–66.

34. His Gujarati master in the Chishti path, Rahmatullah Mutavakkil, was not known for his love of music and visible ecstasy; see Shattārī, *Gulzār-e Abrār*, 204.

35. Eaton, *Sufis of Bijapur*, 141–45, provides information on Shams al-ʿUshshaq Miranji (died 1499), his son Burhan al-Din Janam (died around 1597), and his follower Mahmud Khush-Dahan (died 1617); see also Schimmel, *Islam in the Indian Subcontinent*, 59.

36. Sirāj, *Kulliyāt-e Sirāj*, 678. Ghazal 169 in radīf *yē*; first, second and final couplet out of seven. Its first couplet is: "shab-e hijr mujh par balā lāʾī hai / birah āg sīnē meiṅ sulgāʾī hai."

37. Digby, *Sufis and Soldiers in Awrangzeb's Deccan*; Green, *Indian Sufism since the Seventeenth Century*, 11–19.

38. Ernst and Lawrence, *Sufi Martyrs of Love*, 133; Green, *Indian Sufism since the Seventeenth Century*, 19–23; and Kugle, "Sufi Meditation Manuals from the Mughal Era," 484–88.

39. Scott Kugle, "Sufi Meditation Manuals from the Mughal Era," in Giordani, *Faith and Practice in South Asian Sufism*, 459–89.

40. Green, *Indian Sufism since the Seventeenth Century*; also Alam, *Languages of Political Islam*, 193–94, for similar Naqshbandi opposition to Sufi music in Delhi.

41. Amīr Khūrd, *Siyār al-Awliyā*, 515.

42. Sirāj, *Kulliyāt-e Sirāj*, 452. Ghazal 4 in radīf *lām*, sixth couplet. Its first couplet is: "bāt kar dil satī ḥijāb nikal / ghuncha-ye lab satī gulāb nikal." Sirāj plays on *makhmal* or "velvet," also known as *kām-khwāb* or "dream-work fabric" for its rich, dark quality.

43. Siraj continued to write prose and sent letters to his friends in other cities; eight years before he died, he gathered his favorite Persian poems in a collection called *Intikhāb-e Divān-hā* and wrote a prose introduction to it.

44. Sirāj, *Kulliyāt-e Sirāj*, 63, lists Siraj as the poetry teacher of Zia al-Din "Parwana," Lala-ji Kishan "Bejan," Mirza Mughal "Kamtar," Mir Mahdi "Matin," Mirza Mahmud Khan "Nisar," and Muhammad ʿAta "Zia."

45. Ibid., 73; the last line in Persian reads "rū bi-raḥmān namūd Shāh Sirāj" and adds up to give the year AH 1177.

46. Ibid., 70. The quatrain is "The light of poets, Siraj, who delights imagination made eloquence mourn in cloth black and rent / The day of his passing is fixed in our recollection 'Alas, alas, the lamp of India now lies silent.'" The final line in Persian reads "hay hay, miṣbāḥ-e hind khāmōsh" and gives the value of 1177.

47. Ibid., 73. The line in Persian, "gil gasht Sirāj, ḥaif ay dil," also gives the value of 1177.

48. Ibid.

49. Ibid., 68–69.

50. Ibid., 74. The editor Sarvari notes that in his time (the 1940s), descendants of the *takiya*'s custodians were still active in Awrangabad and it was common to hear Siraj's poems sung in Hyderabad, where he lived and worked. The death dates of these followers of Shah Siraj are not known.

Chapter 6

1. Imān, *Kulliyāt-e Imān*, "Praise of Imam ʿAli in Five-Line Stanzas," 436–38.

2. Sirāj, *Kulliyāt-e Sirāj*, 150–53 — *Būstān-e Khayāl*, couplets 17–57.

3. The word for courtesans here is *āliyāñ*, meaning literally a woman's female friends, but in slang meaning courtesans or prostitutes who are friends of each other since they have no husband to protect them.

4. Most Sunni Muslims have a Sufi orientation to their practice, even if they do not explicitly belong to Sufi orders. This reality is denied by modern anti-Sufi reformers like the Wahhabi and Salafi movements, yet it persists. Folk cultures of countries with the greatest population of Sunnis—such as Indonesia, India, Pakistan, Bangladesh, Nigeria, and Turkey—are all deeply influenced by Sufi personalities and practices, though lay practitioners of such places rarely control the media dominated by reformists and amplified by Western observers.

5. South Asia also housed adherents to the Suhravardi, Naqshbandi, and Shattari orders, among many other minor orders, sometimes termed as the "fourteen families" of Sufis.

6. Such journalistic assertions confuse categories, as if one were to assert of colors that hue and saturation are mutually exclusive. Yet a bright, intense blue and a dark, dull blue are both blue: the hue of blue is not the same as its saturation, meaning whether the color is intense or dull, bright or dark.

7. Discussion of Shiʿism in the Deccan here concerns the Twelver Shiʿi community (iṡnā-ʿāsharī). Its legal school, Jaʿfari maẓhab, developed with the same intellectual and scriptural tools as Sunni schools, though it does not consider the rules passed by early caliphs to be binding.

8. In the Deccan, a *murshid* or spiritual guide could hold allegiance to both Chishti and Qadiri affiliations, passing them both on to their disciples. This was easy to achieve, since both lineages trace their charismatic initiation back to ʿAli, who is the anchor of their *silsila* and connection to the Prophet Muhammad. In addition, the saintly founders of each *tariqa*—namely Muʿin al-Din Chishti and ʿAbd al-Qadir Jilani—claim a Sayyid family lineage as genealogical descendants of ʿAli's sons. Other Sufis in South Asia, like Suhravardi and Shattari silsilas, also trace their initiatic lineage back to ʿAli.

9. Abu Bakr al-Siddiq (died 634) was the companion of the Prophet recognized by Sunni Muslims as the first caliph, whereas ʿAli was the cousin and son-in-law of the Prophet recognized by Shiʿi Muslims as the first imam and only rightful leader though acknowledged by Sunnis as the fourth caliph.

10. Hodgson, *Venture of Islam*, 1:372, coins the term "'Alid loyalty" to mean "the varied complex of special religious attitudes associated with loyalty to the Alid [the family of ʿAli]," whether among Sunnis or among those who identified as Shiʿis.

11. As sung by Jafar Husain Khan Badauni, *Chant Qawwali de l'Inde Nord* (Inedit, 1993).

12. For Sufis, Qawwali was a way to draw close to ʿAli and his sons; see Hyder, *Reliving Karbala*, 105–36; and Scott Kugle, "From Baghdad to Vrindavan: Erotic and Spiritual Love in Qawwali," in Chakravorty and Kugle, *Performing Ecstasy*, 139–78.

13. Nasr, Dabashi, and Nasr, *Shiʿism*, 160. This ḥadīṡ is recorded in the *Musnad* of Ahmad ibn Hanbal; for a discussion of the ḥadīṡ as the "basic ritual song of Sufism in India," see Qureshi, *Sufi Music*, 21–22.

14. Scott Kugle, "The Spirituality of Qawwali," in Cornell and Lawrence, *Blackwell Companion to Islamic Spirituality*.

15. "Turkic" means Central Asians who were Timurid Chaghatais, Uzbeks or Turkomans, Azarbaijanis, or other various Turkic groups.

16. The genealogy of Gesu Daraz is from Husain, but other Sayyid families (especially those associated with the Qadiri Sufi community) were from his elder brother Hasan.

17. Eaton, *India's Islamic Traditions*, 166–71.

18. Hollister, *Islam and the Shia's Faith in India*, 106. In the center are calligraphic representations of Allah, Muhammad, Fatima, ʿAli, Hasan, and Husain (known popu-

larly as Panj-Tan or "Five Pure Members"), while slightly lower to the right are those of Abu Bakr and ʿUmar and on the left are those of ʿUsman and ʿAli (ʿAli's name is depicted a second time, showing his place in the Sunni list as the fourth khalīfa).

19. Hollister, *Islam and the Shia's Faith in India*, 105.

20. Pinault, *Shiʿites*, 79–82.

21. Naqvi, *Qutb Shahi Ashur Khanas*, 74–76.

22. Ruffle, "Bride of One Night," 135–40 and 210–14; see also Ruffle, *Gender, Sainthood and Everyday Practice*. This study chooses to use the term "Desi" Shiʿism to describe this process of South Asian or more particularly Deccan "vernacularization."

23. Howarth, *Twelver Shiʿa as a Muslim Minority in India*.

24. Rizvi, *A Socio-Intellectual History of Isna ʿAshari Shiʿis in India*, 1:311–12, as cited in Ruffle, "Bride of One Night," 136.

25. Naqvi and Rao, *Muharram Ceremonies*; and Ruffle, "Bride of One Night," 137. Hyder, *Reliving Karbala*, 84–85, discusses the lack of boundary between Sunni and Shiʿi in Muharram rituals until the influence of British colonialism; and Green, *Indian Sufism since the Seventeenth Century*, 50 and 86, discusses this "composite culture" of the Deccan that allowed overlap of religious communities. In this sense, "conversion" as an analytic concept may be misleading; "transposition" might be a better term for the process by which religious communities identified their own sacred landscape with those of others. Since for many premodern religious communities, rituals of deference to spiritual heroes were more important than adherence to theological doctrine, the heroes of one religious community could be easily "transposed" with the holy persons of other communities, facilitating coexistence in society or co-participation in rituals without the crossing of religious boundaries implied by "conversion."

26. Wagoner, "Charminar as Chaubara." The structure is a tower with four minarets placed at the crossroads marking the center of the city; it incorporates a madrasa and mosque, but its unique shape resembles a taʿziya (a model of Imam Husain's tomb that is carried in Muharram processions commemorating his martyrdom). On its interior walls are plaster designs carved in the shapes similar to an ʿalam, reminding viewers of an ʿāshūr-khāna. Yet the monument's placement resembles a *chawbara* or local Hindu town-center for meetings at the main crossroads.

27. Naqvi, *Qutb Shahi Ashur Khanas*, 73–74.

28. Nasr, Dabashi, and Nasr, *Shiʿism*, 76.

29. This was a specifically Deccani vernacular idiom, for there were other regional expressions of Shiʿism in North India, especially in Avadh with its capital at Lucknow. North Indian vernacular took shape in the eighteenth and nineteenth centuries and borrowed many devotional forms from the earlier Deccani idiom: the form of building called ʿashur-khana was adopted from the Deccan but was called *Imām-bāra* or "House of the Imams." See Juan Cole, "Popular Shiʿism," in Eaton, *India's Islamic Traditions*, 311–39.

30. Lalaguda was located near the present Malkajgiri, not far from the hill of Mawla 'Ali; in the modern locality of Lalapet there are remains of a medieval wall, which was perhaps the Qutb-Shahi fort were Yaqut stayed.

31. Prasad, *Social and Cultural Geography of Hyderabad City*, 132–34. A pious version that stresses Yaqut's devotion to 'Ali and neglects to mention that he was a eunuch is found in Naqvi, *Qutb Shahi Ashur Khanas*, 25–26. See Scott Kugle, "Courting 'Ali: Urdu Poetry, Shi'i Piety and Courtesan Power in Hyderabad," in Hermann and Speziale, *Muslim Cultures in the Indo-Iranian World*, 125–66.

32. The 'urs of Mawla 'Ali is a separate celebration from 'Ali's birthday, though they are only a few days apart; in practice, mainly Shi'is commemorate the birthday (*mawlid*) on 13 Rajab while the 'urs is wider in popularity with Shi'is, Sunnis, caste Hindus, and tribal Hindus participating in the pilgrimage from 15 to 18 Rajab.

33. Naqvi, *Qutb Shahi Ashur Khanas*, 33, describes the offerings (*sandal*) of sandalwood paste, perfumes, incense, flowers, and other precious substances that are carried on the heads of devotees to venerate the shrine.

34. Sarkar, *Ma'asir-e-Alamgiri*, 174.

35. Ibid., 178.

36. Naqvi, *Qutb Shahi Ashur Khanas*, 18.

37. Nizam al-Mulk's grandfather was killed in a Mughal assault on the Golkonda fort; his father was shot with arrows and humiliated by his failure to scale its walls.

38. Naqvi, *Qutb Shahi Ashur Khanas*, 18.

39. Sirāj, *Kulliyāt-e Sirāj*, 243–44—*Būstān-e Khayāl*, couplets 1126–37.

40. Khūsh-ḥāl Khān's name does not clearly reveal sectarian identity as Shi'i or Sunni. He is said to have been a Kalāvant or Qawwāl and evidently sang in *dhrupad* style with lyrics that are devotionally Islamic rather than Hindu; see Khūsh-ḥāl Khān, *Rāg o Rāginī*, mss.

41. Sirāj, *Kulliyāt-e Sirāj*, 467. Ghazal 10 in radīf *mīm*, last two couplets. Its first couplet reads: "jā bōl ay ṣabā dō dilārām kōñ salām / mērī ṭaraf señ dilbar-e gul-fām kōñ salām."

42. Ibid., 530. Ghazal 75 in radīf *nūn*, last couplet. Its first couplet reads: "ā'ina-rū kē shawq meiñ ḥairāñ huā hūñ maiñ / zulfōñ kōñ us kī dēkh parēshāñ huā hūñ maiñ."

Second Orbit

1. Her court title (*khitāb*) means "Moon Cheek" and is often romanized as Mah Laqa or Mahlaqa (or even Mahlakha Bai or Malika). Confusion arises from the local Deccani pronunciation, which does not distinguish between *laqā* (meaning "cheek") and *liqā* (meaning "meeting") and which often pronounces the letter *q* as *kh* or *k*.

2. There is controversy over whether her death date is 1820–21 or 1824.

3. Māh Laqā Bāī, *Gulzār-e Māh Laqā*, 32. Ghazal 106 in radīf *yē*. Its first couplet: "bahūt makhmūr hūñ sāqī sharāb-e arghavānī dē / na rakh tashna mujhē sāghar birāh-e meherbānī dē." Each publication of her divan orders poems differently, so to

facilitate reference this book provides the first couplet in Urdu transliteration. The standard reference is the earliest lithograph publication from Hyderabad in 1906, titled *Gulzār-e Māh Laqā*, which has the least omissions and errors: page number and ghazal number in endnote references correspond to the ordering in that edition.

4. Kugle, "Courting ʿAli," 125–66.

5. Māh Laqā Bāī, *Gulzār-e Māh Laqā*, 2. Ghazal 1 in radīf *ālif*. Its first line is: "kahāṅ ṭāqat hai rāh-e ḥamd meiṅ jō hō zabān gōyā / keh yahāṅ juz ʿajaz o khāmōshī nahīṅ hai ek jahān gōyā."

6. Dalrymple, *White Mughals*, 124, asserts that Mah Laqa Bai was "the first major woman poet in Urdu," but there were earlier female poets. Rather, she is "major" because she compiled a full divan of Urdu ghazals (meaning at least one ghazal rhyming in each of the thirty-two letters of the Urdu alphabet). Yet the first woman to do this was actually Lutf al-Nisa "Imtiyaz," a contemporary of Mah Laqa Bai discussed in chapter 11. Debates about who was the first female poet to do this continue in the contemporary journal *Sabras* 84, no. 9 (September 2012), published by the Idara-e Adabiyat-e Urdu in Hyderabad.

7. Andrews and Kalpaklı, *Age of Beloveds*, 118.

8. Māh Laqā Bāī, *Dīvān-e Chandā*, mss.

9. Jawhar, *Tajalliyāt-e Māh Laqā*, mss.

10. Earlier in the nineteenth century, her biography was given by traditional Urdu collections, including the 1864 collection by Ranj, *Bahāristān-e Nāz*, 127 (under the name Chanda) and 206 (under the name Mah Laqa), and the 1876 collection by Nādir, *Gulshan-e Nāz*.

11. The standard modern biography is ʿAzmī, *Māh Laqā—Ḥālāt-e Zindagī*. His biography was preceded in 1935 by Sayyid Akhtar Hasan, "Chandā, Māh Laqā Bāī" in Zōr, *Muraqqaʿ-ye Sukhan*, 83–104, and succeeded in 1959 by Shawkat, *Māh Laqā*.

12. Kugle, "Mah Laqa Bai: The Remains of a Courtesan's Dance."

13. Māh Laqā Bāī, *Gulzār-e Māh Laqā*, 3. Ghazal 3 in radīf *ālif*. Its first couplet is: "ṭarapē hai dil payām sē is bē-qarār kā / taskīn-e jān hai vaqt hō jis dam dō-chār kā."

Chapter 7

1. The actress who plays the madam in *Mandi* is the daughter of the actress who plays the madam in *Umrao Jaan*.

2. Published in 1905, *Umrao Jan* is one of the earliest novels in Urdu, and it is ironic that male authors elevated the voice and experiences of a female courtesan to experiment with representing society through the novel, a genre that did not previously exist in Urdu literature; see Matthews, *Umrao Jan Ada*, which is a more accurate translation than that by Khushwant Singh and M. A. Husaini.

3. Oldenburg, "Lifestyle as Resistance," 136–54; see also Sinha and Basu, *History of Prostitution in India*, 238–41.

4. Shawkat, *Māh Laqā*, 36–37. There is controversy over whether Mah Laqa Bai adopted one or two daughters; see chapter 9, note 47.

5. In Persian, the poem is:

> kamān o masjid o ʿāshūr-khāna żīʾl-shān
> ṭarāz-e masjid-e ʿālī ze rāh-e ṣidq o ṣafā
> zahī naṣīb keh Khūsh-ḥāl Khān bi-kōh-e sharīf
> binā nihād bi-qānūn-e khūb o rūḥ-fizā

6. Naqvi, *Qutb Shahi Ashur Khanas*, 28, gives the *abjad* equivalent as AH 1293, but this cannot be correct. This error can be attributed to the numerous printing mistakes in Naqvi. My calculation of *abjad* gives the date AH 1238 (1822–23 CE). Khush-hal Khan died in Mah Laqa Bai's mansion, where he imparted musical skill to the young women trained there; he died before her, so the date of 1822 makes sense, meaning that he died two years before her death in AH 1240 (1824 CE).

7. Jawhar, *Tajalliyāt-e Māh Laqā*, mss., 228.

8. Māh Laqā Bāī, *Gulzār-e Māh Laqā*, 5–6. Ghazal 13 in radīf *bē*. Its first couplet is: "sāqī hai garcha bē-shumār sharāb / nahīñ khūshtar sivā-ye yār sharāb." The first line is different in manuscript copies of her *divan*, and in this translation I follow the London manuscript. See Khūsh-ḥāl Khān, *Rāg o Rāginī*, mss., 11 a–b, for lyrics of Mah Laqa Bai's music teacher that implore ʿAli, the pourer of *kawsar*, to give a spring of sweet water at the hill of Mawla ʿAli.

9. The Qurʾan describes four rivers that flow from springs in paradise: of water, of milk, of wine, and of honey (Q 47:51).

10. Māh Laqā Bāī, *Gulzār-e Māh Laqā*, 34. Ghazal 114 in radīf *yē*. Its first couplet is: "'ajab kyā mai-kashī kā dil meiñ har zāhid kē jōsh āʾē / agar sāghar bi-kaff mehfil meiñ upnā māh-vash āʾē."

11. Gawhar, *Ḥayāt-e Māh Laqā*, 19–20.

12. Ṭāliʿ, *Tażkira-ye Awliyā-ye Haidarābād*, 3:37–38. Shah Tajalli ʿAli was a disciple of Shah Muʿin Tajalli (death date unknown) in the Chishti Sufi order and served as his successor. As a historian, poet, and calligrapher, he was close to Aristu Jah and the second nizam; he participated in court functions and received royal stipends for his services to the court.

13. Gawhar, *Ḥayāt-e Māh Laqā*, 19.

14. Ibid., 21.

15. Jawhar, *Tajalliyāt-e Māh Laqā*, 228, gives a chronogram and date as AH 1218, though Naqvi claims that the well was built in AH 1294 (1877 CE). The information provided by Jawhar—written under Mah Laqa Bai's own direction—is more reliable.

16. In his rise in rank, Aristu Jah earned the titles *amīr-e aʿzam* (prime minister) and *sohrāb-e jang* (hero in battle).

17. Jawhar, *Tajalliyāt-e Māh Laqā*, 213–14; and Gawhar, *Ḥayāt-e Māh Laqā*, 20.

18. Jawhar, *Tajalliyāt-e Māh Laqā*, 215.

19. Ibid., 215–16; and Gawhar, *Ḥayāt-e Māh Laqā*, 24–25. The second nizam gave her this title six months before his death on August 6, 1803, but her noble position was confirmed by his successor.

20. Māh Laqā Bāī, *Gulzār-e Māh Laqā*, 37. Ghazal 124 in radīf *yē*. Its first couplet is: "basant āyī hai mawj-e rang-e gul hai jōsh-e ṣabā hai / khudā kē faẓl sē ʿaish o ṭarab kī ab kamī kyā hai."

21. Khizr appears in the Qurʾan as Moses's companion and as Alexander's servant (Q 18:60–82).

22. John Malcolm, assistant to the British Resident (equivalent to ambassador from the British East India Company to the nizam), commented that dealing with Mah Laqa Bai was the key to getting anything accomplished at the nizam's court.

23. Andrews and Kalpaklı, *Age of Beloveds*, 86–87.

24. Māh Laqā Bāī, *Gulzār-e Māh Laqā*, 19. Ghazal 59 in radīf *ṣuād*. Its first couplet is: "dawr-e sharāb-e surkh hai yahāñ ṣubḥ o shām raqṣ / dekhē kabhī tō yār yeh majlis tamām raqṣ."

25. Tajallī, *Tuzuk-e Aṣafiyya*, mss., 155–57.

26. Ibid., 156, 259, 295, and 317 contain images of dancing courtesans at court and abroad on diplomatic missions (for reproductions of these images, see Nayeem, *Miniature Paintings*, 110, 123, 128, and 131).

27. Tajallī, *Tuzuk-e Aṣafiyya*, mss., 251, possibly depicts Mah Laqa Bai—identified by a crescent moon over her head—leading a troupe of female dancers on May 14, 1782 (for reproduction of this image, see Nayeem, *Miniature Paintings*, 122).

28. Māh Laqā Bāī, *Gulzār-e Māh Laqā*, 13. Ghazal 39 in radīf *dāl*. Its first couplet is: "kuch din karē ṣaiyād kō allah jō merā ṣaid / kar dūñ maiñ sabhī dām sē ek-dam meiñ rahā ṣaid."

29. Gawhar, *Ḥayāt-e Māh Laqā*, 33–34.

30. Māh Laqā Bāī, *Gulzār-e Māh Laqā*, 13. Ghazal 40 in radīf *dāl*. Its first couplet is: "agar hō kuch bhī merī āh kār gar ṣaiyād / rahē na dil meiñ tērē ẓulm kā aṣar ṣaiyād."

31. Ibid., 21–22. Ghazal 69 in radīf *ghain*. Its first couplet is: "tā hai mujh kō dekh kē kyūñ justujū-ye tēgh / sar hai merā ḥabāb-e kaff-e ābjū-ye tēgh."

32. Gawhar, *Ḥayāt-e Māh Laqā*, 20.

Chapter 8

1. Māh Laqā Bāī, *Gulzār-e Māh Laqā*, 18. Third and fifth couplets from ghazal 58 in radīf *shīn*. Its first couplet is: "bulbul kō hō bahār meiñ gulzār kī talāsh / lēkin mujhē sadā hai mērē yār kī talāsh."

2. Ibid., 5. Ghazal 10 in radīf *ālif*. Its first couplet is: "Rahē nawrōz ʿishrat āfarīn jōsh-e bahār afzā / gul afshāñ hai karam tērā chaman meiñ dahr kē har jā."

3. Ibid., 17. Ghazal 52 in radīf *rē*. Its first couplet is: "jab huā ṣaḥn-e chaman meiñ khusrō gul kā guẓar / ʿandalībōñ nē kiyē har simt sē mujrā pukār."

4. Ibid., 28. Ghazal 93 in radīf *nūn*. Its first couplet is: "muhaiyā dawr meiñ jō ʿaish hai tērē sar-e shāhān / na jam sē bhī huā thā is qadr nawrōz kā sāmān."

5. Another poem composed for Basant does not mention ʿAli, and most likely this poem was written in honor of Aristu Jah; see ibid., 37. Ghazal 123 in radīf *yē*. Its first

couplet is: "bahār ʿaish lē kar bāgh meiñ ab yuñ basant āyī / keh bē-taklīf hai shab-nam sē gul kī bāda paimāʾī."

6. Hashmī, *Khavātīn-e Dakkan kī Urdū Khidmāt*, 24.

7. The British—that is, the East Indian Company—had previously refused to dedicate troops to defend the nizam against Maratha incursions under the Triple Alliance pact of 1790, which bound the British, the nizam, and the Marathas into a confederacy against Tipu Sultan; see Dalrymple, *White Mughals*, 130–34.

8. Jawhar, *Tajalliyāt-e Māh Laqā*, 215.

9. Dalrymple, *White Mughals*, 172–73.

10. Jawhar, *Tajalliyāt-e Māh Laqā*, 215; Ṭālib, *Mīr ʿAlam*, 163.

11. Dalrymple, *While Mughals*, 172, 525n30.

12. Mīr ʿAlam, *Sarāpa-ye Māh Laqā*, couplets 1–3.

13. Ibid., couplet 10.

14. Ibid., couplets 19 and 22.

15. Ibid., couplets 55–60.

16. Ibid., couplets 61–65.

17. Ibid., couplet 85, describes Mah Laqa Bai's style and behavior as *fitna*, meaning both temptation and public disorder, a term that is integral to Islamic moral discourse on women's beauty in public.

18. Mīr ʿAlam, *Sarāpa-ye Māh Laqā*, couplets 89–90.

19. Ibid., couplets 99–100 and 103–5.

20. Ibid., couplets 222–24.

21. Māh Laqā Bāī, *Diwan-e-Chanda*, mss.

22. Mudiraj, *Pictorial Hyderabad*, 2:165–66.

23. Ibid., 2:163–65.

24. Shawkat, *Māh Laqā*, 60–62, claims that Raja Rambha Rao was her first promoter.

25. Ibid., 62–63.

26. Quoted in Mudiraj, *Pictorial Hyderabad*, 2:130.

27. ʿAzmī, *Māh Laqā*, 58–59, records these poetic similarities that were first observed by Samina Shawkat in her book on Chandulal. For instance, Chandulal composed a ghazal that opens with the couplet "Tonight I saw a face than the moon more beautiful / Of her the whole world strained to catch an eyeful" ("dēkhā hai shab kō chehrā jō us rashk māh kā"). In the same meter and rhyme, Mah Laqa composed a ghazal that opens, "I told my darling of my longing in words truthful / I'm ready, too, if you desire also to be faithful" ("ham sē karē hai yār bayān apnī chāh kā"), the sixth ghazal in radīf *alif* of her collection.

28. Sarma, *Deodis of Hyderabad*, 26.

29. The major figures of this first generation of Deccan poets during the nizams' rule were Mir ʿAbd al-Vali "ʿUzlat" (who came from Surat in Gujarat to Awrangabad and later to Hyderabad), Asad ʿAli Khan "Tamanna" and Lakshmi Narayan "Shafiq"

(in Awrangabad), and Tajalli ʿAli Shah "Tajalli" (in Hyderabad) along with Nawazish ʿAli Khan "Shaida" and Khwaja ʿInayatullah "Maftun."

30. Iman's father, Muhammad ʿAqil Khan, was a royal historian and court chronicler in Hyderabad, known by the pen name "Naʾik."

31. Imān, *Kulliyāt-e Imān*, 356–58. Jahan-Parvar Begum was the daughter of Maʿali Miyan, a son of the second nizam who was adopted by Aristu Jah. After Maʿali Miyan was killed in the campaign of Khardla, his wife and daughter lived at Aristu Jah's mansion. Dalrymple, *White Mughals*, 201 and 366 misspells her name as "Jahan Pawar Begum."

32. Imān, *Kulliyāt-e Imān*, 29–35; the editor, Sayyida Hashmi Mujeeb, provides this biography.

33. Hashmī, *Khavātīn-e Dakkan kī Urdū Khidmāt*, 24.

34. ʿAzmī, *Māh Laqā*, 89–92.

35. Imān, *Kulliyāt-e Imān*, 49. Qais was a founder of the *rēkhtī* genre; see Carla Petievich, "Feminine Authorship and Urdu Poetic Tradition," in Hansen and Lelyveld, *Wilderness of Possibilities*, 247n22. Most Urdu literary histories credit Rangin of Lucknow (died 1834) with creating the genre, but that may be due to North Indian bias that elides Deccani contributions. See Qais, *Kulliyāt-e Qais*, mss.

36. Imān, *Kulliyāt-e Imān*, 50–51. Another student of Iman who rose to fame was Shaykh Hafiz "Hafiz" (died 1830), a master poet (*mālik al-shuʿarā*) compared to Zawq of Delhi and Nasikh of Lucknow; he was neglected by later generations, and his poetry lies in manuscripts yet unpublished.

37. Ibid., 426–29. The same poem is reproduced in ʿAzmī, *Māh Laqā*, 148–51, but with many errors and unaccounted-for editorial changes.

38. Imān, *Kulliyāt-e Imān*, 426–29, stanza 16.

39. Ibid., stanzas 11–12.

40. Ibid., stanza 13.

41. Ibid., stanzas 15 and 17.

42. Ibid., stanza 19.

43. Shamsur Rahman Faruqi, "The Poet in the Poem or, Veiling the Utterance," in Hansen and Lelyveld, *Wilderness of Possibilities*, 179

44. Jawhar, *Tajalliyāt-e Māh Laqā*, 16–17. The masnavi is reproduced with some lacunae in ʿAzmī, *Māh Laqā*, 151–54, from which translation here was rendered.

45. Jawhar, *Tajalliyāt-e Māh Laqā*, 16–17, couplets 1–2.

46. Ibid., couplets 6–17.

47. Ibid., couplets 22–23.

Chapter 9

1. Māh Laqā Bāī, *Gulzār-e Māh Laqā*, 5. Ghazal 12 in radīf *bē*, last two couplets; its first couplet is: "hō sakē hai kub tērē chehrē kē hamsar āftāb / gō rakhī hai nūr kī khilʿat kō darbar āftāb."

2. Ibid., 14. Ghazal 43 in radīf dāl, first couplet which reads: "garcha gul kī sēj ho tuspar bhī ūṛ jātī hai nīnd / sar rakhūṅ qadamōṅ pe jub tērē mujhē ātī hai nīnd."

3. Hashmī, Khavātīn-e Dakkan kī Urdū Khidmāt, 23.

4. Gawhar, Ḥayāt-e Māh Laqā, 21.

5. Begum, Princess Jahan Ara Begum.

6. Gawhar, Ḥayāt-e Māh Laqā, 33.

7. Ibid., 33–34.

8. Ibid., 34.

9. Mah Laqa Bai's maternal grandfather was named Muhammad Husain Khan, and she asserts that he was a Sayyid of the Zaydi lineage resident in Barhah, a town in North India home to many Shiʿi nobles in the Mughal court after the death of Awrangzeb. Richards, Mughal Empire, 20, reports that soldiers and nobles from Barhah enrolled in the Mughal imperial system starting in the 1560s; known for bravery, their ancestors migrated from Iraq in the thirteenth century CE and claimed a Sayyid lineage.

10. Jawhar, Tajalliyāt-e Māh Laqā, mss., 201. Mah Laqa Bai claims that her maternal grandmother was a Sayyid from the Khwaja lineage of Kathiawar, Gujarat.

11. Suvorova, Masnavi, 135, notes that bhagat-bāz in North India meant a popular entertainer who would perform with comedians (bhāṅḍ) and courtesan dancers (ṭavāʾif). The original meaning of bhagat is a religious devotee (this meaning was preserved among Lambada caravans with whom Mah Laqa Bai's family probably traveled south to the Deccan; see Bhukya, Subjugated Nomads, 204). This suggests that the bhagats were originally religious devotees who crafted devotional song and dance into popular performance to earn a livelihood; their drift into commercial earning may have forced their wives or daughters into prostitution, for in Hindi bhagtānī or "woman of a bhagat family" was slang for prostitute.

12. Shawkat, Māh Laqā.

13. ʿAzmī, Māh Laqā, 11–12.

14. Ibid., 16.

15. This quote is from Dr. Raihana Sultana's introduction to ibid.

16. Quoted in ibid., 13.

17. In Arabic, this proverb is "kullu shaiʾin yarjiʿu ilā aṣlihī."

18. Jawhar, Tajalliyāt-e Māh Laqā, 204.

19. ʿAzmī, Māh Laqā, 35.

20. Jawhar, Tajalliyāt-e Māh Laqā, 207.

21. Ibid., 204.

22. Ibid., 205. The image is taken from Persianate folklore, in which the raindrops of the spring month of Naisān are believed to generate pearls if they fall into oysters (and to generate poison if they fall into snakes' mouths).

23. Ibid., 208.

24. ʿAzmī, Māh Laqā, 35.

25. Jawhar, Tajalliyāt-e Māh Laqā, 208.

26. Ibid., 205, 208; confirmed by Gawhar, *Ḥayāt-e Māh Laqā*, 7–8.
27. ʿAzmī, *Māh Laqā*, 37–38.
28. Jawhar, *Tajalliyāt-e Māh Laqā*, 209.
29. Ibid., 210.
30. Ibid., 206.
31. Gawhar, *Ḥayāt-e Māh Laqā*, 5–6.
32. Ibid., 9–10.
33. ʿAzmī, *Māh Laqā*, 38.
34. Ibid., 37.
35. Gawhar, *Ḥayāt-e Māh Laqā*, 7.
36. ʿAzmī, *Māh Laqā*, 37.
37. Jawhar, *Tajalliyāt-e Māh Laqā*, 208–9.
38. Ibid., 206. Rukn al-Dawla, whose personal name was Mir Musa Khan, is discussed in chapter 7.
39. Ibid., 206; compare to Gawhar, *Ḥayāt-e Māh Laqā*, 10.
40. Gawhar, *Ḥayāt-e Māh Laqā*, 10.
41. Ibid., 8.
42. ʿAzmī, *Māh Laqā*, 42–43.
43. Jawhar, *Tajalliyāt-e Māh Laqā*, 210.
44. Gawhar, *Ḥayāt-e Māh Laqā*, 10–11.
45. The army was then led by Nizam al-Mulk, as explained by Jawhar, *Tajalliyāt-e Māh Laqā*, 205.
46. Gawhar, *Ḥayāt-e Māh Laqā*, 9.
47. Ibid., 31–33. This passage asserts that Mah Laqa Bai adopted only one daughter, named Ḥusn Laqā Bāī, "Madam Beauty Cheek," whereas Shawkat, *Māh Laqā*, 37, asserts that she adopted two daughters, named Ḥusn Afzā Bāī, "Madam Increasing Beauty," and Ḥasīn Laqā Bāī, "Madam Beautiful Cheek." Some contemporary Hyderabadis remember these daughters as Ḥusain Laqā Bāī and Ḥasan Laqā Bāī in an overly devout reading of their names as referring to the early Shiʿi imams (namely the Prophet Muhammad's grandsons Hasan and Husain). It is impossible to tell which information is correct. Gawhar is closer to Mah Laqa Bai's time and seems to have known personally courtesans in her lineage and is therefore a more authoritative source of information; but the name he gives includes terms from each of the compound names that Shawkat mentions, so he might have conflated two women into one. No grave of Mah Laqa Bai's daughter(s) is traceable, so there is no epigraphic verification whether she had one daughter or two or what their names were. In addition to two adopted daughters, Shawkat gives names of several prostitutes (*nawchī*) in Mah Laqa Bai's household who continued to perform after her death: Deepa, Dilaram, Rami, Shama, Muna, and Sharifa.
48. Gawhar, *Ḥayāt-e Māh Laqā*, 30.
49. Khūsh-ḥāl Khān, *Rāg o Rāginī*, mss. ʿAzmi, *Māh Laqā*, 94–100, records some lyrics Mah Laqa Bai composed for religious occasions like the Jashn-e Ḥaidarī (birth-

day of ʿAli) and Jashn-e Ghadīr (day of announcing ʿAli's leadership) and for secular ones like the birthday of rulers or the wedding day of nobles. It includes the song in *rāga bihāg* (a musical mode) that Mah Laqa Bai sang for the wedding of Bala Prasad, son of Maharaja Chandulal. Folio 11 a–b gives an example of *dhrupad khayāl* lyrics in *rāginī bhairavī* (a musical mode) that beseech Imam ʿAli: "Thus give me aid from the unseen, for I am weak and in need of your generosity, O king of men ʿAli, the ruler of all land and sea! I may be just a dancing girl but let me remain joyful in this, Anup's garden—this much please give me for the sake of Hasan and Husain!" (In Hindi mixed with Persian, it reads: "gaib sē dō mū-kō aisō, hūñ nājuk main muḥtāj sakhī shāhimardān ʿAlī, mālik hō tum baḥr o bar kī. Shād-khwār-am rahūñ Anūp dēkh bāgh hō khūsh-ḥāl ṣadkē sē dō mawlā mū-kō Shabbīr o Shabbar kī"). Folio 16 a gives an example of a *khayāl* song in *rāga rāmkalī* (a musical mode) to be sung in *ektāla* (twelve-beat rhythm) based upon a composition by Sada-Rang (died 1748), the *khayāl* singer from the Mughal court of Muhammad Shah: "Preserve the life, honorable Mawla ʿAli, of those who call out for safety and security—make all their troubles easy. I find that, by your grace, Hasan and Husain rule over more than both worlds. Let me be sacrifice sacrifice sacrifice sacrifice for the sake of Mawla ʿAli Mawla ʿAli! Give me faith and righteousness, let me achieve this goal. Look upon me with kindness, Khwaja Muin [Muʿin al-Din Chishti], and aid this humblest follower of faith. Please accept this small request of Sada-Rang and protect us poor beggars" (in Hindi mixed with Persian: "Amn amān keh sē gujarān rakhīyē mawlā ʿAlī jī, mushkil kījīyē āsān. Pāūñ min zād dō jahān kī, karam kijīyē Ḥasan Ḥusain sulṭān. Vār vār vār vār jāūñ mawlā ʿAlī kī, mawlā ʿAlī kī. Dīn īmān dījīyē mū-kōñ yehī murād maiñ pāvān. Karam kī najar kījīyē, kavāja Muīn, dīn pairavīn danī kī pustī. Itnī bintī sun lījē Sada-Rang kī, dījīyē dhayān dharam lāj").

50. Claudia Salazar, "A Third World Woman's Text: Between the Politics of Criticism and Cultural Politics," in Gluck and Patai, *Women's Words*, 98.

51. The Persian phrase—"gōyā mashriq anvār-e ḥusn-e Māh Laqā"—yields the date AH 1229 (1814 CE) when decoded through the *abjad* system.

52. Vanita, *Gandhi's Tiger and Sita's Smile*, 131.

Chapter 10

1. Māh Laqā Bāī, *Gulzār-e Māh Laqā*, 31. Ghazal 101 in radīf *yē*; its first couplet is: "rōktā hūñ jō us-sē mujh sē khafā rehtā hai / dil yeh mērā terē kūchē hī meiñ jā rehtā hai."

2. Petievich, "Feminine Authorship and Urdu Poetic Tradition," 234.

3. Kugle, "Mah Laqa Bai and Gender."

4. Māh Laqā Bāī, *Gulzār-e Māh Laqā*, 33. Ghazal 109 in radīf *yē*. Its first couplet is: "har rōz jō yūñ hī sitam-ījād karōgē / dil ʿāshiqōñ kē sēkṛōñ bar-bād karōgē." Petievich, "Feminine Authorship and Urdu Poetic Tradition," 238, surveyed *tażkira* literature for examples of *rēkhtī* and finds that "actual evidence for women writing *rekhti* is very slim—just four *sheʿrs* [couplets] from one ghazal and another lone *sheʿr*."

5. Petievich, *When Men Speak as Women*, 246–67, gives six of Hashimi's *rēkhtī* ghazals in Urdu with masterful English translations. She gives his pen name as "Hashim," but it should be "Hashimi" because he was a follower of the Mahdawi leader Sayyid Hashim (died 1669); his given name was Sayyid Miran Khan. See Sharīf, *Dakkan meiñ Urdū Shāʻirī*, 747–70; Hashmī, *Dakkan meiñ Urdū*, 231–35; and Argilī, *Rēkhtī*, 8–12. There is difference of opinion about his name and lack of detail about his life. He is known as a court poet of Bijapur but may have settled in Burhanpur and died there. See also Petievich, "Feminine and Cultural Syncretism in Early Dakani Poetry."

6. Māh Laqā Bāī, *Gulzār-e Māh Laqā*, 31–32. Ghazal 104 in radīf *yē*. Its first couplet is: "sañbhāl apnē kō ay shānē na in zulfōñ meiñ uljhālē / charhē haiñ bin ḍasē kē zahr yeh dō nāg haiñ kālē."

7. Ibid., 7. Ghazal 17 in radīf *pē*. Its first couplet is: "tumhārē zulfōñ kē jaisē haiñ pīch o tāb meiñ sāñp / kīsī nē dēkhē nahīñ aisē kālē khwāb meiñ sāñp."

8. Ibid., 34. Ghazal 113 in radīf *yē*. Its first couplet is: "yād ā gaī hai dil kō merē āh kīsī kī / taktā hūñ shab o rōz jō maiñ rāh kīsī kī." The English translation does not show that the speaker is male, for in English a first-person verb is not conjugated according to gender, but in Urdu it is, such that *taktā hūñ* means "I [male] stare" whereas *taktī hūñ* would mean "I [female] stare."

9. Ibid., 8. Ghazal 22 in radīf *tē*. Its first couplet is: "rū-bi-rū kab hō lab-e laʻl kē tāb yāqūt / nām sun jiskā utar jāē hai āb yāqūt."

10. Sirāj, *Kulliyāt-e Siraj*, 151–52—*Būstān-e Khayāl*, lines 29–34.

11. Māh Laqā Bāī, *Gulzār-e Māh Laqā*, 28. Ghazal 91 in radīf *nūn*. Its first couplet is: "kaṭī hai hijr kī shab ab hai vaṣl-e yār kā din / khudā nē ham kō dekhāyā hai phir bahār kā din."

12. Petievich, "Feminine Authorship and Urdu Poetic Tradition," 140–41.

13. Hashmī, *Dakkan meiñ Urdū*, 475–77. Qais was a poetry student of Muhammad Sher Khan Iman (along with Mah Laqa Bai) and was respected as his successor.

14. Tharu and Lalita, *Women Writing in India*, includes one ghazal of Mah Laqa Bai.

15. Poduval, *Re-figuring Culture*, 1.

16. The contemporary effort to raise Mah Laqa Bai to the ranks of a premodern feminist creates backlash in different forms; see one journalist's reaction to a 2002 lecture by Kishwar Naheed at the Institute of Women's Studies in Lahore that cited Mah Laqa Bai. Intizar Husain, *Dawn Magazine*, March 10, 2002, cited at www.dawn.com/weekly/dmag/archive/020310/dmag16.htm.

17. Jameela Nishat, "Dakhini Urdu as a Vehicle of Social Interaction," in Gupta, Parasher-Sen, and Balasubramanian, *Deccan Heritage*, 215.

18. Ibid., 214.

19. Jawhar, *Tajalliyāt-e Māh Laqā*, 698–747.

20. Nishat, "Dakhini Urdu as a Vehicle of Social Interaction," 215.

21. Gawhar, *Ḥayāt-e Māh Laqā*, 31–32.

22. Leonard, *Hyderabad and Hyderabadis*, 378–427.

23. Rustom Dil Khan served as governor of the Deccan province during the era of Awrangzeb, as had his father, Jan Supar Khan, before him. Rustom Dil Khan was executed during the succession dispute following Awrangzeb's death, but he managed to build the Kali Masjid before he died. His mansion was located at Imli Mahal outside Yaqutpura Gate in Hyderabad; see Bilgrami, *Landmarks of the Deccan*, 96–98.

24. Gawhar, *Ḥayāt-e Māh Laqā*, 20.

25. Jawhar, *Tajalliyāt-e Māh Laqā*, 213.

26. *Tavā'if* is a Persian term compounded from two different words in Arabic that sound the same when pronounced in Persian and Urdu but have different root meanings in Arabic. In Arabic, *tavā'if* (with a sharp dental t) means a group, troupe, community, or sect (plural of *tā'ifa*). In contrast, *ṭavā'if* (with a deep retroflex t) means people who move in a circle or form a circle; it is derived from the same root that means circumambulation of the Kaʿba (*ṭavvāf*). These two terms became superimposed because they are pronounced identically in Persian and Urdu to mean a troupe of circling dancers.

27. Margaret Walker, "Courtesans and Choreographers: The (Re)placement of Women in the History of Kathak Dance," in Chakravorty and Gupta, *Dance Matters*, 279–300.

28. Sweta Sachdeva Jha, School of Oriental and African Studies, personal correspondence (August 15, 2008). I am indebted to Dr. Jha for information based upon her dissertation on the history of kathak; see also Jha, "Tawa'if as Poet and Patron: Rethinking Women's Self-Representation," in Malhotra and Hurley, *Speaking of the Self*.

29. ʿAzmī, *Māh Laqā*, 100, claims that Mah Laqa Bai learned to dance from a master named Panna Naqqal. *Naqqāl* means actor or mime and connotes a theater performer rather than a dancer. ʿAzmī cites *Gulzār-e Aṣafiyya*, reporting that Panna Naqqal performed for the first nizam and received a monthly stipend. However, the source says nothing about him teaching Mah Laqa Bai to dance. The first nizam held court in Awrangabad rather than in Hyderabad and died in 1748, long before Mah Laqa Bai was born; so Panna Naqqal's performance in the court in that era does not mean that Mah Laqa Bai learned dance from him. ʿAzmī does not explain how he deduced any relationship between them based on other sources, so his conclusion is highly doubtful. It is more likely that Mah Laqa Bai learned dance from her elder half sister who raised her and had learned from her mother and aunts in an all-female lineage.

30. See, for instance, research of Sweta Sachdeva and Margaret Walker, especially Walker, *India's Kathak Dance in Historical Perspective*.

31. Chakravorty, *Bells of Change*.

32. Māh Laqā Bāī, *Gulzār-e Māh Laqā*, 17. Ghazal 55 in radīf *sīn*. Its first couplet is: "saj kē is taraḥ sē niklā voh taraḥ-dār keh bas / jān o dil hō hī gāyā dēkh gariftār keh bas."

33. Ibid., 21. Ghazal 66 radīf *ẓoē*. Its first couplet is: "Rahē raqīb sē bā-ham voh sīm-bar maḥẓūẓ / huā na āh kā upnē kabhī aśar maḥẓūẓ."

Chapter 11

1. Māh Laqā Bāī, *Gulzār-e Māh Laqā*, 33. Ghazal 110 in radīf *yē*. Its first couplet is: "chashm-e kāfir bhī hai awr ghamza-ye khūn-khwār bhī hai / qatl kō pās sapāhī kē yeh talvār bhī hai."
2. Bukhārī, *Ṣaḥīḥ al-Bukhārī*, 2:732–33 (Kitāb Fażāʾil Aṣḥāb al-Nabī, book 62, ḥadīs 3750).
3. Ibid., 2:732 (ḥadīs 3748–49). Al-Tabari's famous history, in his account of the battle of Uhud, attributes this saying to the angel Gabriel, who said this to Muhammad in praise of ʿAli's heroism.
4. Ibid., 2:733 (ḥadīs 3753), 2:881 (Kitāb al-Maghāzī, book 70, ḥadīs 4460).
5. Māh Laqā Bāī, *Gulzār-e Māh Laqā*, 22. Ghazal 71 in radīf *fē*. Its first couplet is: "kyōn na hō dil in dinōn mein bulbul-e zār-e najaf / hai merī madd-e naẓar mein ṣaḥn-e gulzār-e najaf."
6. Ibid., 5. Ghazal 11 in radīf *bē*. Its first couplet is: "na gul sē hai gharaẓ tērē na hai gulzār sē maṭlab / rahā chashm-e naẓar-e shabnam mein apnē yār sē maṭlab."
7. Ibid., 14. Ghazal 43 in radīf *dāl*. Its first couplet is: "Garcha gul kī sēj hō taspar bhī ūṛ jātī hai nīnd / sar rakhūn qadamōn pe jab tērē mujhē ātī hai nīnd."
8. Muhammad said that Fatima was his special solace, the "coolness of my eye," which in Arabic is equivalent to the English expression "the apple of my eye."
9. Māh Laqā Bāī, *Gulzār-e Māh Laqā*, 17. Ghazal 53 in radīf *zē*. Its first couplet is: "kab hai ṭarīq-e ʿishq mein rah-bar kā gham hanūz / hai chashm-e rah-numā mujhē naqsh-e qadam hanūz."
10. Ibid., 32. Ghazal 106 in radīf *yē*. Its first couplet is: "bahūt makhmūr hūn sāqī sharāb-e arghavānī dē / na rakh tashna mujhē sāghar bi-rāh-e meherbānī dē." In the final couplet, she refers to Husain and Hasan as princes, for if ʿAli is the king of all men (*shāh-e mardān*), as he is popularly known in Shiʿi lore and Urdu poetry, then his two sons Husain and Hasan are princes (*shāhzādē*).
11. Ibid., 6. Ghazal 14 in radīf *bē*. Its first couplet is: "dil hō gayā hai gham sē tērē dāghdār khūb/ phulā hai kyā hī jōsh sē yeh lālazār khūb."
12. Flueckiger, *In Amma's Healing Room*, 79–85, describes a Muslim female spiritual healer in Hyderabad who provides such a charm or amulet (*taʿvīż*).
13. Māh Laqā Bāī, *Gulzār-e Māh Laqā*, 15. Ghazal 45 in radīf *żal*. Its first couplet is: "rōk kō yeh nigah-e bad kē hai qātil taʿvīż / apnē bāzū mein tū rakh kar kē merā dil taʿvīż."
14. ʿAbd al-Ḥai, *Tārīkh-e Awrangābād*, 395. This contemporary historian of Awrangabad claims that Lutf al-Nisa was born and raised in that city but died in Hyderabad.
15. Imtiyāz, *Dīvān-e Imtiyāz*, mss. The collection of poetry of Lutf al-Nisa was compiled in AH 1212 (1797–98 CE) and was in circulation in Hyderabad before Mah Laqa Bai died; it is likely that Mah Laqa Bai read Imtiyaz's poetry but only after Mah Laqa Bai had circulated her own collection. Lutf al-Nisa encodes her date of collection in a Persian couplet: "Since the time this slave-girl of Fatima collected fresh poetry, her heart flourished / With joy, the fortunate date of this book is given by saying,

'Read the divan of Imtiyaz'" (chūn az kanīz-e khātūn darīn zamān ashʿār-e tāra jamʿ shūd dil shagufta shūd / az rū-ye yumn sāl-e humāyūn-e īn kitāb dīvān-e Imtiyāz bi-khwānīd gufta shūd).

16. The collection of poetry of Lutf al-Nisa includes a *qaṣīda* praising the nizam, folios 67–72. Her collection consists of 2,160 couplets of poetry including approximately 178 ghazals and others forms like *rubāʾī*, *mukhammas*, and *musaddas*. I hope to publish an article comparing Mah Laqa Bai and Lutf al-Nisa and offering translations of the latter's work.

17. Henri Corbin, "The Meaning of the Imam for Shiʿi Spirituality," in Nasr, Dabashi, and Nasr, *Shiʿism*, 167–69.

18. Māh Laqā Bāī, *Gulzār-e Māh Laqā*, 13–14. Ghazal 41 in radīf *dāl*. Its first couplet is: "karēgā jō galī meiñ us kē tō apnā gużar qāṣid / sivā-ye āh kē kījō na mērā ḥāl-e sar qāṣid."

19. Ibid., 24. Ghazal 77 in radīf *kāf*. Its first couplet is: "ham-rah thā rāt ṭāliʿ bē-dār yahān talak / āyā thā apnē ghar sē mera yār yahān talak."

20. Ibid., 24. Ghazal 78 in radīf *lām*. Its first couplet is: "ṣāghar sē kis kē chashm kē pī kar sharāb dil / phirtā hai bē-khudāna sā mast o kharāb dil."

21. Gawhar, *Ḥayāt-e Māh Laqā*, 26.

22. Tajallī, *Tuzuk-e Aṣafiyya*, mss., 232, illustrates a procession by the second nizam to the sacred shrine of Mawla ʿAli; see Nayeem, *Miniature Paintings*, 120.

23. Gawhar, *Ḥayāt-e Māh Laqā*, 28.

24. Tajallī, *Tuzuk-e Aṣafiyya*, mss., 338; see Nayeem, *Miniature Paintings*, 135.

25. Gawhar, *Ḥayāt-e Māh Laqā*, 26–27.

26. Ibid., 27.

27. Chishti Sufis also see ʿAbd al-Qadir Jilani as an elder relative of Muʿin al-Din Chishti (or as an elder in their community), so Qadiri and Chishti Sufis overlap in their veneration of him.

28. Gawhar, *Ḥayāt-e Māh Laqā*, 28.

29. Shawkat, *Māh Laqā*, 38–39.

30. Gawhar, *Ḥayāt-e Māh Laqā*, 28–29.

31. Ibid., 29.

Conjunction

1. De Sondy, *Crisis of Islamic Masculinities*, 8.

2. Ibid., 11.

3. Dance was more important as a poetic image than as a form of art. For this reason, poetry has attracted the attention of Sufism scholars specializing in South Asia more than dance has—in contrast to the Turkish practice of "whirling" among Mevlevi Sufis, which has attracted much scholarly attention.

4. See Avery, *Psychology of Early Sufi Samāʿ*; and Lawrence, "Early Chishti Approach to Samāʿ." Among South Asian Sufis, two treatises that outlined these rules while explaining the spiritual purpose of music were especially influential: *ʿAvārif*

al-Maʿārif [Knowers of intuitive knowledge] by Shaikh ʿUmar Suhravardi (died 1234 in Baghdad) and *Kashf al-Maḥjūb* [Unveiling the unseen] by Shaikh ʿAli Hujviri (died 1072 in Lahore).

5. Al-Faruqi, "Music, Musicians and Muslim Law."

6. Kabbani, *Repudiation of "Salafi" Innovations*, 345–49, cites a *fatwa* by Al-ʿIzz ibn ʿAbd al-Salam al-Sulami.

7. Nizami, *Some Aspects of Religion and Politics in India*, 247.

8. Ernst, *Eternal Garden*, 118–54.

9. See Jean During, "Emotion and Trance: Musical Exorcism in Baluchistan," in Caton and Siegel, *Cultural Parameters of Iranian Musical Expression*, whose scholarly approach gives rise to interesting comparisons to ritual music in Shamanistic traditions.

10. Jaffer, *Book of Nizamuddin Aulia*, 122–23.

11. In Hyderabad are the tombs of Shakir Sada Sohag and his followers, in the Rekabganj neighborhood near the hijras' mansion (*baṛī ḥavelī*). They were followers of Musa Sada Sohag, about whom see Kugle, "Dancing with Khusro"; see also Tanvir Anjum, "The Perpetually Wedded Wife of God: A Study of Shaykh Musa 'Sada Suhag' as the founder of the Sada Suhagiyya Silsilah," *Journal of Religious History* (2014).

12. Nasr, Dabashi, and Nasr, *Shiʿism*, 107–8.

13. The terms *vilāyat* and *valāyat* as used in this book (with Persian/Urdu transliteration) have the same meaning as *wilāya* and *walāya* (with Arabic translation) as used in other studies, such as V. Cornell, *Realm of the Saint*, xvii–xxi and 272–74, and Ernst, *Shambhala Guide to Sufism*, 58–59. The terms *vilāyat* and *valāyat* are similar nouns derived from the same Arabic verbal root, from which is formed the noun *valī* or "saint." Nizam al-Din Awliya used *vilāyat* to mean love and intimacy (as in God's love for a saint and a saint's intimacy with God) and *valāyat* to mean power and authority (as in God's granting power to perform miracles to saints and saints' authority over others in society). Cornell observes that these terms are reversed in meaning in North African Sufi discourses on sainthood; it seems that scholars of Shiʿism also use *valāyat* to mean devoted love, as in Shah-Kazemi, *Justice and Remembrance*, 21–22. The same concepts became encoded in language in different ways in these diverse regions or communities of the Islamic world, but this study follows the usage of Nizam al-Din Awliya, as in Lawrence, *Morals for the Heart*, 95.

14. Leonard Lewisohn, "Ali ibn Abi Talib's Ethics of Mercy in the Mirror of the Persian Sufi Tradition," in Lakhani, *Sacred Foundations of Justice in Islam*, 116.

15. Shah-Kazemi, *Justice and Remembrance*, 22–36, presents a beautiful synopsis of ʿAli's spiritual teachings as Neoplatonism.

16. Lewisohn, "Ali ibn Abi Talib's Ethics of Mercy," 132.

17. Māh Laqā Bāī, *Gulzār-e Māh Laqā*, 19–20. Ghazal 62 in radīf ẓuād. Its first couplet is: "rakhtē haiñ mere ashk sē yeh dīda-ye tar faiẓ / dāman maiñ liyā apnē hai daryā nē ghar faiẓ."

18. Sirāj, *Kulliyāt-e Sirāj*, 380–81. Ghazal 3 in radīf ḥē, last couplet; its first couplet reads: "mat karō hum señ zar-garī kī ṭaraḥ / yeh nahīñ banda parvarī kī ṭaraḥ."

19. In his Arabic poetry, the radical Sufi Mansur Hallaj sang, "I have a lover whose passion in my gut does dwell, if he wills the right to tread over my cheek is his / his spirit is my spirit and my spirit is his spirit / If he desires I too desire and if I desire the desire is his"; see Stetkevych, *Reorientations*, 196.

20. Sirāj, *Kulliyāt-e Sirāj*, 330–31. Ghazal 66 in radīf ālif, first and last couplet. The first couplet reads: "sharāb-e shawq pī kar dō jahāñ kā jis nē gham bhūlā / khayāl-e kham-e aflāṭūn o fikr-e jām-e jem bhūlā." This Urdu verse says "delusions of Plato," but this English translation replaces him with Aristotle for a more productive rhyme; the point is to negate Greek philosophy and ancient Near Eastern alchemy.

BIBLIOGRAPHY

Manuscripts

Burhānpūrī, Muḥammad ibn Fażlullah. *Taḥẕīr al-Ṭālibīn ʿan Ruʾiyat al-Amrad liʾl-Vuṣūl ilā Allah* [Warning to the seekers against gazing at beautiful young males as a way to reach God]. Hyderabad: Salar Jung, Taṣawwuf 29: folios 112b–117b. In Arabic.

"Imtiyāz," Luṭf al-Nisā. *Dīvān-e Imtiyāz*. Hyderabad: Salar Jung, Davāvīn o Kulliyāt 536. In Urdu.

"Jawhar," Ghulām Ḥusain. *Tajalliyāt-e Māh Laqā* [alternatively *Tārīkh-e Dil-Afrōz* or *Māh-Nāma*]. Hyderabad: Salar Jung, Tārīkh 364. In Persian.

Khūsh-ḥāl Khān. *Rāg o Rāginī Rōz o Shab* [Male and female ragas from morning to night]. Hyderabad: Salar Jung, Mūṣīqī 2 (acquisition no. 474, catalog no. 433). In Urdu.

Māh Laqā Bāī. *Dīvān-e Chandā* [transliterated in the manuscript catalog as *Diwan-e-Chanda*]. London: British Library, Oriental and India Office Collection, Islamic 2768. In Urdu.

"Qais," Muḥammad Ṣādiq. *Kulliyāt-e Qais*. Hyderabad: Salar Jung, Davāvīn o Kulliyāt 160 and 161. In Urdu.

"Qāqshāl," Afẓal Bēg Khān Awrangābādī. *Tuḥfat al-Shuʿarā* [Gift of the poets]. Hyderabad: Salar Jung, Tażkira 8. Another copy is at Hyderabad: AP State Oriental Manuscript and Research Library, Tażkira 122. In Persian.

Sabzāvarī, Khāksar. *Savāniḥ* [Life and travels]. Calcutta: Asiatic Society of Bengal, P.S.C. 285. In Persian.

"Shafīq," Lakshmī Narāyan. *Gul-e Raʿnā* [Rose of beauty]. Hyderabad: Salar Jung, Tażkira 38. In Persian.

Shāh Bājan, Burhān al-Dīn. *Khazāʾin-e Raḥmat* [Treasuries of divine mercy] (known by the alternate title *Gulshan-e Raḥmat*). Lahore: Punjab University 2282/5289. In Persian and Gujari.

"Tajallī," Shāh Tajallī ʿAlī. *Tuzuk-e Aṣafiyya* [Pomp and glory of the Nizams]. New Delhi: National Museum Manuscript Archive, Persian 59.138. In Persian.

Published Books and Articles

ʿAbd al-Ḥai, Muḥammad. *Tārīkh-e Awrangābād*. Aurangabad: Savera Offset Printers, 2004.

Aga Khan Trust for Culture. *Jashn-e-Khusro: A Collection*. New Delhi: Roli Books, 2012.

Alam, Muzaffar. *The Languages of Political Islam, India 1200–1800*. Chicago: University of Chicago Press, 2004.

Al-Faruqi, Lois. "Music, Musicians and Muslim Law." *Asian Music* 17 (1985): 3–36.

Ali, Kamran Asdar. "Courtesans in the Living Room." *ISIM Review* 15 (Spring 2005): 274–79.

Amīr Khūrd, Muḥammad ibn Mubārak Kirmānī. *Siyār al-Awliyā* [Lives of the saints]. Urdu trans. ʿAbd al-Latīf. New Delhi: Farḥīn Publishing Company, 1996.

Andrews, Walter, and Mehmet Kalpaklı. *The Age of Beloveds: Love and the Beloved in Early-Modern Ottoman and European Culture and Society*. Durham, N.C.: Duke University Press, 2005.

Aquil, Raziuddin, ed. *Literary and Religious Practices in South Asian Sufism*. Studies in Medieval Indian History. Delhi: Manohar Publications, forthcoming 2015.

Argilī, Fārūq. *Rēkhtī: Urdū kē Nāmvar Rēkhtī-gū Shāʾirōn kā Mukammil Majmūʿa* [Rekhti: The complete collection of famous Rekhti poets of Urdu]. New Delhi: Farid Book Depot, 2006.

Austin, R. W. J., trans. *Ibn al-ʿArabi.: The Bezels of Wisdom*. Mahwah: Paulist Press, 1980.

Avery, Kenneth. *A Psychology of Early Sufi Samāʿ*. London: Routledge Curzon, 2004.

Azhar, Ẓuhūr Shehdād. *Urdū Meiñ Shāhid-Bāzī* [Homoerotic contemplation in Urdu poetry]. Srinagar: Gulshan Publishers, 1995.

ʿAzmī, Rāḥat. *Māh Laqā—Ḥālāt-e Zindagī* [Life of Mah Laqa]. Hyderabad: Bazm-e Gulshan-e Urdū, 1998.

Bayaban, Kathryn, and Afsaneh Najmabadi, eds. *Islamicate Sexualities: Translations across Temporal Geographies of Desire*. Cambridge, Mass.: Harvard University Press, 2008.

Begum, Qamar Jahan. *Princess Jahan Ara Begum: Her Life and Works*. Karachi: S. M. Hamid Ali, 1991.

Bhukya, Bhangya. *Subjugated Nomads: Lambadas under the Rule of the Nizams*. Hyderabad: Orient Blackswan, 2010.

Bilgrami, Syed Ali Asghar. *Landmarks of the Deccan: A Comprehensive Guide to the Archaeological Remains of the City and Suburbs of Hyderabad*. New Delhi: Asian Education Services, 1992.

Borah, M. I. "The Life and Works of Amir Hasan Dihlavi." *Journal of the Royal Asiatic Society of Bengal*, Letters VII (1941): 1–59.

Boswell, Jonathan. *Christianity, Social Tolerance and Homosexuality*. Chicago: University of Chicago Press, 1980.

Brooten, Bernadette. *Love between Women: Early Christian Responses to Female Homoeroticism*. Chicago: University of Chicago Press, 1996.

———, ed. *Beyond Slavery: Overcoming Its Religious and Sexual Legacies*. New York: Palgrave Macmillan, 2010.

Browne, Edward. *A Literary History of Persia*. 4 vols. 1902; New Delhi: Goodword Books, 2002.

Bukhārī, Muḥammad. *Ṣaḥīḥ al-Bukhārī*. Liechtenstein: Thesaurus Islamicus Foundation, 2000.

Caton, Margaret, and Niel Siegel, eds. *Cultural Parameters of Iranian Musical Expression*. Los Angeles: Institute of Persian Performing Arts, 1988.

Chakravorty, Pallabi. *Bells of Change: Kathak Dance, Women and Modernity in India*. Calcutta: Seagull Books, 2008.

Chakravorty, Pallabi, and Nilanjana Gupta, eds. *Dance Matters: Performing India*. New Delhi: Routledge Press, 2010.

Chakravorty, Pallabi, and Scott Kugle, eds. *Performing Ecstasy: The Poetics and Politics of Religion in India*. Delhi: Munshiram Manoharlal Press, 2009.

Cornell, Rkia. *Early Sufi Women: Dhikr an-Niswa al-Mutaʿabbidat al-Sufiyyat by al-Sulami*. Louisville, Ky.: Fons Vitae, 1999.

Cornell, Vincent. *The Realm of the Saint: Power and Authority in Moroccan Sufism*. Austin: University of Texas Press, 1996.

Cornell, Vincent, and Bruce Lawrence, eds. *Blackwell Companion to Islamic Spirituality*. New York: Willey-Blackwell, forthcoming.

Dalrymple, William. *White Mughals*. New Delhi: Penguin Books India, 2002.

De Sondy, Amanullah. *The Crisis of Islamic Masculinities*. London: Bloomsbury, 2014.

Digby, Simon. *Sufis and Soldiers in Awrangzeb's Deccan*. New Delhi: Oxford University Press, 2001.

Eaton, Richard Maxwell. *Essays on Islam and Indian History*. Oxford: Oxford University Press, 2000.

———. *India's Islamic Traditions*. New York: Oxford University Press, 2003.

———. *A Social History of the Deccan, 1300–1761: Eight Lives*. New York: Cambridge University Press, 2008.

———. *Sufis of Bijapur, 1300–1700: Social Roles of Sufis in Medieval India*. Princeton: Princeton University Press, 1978.

El-Rouayheb, Khaled. *Before Homosexuality in the Arab-Islamic World, 1500–1800*. Chicago: University of Chicago Press, 2005.

Ernst, Carl. *Eternal Garden: Mysticism, History, and Politics in a South Asian Sufi Center*. Albany: SUNY Press, 1992.

———. "From Hagiography to Martyrology: Conflicting Testimonies to a Sufi Martyr of the Delhi Sultanate." *History of Religions* 25, no. 4 (1985): 308–27.

———. *Shambhala Guide to Sufism*. Boston: Shambhala Press, 1997.

Ernst, Carl, and Bruce Lawrence. *Sufi Martyrs of Love: The Chishti Order in South Asia and Beyond*. New York: Palgrave Macmillan, 2002.
Fārūqī, Mushtāq Illāhī. *Naghmāt-e Samāʿ*. Karachi: Educational Press, 1972.
Flueckiger, Joyce. *In Amma's Healing Room: Gender and Vernacular Islam in South India*. Bloomington: Indiana University Press, 2006.
Foucault, Michel. *History of Sexuality*. Vol. 1. New York: Vintage Books, 1990.
Gawhar, Ghulām Ṣamdānī. *Ḥayāt-e Māh Laqā* [The life of Mah Laqa]. Hyderabad: Niẓām al-Maṭābiʿ, 1904.
Giordani, Demetrio, ed. *Faith and Practice in South Asian Sufism*. Rome: Oriente Moderno, 2013.
Gluck, Sherna Berger, and Daphne Patai, eds. *Women's Words: The Feminist Practice of Oral History*. New York: Routledge, 1991.
Green, Nile. *Indian Sufism since the Seventeenth Century: Saints, Books and Empires in the Muslim Deccan*. London: Routledge, 2006.
———. "Stories of Saints and Sultans: Re-membering History at the Sufi Shrines of Aurangabad." *Modern Asian Studies* 38, no. 2 (2004): 419–46.
Gupta, Harsh, Aloka Parasher-Sen, and D. Balasubramanian, eds. *Deccan Heritage*. Hyderabad: Universities Press, 2000.
Halperin, David. *How to Do the History of Homosexuality*. Chicago: University of Chicago Press, 2002.
———. *One Hundred Years of Homosexuality: The New Ancient World and Other Essays on Greek Love*. New York: Routledge, 1990.
Hansen, Kathryn, and David Lelyveld, eds. *A Wilderness of Possibilities: Urdu Studies in Transnational Perspective*. New Delhi: Oxford University Press, 2005.
Hashmī, Naṣīr al-Dīn. *Dakkan meiñ Urdū*. New Delhi: Qawmī Kōnsil Barā-ye Farōgh-e Urdū Zabān [National Counsel for the Advancement of Urdu Language], 1985.
———. *Khavātīn-e Dakkan kī Urdū Khidmāt* [Advancement of Urdu by women of the Deccan]. Hyderabad: Razzāqī Machine Press, 1940.
Heer, Nicholas, trans. *The Precious Pearl or al-Durra al-Fakhira by Abd al-Rahman Jami*. Albany: SUNY Press, 1979.
Hermann, Denis, and Fabrizio Speziale, eds. *Muslim Cultures in the Indo-Iranian World during the Early-Modern and Modern Periods*, Islamkundliche Untersuchungen Band 290. Berlin: Klaus Schwarz Publishers, 2010.
Hodgson, Marshall. *The Venture of Islam: Conscience and History in a World Civilization*. 3 vols. Chicago: University of Chicago Press, 1974.
Hollister, John. *Islam and the Shia's Faith in India*. Delhi: Kanishka Publishing House, 1988.
Howarth, Toby. *The Twelver Shiʿa as a Muslim Minority in India: Pulpit of Tears*. London: Routledge, 2005.
Hyder, Syed Akbar. *Reliving Karbala: Martyrdom in South Asian Memory*. New York: Oxford University Press, 2006.

"Imān," Muḥammad Shēr Khān. *Kulliyāt-e Imān*. Edited by Sayyida Hāshimī Mujīb. Hyderabad: Khūrshīd Press, 1987.

Jaffer, Mehru. *The Book of Nizamuddin Aulia*. New Delhi: Penguin Ananda, 2012.

Kabbani, M. Hisham. *The Repudiation of "Salafi" Innovations*. Chicago: Kazi Publications, 1996.

Kalīmullāh, Shāhjahānābādī. *Kashkūl-e Kalīmī* [The alms-bowl]. Delhi: Maṭbaʿ-ye Mujtabāʾī, n.d.

Kanda, K. C. *Masterpieces of Urdu Ghazal: From the 17th to the 20th Century*. New Delhi: Sterling Publishers, 1992.

Khān, Bashīr Muḥammad. *Tārīkh-e Awliyā-ye Kirām-e Burhānpūr* [History of the Sufis of Burhanpur]. 2 vols. Burhanpur: Ḥājjī Jamīl Aḥmad Khān Publisher, 1980; second ed., 1998.

Khan, Zia Inayat, ed. *A Pearl in Wine: Essays on the Life, Music and Sufism of Hazrat Inayat Khan*. New Lebanon: Omega Press, 2001.

Kugle, Scott. "Burhan al-Din Gharib: Enduring Sufi Example in the Eternal Garden of Khuldabad." *Deccan Studies Journal* 7, no. 2 (July–December 2009): 82–111.

———. "Mah Laqa Bai and Gender: Language, Poetry and Performance of a Courtesan in Hyderabad." *Comparative Studies in South Asia, Africa and the Middle East* 30, no. 3 (2010): 365–85.

———. "Mah Laqa Bai: The Remains of a Courtesan's Dance." In Pallabi Chakravorty, ed., *Dance Matters II*. Forthcoming.

———. "Movement from Persian to Urdu in the Deccan: The Legacy of Burhan al-Din Gharib, Shah Bajan and Siraj Aurangabadi." Forthcoming.

———. "Qawwali between Written Poem and Sung Lyric . . . or How a Ghazal Lives." *The Muslim World* 97, no. 4 (October 2007): 571–610.

———. "Sufi Meditation Manuals from the Mughal Era." *Oriente Moderno*, n.s., 2 (2012): 459–89.

———. *Sufis and Saints' Bodies: Mysticism, Corporeality, and Sacred Power in Islam*. Chapel Hill: University of North Carolina Press, 2007.

———, trans. *Sufi Meditation and Contemplation: Contemporary Wisdom from Mughal India*. New Lebanon, N.Y.: Omega Press, 2013.

Lakhani, M. Ali, ed. *The Sacred Foundations of Justice in Islam: Teachings of Ali ibn Abi Talib*. Bloomington, Ind.: World Wisdom, 2006.

Lawrence, Bruce. "The Early Chishti Approach to Samaʿ." In *Islamic Society and Culture: Essays in Honor of Professor Aziz Ahmad*, edited by Milton Israel and N. K. Wagle, 69–83. New Delhi: Manohar, 1983.

———. "Honoring Women through Sexual Abstinence: Lessons from the Spiritual Practice of a Pre-modern South Asian Sufi Master, Shaykh Nizam ad-din Awliya." *Journal of Turkish Studies* 18 (1994): 149–61.

———, trans. *Morals for the Heart by Nizam al-Din Awliya*. Mahwah, N.J.: Paulist Press, 1992.

Lawson, Todd, ed. *Reason and Inspiration in Islam: Essays in Honour of Hermann Landolt*. London: I. B. Tauris, 2005.
Leonard, Karen. *Hyderabad and Hyderabadis*. New Delhi: Manohar Books, 2014.
Lewis, Franklin. *Rumi Past and Present, East and West*. London: Oneworld, 2000.
Madanī, Sayyid Zahīr al-Dīn. *Sukhanvarān-e Gujarāt* [Eloquent literati of Gujarat]. New Delhi: Qawmī Kōnsil Barā-ye Farōgh-e Urdū Zabān [National Counsel for the Advancement of Urdu Language], 1999; first ed. 1981.
Māh Laqā Bāī. *Dīvān-e Chandā* [Divan of Mah Laqa Bai]. Lahore: Majlis-e Taraqqī-ye Adab, 1990.
———. *Gulzār-e Māh Laqā* [Divan of Mah Laqa Bai]. Hyderabad: Niẓām al-Maṭābiʿ, AH 1324 (1906 CE).
Malhotra, Anshu, and Siobhan Lambert Hurley, eds. *Speaking of the Self: Gender, Performance and Autobiography*. Durham, N.C.: Duke University Press, 2015.
Malkāpūrī, ʿAbd al-Jabbār Khān. *Maḥbūb żūʾl-Minan fī Tażkira-ye Awliyā-ye Dakkan* [Biographies of Sufis of the Deccan]. 2 vols. Hyderabad: Maṭbaʿ-ye Raḥmānī, 2001; reprint of undated lithograph.
Martin, Richard, and Carl Ernst, eds. *Rethinking Islamic Studies: From Orientalism to Cosmopolitanism*. Columbia: University of South Carolina Press, 2010.
Massad, Joseph. *Desiring Arabs*. Chicago: University of Chicago Press, 2007.
Matthews, David, trans. *Umrao Jan Ada*. New Delhi: Rupa, 1996.
Mir ʿAlam, Sayyid Abūʾl-Qāsim. *Sarāpā-ye Māh Laqā* [Describing head to foot the beauty of Mah Laqa Bai]. Hyderabad: ʿAhd-e Āfarīn Barqī Press, n.d.
Mudiraj, K. Krishnaswamy. *Pictorial Hyderabad*. 2 vols. Hyderabad: Chandrakanth Press, 1934.
Mutālā, Muḥammad Yūsuf. *Mashāʾikh-e Aḥmadābād* [Sufi masters of Ahmedabad]. Meerut: Maktaba Maḥmūdiyya, 1993.
"Nādir," Durga Parshād. *Gulshan-e Nāz* [Garden of grace, biographies of female poets]. Delhi: n.p., 1876.
Naqvi, Sadiq. *Qutb Shahi Ashur Khanas of Hyderabad City*. Hyderabad: Bab-ul-Ilm Society, 1982.
Naqvi, Sadiq, and V. Kishan Rao, eds. *The Muharram Ceremonies among the Non-Muslims of Andhra Pradesh*. Hyderabad: Bab-ul-Ilm Society, 2004.
Narang, Gopi Chand, ed. *Valī Dakkanī: Taṣawwuf, Insāniyāt awr Muḥabbat kā Shāʿir* [Vali Dakkani: Poet of Sufism, humanism and love]. Delhi: Sahitya Academy, 2005.
Nasr, Seyyed Hossein, Hamid Dabashi, and Seyyed Vali Reza Nasr, eds. *Shiʿism: Doctrines, Thought and Spirituality*. Albany: SUNY Press, 1988.
Nayeem, M. A. *Miniature Paintings of Nizam Ali Khan Asaf Jah II and Others from 18th Century Hyderabad (based on Tuzuk-i-Asafia of Tajalli Ali Shah)*. Hyderabad: Hyderabad Publishers, 2014.

Nizami, Khaliq Ahmad. *The Life and Times of Shaykh Nasir-u'd-Din Chiragh-e-Dehli*. New Delhi: Idāra-ye Adabiyāt-e Dillī, 1991.

———. *Some Aspects of Religion and Politics in India during the Thirteenth Century*. New York: Asia Publishing House, 1961.

O'Donnell, Katherine, and Michael O'Rourke, eds. *Queer Masculinities, 1550–1800: Siting Same-Sex Desire in the Early Modern World*. New York: Palgrave, 2005.

Oldenburg, Veena Talwar. "Lifestyle as Resistance: The Case of the Courtesans of Lucknow." In *Lucknow: Memories of a City*, edited by Violette Graff, 136–54. Oxford: Oxford University Press, 1997.

Orsini, Fancesca, ed. *Before the Divide: Hindi and Urdu Literary Culture*. Hyderabad: Orient Blackswan, 2010.

———, ed. *Love in South Asia: A Cultural History*. New York: Cambridge University Press, 2006.

Parvēz, Akhtar. *Shāh Bājan: Ek Muṭāli'a* [Shah Bajan: A study]. Burhanpur: Raja Offset, 2005.

Petievich, Carla. "The Feminine and Cultural Syncretism in Early Dakani Poetry." *Annual of Urdu Studies* 8 (1993): 19–30.

———. *When Men Speak as Women: Vocal Masquerade in Indo-Muslim Poetry*. New Delhi: Oxford, 2007.

Pinault, David. *The Shi'ites: Ritual and Popular Piety in a Muslim Community*. New York: St. Martin's Press, 1992.

Plato. *The Essential Plato*. New York: Quality Paperback Book Club, 1999.

Poduval, Satish. *Re-figuring Culture: History, Theory and the Aesthetic in Contemporary India*. Delhi: Sahitya Academy Publications, 2005.

Pollock, Sheldon, ed. *Literary Cultures in History: Reconstructions from South Asia*. Berkeley: University of California Press, 2003.

Prasad, Dharmendra. *Social and Cultural Geography of Hyderabad City: A Historical Perspective*. New Delhi: Inter-India Publications, 1986.

Pritchett, Frances. *Nets of Awareness: Urdu Poetry and Its Critics*. Berkeley: University of California Press, 1994.

Qureshi, Regula Burkhardt. *Sufi Music of India and Pakistan: Sound, Context, and Meaning in Qawwali*. New York: Cambridge University Press, 1986.

Rahman, Tariq. *From Hindi to Urdu: A Social and Political History*. Hyderabad: Orient Blackswan, 2011.

"Ranj," Faṣīḥ al-Dīn. *Bahāristān-e Nāz: Tażkira-ye Shā'irāt* [Springtime garden of graceful pride: Memorial of women poets]. Edited by Khalīl al-Raḥmān Dāūdī. Lahore: Majlis-e Taraqqī-ye Urdū, 1965.

Richards, John. *The Mughal Empire*. New York: Cambridge University Press, 1995.

Ruffle, Karen. "A Bride of One Night, a Widow Forever: Gender and Vernacularization in the Construction of South Asian Shi'i Hagiography." Ph.D. diss., University of North Carolina at Chapel Hill, Department of Religious Studies, 2007.

———. *Gender, Sainthood, and Everyday Practice in South Asian Shi'ism.* Chapel Hill: University of North Carolina Press, 2011.

Safi, Omid. *The Politics of Knowledge in Premodern Iran: Negotiating Ideology and Religious Inquiry.* Chapel Hill: University of North Carolina Press, 2006.

Sarkar, Jadunath, trans. *Ma'asir-e-Alamgiri: History of the Emperor Aurangzib-Alamgir of Saqi Musta'id Khan.* Calcutta: Royal Asiatic Society, 1947; second ed., Delhi: Oriental Book Reprint Corp., 1986.

Sarma, Rani. *The Deodis of Hyderabad: A Lost Heritage.* New Delhi: Rupa, 2008.

Schimmel, Annemarie. *And Muhammad Is His Messenger: Veneration of the Prophet in Islamic Piety.* Chapel Hill: University of North Carolina Press, 1985.

———. *Islam in the Indian Subcontinent.* Leiden: E. J. Brill, 1980.

———. *Mystical Dimensions of Islam.* Chapel Hill: University of North Carolina Press, 1975.

Sells, Michael. *Approaching the Qur'an.* Ashland, Ore.: White Cloud Press, 1999.

———. *Mystical Languages of Unsaying.* Chicago: University of Chicago Press, 1994.

Shah-Kazemi, Reza. *Justice and Remembrance: Introducing the Spirituality of Imam 'Ali.* London: I. B. Taurus, 2011.

Shaikh, Sa'diya. *Sufi Narratives of Intimacy: Ibn 'Arabi., Gender and Sexuality.* Chapel Hill: University of North Carolina Press, 2012.

Sharib, Zahurul Hasan. *Life and Work of Khwaja Ghareeb Nawaz.* Lahore: Sh. Muhammad Ashraf Publishers, 1990.

Sharīf, Muḥammad Jamāl. *Dakkan meiṅ Urdū Shā'irī Valī sē Pehlē* [Urdu poetry in the Deccan before Vali]. Hyderabad: Idara-ye Adabiyat-e Urdu, 2004.

Shattārī, Muḥammmad Ghawsī. *Gulzār-e Abrār* [Rose-bush of the righteous]. Translated into Urdu by Fażl Aḥmad Jevarī. Agra: Maṭba'-ye Mufīd-e 'Ām, AH 1326.

Shawkat, Samīna. *Māh Laqā: Māh Laqā Bāī Chandā kī Zindagī awr us kē Kalām* [Mah Laqa Bai's life and poetry]. Hyderabad: National Fine Printing Press, 1959.

Sherwani, Harun Khan, and P. M. Joshi, eds. *History of Medieval Deccan.* 2 vols. Hyderabad: Government of Andhra Pradesh, 1972.

Siddiqi, M. Suleman. "Origin and Development of the Chishti Order in the Deccan, 1300–1538." *Islamic Culture* 51 (1977): 209–19.

Sijzī, Amīr Ḥasan. *Favā'id al-Fu'ād: Spiritual and Literary Discourses.* Translated by Ẓiyā'l-Ḥasan Fārūqī. New Delhi: D. K. Printworld, 1996.

Sinha, S. N., and N. K. Basu. *History of Prostitution in India.* New Delhi: Cosmo Publications, 1994.

"Sirāj," Sayyid Sirāj al-Dīn Ḥusainī Awrangābādī. *Kulliyāt-e Sirāj.* Edited by 'Abd al-Qādir Sarvarī. Hyderabad: Majlis-e Isha'āt-e Dakkanī Makhṭūṭāt, 1938.

Stetkevych, Suzanne Pinckney. *Reorientations: Arabic and Persian Poetry.* Bloomington: Indiana University Press, 1994.

Suvorova, Anna. *Masnavi: A Study of Urdu Romance.* Translated by M. Osana Faruqi. Karachi: Oxford University Press, 2000.

Ṭāliʿ, Murād ʿAlī. *Tażkira-ye Awliyā-ye Ḥaidarābād* [Memorial of the saints of Hyderabad]. 4 vols. Hyderabad: Minar Book Depot, 1972.

Ṭālib, Muḥammad Sirāj al-Dīn. *Mīr ʿAlam ke Savāniḥ-e Zindagī* [The life of Mir Alam]. Hyderabad: Shams al-Islām Press, 1930.

Thackston, Wheeler. *A Millennium of Classical Persian Poetry*. Bethesda, Md.: Iranbooks, 1994.

Tharu, Susie, and Ke Lalita, eds. *Women Writing in India: 600 B.C. to the Present*. New York: Feminist Press, 1991.

Vanita, Ruth. *Gandhi's Tiger and Sita's Smile: Essays on Gender, Sexuality and Culture*. New Delhi: Yoda Press, 2005.

———. *Love's Rite: Same-Sex Marriage in India and the West*. New Delhi: Penguin Books, 2005.

———, ed. *Queering India: Same-Sex Love and Eroticism in Indian Culture and Society*. New York: Routledge, 2001.

Vanita, Ruth, and Saleem Kidwai, eds. *Same-Sex Love in India: Readings from Literature and History*. New York: St. Martin's Press, 2000.

Wagoner, Philip. "The Charminar as Chaubara: Cosmological Symbolism in the Urban Architecture of the Deccan." In *Architecture of the Indian Sultanates*, edited by Abha Narain Lambah and Alka Patel, 104–13. Mumbai: Marg Publications, 2006.

Walker, Margaret. *India's Kathak Dance in Historical Perspective*. Surrey: Ashgate Publishing, 2014.

Weir, T. H., trans. *"Whoso Knoweth Himself . . .": The Treatise on Being of Ibn ʿArabi*. Cheltenham, UK: Beshara Press, n.d.

Zōr, Muḥī al-Dīn Qādirī. *Muraqqaʿ-ye Sukhan: Ḥaidarābād Dakkan ke Pachīs Shuʿarā-ye Dawr-e Aṣafiyya* [Patchwork of eloquent speech: Twenty-five poets of Hyderabad State under the Nizams]. Hyderabad: Aʿẓam Steam Press, 1935.

INDEX

Aaron (Harun, the Islamic prophet), 237
ʿAbd al-Latif Shushtari (scientist and philosopher, uncle of Mir ʿAlam, died 1806), 171
ʿAbd al-Qadir Jilani (died 1166), 126, 250, 278 (n. 8), 292 (n. 27)
ʿAbd al-Rahman Chishti (died 1747), 51–53, 57–58, 61, 70, 270 (n. 9)
ʿAbd al-Rasul Khan (disciple of Siraj), 52, 53, 79, 118, 271 (n. 13)
Abjad, 85, 118, 151; chronograms in, 117–18, 156, 209, 274 (n. 52), 277 (n. 46), 282 (n. 6), 282 (n. 15), 288 (n. 51), 291 (n. 15)
Abraham (Ibrahim, the Islamic prophet), 8, 19, 20–21, 268 (n. 22)
Absence, 31–32, 44, 63, 170, 232, 242; of men, 166, 170; as quality of the beloved, 20, 34, 63; of women, 143, 215
Abu Bakr al-Siddiq (first Sunni Caliph, died 634), 126, 278 (n. 9), 279 (n. 18)
Abuʾl-Hasan Tana Shah (seventh Sultan of Qutb-Shahi dynasty, died 1688), 136–37
Adam (the Islamic prophet), 36
Adolescence, 72, 74, 76, 77, 78, 81, 84, 256
Adoption, 147, 151, 153, 154, 170, 179, 189, 192, 205, 206, 226, 255, 281 (n. 4), 285 (n. 31), 287 (n. 47)
Aesthetics, 16, 18, 24, 34, 67, 88, 101, 116, 123, 149, 160–61, 187, 221, 224; as synesthesia, 94, 107, 228–29, 257. *See also* Beauty
Afghanistan, 13, 14, 54, 132, 192
Africa, 8, 267 (n. 6), 293 (n. 13); Berbers from northern, 9; Ethiopians in eastern, 58
Agency, 37–39, 44, 186. *See also* Subjectivity
Agra, 22, 85
Ahmad-e Jam, Abuʾl-Hasan Namiqi (died 1141), 275 (n. 6)
Ahmad Ghazali (died 1120–21), 87–89
Ahmadnagar, 13, 118, 273 (n. 31)
ʿAin al-Qudat Hamadani (died 1131), 87–89
Air (*hava*): as breeze (*saba*), 31, 35, 91, 241, 245; as wind (*bad*), 29, 33–37, 44. *See also* Breath
Akbar (Mughal emperor, died 1605), 23, 230
ʿAlam (battle standards), 130–31, 135, 137–38, 177, 249, 279 (n. 26)
Alchemy, 39, 44, 294 (n. 20). *See also* Fire: in furnace; Sublimation
Alexander (Iskandar or Zuʾl-Qarnayn, the Islamic prophet), 100, 283 (n. 21)
Alid loyalty, 123–29, 133, 278 (n. 10)
ʿAli ibn Abi Talib (died 661), 9, 13, 60, 123–28, 129, 133–34, 136, 138, 142–43, 157, 258, 260–64; addressed in poetry, 146, 147, 160, 161, 162, 163, 164,

166, 169, 182, 184, 214, 232, 238–39, 242, 282 (n. 8), 291 (n. 10); birthday of (*mawlid* or *Jashn-e Haideri*), 135, 248–49, 280 (n. 32), 287 (n. 49); as embodiment of light, 120, 127, 147, 185, 213, 238; as first Shiʿi imam, 10–11, 125, 145, 154, 156, 162, 166, 184, 219, 233–34, 235–53, 237–42, 260–61, 278 (n. 9), 288 (n. 49); as first Sufi saint, 56, 125–27, 154, 248–49, 260–64, 278 (n. 9), 279 (n. 18); as fourth Sunni caliph, 278 (n. 9), 278–79 (n. 18); known as Abu Turab, 237, 246–47; known as Lion of God (*asad* or *haider*), 127, 152, 154, 232, 237, 239, 250; known as Mawla, 120, 127, 153, 162, 166, 167, 288 (n. 49); known as Murtaza, 154; preeminence of (*tafzil*), 260; sword of (*zuʾl-fiqar*), 127, 237
Allegory, 20, 34, 110–14, 183
America, xv, 74, 75, 92, 93, 260
Amir Hasan Sijzi (died 1336) 13, 20–22, 54, 86–87, 104–7, 268 (n. 18), 268 (n. 20)
Amir Khusro (died 1325), 13, 20, 21, 54, 104, 105, 128, 258–59, 268 (n. 18), 274 (n. 47), 276 (n. 27)
Andrews, Walter, 4, 74, 143, 160
Angel, 11, 245; Gabriel, 291 (n. 3); Rizvan (guarding entrance to paradise), 85
Apophasis, 32–33
Arabia, 14; Saudi kingdom in, 264; Gulf Emirates in, 264. *See also* Medina
Arabic language, 19–20, 22, 95, 118, 128, 203, 230, 244, 268 (nn. 16–17), 271 (n. 22), 273 (n. 33), 286 (n. 17), 290 (n. 26), 291 (n. 8), 294 (n. 19); grammar of, 105, 267 (n. 1), 293 (n. 13)
Arab people, 10, 19, 20, 74–75, 133; Bedouin, 19; pagan, 8–9, 126, 275 (n. 55). *See also* Umayyad dynasty

Archery, 106, 162, 280
Architecture, 19, 22, 132, 145, 207; arched gate (*kaman*), 151–52; archway (*rivaq*), 133; gateway (*darvaza*), 155–56; inscriptions on, 124, 151, 155–56, 207; open hall (*dalan*), 152; pavilion (*barah-dari*), 7, 155–56, 161, 177, 251. *See also* ʿAshur-khana; Mansion; Mosque; Samaʿ-khana; Tomb
Aristocracy, 16–18, 38, 74, 82, 93, 97, 100, 113, 149, 153, 169, 187, 202, 207, 213, 255. *See also* Class, social; Courtier
Aristu Jah, Ghulam Sayyid Khan (died 1804), 157–58, 162, 164, 166–73, 175–77, 179, 184, 247, 282 (n. 12); 282 (n. 16), 283 (n. 5), 285 (n. 31).
Asaf-Jahi dynasty. *See* Nizams
Ascension, 1–2, 8, 31, 113, 183, 236, 246, 261–62
Asceticism, 2, 11, 13, 16, 19, 24, 36, 62, 65–68, 97, 101, 113, 139, 153, 155, 236, 248, 250, 251, 258. *See also* Hindu people: ascetic
Asexuality, 76, 87, 256
ʿAshura (commemoration of Karbala on tenth of Muharram), 158, 249. *See also* Muharram
ʿAshur-khana (hall for commemorating martyrs), 124, 128, 130–31, 134–35, 137–38, 151, 177, 249, 279 (n. 26), 279 (n. 29); Badshahi in Hyderabad, 137–38
Autobiography, 26, 53, 57, 77, 78, 82, 95, 97, 101, 138, 160
Awrangabad (also known as Aurangabad), 13, 23, 25–28, 38, 48, 50, 54, 66, 77–78, 81–83, 85, 90, 112–13, 118–20, 136, 137, 138, 158, 179, 193, 199, 200, 203, 223, 244, 259, 269 (n. 3), 270 (n. 2), 273 (n. 21), 277 (n. 50), 284 (n. 29), 290 (n. 23), 290 (n. 29), 291

(n. 14); Shahgunj neighborhood of, 49, 51, 113; fort at, 169
Awrangzeb (Mughal emperor, died 1707), 23, 40, 48, 84, 85, 112, 136–37, 158, 187, 221, 270 (n. 2), 272 (n. 15), 273 (nn. 31–32), 286 (n. 9), 290 (n. 23)
Azad Bilgrami (died 1786), 118, 269 (n. 3)
ʿAzmi, Rahat, 194–95, 196, 198–202, 205–6, 209
Azmi, Shabana (actress), 147
Azmi, Shaukat (actress), 149

Baba Musafir (died 1715), 49, 112, 273 (n. 21)
Baba Palangposh (died 1699), 49, 112, 273 (n. 21)
Baghdad, 14, 39, 126, 250, 268 (n. 6), 293 (n. 4)
Bahmani dynasty, 129, 268 (n. 19)
Bai (address meaning Madam), 188, 189, 201–2
Bajan, Shah Bahaʾ al-Din (died 1507), 90, 108–12, 276 (nn. 26–27), 276 (n. 34)
Banaras (known also as Varanasi), 230
Barahna, Shah (died 1653–54), 41
Basalat Khan (husband of Raj Kanvar Bai, father of Mah Laqa Bai), 192, 204, 227
Beasts, 52, 137, 161; buffalo, 176; camel, 168; elephant, 162, 167, 170, 228; gazelle, 162–63; horse, 118, 177; lion, 127, 239, 250; snake, 62, 213–14, 286 (n. 21); tiger, 250. See also Birds
Beauty (*jamal* or *husn*), 29–32, 39, 51, 58, 60, 64, 68, 71, 82, 83, 89, 91, 92, 98, 106–7, 115, 121–22, 142, 149, 164, 173, 180, 182–83, 209, 242. See also Harmony; Truth
Bedam Varsi (died 1795), 127
Being (*vujud*), 8, 28, 34–36, 39, 44–45, 60–61, 258; unity of (*vahdat al-vujud*),

40, 42, 37, 108, 261–63, 275 (n. 19). See also Nothingness
Benegal, Shyam (film director), 147
Berar, 13
Bewilderment (*tahayyur*), 28–33, 41, 43, 45, 52, 91, 102–3, 107, 149, 263. See also Oblivion
Bhagat (gypsy minstrels), 153, 191, 195–97, 199, 207, 286 (n. 11)
Bidar, 14, 108, 182, 268 (n. 19)
Bijapur, 13–14, 40, 48–49, 111, 118, 125, 213, 269 (n. 9), 276 (n. 35), 289 (n. 5)
Biography, 21, 26, 47, 50, 53, 78–81, 91, 100, 145, 164, 181, 187, 190–94, 198, 205, 206, 225–26, 244, 252, 254, 281 (nn. 10–11)
Birds, 24, 161; chicken, 189; cock, 189; dove, 106; falcon, 106; nightingale (*bulbul* or *andalib*), 33, 45, 68, 95, 238; peacock, 228; songbird, 106. See also Beasts
Birth, 25, 48, 141, 151, 164–65, 191–93, 198, 200–204, 227, 240, 244, 267 (n. 5), 268 (n. 10); death during, 195, 203; miscarriage during, 153–54, 179, 192; rituals after, 157, 227–28. See also Celebration: of birthday; Reproduction
Blessing (*faiz*), 52, 148, 158, 169, 228, 252, 262–63
Blood, 68–69, 95, 154, 235, 239, 240, 245; as family tie, 125, 237, 240, 263. See also Menstruation
Body, 12, 20, 36, 44, 62, 67, 72, 90, 103, 130, 173–74, 182, 210, 227, 236, 272 (n. 33); as corpse, 59, 137, 273 (n. 31); as flesh, 24, 67, 110, 137. See also Bosom; Embodiment; Eros; Eye; Face; Foot; Mouth; Reproduction; Sex
Bosom, 20–21, 111, 174, 232, 250, 268 (n. 22)

Index 307

Boswell, Jonathan, 75
Brand (*dagh*), 52–53, 68, 194. *See also* Fire: burning
Bravery (*shujaʿat*), 127, 177, 237, 241, 286 (n. 9)
Breath (*nafas* or *sans*), 35, 55, 63, 112, 122–23, 148, 163, 164, 172, 214, 235; of God, 35
Bridge, 2, 101, 115, 124, 245
British Resident (East India Company representative to nizams), 172; James Kirkpatrick (died 1805, known as Hashmat Jung), 176; Henry Russell (died 1852), 178. *See also* Colonialism; Malcolm, John
Brooten, Bernadette, 75
Buddhism, 66
Burhan al-Din Gharib (died 1337), 13, 54, 66, 84–88, 89–90, 104–8, 112, 258; dargah of, 50, 77–80, 84–85, 90, 108, 110, 115; followers of called Burhani, 105–6
Burhanpur, 90, 107–9, 111, 193, 200–201, 203, 205, 213, 223, 268, 268 (n. 19), 289 (n. 5)
Burj Kanvar Bai (given name Nur Bibi, maternal aunt of Mah Laqa Bai), 156, 192, 195–97, 202, 208, 290 (n. 29)

Calcutta (known also as Kolkata), 175, 230
Caliph (*khalifa*, political ruler), 10–12, 124, 129, 267 (n. 2), 267 (n. 4), 278 (n. 7)
Calligraphy, 1, 124, 154, 278 (n. 18)
Candle, 28, 52, 60, 68, 69, 139, 142, 165, 228; wax of, 65
Celebration (*taqrib*), 136, 157–60, 175, 247–49, 179, 252–53; of birthday (*sal-gira*), 179, 227–28, 288 (n. 49); of death anniversary (*ʿurs*), 29, 38, 135, 250; and fair (*Mela Khat-Darsan*), 251–52; honoring ʿAbd al-Qadir Jilani (*Gyarwin Sharif*), 250; of Persian New Year (*Nawroz*), 158, 162, 167–68. *See also* ʿAli ibn Abi Talib: birthday of; Mawla ʿAli Shrine: ʿurs at
Celibacy, 65, 86–87; for men, 6, 65–69, 71, 76, 90, 117; for women, 187, 194; Hindu tradition of (*brahmachariya*), 16, 66
Center for Deccan Studies, xv
Central Asia, 23; shamanism in, 293 (n. 9). *See also* Turks
Chakravorty, Pallabi, 231
Charminar (monument at the center of Hyderabad), 132, 189, 279 (n. 26)
Chauvinism, 10, 112, 132, 136, 224, 236
Chanda. *See* Mah Laqa Bai Chanda: pen name of
Chanda Bibi (given name of Mah Laqa Bai), 141, 154, 157–58, 165, 204
Chanda Bibi (maternal grandmother of Mah Laqa Bai), 192, 195–96, 198–99, 252
Chandulal, Maharaja (minister of the third nizam, died 1845), 178, 184, 288 (n. 49); as poet 178–80, 284 (n. 27); with pen name Shadan, 178
Charisma, 126, 128, 241–42, 245, 259–61, 267 (n. 3); of ʿAli, 153–54, 234–38, 240, 248, 260–61, 263; of Muhammad, 11, 142, 250, 264; of Sufi master, 11, 115, 249–50, 278 (n. 8)
Chishti Sufi order, 13, 16, 27, 35, 37–39, 50, 53–54, 58–59, 71, 80, 84–90, 113, 123–29, 154, 251, 255, 268 (n. 18), 273 (n. 21), 278 (n. 8), 282 (n. 12), 292 (n. 27); attitude toward sexuality in, 65–68, 70, 86–89, 94; contribution to Urdu, 22, 48, 102; music promoted by, 69, 90, 102–12, 115, 257–60, 262
Christianity, 10, 75, 92, 240

Class, social, 76, 161, 178, 187–88, 197, 219. *See also* Aristocracy

Cloth covering (*kiswa* or *chadar*), 108, 135, 137

Clothing (*libas*), 37–41, 79, 84, 122, 185, 228, 230, 250, 259, 277 (n. 46); cloak (*khirqa* or *ʿaba*), 20, 38, 50, 65, 106–8, 241; collar, 41; robe (*khilʿat*), 29, 37–40, 50, 162; shawl (*lai*), 187; turban, 83; veil (*hijab*), 2, 29, 37, 41, 153, 216, 242, 246. *See also* Nakedness

Colonialism, 18, 149, 171, 279 (n. 25); Victorian values of, 81, 151, 226, 274 (n. 46). *See also* East India Company

Collyrium (*kohl* in Arabic, *surma* in Urdu), 44

Companion (of the Prophet Muhammad, *sahabi*), 10

Comparison, 5–6, 15, 19, 120–21, 138, 160, 190, 222, 243, 254–55, 259, 262, 264–65

Concubine, 6, 16–18, 170, 176, 185–86, 192, 193, 195–98, 200, 203–4, 208, 252, 256, 268 (n. 10)

Conjunction, 6, 254

Contemplation, 11, 64, 86, 103, 105, 115, 155

Conversion, 9–10, 131–32, 279 (n. 25)

Corbin, Henri, 244

Cosmos (*kawn*), 34, 56, 61, 261. *See also* Space; Time

Couplet (*bait* or *shiʿr*), 21, 30, 45, 53, 63, 81, 85, 100, 109, 138–39, 160, 175, 223, 262; closing (*maqtaʿ*), 43–44, 52, 53, 56, 63, 69, 97, 143, 160, 217, 233–34, 235, 239, 241; knotted (*girah*), 36; independent line of (*fard*), 95, 274 (n. 50), 288 (n. 4); opening (*matlaʿ*), 30–33, 43, 55, 68–69, 91, 95, 159, 215, 245, 281 (n. 2), 284 (n. 27)

Court, 16, 24, 33, 38, 49, 100, 104, 109, 128, 139, 142, 154, 157, 167, 178, 187–88, 207, 219, 230, 238, 257, 258; of God, 51; of justice, 148, 226; politics in, 159, 161–64, 166, 175, 229. *See also* Aristocracy

Courtesan (*tavaʾif*), 24, 37, 76, 93, 143, 153, 171, 185–86, 189, 190, 202–7, 219–20, 229–32, 255–56, 257, 259, 272 (n. 13); as companions to other women (*āliyāñ*), 277 (n. 3); definition of, 17–19, 121, 185, 194, 290 (n. 26); dialect of, 180; in film, 147–51; as poets, 243–44; as Shiʿis, 6, 120, 123, 138, 145, 153, 156, 207, 259–64. *See also* Mah Laqa Bai Chanda: as courtesan; Hindu people: courtesan; Marriage: for courtesans

Courtier (*navvab* or *amir*), 13, 16, 23, 37, 48, 80, 135, 158–59, 162, 169, 187–88, 224, 227–28, 282 (n. 16), 282 (n. 19). *See also* Love: courtly

Cup or goblet, 20, 28, 29, 55–56, 60, 91, 152–53, 161, 182, 214, 217. *See also* Wine

Cyrus the Great (c. sixth century BC, founder of Persian empire), 167

Dalrymple, William, 172, 176, 281 (n. 6), 285 (n. 31)

Dance, 6, 16, 18, 23–24, 44, 121–23, 138, 141–42, 149, 151, 153, 156–57, 161–62, 193–200, 206, 215, 227–34, 249, 255, 257–59, 283 (nn. 26–27); choreography of, 44, 139; circling in, 229–30, 258–59, 290 (n. 26); dancing girl (nautch-girl), 226, 228, 230, 286 (n. 11); expression in (*abhinaya*), 148, 196, 230; kathak form of, 229–31, 257–59, 290 (n. 28), 290 (n. 28); known as *raqs*, 229–30, 283 (n. 24); of Krishna, 34, 229–30; of salutation (*mujra*), 167; in Sufi ritual, 85, 90, 104–7, 257–59, 275 (n. 11), 292

Index 309

(n. 3); women teachers of, 226, 231, 290 (n. 29). *See also* Foot: of dancers; Mah Laqa Bai Chanda: as dancer
Dara Shikoh (Mughal prince, died 1659), 40
Dargah. *See* Tomb: shrine at
David (Davud the Islamic prophet), 19
Dawlatabad, 13–14, 27, 107
Deccan (region of South-Central India), 2–6, 12–15, 22–24, 48, 74, 75, 80, 84–85, 104–5, 107, 110, 116–19, 120, 124–25, 153, 191, 193, 199, 207–8, 220–25, 229, 244, 251, 252, 256, 257, 260–64, 286 (n. 11), 290 (n. 23); Mughal conquest of, 3, 15, 23, 40, 48, 126, 136–38, 221; Persian poetry in, 20; Shi'ism in, 128–33, 135–38. *See also* Urdu language: development of in Deccan
Deccani (dialect of Urdu), 22, 33–34, 48–50, 87, 108–9, 131–32, 220–24, 229, 280 (n. 1)
Delhi, 20, 22, 25, 40, 48, 50, 54, 85, 92, 109, 128, 129, 213, 221, 223, 270 (n.10), 276 (n. 40), 285 (n. 36); Red Fort in, 177
Delhi Sultanate, 13; as Sunni rulers, 15, 128
Demon, 58–59, 136
Deoliya (or Devliya, a locale in Rajasthan or Malwa), 192–201, 207, 208
Desire (*shawq*), 21, 24, 31–33, 41, 51, 53, 68–69, 104, 122, 127, 152, 158, 174, 183, 215, 233, 239, 242, 294 (n. 19); for God, 34, 69; sexual, 67, 87, 89, 96, 203, 121, 186, 188, 219, 255
De Sondy, Amanullah, 256, 272 (n. 13)
Despair (*qabz*), 32, 36, 84, 116, 121, 233
Digby, Simon, 77
Diplomacy, 23, 132, 161–62, 169, 176, 177, 222, 283 (n. 26)
Discernment (*tamyiz*), 29, 37, 39–40, 92, 184

Disciple (*murid*), 13, 27, 38–39, 40, 53, 58–61, 66, 78, 85, 87, 104–5, 108, 110, 118, 263, 270 (n. 10), 278 (n. 8), 282 (n. 12)
Dissent, 10–11, 132
Divan (collection of *ghazal* poetry), 9, 26, 95, 160, 244, 281 (n. 6); of Mah Laqa Bai, xvi, 141–43, 145, 166–67, 169, 176, 178, 181, 210, 212, 222, 232–34, 241, 242, 280 (n. 2), 291 (n. 15); of Siraj, 38, 47, 52–53, 55, 79. *See also* Ghazal; Kulliyat
Dohra, 109
Dominance, 74, 86, 92, 93, 161, 215, 219, 221, 232–33. *See also* Patriachy
Dream, 71, 98, 108, 133, 214, 232, 277 (n. 42)
Drunkenness (*masti* or *nasha* or *sukr*), 28, 40, 55–56, 59–60, 62, 77, 91, 101, 152, 181, 217, 242, 246. *See also* Ecstasy; Wine
Duality, 41, 65, 214, 236, 238, 256, 261, 272 (n. 33)

Earth, 8, 85, 123, 180, 258; as dirt, 38, 98, 101, 148, 155, 187–88; as dust (*khak* or *zarra*), 37, 43–44, 83, 95, 110, 169, 180, 237, 246–47; as soil, 1, 8, 33, 105, 118, 172, 224; topography of, 5, 119–21, 123
East India Company, 145, 170–71, 175–76; cantonment of in Secunderabad, 178; Triple Alliance pact of 1790 (with Nizam and Marathas), 177–78, 284 (n. 7). *See also* British Resident; Colonialism
Ecstasy, 11, 12, 19, 24, 34–35, 38, 53, 62, 104–6, 108, 116, 137, 152, 177, 257–59, 275 (n. 11), 276 (n. 34) ; as bliss, 24, 34, 85, 158, 167, 172, 182; as rapture (*vajd*), 33, 41, 45, 59, 68–69, 77, 100–104, 108–9, 158, 200, 229–31, 258. *See also* Drunkenness

Ego. *See* Self
Elegy (*nasib*), 20, 43
Elements. *See* Air; Earth; Fire; Water
Ellichpur (locale in Maharashtra), 51, 270 (n. 9)
El-Rouayheb, Khalid, 75
Emanation, 40, 56, 261. *See also* Philosophy: Neoplatonic
Embodiment, 2, 19, 56, 120, 174, 211, 217, 232. *See also* Body; Senses
Embrace, 1, 82, 146, 174, 180, 187, 197, 242
Emptiness, 28, 30
Epic (*masnavi*), 109–10, 142, 228, 243; about Mah Laqa Bai, 172–75, 182–83, 228, 285 (n. 44); by Siraj, 26, 47, 78, 81–85, 97–98, 270 (n. 1). 270 (n. 13), 272 (n. 15), 274 (n. 49), 274 (n. 52). *See also* "Fragrant Garden of Imagination, The"
Erasure, 44, 79–81, 90, 221
Eros, 6, 24, 26, 66–69, 71, 80, 258–59, 272 (n. 13)
Essence (*zat*), 31, 51, 115, 128, 173, 238, 245, 260, 263
Ethics (*akhlaq*), 13, 15, 65, 93, 127, 260–61, 263–64; of ʿAli, 237, 248, 258, 260; virtues in, 86, 95, 103, 124, 142, 168, 172, 182–83, 185, 200, 205
Eunuch (*khawaja sara*), 6, 16, 74–75, 93; named Yaqut, 133, 135, 280 (nn. 30–31)
Europe, 5, 7, 74–75, 230, 268 (n. 20); as the West, 22, 81, 277 (n. 4). *See also* Colonialism; East India Company; France; Greece
Exile (*hijra*), 28, 50, 53, 58, 61, 78, 80, 95, 126, 148, 171, 217, 245
Extinction (*fanaʾ*), 35, 41, 59–61, 246; in Qurʾan, 55
Eye, 44, 84, 122, 146, 161, 162, 173, 213, 241, 242, 245, 246; eyebrow, 64, 91, 213, 235; eyelash, 241; wink, 106, 146, 173, 180, 235, 276 (n. 27). *See also* Sight; Tear

Face, 30, 37, 43, 51, 60, 62, 63, 69, 95, 97, 98, 106, 149, 153, 174, 180, 217, 241; brow, 25, 139, 173, 181, 214, 217, 235, 242; cheek, 48, 58, 63, 91, 106, 142, 173, 196, 214, 241, 246, 280 (n. 1), 294 (n. 19); chin, 52; forehead, 62, 173. *See also* Eye; Mouth
Fairy (*pari*), 32, 58–59, 122, 180, 200
Faith (*iman*), 3, 55, 210, 236, 268 (n. 16), 288 (n. 49); infidelity, 235–36
Fakhr al-Din Awrangabadi, Mir or Mawlana (died 1785), 54, 80, 273 (n. 20)
Fakhr al-Din ʿIraqi (died 1289), 36–37
Fakhr al-Din Zarradi (died 1337), 104
Faridun (mythic Persian king), 167–68
Faruqi, Shamsur Rahman, 181
Faruqi dynasty, 107. *See also* Khandesh
Fatima (daughter of Muhammad, died 632), 11, 127, 138, 160, 237, 238, 240–42, 278 (n. 18), 291 (n. 8), 291 (n. 15); immaculate conception attributed to, 11; known as Batul, 240; known as Qurrat al-ʿAin, 241. *See also* Muhammad: family of
Fear, 10, 20, 86, 90, 153, 164, 238, 239; fearlessness, 30, 43, 45–46, 82, 127, 153, 185, 237, 239
Femininity, 6, 73, 92–93, 184, 210–12, 231–33, 239, 240, 255, 256; in language, 221–23; in men as effeminacy, 72, 74, 211, 274 (n. 46)
Feminism: as liberation of women, 92, 143, 145, 147, 209, 210–11, 217–20, 221–23, 225, 233, 241–42, 255, 289 (n. 16)
Festival. *See* Celebration
Films, 37, 92, 147–51; *Mandi*, 147–48, 149, 151, 281 (n. 1); *Umrao Jaan*, 148–51, 281 (n. 1)

Index 311

Fire, 20, 43–45, 61, 95, 110, 111; ash from, 30, 43–44; boiling with, 35, 41, 122, 241; burning with, 29–30, 32, 35, 42–43, 60, 103, 106–7, 117, 123, 236, 241, 242, 246; in furnace, 20–21, 59, 268 (n. 22); melting with, 32, 59, 122. *See also* Alchemy

Flowers, 33–37, 65, 68, 82, 97; bud, 29, 33, 36, 65, 68; hyacinth, 180–81; narcissus, 33, 48, 241, 246; rose, 24, 33, 37, 45, 48, 52, 68, 95, 97, 127, 166, 167, 172, 186, 228, 236, 238, 241, 246; tulip, 33, 228, 242

Foot, 38, 44, 65, 83, 108, 164, 166, 174, 186, 241; footprint, 102; of dancers, 122, 196, 258; shoes related to, 150, 187–88

Foucault, Michel, 74

"Fragrant Garden of the Imagination, The" (*Bustan-e Khayal*, a *masnavi* by Siraj), 78, 81–84, 95, 97–98, 121–23, 138

France, 23; mercenaries of, 170. *See also* Raymond, Michel Joachim Marie

Garden, 9, 49, 56, 68–69, 85, 121–23, 155, 197, 269 (n. 22); in poetry, 20–21, 24, 29, 32, 33–37, 43, 48, 52, 97, 127, 167, 238, 239, 288 (n. 49). *See also* Flowers; Paradise

Gawhar, Mawlvi Ghulam Samdani (died after 1894), 193, 205–6, 248, 252

Geet, 109, 223

Gender, 1, 2, 3, 15–19, 24, 66, 70, 76, 82, 87, 92, 120–21, 188, 210–35, 254–57, 265; ambiguity in, 21, 73–74, 83, 91, 211–17, 225, 254, 256; as performance, 225–34, 254–56; dysphoria in, 73; in grammar, 1, 21, 91, 210–15, 289 (n. 8); heteronormative, 2, 73, 254–55; as identity, 72–74, 143, 224, 231, 254, 256; nonnormative, 185, 205–7, 212, 255;

norms of, 5, 17, 26–27, 75, 77, 217–19, 254–55, 274 (n. 51); segregation by, 16, 74, 76, 213. *See also* Duality; Femininity; Hijra; Masculinity; Parda

Gender studies, 3, 145, 256, 289 (n. 16)

Genealogy, 11, 38, 190, 194, 207, 248, 250, 263, 278; legitimacy in, 77, 200–2, 204, 240. *See also* Blood: as family tie; Sayyid

Generosity, 13, 71, 83, 156, 157–58, 166–69, 178, 182–83, 194, 196, 218, 226, 232, 248, 250–52, 263, 288 (n. 49)

Genitalia, 40, 74, 174, 240; circumcision of, 267 (n. 5); as gendered anatomy, 256

Gesu Daraz, Sayyid Muhammad Husaini (died 1422, known as Khwaja Banda Navaz), 54, 105, 129, 278 (n. 16)

Ghazal, 3, 4, 20–22, 30–31, 63, 77, 82, 110, 113, 115, 268 (n. 20), 270 (n. 13); as biography, 78, 160; that returns to its starting phrase (*baz-gasht*), 63–64; in Urdu, 25, 28, 61, 95, 117, 120, 167–68, 180, 215, 217–18, 220–21, 223, 225, 233, 239, 243, 245, 257, 274 (n. 46), 292 (n. 16)

Gift or offering (*nazr* or *nazrana*), 37–39, 130, 135, 167, 197–98, 216, 222, 246, 249, 250, 252, 280 (n. 33)

Grant of land (*jagir*) or stipend (*madad-e ma'ash*), 118, 135, 158, 167–68, 179, 186, 206, 218, 226, 282 (n. 12), 290 (n. 29)

Greece, 19, 58, 294 (n. 20); known as Byzantium, 169. *See also* Philosophy

Green, Nile, 38, 57, 272 (n. 10)

God (*Allah*), 2, 8–12, 15–16, 19, 95, 97, 104, 114, 239, 261; as creator, 15, 51, 56, 69, 115, 200; awareness of, 11, 55; breath of, 35; court of, 51; desire for, 34, 69; face of, 55; hand of, 127; love for, 27, 66, 71, 78, 83, 91, 94, 95,

312 *Index*

113, 239, 255, 261–62; majestic might (*jalal*) of, 1, 35, 51, 142; mercy and compassion of (*rahma*), 88, 102, 115, 240; names and qualities of, 35, 52, 55, 118, 183, 243, 267 (n. 2); praise of, 55, 142, 155, 205, 243–244, 247, 270 (n. 1); singleness of, 8, 55–56, 236–37, 258; speech of, 55–56, 110, 120

Gods, 8–9, 15–16, 19; goddess, 15. *See also* Hindu deities

Golkonda, 13, 22–23, 49, 125, 130, 133–34, 136–37, 270 (n. 10), 280 (n. 37)

Gujar, 132

Gujarat, 14, 54, 58, 107–9, 153, 190–92, 223, 230, 269 (n. 9), 273 (n. 22), 275 (n. 17), 276 (n. 34), 286 (n. 10); Ahmedabad in, 54, 108, 153, 191, 192, 195, 207–8, 259; Surat in, 284 (n. 29)

Gujari (dialect of early Urdu), 48, 109, 111, 275 (n. 17)

Gulbarga, 54, 105, 129; *jamiʿa* mosque at, 129

Hadis (reports about Muhammad's sayings and deeds), 55–56, 57, 60, 108, 249, 250, 258, 271 (n. 22); about ʿAli, 127–28, 237, 291 (n. 3); experts in, 126. *See also* Muhammad: public example of

Hafiz of Shiraz (died 1389), 20, 54, 268 (n. 19)

Hair, 31, 63, 157, 173, 214; braid, 150, 213–14; curls (*zulf*), 20, 52, 58, 62, 84, 162, 180–81; facial (*khatt*), 83

Hallaj, Mansur (died 922), 95, 294 (n. 19)

Halperin, David, 74

Harmony, 1, 9, 107, 110, 228. *See also* Beauty; Truth

Hasan Basri (died 728), 126

Hasan ibn ʿAli (grandson of Muhammad and elder brother of Husain, died 670), 160, 240–42, 250, 278 (nn. 16–17), 287 (n. 47), 288 (n. 49), 291 (n. 10)

Hashimi, Sayyid Miran Khan Bijapuri (died 1697), 213, 289 (n. 5)

Hashmi, Nasir al-Din, 179, 186

Hatim Tai (Arab poet, died c. 578), 167–68

Head-to-foot (*sarapa*), 65, 172–75, 182–83, 238

Healing, 154, 164, 250; by doctor, 95, 103, 180; by Islamic spiritual medicine (*runani tibb*), 291 (n. 12); with Islamic traditional medicine (*unani tibb*), 62, 103

Heart (*dil* or *qalb*), 20, 29, 39, 42, 43, 53, 55, 58, 65, 68, 83, 91, 97, 102–3, 106, 110, 118, 121, 141, 142, 146, 162, 163, 167, 173, 174, 180, 212, 215, 232, 238, 239, 242, 244, 246, 247. *See also* Blood

Heaven, 1, 5, 9, 84–85, 123, 142, 158, 167, 180, 183, 228, 239, 246, 248, 249, 258. *See also* Paradise

Henna (*mehndi*, red staining of hands and feet), 122, 215–16

Heterosexism. *See* Gender: heteronormative

Hijra (third gender persons), 73–74, 259, 293 (n. 11)

Hindi language, 22, 79, 108–9, 191, 230, 269 (n. 1), 286 (n. 11), 288 (n. 49); Hindavi dialect of, 109

Hindu deities, 130; Krishna, 34, 229–30, 273 (n. 23); Saraswati, 159; Shiva, 44

Hinduism, 16–17, 23, 66, 230–31, 280 (n. 40); bhakti in, 229–30

Hindu people, 13, 44, 81, 83–84, 112, 130–32, 135–36, 158–59, 191, 229–31, 249, 257, 264, 273 (n. 23), 279 (n. 26), 280 (n. 32); ascetic (*bairagi* or *yogi*), 44, 251; Brahmin, 34, 236; courtesan, 147, 287 (n. 47); noble, 23, 176–78, 197, 202, 247. *See also* Rajput

Homosexuality, 2, 21, 24, 71–78, 81–84, 88, 212, 255, 256, 274 (n. 46); cultural responses to, 72, 75, 76, 77; defined as same-sex love, 75, 77, 272 (n. 15); as homoerotic bonding, 70, 78, 85, 86, 88, 90–92, 96, 273 (n. 30), 274 (n. 42); as part of personality, 72; as "socially constructed" category, 75

Homosocial relationships, 76–77, 255, 256

Hope (*umid*), 28, 31–32, 36, 51, 60, 98, 138, 168, 174, 197–98, 213, 238, 240, 246

Hospice, Sufi (*khanqah* or *takiya*), xvi, 16, 27, 49, 84, 102, 105, 108, 118, 277 (n. 50)

Howarth, Toby, 131

Hujwiri, ʿAli (died 1072), 293 (n. 4)

Human (*insan*), 12, 35–36, 55–56, 67, 69, 88–89, 95, 110, 183–84, 236, 258, 260–63. *See also* Adam; Body; Senses

Humility, 28, 36, 60, 98, 162, 182–83, 187, 258, 288 (n. 49); through courting blame (*malamat*), 39–40, 88, 98

Humor, 21, 118, 187–89, 207, 212–13, 218, 259, 286 (n. 11)

Hunting, 162–63, 169, 170

Husain ibn ʿAli (died 680, grandson of Muhammad and Shiʿi Imam), 13, 38, 124, 126–30, 136, 138, 142, 160, 238, 240–42, 249–50, 263, 279 (n. 26), 287 (n. 47), 288 (n. 49), 291 (n. 10)

Husain Vaʾiz Kashifi (died c. 1501), 131

Husn Laqa Bai (adopted daughter of Mah Laqa Bai), 151–52, 179, 226, 255, 281 (n. 4), 287 (n. 47)

Hyderabad, 23–24, 48, 54, 81, 83, 119–20, 125, 133–38, 141, 145–46, 151, 153–54, 158, 164, 161, 175, 179, 204, 207–8, 210, 218, 222–24, 229, 244, 248, 250, 262, 264, 273 (n. 21), 277 (n. 50), 285 (nn. 29–31), 291 (n. 12), 291 (nn. 14–15); founding of, 13, 130–31; Mughal conquest of, 40–41, 136–38, 158–59, 280 (n. 37)

Hyderabad neighborhoods, 134, 259, 293 (n. 11); Adikmet, 251; Lingampally, 226; Lalaguda, 133, 280 (n. 30); Mughalpura, 137; Nampally, 218, 226; Secunderabad, 178; Yaqutpura, 290 (n. 23). *See also* Golkonda; Mawla ʿAli Shrine

Hypocrisy, 39, 106–7

Ibn ʿArabi (died 1240), 33, 60, 275 (n. 19)

Ibrahim ʿAdil-Shah (died 1627, Sultan of Bijapur), 49

Ibrahim Qutb-Shah (died 1580, fourth Sultan of Qutb-Shahi dynasty), 133–34

Ideology, 12, 74–75, 125, 128, 221, 224, 264–65

Idolatry, 98, 236; idol, 8, 25, 30, 34, 97–98, 102, 106, 236–37, 263. *See also* Infidelity

Illness, 103, 117, 172; with fever, 29–30, 32, 50, 62, 149, 171; from love, 172, 174–75, 180–81, 216; with plague, 133. *See also* Healing

Image, 30, 43, 69, 292 (n. 3); of the beloved, 32, 42, 44; of Sufi master (*tasavvur*), 59–60

Imagination (*khayal*), 2, 4–5, 36, 50, 78, 115, 155, 160, 209, 255, 277 (n. 46); realm of, 2, 36, 120, 254

Imam, 11–12, 125, 127, 129–31, 138, 142, 158–59, 166–67, 169, 219, 233–34, 238, 239, 242, 244, 245, 250, 260, 262, 263, 267 (nn. 3–5), 287 (n. 47); designation of (*nass*), 11, 263

Iman, Muhammad Sher Khan (died 1806, poetry teacher of Mah Laqa Bai), 120, 179–81, 184, 223, 285 (n. 30), 285 (n. 32), 285 (n. 36), 289 (n. 13)

India: northern (Hindustan), 22, 25, 48, 58, 109, 220-23, 228, 229, 251, 285 (n. 35), 286 (n. 11). *See also* Deccan; South Asia
Infidelity (*kufr*), 235-36
Initiation (*bai'at*), 37-38, 50, 52, 54, 77-78, 94, 107, 126, 249, 261, 263
Inspiration (*ilham*), 19, 47, 101, 159, 260, 261
Intention (*niyya*), 60, 88, 96, 151-52, 243
Intercession (*shafa'at*), 238-40, 262
Intimacy (*qurb* or *ulfat*), 35-36, 41, 51, 55, 56, 84, 91, 94, 95, 97-98, 127, 162, 163, 170-73, 180, 200, 236, 239, 258-59, 261, 293 (n. 13)
Iran, 13, 20, 23, 54, 87, 128-29, 131-33, 136-37, 164, 168, 171, 224, 262, 264, 267 (n. 5); classical music in, 262; Isfahan in, 14, 131. *See also* Persian people
Iraq, 128, 238, 264, 270 (n. 10), 286 (n. 9). *See also* Baghdad; Karbala; Najaf
Islam, 15-16, 56, 81-82, 109, 157, 236; reform movements in, 18, 81, 195, 199, 209, 274 (n. 46), 277 (n. 4); spread of, 9-15
Islamic studies, 6, 256, 257, 292 (n. 3)

Jahan Ara (died 1681, Mughal princess and daughter of Shahjahan), 187
Jainism, 66
Jami, Mawlana 'Abd al-Rahman (died 1492), 36-37, 42, 54
Jamshed (mythic Persian king), 168-69, 263
Jawhar, Ghulam Husain (died after 1814), 172, 182-83, 184, 190, 193-200, 208, 222, 227-29, 248
Jesus ('Issa, the Islamic prophet), 8, 19, 159, 180
Jewels, 38, 122, 137, 162, 162, 228; diamond, 130; gem, 53, 104, 215-16; jewelry, 97, 226, 228; of Solomon's ring, 58; ruby, 59, 167, 216, 242
Jews and Judaism, 10, 269 (n. 22)
Jinn (disembodied beings created from fire), 19. *See also* Demon
Joseph (Yusuf, the Islamic prophet), 82
Joy (*bast* or *khushi*), 36, 53, 69, 85, 95, 99, 103, 152, 228, 249, 258, 288 (n. 49)
Judgment day and resurrection (*qiyama*), 115, 146, 152, 213, 236, 238, 240, 250, 254
Junaid of Baghdad (died 910), 39
Justice, 11, 138, 159, 238, 247, 263; injustice, 15, 163, 177

Ka'ba, 98, 106, 237, 290 (n. 26)
Kalavant, 157, 249, 280 (n. 40); Sada-Rang (died 1748), 288 (n. 49). *See also* Khush-hal Khan
Kalimi (or Kaleemi), xvi, 53-54, 112, 273 (n. 21)
Kalimullah Shahjahanabadi (died 1729, estblished the Kalimi Sufi order), 31, 54, 113
Kalpaklı, Mehmet, 4, 75, 143, 160
Kannada, 220
Karbala, 13, 14, 128; battle of, 130-31
Kathak. *See* Dance: kathak form of
Khaksar Sabzavari, 26-27, 84-85
Khandesh, 13, 107, 108
Khardla (locale in Maharashtra), 14, 169-70, 285 (n. 31)
Khizr (immortal wise companion to Islamic prophets), 158-59, 283 (n. 21)
Khuldabad, 14, 27, 49, 54, 84-85, 107-8, 137, 273 (n. 31)
Khush-hal Khan (died 1822-3), 138, 151-52, 157, 280 (n. 40), 282 (nn. 5-8); with pen name Anup, 287 (n. 49)
Kidwai, Saleem, 75, 82
King (*malik* or *shah*), 10-13, 15, 29, 37-38, 71, 83, 84, 107, 124, 129-30, 158,

Index 315

161, 167–69, 201, 267 (n. 2), 291 (n. 10); as address for groom, 112; as address for Sufi master, 37–41, 51–52, 118, 251

Kiss, 35, 38, 141, 142, 146, 158, 173, 215–16, 232, 242, 245

Kruitzer, Gijs, 77

Kulliyat (poet's collected works in various genres), 26–27, 274 (n. 50), 276 (n. 27), 291 (n. 15), 292 (n. 16). *See also* Divan

Laila. *See* Majnun

Lament, 41, 86, 97, 102, 112, 116, 241, 247; as genre of poetry (*marsiya*), 22, 131, 142, 223, 239, 249; as genre of song (*soz*), 249

Law (*fiqh*), 10, 18, 56, 82, 89, 219, 236; Hanbali school of, 250; Hanafi school of, 84, 245; Islamic school of (*mazhab*), 124–25; Jaʿfari school of, 125, 204, 245, 278 (n. 7); jurists as experts in, 36, 87, 124, 126, 132, 135, 207, 258–59, 267 (n. 3). *See also* Shariʿa

Leonard, Karen, 226

Letter (of Urdu alphabet), xi–xii, 85, 118, 156, 280 (n. 1), 281 (n. 6); alif, 65; mim, 55–56

Light, 1, 20, 51, 165, 183, 201, 245, 246, 249, 262, 263, 269 (n. 1); ʿAli as embodiment of, 120, 127, 147, 185, 213, 238; of Muhammad, 11–12, 56, 238

Litany (*vird* or *vazifa*), 155, 271 (n. 19)

Literature, 4, 13, 19–22, 74, 100, 172, 182, 206, 220, 254–57, 261–62; history as, 208–9; in literary criticism, 145, 160, 210, 212, 219–22; literacy, 9, 255

Liver. *See* Heart; Passion

London, 5, 222, 282

Love, 2, 27, 29–33, 39, 41, 45, 47, 58–60, 68, 71, 82, 98, 111, 139, 146, 149, 181–82, 225, 230, 239, 242, 246, 252; for ʿAli, 244–47, 252–53, 259–64; courtly, 9, 20, 159; erotic, 37, 47, 61–65, 74–76, 113, 116, 173–75, 183, 212–13, 255; for God, 27, 66, 71, 78, 83, 91, 94, 95, 113, 239, 255, 261–62; religion of (*mazhab-e ʿishq*), 64, 100, 244, 252, 262; spiritual, 25–26, 37, 49–50, 103, 182, 211, 253; stages of, 87, 99, 116. *See also* Eros; Homosexuality: defined as same-sex love; Illness: from love; Romance

Lucknow (capital of Avadh), 149, 213, 221, 229–31, 279 (n. 29), 285 (nn. 35–36)

Lust (*shahwa*), 72, 78, 86, 88, 113, 117, 136, 173–74, 183, 188, 211, 216, 227, 233–34, 235. *See also* Desire: sexual; Urges

Lutf al-Nisa Imtiyaz (died after 1798), 143, 243–44, 281 (n. 6), 291 (nn. 14–15), 292 (n. 16)

Madari Sufi order, 251

Madho Rao (Maratha chieftain, died 1795), 161–62

Madness, 29–32, 47, 53, 78–80, 82–84, 85, 149, 263; as divine attraction (*majzub*), 40, 50; as *mania*, 19

Magic (*jadu*), 121; as sorcery (*sihr*), 9, 63, 84, 199; through protective charm (*taʿviz* or *tilsim*), 173, 242–43, 291 (n. 12)

Mah Laqa Bai Chanda (1768–1824), 2–7, 15, 18–19, 24, 77, 119, 138–39, 141–47, 151–65, 166–84, 185–91, 196, 205–9, 254–57, 262, 264, 286 (n. 9); as builder, 145–46, 151–53; childhood of, 154–57, 227–28; as courtesan, 24, 120–21, 139, 141, 143, 163–64, 169, 173, 184–85, 188, 193–94, 216, 224, 225–27, 243, 249, 255, 264, 284 (n. 17), 287 (n. 47); court title of, 141, 158, 173, 186, 280 (n. 1), 282 (n. 19); as dancer, 120,

160–62, 166, 190, 224, 227–33, 252; as mystic, 120, 142, 244–53; as patron of arts, 179–80, 182–84, 190; pen name of, 139, 141, 160, 214, 235, 242; as poet, 120, 141–43, 210–27, 231–34, 256, 284 (n. 27), 289 (n. 13); as Shi'i, 121, 142–43, 184, 224, 233–34, 235–53; tomb of, 145, 151, 155–56, 159. *See also* Divan: of Mah Laqa Bai

Mahmud, Sultan (ruler of Ghazna, died 1030), 19

Mah-nama ("Moon Chronicle," a history of Hyderabad), 145, 182, 183, 190, 193, 208, 222

Mahtab Kanvar Bai (elder half sister of Mah Laqa Bai), 154–55, 170, 192, 199–203, 227, 290 (n. 29)

Majnun-Laila, 32, 181

Malcolm, John (died 1833), 175–76, 222, 283 (n. 22)

Malfuzat (oral teachings of Sufi master), 108; titled *Fava'id al-Fu'ad*, 86

Malkapuri, 'Abd al-Jabbar Khan, 100

Malwa, 107, 199, 229–30

Mangi, Shah (died 1713), 40

Man Kanvar Bai (half sister of Mah Laqa Bai), 192, 202–3

Mansion, 134, 148, 175, 206, 216, 226–28, 285 (n. 31), 290 (n. 23), 293 (n. 11); without surrounding wall (*haveli*), 134, 146, 189, 218, 226, 249, 282 (n. 6); with surrounding wall (*devrhi*), 157

Manuscript, 26, 79–81, 193, 222

Maratha people, 132, 136, 161–62, 169–71, 176–78, 223, 284 (n. 7); Marathi language, 220

Marketplace (*bazar*), 49, 58, 147, 134, 173, 205

Marriage, 17, 65–66, 77, 117, 121, 127, 149, 183, 185, 188, 195, 202–4, 207, 213, 219, 254–55, 288 (n. 49); allowing for divorce, 16; contract of, 16, 203–4; for courtesans, 185–87, 226; dowry in, 68; rituals in, 62–63, 112, 135; temporary (*mut'a* or *izdivaj-e muvaqqat*), 16–18, 204, 268 (n. 12).

Martyr, 22, 124, 128, 131, 240, 249–50, 263

Mary (mother of Jesus), 240

Masculinity, 26, 65–68, 73–74, 86–89, 92–97, 181, 184, 188, 210–11, 217–18, 220–21, 233–34, 255, 256, 274 (n. 51); of heroic youth (*fata* or *javan*), 142, 237; of young men (*amrad*), 69, 83, 88, 90–91, 214, 228. *See also* Dominance; Gender; Patriarchy

Masnavi. *See* Epic

Massad, Joseph, 74

Mas'ud Bakk (died 1387), 37, 54, 108, 275 (n. 19)

Mawla 'Ali Shrine, 133–36, 148, 154, 156, 224, 251, 280 (n. 30), 282 (n. 8); building at, 135, 138, 145, 151–53, 177, 207, 247; 'urs at, 135, 158, 247–48, 280 (n. 32), 292 (n. 22). *See also* 'Ali ibn Abi Talib: known as Mawla

Mawlvi (religious teacher), 149, 189, 249, 251

Medina, 10, 14, 54, 126, 237, 267 (n. 1)

Meditation (*zikr*, reciting God's names and qualities), 12, 13, 35, 53, 55, 98, 106–7, 113, 126, 155, 257. *See also* Contemplation; Music: ritual listening to

Menstruation, 16, 240. *See also* Blood; Reproduction

Messiah (*masih*), 11; *mahdi* as, 138, 267 (n. 3); nizam as, 158–59. *See also* Jesus

Metal, 36, 59, 130, 189, 243; gold, 20, 61–62, 95, 122, 137, 162, 167, 187, 216, 228; lead, 39, 44; mercury, 61, 95; silver, 58, 129, 173, 174, 187, 189, 228, 232

Metaphor (*majaz*), 2, 31, 34, 41–42, 49–50, 81, 90, 101–3, 110, 114, 182, 211, 246

Index 317

Mind (*dimagh*), 59, 67, 83, 91, 181, 214, 239, 246, 263, 272 (n. 33); mindfulness, 1, 35. *See also* Reason

Miracles, 52, 97, 154, 196, 237, 242, 254, 267 (n. 5); of prophets (*mu'jiza*), 9, 246; of saints (*karamat*), 109–10, 133, 250, 293, 293 (n. 13)

Mir 'Alam, Abu'l-Qasim Husaini (died 1808), 169–78, 181, 183–84

Mir Muhammad Mum'in Astarabadi (died 1625), 13, 131–32

Mirror, 30, 36–37, 41, 43, 60, 63, 65, 83, 100, 153, 174, 180, 183

Mir Taqi Mir (died 1810), 50, 270 (n. 7)

Mirza Hadi Rusva (died 1931), 149, 231, 281 (n. 2)

Mongol, 12

Money. *See* Wealth

Monotheism, 8–9

Moon, 1–2, 8–9, 15, 24, 119, 138–39, 141, 157, 254; as crescent, 1, 25, 181; in poetry, 20, 82, 120, 142, 146, 173–74, 180–81, 182, 217, 232; splitting of, 9

Moses (Musa the Islamic prophet), 8, 19, 110, 237, 246, 283 (n. 21)

Mosque, 74, 108, 129, 131, 151, 155, 269 (n. 1), 279 (n. 26)

Mouth, 58, 68, 142, 173; lip, 122, 141, 142, 152, 216, 232, 242; tongue, 29, 52, 55, 57, 142, 164

Mughal Empire, 3, 6, 22–23, 112, 119, 132, 158, 179, 193, 197, 286 (n. 9); culture of, 66, 76, 78, 82, 92–94, 117, 160, 221–25, 229–31; rulers of, 40, 153, 177, 223; as Sunni rulers, 23, 84, 132

Muhammad (the Prophet), 2, 8, 19, 38, 55, 108, 113, 114, 126, 236, 275 (n. 55); death of, 10, 12, 120, 237, 241, 249, 260–61; family of (*al-e bait*), 10–11, 120, 123–28, 130–31, 138, 142, 160, 236, 238, 240–43, 249, 259, 261, 263, 291 (n. 3), 291 (n. 8); family of known as *panj-tan*, 241, 279 (n. 18); known by the name Ahmad, 55–56; public example of (*sunna*), 66, 126, 258; as ruler, 10, 56. See also *Hadis*; Prophets

Muhammad ibn Fazlullah (died 1619–20), 90

Muhammad Quli (fifth Sultan of Qutb-Shahi dynasty, died 1611), 49

Muharram, xvi, 130–32, 135, 151, 177, 249–50, 279 (n. 25)

Mu'in al-Din Chishti (known as *Khwaja Gharib Navaz*, died 1236), 13, 20, 27, 123–24, 273 (n. 31), 278 (n. 8), 288 (n. 49), 292 (n. 27)

Murtaza Qadiri, Shah (died 1613), 40

Musa Sada Sohag (died 1449), 258, 274 (n. 47), 293 (n. 11)

Musha'ira (poetry recital), 9, 82, 100, 142, 167, 178–80, 184, 257

Music, xvi, 12, 13, 17–18, 23, 35–36, 46, 56, 100–117, 121, 128, 148, 156, 193, 196, 228, 257–59; ethnomusicology, 258, 293 (n. 9); forbidden in Islam, 36, 87, 117, 258; institution for learning, 196–98, 206, 208, 282 (n. 6); master of, 108, 149, 151, 157, 186, 196, 199, 206, 228; ritual listening to (*sama'*), 38, 41, 45–46, 47, 53, 68–69, 78, 86, 90, 95, 100–107, 126, 257–59, 292 (n. 4); tent for performing (*muzrib khiyam*), 161, 200. *See also* Harmony; Musical instrument; Qawwali; Raga; Song

Musical instrument (*sazang*), 36, 48, 104, 206, 228, 271 (n. 30); drums, 82, 111–12, 158, 206, 249; flute (*nai*), 110–12; lute (*rabab* or *chang*), 110, 206, 228; water chimes (*jaltarang*), 206; zither (*qanun*), 206

Muzaffar Ali (film director), 148

Mysore, 14, 134, 170, 175, 178; fortress of, at Srirangapatnam, 175
Mysticism, 6, 11, 53–56, 261–64; knowledge in (*ma'rifa*, *'irfan*, or gnosis), 12, 34, 58, 60, 155, 236; in music, 105; in poetry, 19–20, 25, 48–50, 55–56, 61, 64, 244; in Shi'ism, 125, 235–36, 240, 244–47, 252–53, 260–64

Najaf, 14, 128, 214, 215, 238, 245
Nakedness (*barahnagi*), 29, 38–41, 50, 77, 270 (n. 10)
Naming, 5, 7, 21, 25, 141, 149, 157–58, 165, 193, 199, 201–5, 207, 237, 239, 241
Nana Phadnavis (chief minister of the Marathas, died 1800), 177
Nanded (locale in Maharashtra), 177
Naqshbandi Sufi order, 27, 49, 77, 112–13, 126, 273 (n. 21), 276 (n. 40), 277 (n. 5)
Nasir al-Din Chiragh-e Delhi (died 1356), 54, 67 85, 105
Nasr, Seyyed Hossein, 260
Negligence (*ghaflat*), 29, 62, 98, 163, 182, 242; of forgetting (*nisyan*), 35, 163, 263; of indifference (*taghafful*), 21, 64, 68, 212, 219, 215, 232, 235, 276 (n. 27)
Nishat, Jameela (Urdu poet and women's rights activist), 221–23
Nizam al-Din Awliya (known as *Sultan al-Masha'ikh* and *Mahbub-e Ilahi*, died 1325), 13, 54, 66–67, 85–89, 104–5, 110, 116, 258–59, 273 (n. 36), 274 (n. 42), 293 (n. 13)
Nizam al-Din Awrangabadi (leader of the Kalimi Sufi order, died 1729), xvi, 29, 50, 51, 54, 58, 80, 112–13, 270 (n. 9)
Nizam 'Ali Khan (second Asaf Jah, died 1803), 137, 143, 157–59, 161–62, 164, 166, 169–71, 172, 175, 176, 178, 179, 183, 202, 224, 244, 248–49, 282 (n. 12), 282 (n. 19), 284 (n. 7), 292 (n. 22)

Nizam al-Mulk (prime minister of Mughal Empire, ruler of the Deccan as first Asaf Jah, died 1748), 23, 49, 80, 137, 153, 177, 193, 280 (n. 37), 287 (n. 45), 290 (n. 29)
Nizami, Khaliq Ahmad, 67
Nizam Mahboob 'Ali Pasha (sixth Asaf Jah, died 1911), 206
Nizam Sikander Jah (third Asaf Jah, died 1829), 143, 152, 164, 170–71, 175, 178–79, 184
Nizams of Hyderabad, 118–19, 177, 221, 223, 225–26; alliance with British, 175–76, 177–78, 284 (n. 7); army camp of, 199–203, 205, 207, 223–24; as Sunni rulers, 23, 137–38, 143, 145, 154, 157–59, 164, 184, 224, 247–48
Nothingness (*nisti*), 28, 36, 60–61, 142–43, 239. *See also* Emptiness; Erasure; Oblivion
Novel: in Urdu, 149, 220, 231, 281 (n. 2)

Object, 21, 31–32, 74–75, 215; in ritual, 130, 137
Oblivion (*be-khudi*), 29, 34, 37–40, 44, 50, 77
Ode (*qasida*), 166–68, 179, 180, 183, 239, 243, 270 (n. 13), 292 (n. 16); Arabic, 19–20
Orbit, 5, 25–26, 141
Osmania University, 194, 251
Ottoman Empire, 4–5, 75; culture in, 160

Paan (digestive condiment of tambul leaf and betelnut), 122, 189, 216
Pain, 28, 29, 31, 33, 35–36, 44–45, 62, 63, 90, 93, 95, 101, 116, 123, 181, 182, 213, 215, 241, 256
Painting and illustration, 19, 22, 41, 144–45, 154, 157, 161, 207, 214, 249, 283 (nn. 26–27), 292 (n. 22)

Index 319

Pakistan, 277 (n. 4), 289 (n. 16), 293 (n. 4)
Paradise (*firdaws* or *jannat*), 24, 34, 56, 84–85, 152–53, 238
Paradox, 24, 33–36, 41, 45, 98–99, 145, 225
Parda (female seclusion), 188, 193, 197, 198, 205, 211. See also Gender: segregation by
Party or gathering (*mehfil*), 9, 38, 41, 46, 65, 68–71, 78, 87, 96, 100, 102, 105–7, 158, 161, 175, 184, 214, 224
Passion (*'ishq*), 19, 30, 32, 41–45, 72, 76, 77, 81, 82–83, 86, 102, 139, 153, 167, 173, 174, 181, 230, 236, 239, 245–47, 252; housed in liver (*jigar*), 67, 103, 294 (n. 19)
Patel, Smita (actress), 147
Patriarchy, 6, 16–17, 26, 73, 75–77, 80, 82, 89, 92–94, 121, 143, 157, 184, 188, 194, 216, 217–19, 233, 255, 259, 274 (n. 51)
Patronage, 17–20, 40, 49, 63, 84, 108, 113, 121, 125, 135, 149, 164, 166–71, 173, 175, 177, 184, 221, 224, 257; dependence upon, 154, 163, 169, 178–79, 185, 193, 203, 219, 252; in Qawwali, 26, 46, 117. See also Mah Laqa Bai Chanda: as patron of arts
Pearl, 20, 21, 183, 189; related to oyster, 197–98, 286 (n. 21)
Pen name (*takhallus*), 20, 25, 43
Performance, 45, 82, 104, 114, 116, 131, 147–48, 150, 189, 224–34, 257, 290 (n. 29); in public, 186, 191, 194, 196, 198–202, 205–6, 233, 259
Persianate culture, 16, 19, 230, 261–62, 286 (n. 21). See also Vernacular: Persianization
Persian language, 22, 87, 108–9, 128, 132–33, 145, 157, 171, 191, 193, 194, 195, 196, 199, 200, 202, 211, 230, 250, 261, 268 (n. 17), 269 (n. 1), 288 (n. 51), 290 (n. 23); expressions in Urdu, 32, 211, 220–22, 229
Persian people, 8, 111, 136, 164; known as *afaqi* in South Asia, 128–29
Persian poetry, 19–22, 26, 36, 48, 50, 104–5, 118, 123–24, 131, 156, 182, 211, 217, 224, 261. See also Siraj Awrangabadi: Persian poetry of
Petievich, Carla, 212, 217–18, 220
Philosophy, 11, 39, 42, 62; Neoplatonic, 36–37, 261–62; Socrates in, 19; Aristotle in, 273, 294 (n. 20); Plato in, 294 (n. 20)
Piety, 11, 13, 20, 51, 187, 195, 200, 202, 205, 240, 242, 250, 259, 263
Pilgrimage, xv, 134–35, 148, 151–52, 247, 280 (n. 32), 292 (n. 22); to Mecca (*hajj*), 108, 127; to tombs of holy people (*ziyarat*), 27, 41, 84–85, 148, 154, 238
Pir. See Sufism: master in
Poetry, 6, 9, 37, 42, 48, 57, 63, 69, 83, 255, 257–59; denunciation of, 19, 113; in five-line stanzas (*mukhammas*), 120, 270 (n. 13), 292 (n. 16); orality in, 100–101, 131, 224; in six-line stanzas (*musaddas*), 180–81, 292 (n. 16); sensitivity toward, 93. See also Abjad; Couplet; Epic; Ghazal; Lament; Persian poetry; Quatrain; Urdu poetry
Poets, 2–6, 16, 18–20, 22, 26, 36–37, 49–50, 54, 79–80, 100–101, 109, 113, 141–43, 178–80, 209, 217–18, 221–23, 284 (n. 29); as soothsayers, 19.
Poison, 95, 107, 170, 171, 199, 213, 286 (n. 21)
Popular religion, 13, 66, 111, 131–33, 135, 191, 250, 280 (n. 32)
Pourjavady, Nasrollah, 89
Poverty, 50, 79, 110, 183, 186, 191, 193, 195–96, 204–5, 288 (n. 49); voluntary, 17, 38, 57, 65, 68, 103, 250–51, 261

Praise, 59, 84, 96, 126–27, 159, 166–68, 173, 175, 180, 182, 220, 232, 242; of ʿAli, 120, 145, 159, 184, 206, 232, 237–43, 277 (n. 1), 291 (n. 3); of God (*hamd*), 55, 142, 155, 205, 243–44, 247, 270 (n. 1); of Muhammad (*naʿat*), 55–56, 142

Prayer, 1, 9, 11, 85, 102–3, 107, 162–63, 206, 237, 251; beads (*tasbih*), 106–7, 236; call for, 189; carpet for (*sajjada*), 20, 96; direction of (*qibla*), 51, 106; in Sufism, 12, 59

Prophets, 8, 56; in relation to imams, 11, 237–38, 240

Propriety, 24, 29, 40, 65, 82, 88, 150, 212; of etiquette (*adab*), 41, 68, 69–70, 104, 185; in restraint (*hilm*), 41, 57, 60, 66, 70, 76, 89, 159, 237, 253

Prostitution, 18, 147–51, 186–87, 189, 190, 220, 226, 268 (n. 12), 277 (n. 3), 286 (n. 11); brothel for (*kotha*), 147, 149–50, 230; related to Mah Laqa Bai's family, 155, 194, 202, 205–6, 252, 287 (n. 47)

Prostration (*sujud*), 15, 38, 102, 237; bowing, 9, 139, 237, 245

Psychology, 71–72, 74, 76, 86, 90, 233, 256

Pulan Kanvar Bai (given name Pulan Bibi, maternal aunt of Mah Laqa Bai), 156, 192, 195–97, 203, 208, 290 (n. 29)

Pune, 14, 161, 170, 176, 177

Punishment, 16, 136; by being chained, 50, 79–80, 83–84; by being executed, 63; by ruler's decree (*taʿzir*), 84, 273 (n. 30)

Purity, 44, 59, 85, 98, 151, 152, 174, 181, 194; lack of, 187, 220–22, 240; of members of Muhammad's family (*maʿsum*), 138

Qadiri Sufi order, 27, 113, 124–26, 250, 251, 260, 262, 278 (n. 8), 292 (n. 27)

Qais, Muhammad Sadiq (died 1815), 180, 218, 285 (n. 35), 289 (n. 13)

Qalandar, 27

Qaqshal, Afzal Beg Khan, 26, 52, 79, 271 (n. 15)

Qawwali, 21, 29, 38, 45–46, 57, 64–65, 70, 96, 100, 109–10, 112–17, 123–28, 135, 138–39, 230, 249, 255, 276 (n. 27), 280 (n. 40); sung by the Warsi Brothers, 148. *See also* Music: ritual listening to; Performance

Qonya, 14, 110

Quatrain (*rubaʿi*), 40, 118, 123–24, 152, 270 (n. 13), 277 (n. 46), 292 (n. 16)

Queer studies, 4. *See also* Gender studies

Qurʾan, 1–3, 8–9, 15, 19, 35, 42, 55–56, 105, 126, 137, 152, 159, 236–37, 243, 254, 268 (n. 16), 269 (n. 22), 269 (chap. 2, n. 1), 270 (n. 12), 275 (n. 55), 282 (n. 9), 283 (n. 21); translation of, 267 (n. 1).

Qutb al-Din (known as Khwaja Bakhtiyar Kaki, died 1235), 102–4

Qutb-Shahi dynasty, 13, 125, 130–37, 158, 224, 262, 270 (n. 10), 280 (n. 30)

Raga (mode of Indian music), 100, 109, 196, 206, 288 (n. 49); known as *parda*, 109

Rahmatullah Mutawakkil (died c. 1500), 108, 276 (n. 34)

Raj Kanvar Bai (mother of Mah Laqa Bai, known as Mida Bibi, died 1792–93), 138, 153–56, 170, 186–87, 191–205, 227–28, 252, 290 (n. 29)

Rajput, 132, 136, 193, 196–202, 207; Rajputana (known also as Rajasthan), 13, 14, 191, 202, 208, 229; Jaipur in, 230.

Ramazan (Islamic month of fasting and piety), 151

Rambha Rao Jayawant, Raja (died c. 1800, Maratha noble), 176–78, 284 (n. 24)
Raymond, Michel Joachim Marie (French mercenary commander, died 1798), 170
Reason (ʿaql), 24, 30, 31, 34, 39–40, 41–43, 45, 56, 84, 106, 208, 236, 263
Rebellion, 8, 11, 94, 127, 129, 132, 171
Rekha (actress), 149
Rekhta (early poetry in mixed language, later Urdu poetry written in male voice), 52–53, 79, 109, 211–17, 223, 225, 233, 270 (n. 7), 276 (n. 27). See also Masculinity
Rekhti (Urdu poetry written in a female voice), 180, 211–13, 217–18, 221, 285 (n. 35), 288 (n. 4), 289 (n. 5). See also Femininity
Relic: Shiʿi shrine for, 13, 133, 135, 247–48. See also Mawla ʿAli Shrine
Religious studies, 27, 145, 256–57, 279 (n. 25)
Repentance (tawba), 31, 90, 187
Representative (khalifa), 37–38, 85, 95
Reproduction, 2, 4, 17, 77, 86–87, 197–98, 255–56, 268 (n. 10); fertility, 15, 148, 172, 189, 197, 240, 274 (n. 55); infertility, 189; womb, 72, 200, 240. See also Birth; Menstruation
Resignation (riza), 31, 106
Rhyme, 9, 19, 20, 45, 56, 64, 101, 160, 215, 294 (n. 20); rhyming phrase (qafiya), 21, 32, 63, 284 (n. 27); rhyming sound (radif), 21, 30, 43, 178, 214, 216, 232, 238, 239, 242, 247, 262
Rhythm, 45, 56, 107–8, 114, 122, 148, 235; in Indian music (tala), 206, 288 (n. 49); as poetic meter, 100, 160, 178, 215, 228, 234, 284 (n. 27)
Rival (ghair), 62, 81, 161, 163, 167, 177, 212, 220, 228, 232

River, 13, 161; Musi, 137; Narmada, 199; of paradise (kawsar), 107, 282 (n. 9); Tapti, 107
Romance, 16, 19–20, 34, 41, 48–50, 61–64, 106, 159–60, 163, 175–76, 245, 253
Ruffle, Karen, 131
Ruin (kharabat), 27, 48, 53, 65, 103, 122, 212.
Rukn al-Dawla, Mir Musa Khan (prime minister of second nizam, died 1775), 134, 154–55, 161–62, 169, 192, 202–4, 227, 229, 287 (n. 38)
Rumi, Mawlana (died 1273), 110–11, 275 (n. 11); followers of (Mevlevi), 106, 292 (n. 3)
Rustom (legendary Persian hero), 169
Rustom Dil Khan (Mughal governor of Hyderabad, died 1707), 227, 290 (n. 23)

Sacrifice (balihari or qurban), 92–96, 124, 127–28, 151, 167, 168, 212, 233, 238, 239, 241, 242, 245, 249, 252, 263, 288 (n. 49). See also Martyr
Sada Sohagi Sufi order, 258, 293 (n. 11)
Saʿdi of Shiraz (died 1292), 20, 268 (n. 18)
Safavid dynasty, 13, 23, 129–32, 137, 262
Saint or sage (vali, plural awliya), 12, 27, 29, 38, 40, 56, 84, 114, 194–95, 247–49, 251, 253, 260–61, 262, 293 (n. 13); authority of (valayat), 37–39, 57, 108, 115, 127–28, 244–45; personal sanctity of (vilayat), 104, 105, 244, 259–61, 259–61. See also Miracles: of saints; Sufism: master in
Salafi, 277 (n. 4). See also Islam: reform movements in
Salam (respectful greeting), 25, 139, 167
Salim Singh (Raja of Deoliya, Rajput prince), 192, 193, 196–99, 200, 207

322   Index

Samaʿ. *See* Music: ritual listening to; Qawwali
Samaʿ-khana (hall for ritual listening to music), 123–24, 128
Sanskrit, 230, 231
Sarcasm, 21, 32, 61–62, 186. *See also* Humor
Sarmad Shahid (died 1662), 40–41, 270 (n. 10), 274 (n. 47)
Sarvari, Abdul Qadir, 79–80, 82, 277 (n. 50)
Sayyid (descendant of Muhammad through Fatima), 25, 38, 78, 79, 105, 193, 194, 207–8, 248, 249, 250, 278 (n. 8), 278 (n. 16); from Barhah, 208, 286 (n. 9); from Kathiawar, 192, 286 (n. 10). *See also* Genealogy
Schimmel, Annemarie (died 2003), 22
Schofield, Katherine Butler (née Brown), 82
School (*madrasa* or *dars*), 41–42, 50, 79, 171–72; for young women, 157, 218, 226, 255
Script: Persian, 22, 268 (n. 17); Devanagari, 22
Sea, 20, 93, 100, 182–83, 228, 238, 288 (n. 49); Arabian, 23, 128; Bay of Bengal, 23, 130
Sects, 9, 10, 12, 15, 17, 19, 23, 124–25, 128, 132, 135–36, 138, 236, 241, 244, 290 (n. 26); coexistence between, 6, 10, 15, 23, 124–25, 133, 279 (n. 25); concealment of (*taqiya*), 129, 247; cooperation between, 121, 123–24, 247–52, 257, 259–65
Seduction, 2, 17, 24, 31, 48, 60, 82–83, 145, 154, 156, 160, 162–64, 173, 180, 201–4, 207, 211, 225–28, 230, 233, 252, 255
Self, 28, 29–33, 34, 64, 93, 95, 103, 108, 116, 127, 149, 247, 258. *See also* Subjectivity; Worship: as self-awareness

Sells, Michael, 33, 267 (n. 1)
Senses, 31, 62, 108, 153, 227, 229; experience through, 101, 114–15. *See also* Sight; Smell; Sound; Taste; Touch
Separation (*firaq*), 31–32, 41, 45, 65, 112, 230, 246, 252, 261. *See also* Duality
Sermon (*khutba*), 130, 135, 137; of mourning (*rawza-khwani*), 131, 249; preacher (*khatib* or *vaʾiz*), 107, 126, 153
Sex, 9, 15–16, 66–67; acts of, 72, 76, 84, 86–89, 181, 268 (n. 10); as ritual, 15
Sexuality, 4, 17, 24, 66, 70, 71–78, 92, 120–21, 149, 164, 255–56; asexuality, 76, 87, 256; orientation in, 6, 24, 72–77, 82, 89–90, 255; studies of, 4, 145; of women, 194, 195, 203, 210, 211, 215–16, 240, 255. *See also* Homosexuality
Shafiq, Lakshmi Narayan Awrangabadi (died 1809), 26, 53, 118
Shah ʿAlam (Mughal emperor, died 1806), 80
Shah Chiragh (disciple of Siraj), 118
Shahjahan (Mughal emperor, died 1666), 85
Shaikh. *See* Sufism: master in
Shame, 78, 83, 98, 141, 208, 242; as disgrace (*sharm*), 82, 171, 176, 185, 187–88, 201, 202, 205; as modesty (*haya*), 97, 174, 185
Shariʿa (system of Islamic moral order), 2, 10, 16, 67, 207, 244, 284 (n. 17)
Shattari Sufi order, 27, 277 (n. 5), 278 (n. 8)
Shawkat, Samina, 193, 284 (n. 27), 287 (n. 47)
Sherani, Hafiz Mahmud, 109
Shiʿi Muslims (*Shiʿat ʿAli*, Partisans for ʿAli), 2, 5–6, 10–11, 124–25, 128–33, 136, 158–59, 166, 168, 205, 223, 257, 264, 293 (n. 13); Desi (local to India), 125, 128–33, 135, 138, 154, 224, 260–64,

Index 323

279 (n. 22); Isma'ili community of, 267 (n. 4), 267 (n. 6); in Qutb-Shahi realm, 13, 22, 125, 158; as state religion, 129–30, 262; theology or law of, 11, 16–17, 236–40, 252, 260, 268 (n. 12); Twelver community of (*isnā 'asharī*), 11–12, 240, 267 (nn. 3–4), 278 (n. 7). *See also* 'Ali ibn Abi Talib: as first Shi'i imam; Imam; Mysticism: in Shi'ism; Prophets: in relation to imams

Shirin (heroine in the *Shahnama*, lover of Khusro, beloved of Farhad), 181, 232

Shivaji Bhonsle (king of the Marathas, died 1680), 176–77

Shuja' al-Mulk, Mir Muhammad Sharif Khan (brother of second nizam), 203

Sight, 173, 180, 254; blindness, 213, 236; gaze, 29, 59–60, 152, 169, 173–75, 214–15, 225, 227, 232, 235, 239; glance, 58–60, 106, 122, 152, 163, 164, 167, 246, 262. *See also* Eye

Sikh, 23

Silence (*khamoshi*), 57, 62–64, 81, 82, 99, 142, 153, 155, 174, 189, 215, 277 (n. 46); imposed by Sufi master, 47–48, 57–58, 61, 65, 70, 71, 95, 117, 255

Sin, 86, 88, 113, 136, 149, 153, 238; protection from ('*isma*), 11, 261

Sincerity (*sidq*), 42, 68–70, 97, 118, 151, 188–89, 234–35, 243, 259

Sindh, 40

Siraj Awrangabadi (1715–63), 2–7, 15, 18–19, 23–24, 25–46, 47–70, 71, 76–85, 90–92, 94–99, 100–103, 111–12, 115–19, 120–23, 137–39, 149, 216, 221, 254–57, 262, 263, 264, 273 (nn. 21–23); death of, 26, 117–19; divan of, 38, 47, 52–53, 55, 79; epic by, 26, 47, 78, 81–85, 97–98, 270 (n. 1), 270 (n. 13), 272 (n. 15), 274 (n. 49), 274 (n. 52); pen name of,

30; Persian poetry of, 51–52, 57, 78, 79, 101, 271 (n. 15); Sayyid Darvesh (father of), 50, 79; tomb of, 27–28, 118, 269 (n. 6). *See also* "Fragrant Garden of Imagination, The"

Slave, 16, 18, 73–74, 167, 232, 268 (n. 10); female (*kanizak*), 92–93, 143, 149, 156, 189, 206, 210, 213, 219, 238, 291 (n. 15). *See also* Concubine

Smell, 33–34, 62, 65, 95, 97, 259, 127, 228, 241, 259; of ambergris, 228; of camphor, 228; of incense, 135, 154, 280 (n. 33); of musk, 152; of rosewater, 62; of sandalwood, 61–63, 280 (n. 33)

Social order, 3–5, 12, 65, 72–77, 82, 86–87, 92–94, 151, 207, 218–20, 226, 263–65

Soldiers, 24, 39, 48, 58, 81, 83, 118, 132, 149, 158, 164, 175, 235, 237–39; warrior ethos of, 92–93, 127, 162–63, 176–78, 205, 224, 227, 263. *See also* Nizams of Hyderabad: army camp of

Solomon (Sulaiman, the Islamic prophet), 58–59, 161

Song, 1, 6, 27–28, 36, 38, 57, 60, 100, 104, 108, 111, 123, 148–49, 196, 224, 228, 249, 255, 286 (n. 11); *dhrupad*, 157, 249, 280 (n. 40), 288 (n. 49); *khayal*, 157, 288 (n. 49); lament as genre of (*soz*), 249; lyrics, 45, 71, 96, 109, 116, 148, 206, 211, 242, 249, 280 (n. 40), 282 (n. 8), 287–88 (n. 49); melody in, 45, 47, 102, 106–7, 114, 121, 128, 148, 162, 196, 206, 228, 249; *taranna*, 128; *thumri*, 230. *See also* Geet; Music; Qawwali

Sorcery. *See* Magic

Sorrow, 28, 52, 65, 68, 95–96, 212; as grief, 118, 249–50; as melancholy, 41, 122–23, 138

Soul (*nafs* or *jan*), 3, 35–36, 44, 51, 55, 72, 95, 101, 102, 106, 111, 122–23, 141, 142,

146, 153, 163, 173, 232, 238, 239, 242, 245, 261
Sound: hearing of, 108, 116, 153, 167–68, 174, 215, 216, 228, 246, 258, 268 (n. 16); resonance, 36, 110, 113. *See also* Harmony; Music
South Asia, 19, 22, 66, 81, 92, 125, 131, 150, 160, 189, 219, 247, 256, 257, 261–62, 264, 277 (n. 5), 292 (nn. 3–4)
Space (*makan*), 3, 7, 34, 77, 133, 226; of ritual, 69, 96, 114, 117, 128, 130; spacelessness, 34
Spirit (*ruh*), 20, 35, 72, 268 (n. 16), 294 (n. 19); spirituality, 2, 18, 24, 26, 38, 56, 65, 71, 86, 88–89, 98–99, 151, 183, 205–7, 234–35, 244, 249, 251–52, 260; as unseen (*ghaib*), 1, 29, 33–36, 110, 267 (n. 3), 288 (n. 49)
Spring (*bahar*), 33, 35, 68, 158, 162, 167, 198, 217, 242–43; festival of (*basant*), 158–59, 167, 283 (n. 5); Persian month of (*Naisan*), 286 (n. 21). *See also* Celebration: of Persian New Year
Stage or station (*maqam*), 31, 38, 91, 245–47, 261; of no-station, 33
Stars, 8, 161, 246; in astrology, 121, 165, 243; constellations, 1, 121, 201; milky-way, 85; Venus, 181, 216–17, 228. *See also* Conjunction; Orbit; Transit
Subjectivity, 2–3, 32, 43, 44–45, 74, 108, 258. *See also* Self
Sublimation, 24, 44, 64, 67–69, 71, 78, 89, 183, 255; as refinement, 15–16, 21, 35, 37, 55, 57, 91, 94, 101, 113, 116–17, 181, 233, 245–46
Submission, 9, 15, 38, 76, 93, 102–4, 124, 161, 211, 236; to Shiʻi imam, 219, 233, 239, 260; to Sufi master, 59, 71, 255
Suffering, 11, 58, 60, 78, 99, 102, 103, 106, 131, 138, 186, 190, 232–33, 241, 245, 247. *See also* Pain

Sufi master (*shaikh*), 26–27, 38–39, 47, 50, 56, 58–59, 66, 78, 95, 100, 125, 127–28, 249–51, 255, 258, 259, 263; charisma of, 11, 115, 249–50, 278 (n. 8); image of (*tasavvur*), 59–60; king, as address for, 37–41, 51–52, 118, 251; silence imposed by, 47–48, 57–58, 61, 65, 70, 71, 95, 117, 255; submission to, 59, 71, 255;
Sufism, 5, 11–15, 39, 56, 94, 135, 230, 236, 245, 246–47, 250–51, 255, 257–64; follower of (dervish), 50, 106; lineage of (*silsila*), 11–12, 37–38, 54, 126, 260, 263, 278 (n. 8); order in (*tariqa*), 12, 50, 66, 124–26, 249, 251, 262, 263, 277 (n. 5); women in, 17, 87, 116, 273 (n. 36), 291 (n. 12). *See also* ʻAli ibn Abi Talib: as first Sufi saint; Dance: in Sufi ritual; Hospice, Sufi; Mysticism; Saint; Sunni Muslims: soft (oriented toward Sufism); Tomb: shrine at
Suhravardi, ʻUmar (died 1234), 293 (n. 4)
Suhravardi Sufi order, 113, 277 (n. 5), 278 (n. 8), 293 (n. 4)
Sultan (ruler by might), 12, 19–20, 124–25, 267 (n. 2). *See also* Delhi Sultanate
Sultan Quli Qutb-Shah (first Qutb-Shahi ruler of Golkonda, died 1543), 13, 130
Sun, 1–2, 8–9, 15, 24, 35, 118, 138–39, 141, 251, 254, 269 (n. 1); in poetry, 20, 25, 63, 71, 95, 110, 120, 142, 147, 163, 167, 169, 174, 180–81, 185, 213, 242
Sunni Muslims (*Ahl al-Sunna waʼl-Jamaʻa*, supporters of the Prophet's custom and community), 2, 5, 10, 120, 123, 129, 132–33, 168, 236, 242, 257, 262, 264, 268 (n. 6); hard (oriented against Shiʻis), 126, 264; soft (oriented toward Sufism), 124–28, 154, 159, 245–47, 249, 250, 260–64,

Index 325

277 (n. 4), 280 (n. 32); theology or law of, 16–17, 66, 260, 268 (n. 12)
Sunni rulers: Delhi Sultanate as, 15, 128; Mughal Empire as, 23, 84, 132; Nizams of Hyderabad as, 23, 137–38, 143, 145, 154, 157–59, 164, 184, 224, 247–48
Symbol, 4–5, 45, 84, 85, 113, 124, 129, 133, 136, 153, 177, 219, 259. *See also* Metaphor
Syncretism, 13, 22–23, 130, 135, 177, 230
Syria, 10, 34, 264

Tajalli ʿAli Shah (died 1800), 138, 154, 157, 161–62, 179, 249, 282 (n. 12), 285 (n. 29)
Tajalliyat-e Mah. See *Mah-nama*
Takiya. *See* Hospice: Sufi
Taste, 60, 101, 116; of honey, 83, 98, 282 (n. 9); of sweetness, 62–63, 84, 101, 106, 146, 152, 232
Tavern, 9, 33–34, 153. *See also* Wine
Tears, 44, 68, 69, 122–23, 129, 142, 174, 240, 246, 249
Teasing and flirtation, 28, 61, 91, 101–2, 106, 121, 156, 162, 173–74, 243, 217
Telangana, 130
Telugu people, 132; Telugu language, 220
Temple (*mandir*), 34, 98, 231. *See also* Hinduism; Idolatry
Temptation (*fitna*), 113, 173, 273 (n. 33), 284 (n. 17)
Theology, 27, 36, 39, 42, 56, 126, 135, 279 (n. 25); of beauty, 35, 68–69, 101–2; mystical, 111, 126, 262. *See also* Shiʿi Muslim: theology or law of; Sunni Muslims: theology or law of
Thirst, 44, 62, 152, 242
Time (*zaman*), 3, 4, 9, 35, 114, 254; eternity, 28, 34–35, 60, 61, 115, 159, 161–62, 242–43, 252, 263; medieval, 7, 12, 19–20, 75, 107, 220, 260–61; modern, 18, 81, 93, 151, 194, 205–6, 214, 218–20, 225–26, 230–31, 264. *See also* Judgment day; Space
Tipu Sultan (died 1799, ruler of Mysore), 170, 175–76, 178, 284 (n. 7)
Tomb: of Mah Laqa Bai, 145, 151, 155–56, 159; processional replica of (*taʿziya*), 250, 279 (n. 26); shrine at, 13, 23, 27–28, 41, 50, 51, 84–85, 108, 114, 124, 129, 139, 148, 248, 250, 273 (n. 32); of Siraj, 27–28, 118, 269 (n. 6). *See also* Pilgrimage: to tombs of holy people
Transit, 5, 119, 120–21
Translation, 109, 131; into English, 4, 6, 21, 24, 25, 29–30, 45, 63, 91, 141, 174, 180, 213, 232, 239, 241, 271 (n. 15), 271 (n. 24), 271 (n. 26), 271 (n. 28), 271 (n. 30), 274 (n. 42), 289 (n. 5), 289 (n. 8), 294 (n. 20); of Qurʾan, 267 (n. 1); into Urdu, 87, 109, 193, 198, 248, 262
Transvestite, 6, 211–12, 259. *See also* Clothing; Gender: ambiguity in
Tribal (Indian designation for indigenous people outside caste norms), 132, 280, 280 (n. 32); Lambada, 286 (n. 11)
Truth (*haqq*), 2, 28, 36, 181, 215, 252, 263; as name of God, 8, 60–61, 95, 142, 236. *See also* Beauty; Harmony
Turks, 9, 106, 111, 128, 132, 278 (n. 15); Turkoman, 130; Uzbek, 278 (n. 15). *See also* Ottoman Empire
Turkish language, 4, 22, 160
Tuzuk-e Asafiyya ("Pomp and Order of the Asaf Jahi Dynasty"), 154, 162, 179

Umangi, Shah, 40
ʿUmar ibn al-Khattab (second Sunni Caliph, died 644), 268 (n. 12), 279 (n. 18)

Umayyad dynasty, 10, 124. *See also* King

Union (*visal*), 34, 41, 44–45, 63, 64, 68, 95–96, 103, 112, 116, 146, 230, 238, 241, 245, 246–47, 254, 258, 262

Urdu language, xi–xiii, 22, 93, 145, 171, 187, 190, 205, 229, 262; development of in Deccan, 6, 22, 25, 46, 48–49, 109, 111, 141–42, 160, 213, 220–24, 230, 270 (n. 7), 275 (n. 22), 276 (n. 35), 285 (n. 35), 290 (n. 26); grammar in, 91, 289 (n. 8); novel in, 149, 220, 231, 281 (n. 2)

Urdu poetry, 2, 6, 19–22, 24, 34, 48–50, 81, 141–42, 157, 160, 178, 210–25, 284 (n. 29); women authors of, 179, 210–11, 215–20, 223, 225, 231, 281 (n. 6), 288 (n. 4), 291 (n. 15). *See also* Couplet; Ghazal; Kulliyat; Musha'ira; Poetry; Rekhta; Rekhti; Rhyme; Ustad

Urges (*jazbat*), 50, 67, 72, 78, 113, 116. *See also* Desire: sexual; Eros; Lust

Ustad (poetry teacher), 120, 172, 179–80, 223, 285 (n. 36), 289 (n. 13). *See also* Music: master of

Vajid 'Ali Shah (king of Avadh, died 1887), 230

Vali Deccani (died 1707), 25, 48–50, 54, 221, 270 (n. 7)

Vanita, Ruth, 75, 209, 212,

Vernacular, 22, 108; Indianization, 125–26, 130–32; Persianization, 221–24; vernacularization as a cultural process, 22–23, 131–33, 279 (n. 22)

Vijayanagar, 13

Violence, 12, 73, 132, 149, 186, 221; as rape, 203

Virgins, 180–81, 240

Wahhabi, 277 (n. 4). *See also* Islam: reform movements in

Water, 8, 98, 122, 152, 161, 189, 216; building for drinking (*abdar-khana*), 152; dewdrops, 37, 214, 239, 246; Husain Sagar reservoir, 162; in paradise (*salsabil*), 152–53, 282 (n. 9); rain, 20, 137, 197–98, 251, 286 (n. 21); reservoir of, 131, 152–53; spring of, 134, 282 (nn. 8–9); step-well for access to, 146, 152, 155, 282 (n. 15). *See also* River; Sea

Wealth, 18, 23, 38, 48, 63, 65, 92, 93, 94, 109–10, 148, 149, 157, 161–62, 169, 183, 186, 191, 205, 247–48, 250, 255, 258; as property, 77, 179, 218, 233. *See also* Poverty

Weapons, 163; dagger, 58–59; knife, 102, 104; lance, 106; saber, 164, 235; sword blade, 40, 122, 127, 164, 181, 237. *See also* Archery; Soldier

Wilderness (*bayaban*), 32, 47, 50, 52, 79, 83–84, 136

Wildness (*vahshat*), 50, 78, 80, 123

Wine (*sharab*), 19, 20, 35, 37, 44, 55, 58–60, 65, 82, 152–53, 158, 161, 167, 182, 242, 246, 263; companion in drinking, 28, 180; of paradise (*kawsar*), 56, 182; pourer of (*saqi*), 53, 56, 60, 62, 91, 152, 182–83, 214, 217, 242; vat of, 29. *See also* Cup or goblet; Drunkenness; Tavern

Wisdom (*hikmat*), 11, 39, 41, 42, 51, 60, 154, 159, 236, 251. *See also* Khizr

Witness play (*shahid-bazi*), 69–70, 87–92, 96–98, 115. *See also* Beauty; Contemplation

Women, 76, 142–43, 148, 157, 237; as authors of Urdu poetry, 179, 210–11, 215–20, 223, 225, 231, 281 (n. 6), 288 (n. 4), 291 (n. 15); as cause of discord (*fitna*), 173, 284 (n. 17); companionship with men, 171–72, 180, 188; empowerment of, 146, 169, 202, 210, 213, 218–21, 233–34, 255; feminism

Index 327

as liberation of, 92, 143, 145, 147, 209, 210–11, 217–20, 221–23, 225, 233, 241–42, 255, 289 (n. 16); of Mah Laqa Bai's family, 195–209; as mother, 93, 157, 200–201, 250; polygyny among, 16; sexuality of, 194, 195, 203, 210, 211, 215–16, 240, 255; in Sufism, 17, 87, 116, 273 (n. 36), 291 (n. 12); as widow, 157, 171; as wife, 65, 66, 69, 92–93, 149, 154, 170, 176, 188, 196–99, 204, 252, 255, 256. *See also* Gender; Marriage; Prostitution; Virgin

Worship, 8, 28, 60, 86, 90, 103, 105, 118, 155, 177, 206, 219, 230, 237, 240, 257; as self-awareness, 28, 98; fasting in, 67. *See also* Music: ritual listening to; Piety; Prayer

Yazid ibn Mu'aviya (second king of the Umayyad dynasty, died 683), 124

Yusufain, Yusuf and Sharif al-Din Chishti (died 1710), 54, 134, 273 (n. 21)

Zahra. *See* Fatima

Zainab bint 'Ali (granddaughter of Muhammad and sister of Husain, died 682), 241–42

Zia al-Din Parwana (a follower of Siraj), 118, 277 (n. 44)

Islamic Civilization and Muslim Networks

SCOTT KUGLE, *When Sun Meets Moon: Gender, Eros, and Ecstasy in Urdu Poetry* (2016).

KISHWAR RIZVI, *The Transnational Mosque: Architecture, Historical Memory, and the Contemporary Middle East* (2015).

EBRAHIM MOOSA, *What Is a Madrasa?* (2015).

BRUCE LAWRENCE, *Who Is Allah?* (2015).

EDWARD E. CURTIS IV, *The Call of Bilal: Islam in the African Diaspora* (2014).

SAHAR AMER, *What Is Veiling?* (2014).

RUDOLPH T. WARE III, *The Walking Qur'an: Islamic Education, Embodied Knowledge, and History in West Africa* (2014).

SAʿDIYYA SHAIKH, *Sufi Narratives of Intimacy: Ibn ʿArabī, Gender, and Sexuality* (2012).

KAREN G. RUFFLE, *Gender, Sainthood, and Everyday Practice in South Asian Shiʿism* (2011).

JONAH STEINBERG, *Ismaʿili Modern: Globalization and Identity in a Muslim Community* (2011).

IFTIKHAR DADI, *Modernism and the Art of Muslim South Asia* (2010).

GARY R. BUNT, *iMuslims: Rewiring the House of Islam* (2009).

FATEMEH KESHAVARZ, *Jasmine and Stars: Reading More than "Lolita" in Tehran* (2007).

SCOTT KUGLE, *Sufis and Saints' Bodies: Mysticism, Corporeality, and Sacred Power in Islam* (2007).

ROXANI ELENI MARGARITI, *Aden and the Indian Ocean Trade: 150 Years in the Life of a Medieval Arabian Port* (2007).

SUFIA M. UDDIN, *Constructing Bangladesh: Religion, Ethnicity, and Language in an Islamic Nation* (2006).

OMID SAFI, *The Politics of Knowledge in Premodern Islam: Negotiating Ideology and Religious Inquiry* (2006).

EBRAHIM MOOSA, *Ghazālī and the Poetics of Imagination* (2005).

MIRIAM COOKE and BRUCE B. LAWRENCE, eds., *Muslim Networks from Hajj to Hip Hop* (2005).

CARL W. ERNST, *Following Muhammad: Rethinking Islam in the Contemporary World* (2003).